Renaissance Rereadings

Renaissance Rereadings

Intertext and Context

EDITED BY

Maryanne Cline Horowitz
Coordinating Editor

Anne J. Cruz
Coeditor

Wendy A. Furman
Coeditor

University of Illinois Press
Urbana and Chicago

A work supported by the Renaissance Conference
of Southern California

Library of Congress Cataloging-in-Publication Data

Renaissance rereadings : intertext and context / edited by Maryanne
  Cline Horowitz, coordinating editor, Anne J. Cruz, co-editor, Wendy
  A. Furman, co-editor.
      p. cm.
  Based on papers presented at the Thirty-first Annual Meeting of
the Renaissance Society of America, held Mar. 21–23, 1985, at the
Huntington Library, Occidental College, and the J. Paul Getty
Museum.
    Includes index.
    ISBN 0-252-01489-8 (cloth) ISBN 0-252-06009-1 (paper)
    1. European literature—Renaissance, 1450–1600—Criticism and
interpretation—Congresses.   2. Renaissance—Congresses.   3. Arts.
Renaissance—Congresses.   I. Horowitz, Maryanne Cline, 1945–
II. Cruz, Anne J., 1941–   .   III. Furman, Wendy Ann, 1949–
IV. Renaissance Society of America. Meeting (31st : 1985 :
Huntington Library, etc.)
PN721.R46 1988
809'.03—dc19   87-27228
                                                                          CIP

Contents

Acknowledgments   vii

Introduction   ix

INTERTEXTUALITY

I. STRATEGIES OF WRITING

Bacon's Poetics   HARRY LEVIN   3

The Boundaries of Interpretation: Self, Text, Contexts in
Montaigne's *Essays*   RICHARD L. REGOSIN   18

The Singer's Voice in Elizabethan Drama   ELISE BICKFORD JORGENS   33

II. MODES OF IMITATION

Jewish Adaptation of Humanist Concepts in Fifteenth- and
Sixteenth-Century Italy   ARTHUR M. LESLEY   51

Between Homer and Virgil: Mimesis and Imitatio in Ronsard's
Epic Theory   FRANÇOIS RIGOLOT   67

Spanish Petrarchism and the Poetics of Appropriation:
Boscán and Garcilaso de la Vega   ANNE J. CRUZ   80

Translation and Imitation in the Development of Tragedy
during the Spanish Renaissance   MARÍA CRISTINA QUINTERO   96

III. INTERDISCIPLINARY RELATIONS

To Paint Poetry: Raphael on Parnassus   PAUL F. WATSON   113

Wanton Discourse and the Engines of Time: William Camden—
Historian among Poets-Historical   WYMAN H. HERENDEEN   142

CONTEXTUALITY

IV. RELATIONS OF POWER

The Poet Laureate as University Master: John Skelton's
Woodcut Portrait   JULIE A. SMITH   159

The Tribulations of a Young Poet: Ronsard from 1547 to 1552
PHILIPPE DESAN   184

V. CULTURAL REPRESENTATIONS

The Death of the Child Valerio Marcello: Paternal Mourning
in Renaissance Venice   MARGARET L. KING   205

Demons, Portents, and Visions: Fantastic and Supernatural
Elements in Ronsard's Poetry   LANCE K. DONALDSON-EVANS   225

Michel de Montaigne's Stoic Insights into Peasant Death
MARYANNE CLINE HOROWITZ   236

VI. TEXT IN COMMUNITY

Renaissance Hermeticism as a Formula for Peace: Some
Responses along Confessional Lines   JEANNE HARRIE   255

Rabbi Leon Modena and the Christian Kabbalists
HOWARD ADELMAN   271

Notes on Contributors   287

Index   290

Acknowledgments

The present volume of collected essays honors a gathering distinguished annually by the prestige of its participants and by the diversity and broad range of their intellectual concerns. On March 21, 22, and 23, 1985, the Renaissance Conference of Southern California hosted the National Conference of the Thirty-first Annual Meeting of the Renaissance Society of America at The Huntington Library, Art Collections, and Botanical Gardens; Occidental College; and the J. Paul Getty Museum. This book grew out of several of the papers presented at that conference—essays that exemplify the relationship between intertext and context in Renaissance studies today. We would like to thank the chairs, commentators, audience participants, and the eighty-nine presenters of papers on diverse aspects of the Renaissance. And we hope this text of many voices continues to foster the same kind of dialogue among disciplines which characterized the national conference.

We also wish to express our deepest gratitude to the Renaissance Conference of Southern California, who generously subsidized this volume, and to its Executive Editorial Advisory Board, whose members spent many hours in the initial selection of papers. The committee is chaired by Edward Gosselin, Department of History, California State University, Long Beach. Members include Sara M. Adler, Department of Italian Literature, Scripps College; Anne J. Cruz, Department of Spanish and Portuguese, University of California, Irvine; Wendy A. Furman, Department of English, Whittier College; Maryanne C. Horowitz, Department of History, Occidental College; Richard Ide, Department of English, University of Southern California; Ricardo J. Quinones, Department of Comparative Literature, Claremont McKenna College; and Jean Weisz, Department of Art History, University of California, Los Angeles. Appreciation extends to the conscientious staff of the University of Illinois viii | *Acknowledgments*

Press, especially Ann Weir, Patricia Hollahan, and Barbara Cohen. Finally, we would like to thank Occidental College; University of California, Irvine; and Whittier College for their ongoing support of this endeavor.

Introduction

As editors of this volume, we are proud to bring to press a selection of essays that by its diversity and its unity reflects the prevailing interests of Renaissance scholars. The essays signal the variety of critical theories and modes of interpretation and analysis that are currently being applied in Renaissance studies, whether in literature, history, art, religion, music, or philosophy. The thematics of intertextuality and contextuality evidenced in these essays reveal an overarching concern for a revisionist approach to the Renaissance—an approach which blurs the intrinsic and extrinsic distinctions of textual interpretation, and concurrently embraces expanding fields of interest and increasingly diverse methodologies.

In keeping with this dual emphasis, the volume is divided formally into two interrelated sections: first the intertextual discourses originated in and by texts, then the contextualities within which these same discourses are generated. While intertext and context are not mutually exclusive categories, essays have been assigned their place according to their dominant concern. By naming the first section of the book "Intertextuality," we refer not only to the reading of one text in conjunction with another, but to the actualization of a given text by the relationship it establishes with others. Similarly, in naming the second section "Contextuality," we fully recognize the importance of the texts' social, cultural, and historical parameters. The essays in this volume thus address the complex relationships between Renaissance texts and other discourses, as well as the different contexts from which these texts emerge. In so doing, these critical rereadings offer novel and timely perspectives on the continuous interactions between Renaissance texts and their culture, society, and history.

The first subsection, "Strategies of Writing," focuses not on the text as representative of an essential authorial truth but on the practice of writing itself. The importance of rhetoric as praxis is underscored in the centrality accorded to the nature and role of language. In the leading essay of the volume, Harry Levin thus reconsiders Francis Bacon's place in literary history, adducing from his writings a well-formed and ultimately well-intentioned poetics that is structured on Bacon's equivocal view of poetry as "feigned history." If Bacon's undertakings are weighted more toward scientific inquiry than toward the literary tradition, Levin rightly reminds us that the imbalance is only apparent. For Bacon, the imagination and its constructs—which are of necessity *verbal* constructs—remain the unifying force between the human psyche and the physical universe and, by creating worlds with words, destroy any illusion of difference between the fictive and the real.

Richard L. Regosin's revisionary study of Montaigne's *Essays* exemplifies poststructuralist trends in literary criticism, as his analysis puts into practice what he argues Montaigne accomplishes in his text: bringing into question the signifying capacity of language, the status of representation, and the value of interpretation itself. Regosin explores the textuality of the *Essays* as both historical and literary interaction, thereby emphasizing their coherence as a result of their own textual dynamics—stressing that context is due to the text, and is fully as complex and as open to interpretation. Another contribution of import to this section is Elise Bickford Jorgens's essay, "The Singer's Voice in Elizabethan Drama," which speculates on the rhetorical purpose of emotionally arousing songs in English Renaissance plays. Jorgens maintains that the singer's voice carries on the wider cultural debate about the efficacy of music, presenting both the conventionally accepted response to a dramatic situation and the playwright's own rejection of the various critical opinions on music current at the time. The intertext of music in the plays, Jorgens argues, seems to assert that Elizabethans reveled in its moral ambiguity.

Positing the problematics of mimetic representation, the second subsection, "Modes of Imitation," studies various methods of imitation central to the development of Renaissance literature. Several of the essays in this subsection reflect the expanding interest of Renaissance scholars into such hitherto lesser-known areas of study as Spanish and Hebraic literatures, and acknowledge the parallels between their imitative practices and those of other Renaissance literatures. As an example of the latter, Arthur M. Lesley investigates the intellectual means by which Jewish scholars in Italy selected and adapted into Hebrew humanist norms for rhetoric, poetry, history, and political philosophy, all the while redirecting attention to their biblical heritage.

That one of the primary purposes of humanist imitation is the elevation of vernacular literatures and languages to the same stature as their classical models is illustrated in François Rigolot's incisive essay on Ronsard's epic theory, which demonstrates the French poet's awareness of alternative modes of imitation available to him and their significance in establishing the autonomy of his *oeuvre*. Similarly, Anne J. Cruz compares the poetics of Juan Boscán and Garcilaso de la Vega, and illustrates how their contrasting applications of the modes of imitation recommended by Bembo and Gianfrancesco Pico della Mirandola appropriate Italian conventions, giving rise to Spanish Petrarchism. As María Cristina Quintero's essay on the development of tragedy in the Spanish Renaissance amply demonstrates, translation proves a literary activity in its own right. She perceptively points out that while translation creates an integral link between classical and vernacular texts, it nevertheless distinguishes vital differences between the two literatures.

As the essays in this subsection confirm, intertextual relationships function both diachronically and synchronically, through time and across social, political, and geographical boundaries. The subsection "Interdisciplinary Relations" affords another view of how different disciplines interact and affect one another while serving as paradigms each to the other: history to poetry, poetics to art, music to literature. Paul F. Watson, in his essay on Raphael's dramatization of poetic theory, considers the complex interaction between disciplines—at times conciliatory, at times adversarial—suggesting the validity of analogies between the painter and the poet. Wyman H. Herendeen reveals a similar interrelation in his thoughtful analysis of the historian Camden's influence on historical poets. To Herendeen, Camden clearly differentiates poetry from mythology, while offering a model for poets in his *Britannia*.

The essays which deal particularly with the contextuality of Renaissance disciplines are also divided into three subsections. The first, "Relations of Power," centers on the hierarchical constructs of power under which poets and artists labored, and the explicit and implicit resolutions incurred by such relations. An example of the involved attitudes elucidated in this section is Julie A. Smith's keen analysis of the iconography of poet portraiture. The representation of John Skelton and subsequent poets as university master reveals the efforts of both authors and printers to create and promote an exalted image of the author and his works.

The issue of patronage has been increasingly central to recent studies of Renaissance art and literature. This trend is well illustrated by Philippe Desan's essay on the patronage opportunities and political ambitions of Ronsard as a fledgling poet. Desan shows how Ronsard's *Odes* reveal a contradictory combination of flattery and poetic arrogance in order to obtain acceptance at court. Thus, despite the subordinate role of artists in Renaissance society, the essays in this subsection disclose the artists' subversive potential through the control of their medium.

The second subsection, "Cultural Representations," emphasizes divergent representations of values, attitudes, and modes of perception in the various Renaissance literary texts. Comparing the many consolations written for the death of a young Venetian boy, Margaret L. King investigates the expression of grief, both as a literary genre and as a measure of familial affection. She concludes that such records afford a means of understanding the values—literary and emotional—of the times.

Lance K. Donaldson-Evans's intriguing essay on the fantastic in Ronsard's poetry points out the intrusion of mysterious elements in such forms as demons and visions. Donaldson-Evans views these apparitions as manifestations of the superstitious fears the poet shares with his culture. In her essay, Maryanne Cline Horowitz illuminates the tensions in Montaigne's Stoic attitude toward death, and affirms that he projects his own values onto the French peasants whom he observes dying. Through these essays, we become aware of how each text reacts to and interacts with its surroundings—an awareness fostered by these scholarly explorations which shed light on both the texts and their social, cultural, and historical foundations.

The last subsection under "Contextuality," "Text in Community," refers specifically to the implications of social change for religious and political communities. In her study of Gabriel du Préau, Jeanne Harrie questions the assertion that Hermeticism promoted a conciliatory attitude on questions of doctrine to quell religious strife, noting du Préau's strong anti-Protestant stance in his later works. Howard Adelman traces Venetian rabbi Leon Modena's changing attitudes toward the Kabbalah to his close contacts with Christian Kabbalists and to his concerns for the Jewish community. These essays show how the pace of change and increasing diversity in the critical interpretations of texts developed concomitantly with the changing identities of the communities in which they were produced.

The essays in *Renaissance Rereadings: Intertext and Context* work together toward an understanding of Renaissance disciplines and texts, but they do so through a range of different interpretations, methodologies, and reading strategies. In their analyses, the essays themselves mirror the complexities of the writing process so well confronted by them. While we do not assert that each essay in the volume offers the definitive interpretation of its chosen subject—on the contrary, we would deny the possibility of such a reading—we believe that they challenge the reader to reconsider the Renaissance text, whether literary, historical, musical, philosophical, or religious, from the perspective of its articulation with other discourses and interrelated contexts.

Maryanne Cline Horowitz
Anne J. Cruz
Wendy A. Furman

I

INTERTEXTUALITY:
Strategies of Writing

HARRY LEVIN

Bacon's Poetics

Since Francis Bacon was both willing and able to play the Renaissance man in so many other respects, it may be significant that he professed "not to be a poet."[1] He could hardly have been blamed if the sonnet that prompted this admission, composed in a last-minute effort to heal the breach between the earl of Essex and Queen Elizabeth, had been as uninspired as it would prove ineffectual. The single lyric from his prolific pen that sometimes turns up in anthologies, a paraphrase from the Greek with the comprehensive Latin title *In vita humana*, seems to be no less coolly detached nor sweepingly sententious than his *Essays*. His metrical translations from the Psalms seem much more prosaic than those of his contemporaries who rendered them, without benefit of meter, for King James's Authorized Version. One of his *Apophthegms* records the "opinion touching poets" of Sir Henry Savile, who had been the queen's tutor and would be one of the king's translators: "He thought them the best writers, next to those that write prose."[2] Such was Bacon's preference, or at least his priority, which may well have suited his own temperament. Thus he shows "a lack of poetic instinct" in his mythological commentaries, according to a modern commentator, the late Jean Seznec.[3] Yet D. G. James, in some paradoxical Oxford lectures, placed him at the other extreme—a position complementary rather than antithetical to Shakespeare's—as, "by nature and endowment, more a poet than a scientist or a philosopher."[4]

Bacon's reputation, over the centuries, has zigzagged strikingly between such extremes. Attacks upon it by uneasy poets have ranged from the damning superlatives of Alexander Pope to the prophetic denunciations of William Blake. Yet, for every detractor, Bacon has had an admirer. By the most cerebral among the English Romantics, Samuel Taylor Coleridge and Percy Bysshe Shelley, he could not have been evaluated more highly. But, having done his utmost to repudiate the scholastic authority of Aristotle, he never fitted into the speculative part that they both assigned

him as "the British Plato."[5] From a more empirical standpoint, he had
personified—in Abraham Cowley's simile—a new Moses, preparing for
if not staking out those promised lands of seventeenth- and eighteenth-
century science, the Royal Society and the *Encyclopédie*. His only noteworthy experiment—noteworthy because the chill was fatal to him—had
been a problem in domestic technology, which involved deep-freezing
an eviscerated hen, and which is so easily solved and so abundantly
replicated through the supermarkets today. Had it succeeded, it would
have been classified among his *experimenta fructifera* rather than *lucifera*,
experiments bearing fruit rather than bringing light.[6] Most of the projects he mentions would have come under the former rubric, involving
the procedures of observation, collection, classification, application, and
organization. At this distance, his programmatic description of Salomon's
House, in *The New Atlantis*, may sound more like a museum than a
laboratory.

Generally speaking, Baconianism has served as a confident ideology
for progress, enlightenment, and utilitarianism—for main historical currents no longer looked upon as inevitable or even indisputably auspicious.
And, since his all-too-worldly career had conveyed him from the very
summit of England's legal hierarchy—the Lord Chancellorship—into the
professional disgrace of impeachment, Bacon's advocacy has exposed discussions of his outlook to *ad hominem* considerations. The metaphori-
cal mascot that trails him through critical arraignment and novelistic
biography, from Lord Macaulay to Lytton Strachey, could not have been
anything less ambiguous than a serpent. Though this beast is evoked
conventionally as an emblem of the subtle wisdom enjoined by Jesus
upon his disciples, together with a lamblike innocence, no one could
have forgotten its underlying activity as the persistent agent of man's fall.
But, when Bacon himself looks back to the very beginning of the beginning,
the first chapters of Genesis, his overwhelming symbol is the primordial
image of light—if indeed that can be viewed as an image and not an
effulgence. "God's first creature" he liked to phrase it, and it dominates
his imagery from first through last.[7] The Deity is "the Father of lights,"
as venerated by the Epistle of James; a "dry light [*lumen siccum*]," formulated by Heraclitus, is precisely that which philosophers should cultivate;
and "the light of nature" would account for much that had been hitherto
ascribed to divine revelation.[8] His neo-Atlantic voyagers are "merchants
of Light."[9] Caroline Spurgeon has graphically demonstrated how "Light,
indeed, to Bacon, very noticeably represents all good things."[10]

Its Manichaean adversary was darkness, inert, chaotic, encircling, and
stubbornly grounded in the past. Bacon shared, with the lesser projectors
of his age, an acute sense of timing; innovation was always opening up,
obsolescence always closing in. His most resounding titles are advertise-

ments for renewal: *The Advancement of Learning, De Augmentis Scientiarum, Novum Organon, Instauratio Magna*. If he was acknowledged as the herald — literally the trumpeter — of modernity (*buccinator novi temporis*), it was because he deliberately presented himself in that part.[11] Given an intellectual heritage heavily overloaded with dogmatic presuppositions and farfetched deductions, it would be his contribution to propose the farthest-reaching critique. Once the diagnostic analogue was admitted, treatment could be dealt with as a matter of curing distempers or purging the peccant humors. He had started from, and often returned to, polemics; a favorite mode of discourse, perhaps for lawyerly reasons, was *redargutio* or refutation. He pounced upon elenchs (or exposable sophistries) with the collector's zeal of a Sir Thomas Browne compiling vulgar errors. Among the four classes of Idols that had bemused men's minds with erroneous notions, he attacked his final set with a special iconoclasm. In calling them *Idola Theatri,* he linked together his own skeptical attitudes toward traditional philosophy and toward theatrical illusion. "In my judgment," he redargued, "all the received systems are but so many stage-plays, representing worlds of their own creation after an unreal and scenic fashion."[12]

Voltaire likened Bacon's achievement to a scaffolding, essential for the construction of New Philosophy but soon to be outmoded by the edifice itself.[13] Probably Bacon had contributed less to the actual building than to the preliminary demolitions and excavations. Outdating was a normal aspect of the continuous process he contemplated, in viewing scientific advance as a "conjunction of labours," the collective accumulation of an institutional enterprise.[14] In his much-trumpeted letter to Lord Burghley, wherein he spoke of taking "all knowledge to be [his] province," he had momentarily considered giving up his public and personal ambitions in order to retreat into research, "to be a true pioneer [a digger in the earth, as originally construed] in that mine of truth" — if only some supporting institution could be established.[15] But royal patronage was otherwise disposed, and individualism guided his subsequent course to its compromised outcome. His collected works, which badly need reediting, were by-products from unsought and unpredictable moments of leisure. In spite of their methodological catchwords and frequent calls to order, they tend to be somewhat rambling, repetitious, and anecdotal, albeit redeemed again and again by memorable phrases, eloquent fragments, pithy outlines, and fascinating lists of unwritten treatises. The clearest plans among them are seldom the most promising; they are the ones that run to inventories and taxonomies more than to inventions or discoveries. But the tone is charged with that inherent feeling for greatness which, transcending mundane complications, seeks to sponsor grand designs.

Bacon's declared purpose in *The Advancement of Learning,* amplified and Latinized in *De Augmentis Scientiarum,* was to put together "a small Globe of the Intellectual World."[16] His starting point, the intellect itself, could unfortunately not be typified as a sheer illuminating transparency: "Nay, it is rather like an enchanted glass, full of superstition and imposture, if it be not delivered and reduced."[17] And science was deliverance and reduction from enchantment, from the magical pretensions of alchemy and astrology, from the benighted sphere of idols and "false appearances." Anatomy was still vague in relating the functions of the mind to the lobes of the brain. Phrenology would be unduly specific, two centuries afterward, in attaching psychological traits to cranial organs. Descartes did not resolve his metaphysical dualism by singling out the pineal gland as the abode of the soul. Bacon took little interest in the material basis of the mental processes that he delineated; yet Freudian psychoanalysis, after all, offers no organic evidence for the existence of the Ego, the Superego, and the Id. Bacon was content to draw his conceptual triad from the ancient apparatus of faculty psychology: Memory, Imagination, Reason. (Albertus Magnus would have located them at the back, the middle, and the front of the head respectively.) Moreover, the Baconian universe, though more open than most of its precursors, remained anthropocentric, corresponding neatly to his tripartite pattern of human understanding. Each of those three faculties correlated with an appropriate domain of knowledge: memory with history (storage and arrangement for the mind's perceptions), reason with philosophy (the dynamics and consequences of the mind's operations), and—somewhere between them—poesy (an inner, darker, yet freer area of speculation and recombination, harboring both illusory and creative potentialities). Bergson, less rationalistically, would locate his *fonction fabulatrice* between the spheres of cognition and intuition.

Bacon's deepest commitment is to the comprehensive span of the whole, and to unifying the paradigms that he sought through an intrinsic *philosophia prima.* Among the ternary branches of learning, the one that clearly interested him most was philosophy. Within that sphere, as within the others, there may still reside a theological component, which can be bracketed—if not taken for granted—by his profession of Fideism. By keeping religion in a separate category, he is enabled to isolate it from his other categories. His credo, "*Da fidei quae fidei sunt* (Give to faith what belongs to faith)," carries an unspoken corollary: "And be careful not to take anything else on faith—above all, never mix up faith with reason."[18] Hence he is free to pursue his central concern, the augmentation of the sciences through Natural Philosophy. On the subject of history, Bacon can speak both as a participant and as a chronicler. Having accorded due notice to Natural, Civil, and Ecclesiastical History, he goes on to enumerate a fourth kind, not yet existent but seriously desiderated. This, termed "Literary History," seems to reach beyond belles lettres to broader conceptions of cultural movement: what the Germans term *Geistesgeschichte* or the French *histoire des mentalités*. Its absence from the records of civilization would be like the blinded eye in a statue of Polyphemus, "that part being wanting which doth most shew the spirit and life of the person."[19] This similitude is so grotesquely striking that we forget to wonder why civilization itself should be likened to, of all creatures, a Cyclops.

Comparably, Aristotle's *Poetics* had situated its theme between history and philosophy. On the grounds of probability — the difference between the particulars of some immediate happening and the universals of widely tested experience — it had asserted that poetry was more philosophic than history. S. H. Butcher's commentary begs a serious question by quoting Bacon in support of that view.[20] Actually, Bacon made no appeal to philosophy in this connection, and had referred to history only by way of an invidious comparison: his concept of Poesy, apart from its more formal characteristics, was "nothing else but Feigned History."[21] This could be both better and worse than straightforward historical verity. It could improve upon the status quo by offering "some shadow of satisfaction to the mind of man in those points wherein the nature of things doth deny it." It can depart from ordinary events to envisage more heroic adventures; it can intervene, when providence does not, to bring about poetic justice; and consequently it surpasses "true history" in conducing to "magnitude, morality, and to delectation." But that last effect is problematic, inasmuch as it invokes the pleasure principle. Setting aside his fideistic reserve, Bacon is even ready to align poetry with religion, at a lofty but nebulous height, before he presses on to an incisive distinction: "And therefore [poesy] was ever thought to have some participation of divineness, because it doth raise and erect the mind, by submitting the shews of things to the desires of the mind; whereas reason doth buckle and bow the mind to the nature of things." The mind exalted by its subjective desires may find itself living with shadows that darken its light; the mind that faces objective realities will be constrained to buckle and bow; but critical realism allows no choice. Many a scientist must have encountered a guiding presumption, as B. F. Skinner attests, in the Baconian aphorism: "Nature, to be commanded, must be obeyed."[22] As between the shows or shadows of things (*umbrae rerum*) and the nature of things (*rerum natura*), Bacon had already made a prolegomenal decision: "Those however who aspire not to guess and divine, but to discover and know; not to devise mimic and fabulous worlds of their own [*simiolas et fabulas mundorum*], but to examine and dissect the very nature of this world itself; must go to facts themselves for everything."[23]

In other words, in words less ornate and more up-to-date, the pleasure principle (*Lustprinzip*) must yield to the reality principle (*Realitätsprinzip*).

Freud's terminology can be rather too glibly superimposed upon some of his predecessors; but, in this case, it is Bacon whose ideas are reflected, refracted, and virtually parodied by Freud. In a crowded paragraph concluding one of his *Introductory Lectures,* the latter speculated about the workings of the artistic imagination. He saw the artist as an introvert, ineffectually and hence neurotically longing for honor, power, riches, fame, and the love of women. Though there must be large numbers of ungifted people who also have such daydreams, the artist has a talent for sublimating and projecting these fantasies out of the libido into art. In that guise they are enjoyed vicariously by the others, and he is thereupon honored by the rewards he has longed for, having, as Freud would put it, "won— through his phantasy—what before he could only win in phantasy."[24] This reductive and philistine case history seems quite unworthy of its searching proponent. The painter-critic Roger Fry took sharp exception to it, pointing out how it vulgarized the artist's motivation and overlooked the aesthetic dimensions of his accomplishment. In a brief early paper on imaginative behavior, "The Relation of the Poet to Day-dreaming," Freud had paid some attention to literary technique, "the essential *ars poetica.*"[25] In his later *Autobiography,* confronting the successive stages of his own psychoanalytic development, he refined to some extent upon his simplistic formula.[26]

Bacon is far less concerned than Freud with the individual; yet they seem agreed in their willingness to equate fantasy with wish fulfillment. Both the Greek φαντασία and the Latin *imaginatio* have a similarly modest origin, rooted in visual perception, implying little more than the mind's ability to visualize again what the eyes have seen before. Since that second sight is no longer controlled by literal circumstance, it is through this area of reproduction and variation that the possibilities for novelty and creativity can enter the picture; and that is why Joseph Addison dwelt upon what he described as "the secondary imagination." Only God may be presumed to create *ex nihilo,* but through the senses He has provided mankind with materials for something like creation. Naturally, young persons are more receptive than their elders: "Imaginations stream into their minds better, and as it were more divinely," Bacon says in his essay "Of Youth and Age."[27] In general, he has much more to say from a positive angle than Montaigne, whose essay *"De la force de l'imagination"* is a series of warnings against being led astray. Most of the Elizabethan testimony is equally negative, stressing the distortions, delusions, and dangers of so wayward a faculty. So is Dr. Johnson's caveat in *Rasselas* on the dangerous prevalence of imagination. Shakespeare's purple passage in *A Midsummer Night's Dream* grants full recognition to the unconscious and irrational elements:

> Lovers and madmen have such seething brains,
> Such shaping fantasies that apprehend
> More than cool reason ever comprehends.

But the poet's function is counterbalanced. On the one hand, his eye rolls "in a fine frenzy," the *furor poeticus*. On the other, those inchoate fancies are shaped and named and localized by his pen. This internalizes, at all events, the primitive notion of genius (as a tutelary spirit) or inspiration (as a supernatural incitement) or a Muse (as a goddess feeding the poet his lines), which had metaphorically implied that his poetic expression somehow originated outside of himself.[28]

More than once Bacon, who was no prolocutor for the Church Fathers, cites the patristic suspicion that poetry may be a diabolical intoxicant (*vinum daemonum*), "because it filleth the imagination; and yet it is but with the shadow of a lie" (here again the votary of light recoils from shadow).[29] This is cited from his essay "On Truth," where lies are obviously inadmissible, though they "make for pleasure as with poets," and on occasion sustain flagging spirits with "flattering hopes ... and the like." It remained for Addison to expatiate on "the pleasures of the imagination." The perennial quarrel between poetry and philosophy can be traced to the pre-Socratic imputation that poets—by instinct, habit, and vocation—were liars. The duplicity of their role was bound up with the double meaning of their craft: in Greek ποίησις, in late Latin *fictio*, in plain English *making*. All of these synonyms cast the poet as, in George Puttenham's Elizabethan phrase, "both a maker and a counterfaitor."[30] Making can be reduced to make-believe: the craftsman, *homo faber*, is one who fabricates. Fiction, though it begins as something solidly formed or convincingly shaped, ends by acquiring an overtone of fictitiousness. Bacon's key word underlies this equivocal implication. The modifying participle in "feigned history" goes back to the *fingo* in "*historia conficta*."[31] This, in turn, is cognate with what Isaac Newton seems to have meant by his repeated declaration, "*hypotheses non fingo*."[32] The English verb he used at one point ("feign," not "frame") signalized not so much a refusal to make hypotheses as a denial that he was making them up as he went along.

Insofar as hypothesis consisted of heuristic theory unsupported as yet by inductive fact, Bacon put even less trust in it than Newton. And Newton must have been following Bacon's example when he dismissed conjecture as "romance." But he had never undertaken, though Bacon implicitly had, to consider romance upon its own ground—or, at least, within its own stratosphere. Significantly, Bacon turned from *The Advancement of Learning* to *The Wisdom of the Ancients* (*De Sapientia Veterum*) and, when he came back to *De Augmentis Scientiarum*, he emphasized and enlarged his discussion of Parabolical Poesy, illustrating with detailed interpretations from the earlier mythographical treatise: with parables on Pan, or Nature; Perseus, or War; and Dionysus, or Desire. Along with the march of intellect, he predicated a rediscovery of the secret lore that darker ages had embodied through myths: "as hieroglyphics were before letters, so parables were before arguments."[33] (The Latin version adduces the instance, so dear to the Elizabethans, of Menenius Agrippa's fable about the belly and the members, used by Shakespeare in *Coriolanus* to draw a rather sophistical analogy.) Classical mythology furnished Bacon, as it did so many European writers, with a typology of human nature. However, he went far beyond allusion into hermeneutics, allegorizing morals and rationalizing meanings out of the fabulous improbabilities that he reinterpreted. Myth could be assimilated to science if, "Under the Person of Proteus, Matter, the most ancient of all things next to God, is meant to be represented."[34]

As a mythographer Bacon was the acknowledged forerunner of Giambattista Vico, whose *Scienza Nuova* would present a synchronic method for recovering prehistory by rereading Homer, the ancient lawgivers, and other archetypal sources of prelogical knowledge—in short, a reinterpretation of poetic wisdom. (Among the many fables, inevitably, would be that of Menenius Agrippa.)[35] Bacon's surveys reported "no other deficiency in Poesy" beyond the one he had attempted to fill with *The Wisdom of the Ancients*.[36] Poetry was like a plant, or possibly a weed "(*herba luxurians*)," that had "sprung up" from the spontaneous richness of the soil and "spread abroad more than any other kind."[37] That lack of deliberate cultivation, the notion of running wild, applies to its content and not its form, since it is said to be restrained in wording (*"verbis astrictum"*) but "free and licensed [*solutum et licentiosum*]" in other matters.[38] Poetic license is more affirmatively treated in *A Description of the Intellectual Globe* (*Descriptio Globi Intellectualis*). Knowledge, in dealing with individuals, usually exercises itself, but sometimes it sports. *Historia* "is the exercise and work of the mind"; *poesis* "may be regarded as its sport [*lusus*]. In philosophy the mind is bound to things; in poesy it is released from that bond, and wanders forth, and feigns what it pleases [*fingit quid vult*]."[39] Bacon here reverts to his triple scheme for the understanding, while relieving the imagination of all responsibilities. What is left, to be positively developed by Kant and Schiller, is the aesthetics of *der Spieltrieb*, the impulse to play.

This is confirmed when Poesy is described by *The Advancement of Learning* as "rather a pleasure or play of imagination, than a work or duty thereof."[40] It has therefore produced no science, though there could be a science about it. But Imagination turns out to be Janus-faced, looking toward Reason, "which hath the print of Truth," and likewise toward — not Memory, but on another plane apparently — Action, "which hath the print of Good." Rhetoric is the intermediate province of "Imaginative or Insinuative Reason" ("insinuative," I suppose, because it works not directly nor explicitly), whereas Religion, on the other side, sets Imagination over Reason. On both sides the inquiry shades off into ethics: in Delphic terms, *"the knowledge of ourselves."*[41] With regard to emotional conduct, "the passions" and "the affections," poets have more to teach than philosophers.[42] Bacon is less mindful of other poetic genres than the parabolical, though he expatiates on two of them more fully in *De Augmentis Scientiarum.* Narrative poems aspire to be heroical, and to celebrate "the dignity of human nature."[43] Drama, which has the advantage of making a direct impression on a social group, could become a sort of plectrum for playing upon their minds. This influence, among the ancients, acted as a discipline, whereby they could be educated to virtue. Such aims, among the moderns, have fallen off into corruption. Writing in the heyday of Shakespeare and Ben Jonson, Bacon recorded his measured opinion that "play-acting is esteemed but as a toy [*pro re ludicra*]."[44] His consistent suspicions of the drama would work, if nothing else did, against the attempts to identify him as Shakespeare's ghostwriter.

The deprecatory English monosyllable, *toy,* was common usage for the Jacobeans. To them it did not signify a child's plaything but stood more broadly for any trifle or else for dallying, with a possible touch of sexual innuendo. "These things are but toys" — so Bacon apologized for, and rapidly dismissed, the subject matter of his late and slight essay, "Of Masques and Triumphs."[45] He himself had participated in one such courtly entertainment, the uproarious *Gesta Grayorum,* enacted by fellow lawyers for the queen at Gray's Inn, where elaborate spectacle was combined with politic counsel. As for dramatic action, that was then supplied by the afterpiece, Shakespeare's *Comedy of Errors,* appropriately or not. Bacon's own distrust of plays comes out again, in defining the Idols of the Theater, when he criticizes wishful thinking.[46] When *The Advancement of Learning* moves on from literary to philosophical exposition, his satisfaction is proclaimed by his tropes: "But it is not good to stay too long in the theatre. Let us now pass on to the judicial place or palace of the mind, which we are to approach and view with more reverence and attention."[47] During the next generation Henry Reynolds would be outraged by this dictum; and, in his Neoplatonic tract *Mythomystes,* he accuses Bacon of inconsistency for expressing such positivistic impatience after having devoted other studies to the allegorical exegesis of myths.[48] But the dismissive contrast is strengthened by Bacon himself in his Latin continuation, when he takes his leave from Poesy's "dream of learning (*doctrinae somnium*)" and awakens to Science's clear air.[49]

Leonardo da Vinci, a century before, had deprecated poetry from the vantage point of painting. That was a bolder step, since visual art had been played down by the humanistic authorities, who categorized it among the mechanical rather than liberal arts. Furthermore, or so Leonardo contended, it outranked its verbal counterpart by qualifying as a science. Pictorial representation came much closer to nature than written texts could do because it dealt with facts and not with words.[50] (Addison would speak to the contrary argument.) Poetry—for Leonardo— was imaginary, whereas painting was real, appealing to our noblest sense, the vision, and mirroring God's creation rather than man's. The interrelationship was that of mind to body, or of moral to natural philosophy. Now the painter could address himself to phenomena more directly than the poet, true enough. But Leonardo's opportune ambition to accredit his medium had run away with his logic. It was fallacious to assume that pigments, because they existed so tangibly, were as alive as the scenes that they had been employed to depict. Theirs too was still a technique of imitation, though it was more likely than sounds or letters to be confused with what it was imitating. The manuscript expounding these views, *Paragone*, redacted from Leonardo's notes by his pupils, could not have been known to Bacon, in any case. If the latter alludes to the classic tag, *"Pictoribus atque poetis, &c.,"* it is because this parallel does not answer—indeed it heightens—the questions he raises concerning artifice and unreality.[51]

Undoubtedly Bacon was well acquainted with Sir Philip Sidney's *Defence of Poesie*, which was not only the most influential of Elizabethan critical statements but—as J. E. Spingarn pointed out—"a veritable epitome of the literary criticism of the Italian Renaissance."[52] Its posture of defense, or the *Apologie* of its alternate title, had been provoked by Puritan attacks, and may help to account for its moralistic premises. Yet it is really a panegyric or eulogy, a teeming survey and sprightly appraisal, a large-minded synthesis of conventions and improvisations, not excluding the familiar—if dubious—object lesson of Menenius Agrippa. In Sidney's perspective, as in Bacon's, Poesy is flanked by Philosophy and History, but the relations that Sidney works out are based upon the original Aristotelian poetics. Philosophy has its precepts, history its examples; and, if the poet can derive precepts from the historian's examples, he can also devise examples for the philosopher's precepts. He can universalize the particular, as Aristotle had more or less observed; Sidney would add that he can particularize the universal. Turning to Plato, who is warmly welcomed as "our Patron, and not our adversarie," Sidney's approach is less defensive than conciliatory.[53] To the Platonic charge that poetry is falsehood, he responds: "Now for the *Poet*, he nothing affirmeth, and therefore never lieth."[54] Why, then, should we be expecting him to tell the factual truth? Yet, though poetic truth may be a paradox, it has aesthetic canons and ethical standards. These "should be εἰκαστική, . . . figuring foorth good things," rather than "φανταστική: . . . which doth contrariwise infect the fancie with unwoorthy objects." Sidney was nothing if not an idealist.[55]

It would remain for I. A. Richards, in the early twentieth century, to suggest that a poet's propositions were "pseudo-statements." To accept them on their own terms depended, not upon epistemological verification, but upon what the Romanticists had campaigned for: a "willing suspension of disbelief." During an epoch when faiths were stronger, Sidney must have found it easier to uphold belief in what—preceding Bacon—he had designated "the fained Image of Poetrie."[56] He realized that nature exerted its primary claims upon everyone; but all the learned professions —historians, philosophers, astronomers, arithmeticians, physicians, musicians, grammarians, yes, and lawyers—reacted by their several lights. "Onely the Poet disdeining to be tied to any such subjection, lifted up with the vigor of his own invention, doth grow in effect into another nature: in making things either better then nature bringeth foorth, or quite a new, . . . so as he goeth hand in hand with nature. . . ."[57] He could rival and, because he did not need to buckle or bow, he conceivably could outdo nature: "her world is brasen, the Poets only deliver a golden." Here Sidney is not simply swept along by his own idealistic ardor. He is closely echoing the exordium of the weighty handbook on poetics by the Veronese humanist, Julius Caesar Scaliger, who had pushed the argument even farther: the creator of that other world (*"natura altera"*) must be another God (*"Deus alter"*).[58] And Scaliger, in his formulation, had been adapting the myth of Plato's *Timaeus* about the demiurge who creates a heterocosm. But that had been an imperfect copy of an ideal cosmos, whereas Sidney's imitation constitutes an improvement on nature—a re-creation larger and better than life, whose warrant is its uplifting impact on life. This attitude prefigures the neoclassical doctrine of *la belle nature,* exemplified in Pope's conception of "nature to advantage dressed." Ultimately it exposes itself to the charge of becoming too prettified, too limited, and accordingly too artificial. It points, in an escapist direction, toward the "golden world" that Shakespeare satirizes in the pastoral landscape of *As You Like It.* Yet it is the clown, Touchstone, in that same play, who argues that "the truest poetry is the most feigning."

Bacon was heavily pledged to discriminate substance from shadow, and authentic brass from the gold of the alchemists. To the idealism of Sidney he would have counterpoised the realism of "Machiavel and others, that write what men do and not what men ought to do."[59] Not that Bacon, as a practising advocate and parliamentary orator, was unconcerned with telling men what they ought to do. Just as language was the field of his greatest mastery, so rhetoric was the middle ground between his professional and his intellectual interests. His *Table of Colours or Appearances of Good and Evil,* demonstrating how the art of persuasion could put the best face upon any cause, is well versed in the uses of the optative mood. This invites a moral skepticism and is posited upon a relativistic sense of values; yet Bacon's juridical training had accustomed him to entertaining opposite points of view, and his dialectical habit was flexible enough to hold them in ambivalent suspension. Future generations would have to oscillate, wavering between a tough and bleak materialism and a sensitive and elusive transcendence, between Thomas Hobbes's mechanistic definition of Fancy and Coleridge's ineffable mystery of Imagination. Ever since the seventeenth century, culture as a whole has been suffering—in the diagnosis of T. S. Eliot—from a "dissociation of sensibility." Bacon has been accused of fostering, if not of having initiated, that mutually detrimental rift disjoining what C. P. Snow has taught us to call the two cultures.[60]

To Bacon such an allegation would have been inconceivable. Knowledge was for him an indivisible totality, though—in his timely endeavors to make room for scientific experimentation and to cut down on verbalistic tradition—he did much to animate a reversal of that imbalance, a shift to the other side. It has been claimed that he became perfunctory and derivative whenever he theorized about literature, and that he would never have bothered to do so if he had not engaged himself to complete an undertaking of encyclopedic scope.[61] As it happened, though many of his undertakings stand uncompleted, he did leave a substantial and interesting sequence of literary animadversions. He took some pains—as we have just noted—to reconsider the arguments of the leading previous English critic, disparate from his own outlook as they were, and to meet them halfway. At that midpoint the romancer of the *Arcadia* and the science-fiction writer of *The New Atlantis* seem to unite in attesting the value of imagination, and of hypothetical constructs as a means of adjustment between the human psyche and the physical universe. Philosophy might not be so austerely remote from Poesy, in the long run, as Baconian rigor had presupposed. Jeremy Bentham would sketch a theory of fictions; Hans Vaihinger would systematize a "philosophy of as if [*als ob*]"; more recent philosophers would concern themselves with the accommodations of thought to language. The continuing presence of myth as an active force in history, even when unmasked as "the big lie," could be deplored but not ignored. As Wallace Stevens would conclude in *Notes toward a Supreme Fiction:*

> the bride
> Is never naked. A fictive covering
> Weaves always glistening from the heart and mind.

Bacon had ample occasion to distinguish the fictive from the real in courts of law, as well as to confound them at the courts of royalty. During the five final years that he spent in the shadows, he must have felt the fullest rigors of the *rerum natura*. Forced at last to give up the civil for the contemplative life, he may have come to believe more fully in the existence of worlds beyond worldliness, in a plurality of those not-quite-impossible worlds which had been conceived as fables or romances. He could scarcely have lived up to the motto *plus ultra* by sticking to known facts. Stimulated by the "feigned commonwealth" of a less worldly lord chancellor, he had briefly indulged in his own dream of learning.[62] That posthumous fragment, with its glistening vision of Salomon's House, "enlarging the bounds of Human Empire, to the effecting of all things possible," would have greater influence on the future than the wide shelf of Bacon's more discursive prospectuses. Its story begins — in spite of, or else because of, its author — with a scriptural miracle, "a pillar of light." *The New Atlantis* would be, for Joseph Glanvill and his colleagues, "a Prophetick Scheam of the ROYAL SOCIETY."[63] A. G. Baumgarten, the rationalistic philosopher who would introduce the study of aesthetics, redefined a poem as a heterocosmic version of actuality.[64] Sidney had long before pleaded that Plato's model commonwealth, *The Republic*, and Xenophon's portrait of a model ruler, Cyrus the Great, along with More's *Utopia*, should be accepted as poetry. If a poet may be character-ized as a designer of models, then it is hard to think of any poet whose imaginings have reverberated farther than Bacon's. His involvements with reason and memory remain significant; and he would be restless and skeptical in any of his three spheres; but if one of them accords with his disposition better than the others, shadowy and precarious though it may be, it is imagination. And today we can observe what Addison fore-saw, that "there are none who more gratifie and enlarge the Imagination, than the Authors of the new Philosophy."[65]

NOTES

1. Francis Bacon, *The Letters and the Life*, ed. James Spedding and R. L. Ellis (London: Longman, Green, 1868), III, 149 ("Apology Concerning the Earl of Essex").

2. Francis Bacon, *Works*, ed. James Spedding, R. L. Ellis, and D. D. Heath (Boston: Brown and Taggard, 1861–65), VIII, 135 (hereafter cited as *Works*).

3. Jean Seznec, *The Survival of the Pagan Gods: The Mythological Tradition and Its Place in Renaissance Humanism and Art*, trans. Barbara F. Sessions (New York: Harper and Row, 1953), p. 250n.

4. D. G. James, *The Dream of Learning: An Essay on the Advancement of Learning, "Hamlet" and "King Lear"* (Oxford: Oxford University Press, 1951), p. 3.

5. S. T. Coleridge, *The Friend,* ed. B. E. Rooke (Princeton, N.J.: Princeton University Press, 1959), p. 488; cf. P. B. Shelley, *Complete Works,* ed. Roger Ingpen and W. E. Peck (London: Ernest Benn, 1929), VII, 114 ("A Defence of Poetry").

6. *Works,* VIII, 135.

7. *Works,* V, 384.

8. *Works,* VI, 95, 88.

9. *Works,* V, 410.

10. C. F. E. Spurgeon, *Shakespeare's Imagery and What It Tells Us* (Cambridge: Macmillan, 1936), p. 18.

11. See *Works,* II, 309 (*De Dignitate et Augmentiis Scientiarum*).

12. *Works,* VIII, 78.

13. Voltaire, *Lettres sur les Anglais,* ed. Arthur Wilson-Green (Cambridge: Cambridge University Press, 1931), p. 41 (xii).

14. *Works,* VIII, 396.

15. Bacon, *Letters and Life,* ed. Spedding and Ellis (London: Longman, Green, 1861), I, 109.

16. *Works,* VI, 412.

17. *Works,* VI, 276.

18. *Works,* VI, 212.

19. *Works,* VI, 183.

20. S. H. Butcher, *Aristotle's Theory of Poetry and Fine Art* (London: Macmillan, 1927), pp. 36f.

21. *Works,* VI, 202f.; cf. VIII, 440f.

22. B. F. Skinner, *A Matter of Consequence: Part Three of an Autobiography* (New York: Alfred A. Knopf, 1983), p. 407; *Works,* VIII, 68.

23. *Works,* VIII, 46; I, 221.

24. Ernest Jones, *The Life and Work of Sigmund Freud* (New York: Basic Books, 1957), III, 410.

25. In Sigmund Freud, *Delusion and Dream,* ed. Philip Rieff (Boston: Beacon Press, 1956), p. 133.

26. Jones, *Life and Work of Sigmund Freud,* III, 421.

27. *Works,* XII, 223.

28. See William Rossky, "Imagination in the English Renaissance: Psychology and Poetics," *Studies in the Renaissance* 1 (1958), 49ff.

29. *Works,* XII, 82; cf. VI, 340.

30. George Puttenham, *The Arte of English Poesie,* ed. G. D. Willcock and Alice Walker (Cambridge: Cambridge University Press, 1936), p. 3.

31. *Works,* VII, 285 and passim.

32. See Henry Guerlac, "Newton and the Method of Analysis," in *Dictionary of the History of Ideas* (New York: Scribner's, 1973), III, 385; Gerald Holton, *Thematic Origins of Scientific Thought: Kepler to Einstein* (Cambridge, Mass.: Harvard University Press, 1973), pp. 50f.; and I. B. Cohen, *Revolution in Science* (Cambridge, Mass.: Harvard University Press, 1985), p. 149.

33. *Works,* VI, 204; cf. VIII, 442.

34. *Works,* XIII, 117.

35. Giambattista Vico, *The New Science,* trans. T. G. Bergin and M. H. Fisch (Ithaca, N.Y.: Cornell University Press, 1948), pp. 40, 108, 150f.

36. *Works,* VIII, 444.

37. *Works,* VI, 204.

38. *Works,* VI, 202; VIII, 439; II, xiii.

39. *Works,* II, 220; cf. VI, 202.

40. *Works,* VI, 259, 258.

41. *Works,* VI, 236.

42. *Works,* VI, 206, 237.

43. *Works,* VIII, 440; cf. II, 221.

44. *Works,* VIII, 441; II, xiii.

45. *Works,* XII, 209.

46. *Works,* VIII, 90.

47. *Works,* VI, 206.

48. In J. E. Spingarn, *Critical Essays of the Seventeenth Century* (Oxford: Oxford University Press, 1949), I, 177.

49. *Works,* II, 250.

50. Leonardo da Vinci, *Paragone: A Comparison of the Arts,* ed. and trans. I. A. Richter (Oxford: Oxford University Press, 1908), pp. 52, 49, 53, 57, 65.

51. *Works,* VI, 202.

52. J. E. Spingarn, *A History of Literary Criticism in the Renaissance* (New York: Columbia University Press, 1908), p. 268.

53. Sir Philip Sidney, *Complete Works,* ed. Albert Feuillerat (Cambridge: Cambridge University Press, 1923), III, 12ff., 34.

54. Sidney, *Works,* III, 29.

55. Sidney, *Works,* III, 30.

56. Sidney, *Works,* III, 15.

57. Sidney, *Works,* III, 8.

58. J. C. Scaliger, *Poetices Libri Septem* (Lyon, 1561), facsimile (Stuttgart: Fromann, 1964), p. 3.

59. *Works,* VI, 327.

60. See L. C. Knights, "Bacon and the Seventeenth-Century Dissociation of Sensibility," in *Explorations: Essays in Criticism* (New York: George W. Stewart, 1947), p. 108; also T. H. Jameson, *Francis Bacon: Criticism and the Modern World* (New York: Praeger, 1954).

61. M. W. Bundy, "Bacon's True Opinion of Poetry," *Studies in Philology* 27 (April 1930), 2, 244ff.

62. *Works,* V, 371, 398.

63. Joseph Glanvill, *Scepsis Scientifica: An Essay of the Vanity of Dogmatizing,* ed. John Owen (London: Kegan, Paul, 1885), p. iii.

64. See A. G. Baumgarten, *Reflections on Poetry* (*Meditationes philosophicae de nonnullis ad poema pertinentibus,* 1735), trans. and ed. Karl Aschenbrenner and W. B. Holther (Berkeley: University of California Press, 1954).

65. Joseph Addison, *The Spectator,* ed. D. F. Bond (Oxford: Oxford University Press, 1965), III, 574 (No. 420, July 2, 1712).

RICHARD L. REGOSIN

The Boundaries of Interpretation: Self, Text, Contexts in Montaigne's Essays

On all its various routes toward the object, in all its directions, the word encounters an alien word and cannot help encountering it in a living, tension-filled interaction. Only the mythical Adam, who approached a virginal and as yet verbally unqualified world with his first word, could really have escaped from start to finish the dialogic inter-orientation with the alien word that occurs in the object.

M. M. Bakhtin, *The Dialogic Imagination*

I

Montaigne's *Essays,* it could be argued, present themselves as historical truth, as the faithful self-portrait of the writer, the accurate first-person account of those trials of judgment which are both the record of the essayist's experience and the very composition of the text. The insistence on the sincerity and good faith of the presentation with which the work opens, the assertion of consubstantiality of writer and text, the metaphor of portraiture itself, urge acceptance of the essays as historical document, intimately personal and intellectual, and broadly social at the same time. The text's own claim to represent the life, the mind, and the times would appear to authorize a confident extrapolation either from the writing to its source in the existential man and his milieu (to know Montaigne's text is to know the essence of Montaigne and Renaissance France) or from the outside world as source to the writing (to know Montaigne's life and times is to know the essence of the text). To read the essays as document apparently fulfills the intentions of the text.

While the *Essays* thus situate themselves in terms of factual or literal dimensions and with reference to empirical reality, they also prominently display dimensions which are imaginative, transformative, and interpretative, which operate through linguistic and tropological structures, through rhetorical designs and textual strategies. The essays seek to impose upon the reader norms which they valorize as inevitable and irresistible: nature, ignorance, humility, spontaneity, and the activity of self-study itself. They intend that the written be taken as the spoken word and prized as original and authentic; they attempt to convince that writing is doing and making, that the word materializes as flesh and bone (and evaporates as air) and that the text is consubstantial to the man. The writing reinvents Socrates as a literary persona and takes him as the model of Montaigne's invention of himself and as the authority for the essayist's role as author of self and of book.[1]

I would argue that it is only in the juxtaposition and interaction of these diverse and divergent tendencies of the text—that is, of what we might call the documentary function of the writing and its literary-rhetorical elements—that Montaigne's *Essays* illustrate and enact their specificity as a text. Indeed, the essays make the relationship between these textual components—developed perhaps in *all* written discourse to different degrees and related to one another in a variety of ways—an explicit concern of the writing itself. The essayist inquires restlessly into the nature and function of his own discursive practice and into its relationship with all that would claim to explain, condition, and determine it as origin, influence, or referent.

This interaction or dialogue between seemingly incompatible inclinations generates tensions which are only heightened by the essayist's obsessive probing of the signifying capacity of language, the status of representation, and the value of interpretation itself. Traditional interpretive practices, however, uncomfortable with irresolution, have sought through a variety of strategies to reduce, control, or repress the tensions produced by it. Synoptic content analysis, for example, has allowed its interpretive narratives to exclude specific literary elements, textual gaps, and indeterminacies; biographical study and the focus on ideas has authorized the extrapolation of selected fragments without inquiring into their function in the writing or their specific articulation as language.[2] And some recent formalist approaches (both new critical and poststructuralist) which have sought to counteract the preponderance of documentary studies have neutralized the discrepant historical dimension by having the writing derive primarily from aesthetic and rhetorical sources.

The complexity of Montaigne's text, then, its own insistence that it be read as both "historical" *and* "literary"—and as their interaction—and its persistent questioning of its own status as discourse, would seem to encourage a reading of the *Essays* that explores the problematical nature of textuality itself. In their concern with the relationship of text and context, with the interaction between the "inside" and the "outside" of writing, the *Essays* set before the reader issues central to the understanding of all written discourse, including that produced by the reader in his or her own interpretive dialogue with the text.

II

Montaigne's text clearly affirms the distinction between the historical and the literary. In terms which recall the traditional Aristotelian antithesis between history and poetry, the essayist distinguishes between his own choice of material that *could* have happened and the use others make of that which *did* happen. "Fabulous testimonies," he claims in "On the power of the imagination," "provided that they are possible, serve [him] as well as true ones" (I, 27, 75).[3] Montaigne's criterion is not truth but utility; if the story exemplifies some aspect of human potential and profit can be drawn from its recounting, then the didactic and moral ends of the writing are served. In the study Montaigne claims to make of behavior and motives, historical accuracy has no special status. The verisimilar, as the traditional sign of the poetic or literary, or of what the essayist himself calls "shadow" (*umbre*), as opposed to "substance," provides him with a means to truth.

If in Aristotelian terms Montaigne's text appears to set itself apart from history, it remains at the same time entirely consistent with the practices of Renaissance historiography. Although history was already being discussed as a mode of scientific inquiry, it was still considered primarily as a branch of literature, an art of representation. In their concern with the ethical dimension of culture and with the mediation of exemplary action attributed to the past, humanist historians made use of aesthetic and rhetorical criteria both for judging moral action and for writing history itself. They reconstructed and evaluated the past in terms of decorum, eloquence, copia, and harmonia and they informed their writing according to the same principles.[4] History's purpose was to persuade to virtuous behavior, and it called upon the resources of rhetoric to argue by example, to teach precept through image, to focus the vision of man on his own action through illustration, *enargia.* As long as the example, as the primary figure of history, moved the reader to moral action, it mattered little whether it was true or invented. Montaigne articulates this view in "Of the power of the imagination": "Plutarch might well say to us," the essayist writes, "that the credit belongs to others if his examples are wholly and everywhere true; but that their being useful to posterity, and presented with a luster which lights our way to virtue, that is his work" (I, 27, 76). "There is no danger," Montaigne adds in closing the essay, "as there is in a medicinal drug—in an old story being this way or that."[5]

Montaigne, of course, does not claim to be writing history. He declares his natural inability to sustain an extended narrative and through the use he makes of historical material drawn from his reading, he renders its exemplary status problematical. In the context of the *Essays,* the lessons of history as teacher, in any broad sense, are uncertain and unreliable, as the titles of so many of the individual essays attest: "By diverse means we arrive at the same end" (I, 1); "One man's profit is another man's harm" (I, 22); "Various outcomes of the same plan" (I, 24); "Of the inconsistency of our actions" (II, 1).[6] But this unwillingness to impose an ordered structure or a coherent form on history, and the essayist's proliferation of individual examples, intended sometimes to teach "à contre-poil," do not lessen the essay's proximity to historical practice and its implications for our understanding of the relationship of text and context.

The conflation of *historia* and *fabula,* both in historiography and in the *Essays,* discloses that the text is not determined or driven in any simple way by that which might be taken as its "outside." Without relinquishing its foothold in existential reality, the writing is not bound by a uniquely referential or mimetic function. Its content or matter is not generated to represent scrupulously the empirical world; rather, it derives as well from itself, and finds its source in the very power of the literary and rhetorical imagination which stimulates Montaigne both to recount fabulous examples and testimonies and to raise questions about the status of his discourse. To fulfill its moral and didactic purpose, the writing can separate itself from any necessary concern for historical accuracy.

The turn to rhetoric both illustrates and enacts the complex interaction of text and context, for rhetoric is *both* what we might call "in itself" and "beyond itself." That is, rhetoric serves first as the source and the means of textual production. It provides the topics and structures of invention and disposition, the figures of style, the rules of eloquence and decorum which serve as criteria for judgment. But the rhetorically generated text is not exclusively "in itself"; its telos exists outside in the reader who must be persuaded to virtuous action if the rhetoric is to fulfill its function. Moreover, as I mentioned earlier, rhetorical criteria such as harmony, gravity, and decorum which serve to determine aesthetic worth become both grids imposed on empirical material to disclose and evaluate historical patterns *and* norms for determining individual moral behavior. When Montaigne refers to his essays as "the study I am making of our behavior and motives" in "Of the power of the imagination," and in that context justifies the use of "fabulous testimonies," his purpose seems moral and epistemological, but can either be separated from the rhetorical? Textual practice, its figures or tropes, and style itself, are inseparable from action *and* knowledge. Aesthetic and rhetorical considerations inform both literature and life and confound the simple distinction between them. The notion that the verisimilar is the means to verity suggests not only that the boundaries between history and fiction, life and literature, context and text are crossed, but that in a more radical way each domain is implicated in the other, always already informs and defines the other. Any simple designation of source, any simple mimetic theory or interpretation of cause and effect, risks reducing and distorting the designation of the boundary as a threshold where seeming opposites enter into tensely charged relationships.[7]

III

In the same essay "Of the power of the imagination," the essayist further complicates the status of context by raising questions about its accessibility. Montaigne wonders quizzically how what he calls "people of exquisite and exact conscience and prudence" (76)[8] could undertake to write history in any Aristotelian sense, given the difficulty of determining accurately "what has happened," even in terms of present events. It is less hazardous, he states, to write of things past than present, since the writer has only to give an account of a borrowed truth.

But borrowed truth, of course, is no less problematical than the partial and conjectured truth of current events. The borrowed truth of past events exists only as texts which either (1) record only their own hypothetical present, or (2) reconstruct their past only in reference to other texts, other borrowed truths. The project of documentary history thus finds itself in a double bind, caught between the imagined (or imaginary) truth of a present at first hand and the secondhand truth of a past already mediated by prior writing, prior narrative. In neither case does context allow for the immediate apprehension of reality, or its unproblematical representation as text. Between the two, the reader must confront the aporia that interpretation seeks endlessly to overcome through the generation of further writing.

Traditionally unconcerned with the problematical status of context which Montaigne's text underscores, the literary historian has too often gone about reconstructing the historical milieu from legal records and documents, personal memoirs, first-person accounts, and the *Essays* themselves, without regard either for the complex textuality of the documentation or the literary implications of the narrative practice. In the legitimate concern with context, the historian is always confronted with *textualized* remainders of the past. The historical task is always one of the reading and interpretation of written evidence from the past, of the multiple elements of cultural, social, political, and religious life which form vast signifying networks, and of the historical works which have already been written. The context, like the text itself, is multiple and complex, composed of diverse and contradictory tendencies and voices, conflictual and open-ended. It is no less opaque, no more readily accessible than the written itself; and just as textual gaps and indeterminacies, paradoxes and silences cannot be glossed over without losing the specificity of the work, so the pluralities, inconsistencies, and oppositions of context cannot be meaningfully confronted by a methodology that too hastily unifies or totalizes.

IV

The metaphor of reading context informs the *Essays* themselves, where the art of physiognomy serves as the emblem for the problematical act of interpretation. What is at stake here is not only the integrity of Montaigne's literal face as the sign of his character, or the unreliability of Socrates' face, or even the meaning of the figurative faces of current history, of war, of death, and most significantly, of nature itself. "The face is a weak guarantee," the essayist declares in "On physiognomy," "yet it deserves some consideration" (III, 12, 811), as if to underscore the inability of any act of reading to master fully its object.[9] What concerns the essayist most centrally is the problem of reading or situating his own discourse with regard to context, that is, of determining to what degree it is original and authentic and to what degree borrowed or alien.[10] The weight of what the essays take from their multiple contexts — historical, literary, philosophical, social — is enormous and threatens always to overwhelm the expression of a self which Montaigne claims as his own.

Montaigne's concern can be phrased as the question, "How does the self constitute itself in history?" What is its relation to a past which has already articulated the attitudes, values, and beliefs, the norms and truths that a man might pretend were his "own" and to a present which constantly draws him out and away from what he might name as "himself"? The opening lines of the essay establish the opposition between self and other, private and public, in the framework of an overpowering tradition ("Almost all the opinions we have are taken on authority and on credit," [792]) and a debilitating contemporary context ("So feeble an age") which undermine from the outset the possibility of an integral self.[11] The essayist's insistence here, and through the essays as a whole, on the force of ambition, the lure of glory and the attraction of pomp and ostentation may be offset by his realization of their emptiness ("Our world is formed only for ostentation; men inflate themselves only with wind, and go bouncing around like balls" [793]), but this knowledge does not negate their power or diminish their pull once and for all.[12] Similarly, the bookish tradition to which Montaigne is drawn, and from which he in turn draws conventional learning, exerts a powerful influence on the formation of his ideas and the composition of his book. The ubiquitous quotation in the essays attests to the weight of a cultural tradition and the strength of common practice to which the essayist bows: "Indeed I have yielded to public opinion in carrying these borrowed ornaments about on me. . . . I load myself with these borrowings more and more heavily every day beyond my intention and my original form, following the fancy of the age and the exhortation of others" (808).[13]

In this context, the figure of Socrates is "presented to the world as an example" (793) as if it were possible to follow that model, to fashion a self "by itself," without going outside itself.[14] Montaigne's Socrates responds in opposition to that very intellectual tradition and social environment which threatens to engulf the nascent self. The essay depicts a Socrates situated in a remote historical past, an original, primordial self constituted outside of tradition and culture, the negation of the institutions and practices of his time. In supremely performative discourse which both illustrates and enacts his being, Socrates represents "the pure and primary impression and ignorance of Nature" (807).[15] His language is that of ordinary or natural man, a language unencumbered by culture or learning; its inductions and similes are drawn from the commonest actions; its thoughts represent ordinary and common ideas. Socrates needs no more than the pure and simple notions of a child to produce the most beautiful achievements of our soul. The child, the peasant, cobblers, masons, and women, marginal figures who lie outside of (high) culture serve Montaigne and his Socrates as examples of the natural, innocent self.

To what extent can *this* Socrates serve as a model to a Montaigne situated inextricably in culture, a Montaigne so drawn to his contexts that he must constantly remind himself to keep to himself: "I have long been preaching to myself to stick to myself and break away from outside things; nevertheless I still keep turning my eyes to one side" (800).[16] The reader of "Of physiognomy" confronts personae diametrically opposed: a self-sufficient Socrates and dependent Montaigne, a sage who would not borrow from the great orator Lysias a written speech to save his own life, who would not commit his fate to art and its ornaments "to bedeck itself with the make-up of the figures and fictions of a memorized oration" (807),[17] and an essayist who commits the very composition of himself to a written composition, who gathers borrowed flowers to make something of his own, who dresses himself up in learned figures to learn something about himself. If Socrates is the "interpreter of the simplicity of nature" (805),[18] Montaigne is the interpreter of books, the reader of Plutarch and Seneca, of Cicero, where he seeks knowledge of life and death. Nature stands in opposition to *science, doctrine,* and *art,* the self to that which is foreign to it, to contexts outside itself, to culture, to history. That which is characterized as pure (nature, the child) opposes that which is by implication impure.

If Socrates is needed to interpret the simplicity of nature, it is because nature has been contaminated by *science, doctrine,* and *art* and so no longer stands integrally on her own: "And men have done with Nature as perfumers do with oil: they have sophisticated her with so many arguments and farfetched reasonings ['appellez du dehors'] that she has become variable and particular for each man, and has lost her own constance and universal countenance ['visage']."[19] The image is one of a mixing of elements that corrupts an original entity, a bringing in from "outside" of a foreign substance which renders impure and falsifies, which deceives all who would pretend to see (know, read) it. In fact, mixture is the dominant metaphor of "Of physiognomy." Montaigne himself cannot keep himself separate from foreign things, as the lines cited above indicate. Not able to "stick to himself," he mixes himself in an outside which is elsewhere (*ailleurs*) and alien (*estrangere*) to the self. The book, as the essayist allows, could be considered a "bunch of other people's flowers" ['fleurs étrangères'], perhaps not too different from the "concoctions of common places" (808) which are his source books. These mixtures, made of "borrowed ornaments," confound inside and outside and contaminate "what is naturally my own" (808).

The social and political upheaval in contemporary France, which Montaigne incorporates in the essay as its historical context, mirrors the confounding of elements which obscures what is real. Wickedness covers itself with the cloak of virtue, and disguises its true face in what the essayist calls "this confusion that we have been in" (800).[20] Even his personal situation is contaminated, his affections and political loyalties beclouded by the situation of his house and his friends which present him with one face, and his life and actions which give him another: "there is never a lack of apparent grounds in such a mixed-up confusion" (799).[21] The civil war raging in the country upsets the proper disposition of the state and turns it unnaturally against itself in the devastating confusion of inside and outside: "Monstrous war! Other wars act outward ['au dehors']; this one acts also against itself, eats and destroys itself by its own venom" (796).[22] France is sick, the essayist claims, employing the commonplace figure to describe the body politic in its state of turmoil and contamination: "In these epidemics one can distinguish at the beginning the well from the sick; but when they come to last, like ours, the whole body is affected, head and heels alike; no part is free from corruption" (796).[23]

This profound confusion of original distinctions, of the discrete oppositions which organize and order thought and experience, is dramatically signified in the problematical medicine brought to the cure, for what is meant to heal poisons and kills: "It [war] comes to cure sedition and is full of it, would chastise disobedience and sets the example of it; and employed in defense of the laws, plays the part of a rebel against its own laws. What have we come to? *Our medicine carries infection*" (796; my emphasis).[24] Is there any political disease so bad, Montaigne asks, that it is worth combating with so deadly a drug? But if the state cannot take what belongs properly outside and introduce it as a remedy without poisoning itself, neither can the individual take on what is exterior to itself to cure its ills. In this central concern of the essay, Montaigne employs the same vocabulary of the cure that infects to represent the danger of ingesting *science* and *doctrine:* "But learning ['les sciences'] . . . There is some of it that only hampers and burdens us instead of feeding us, and also some which, under color of curing us, poisons us" (794).[25] This remark immediately precedes his denigration of "the study of books" and his argument that learning is superfluous to living: "We need hardly any learning [*doctrine*] to live at ease. And Socrates teaches us that it is in us. . . . All this ability of ours that is beyond the natural is as good as vain and superfluous" (794).[26] Learning is dangerous and unnecessary, or it could be argued that it is dangerous *because* unnecessary; it is surplus, beyond the natural, beyond what is authentic and original, what is "in us." Only in the "feverish excesses of our mind" does man seek what is itself excess, does he abandon the real, seduced and deceived by a dangerous supplement which misleads his disordered desire from the straight and natural path into error: "The dangerous supplement breaks with nature."[27]

In an ironic play with traditional Christian terminology, Montaigne condemns the allure of books which tempt and stimulate the appetite of the mind and what he calls the voluptuous complacency of the soul, and tickle them with the notion of being learned. To curb this disordered appetite and blunt the cupidity which pricks men to study, the essayist cites the religious vows of poverty and chastity as examples. To safeguard the purity of the mind from intellectual corruption, men would live destitute of learning and would, as Montaigne says, "castrate our disorderly appetites" (794).[28] By the dramatic act of intellectual self-mutilation, the essayist would cut himself off from what is exterior to himself, everything that is supplementary and therefore unnatural, thus making himself resistant to temptation and immune to pollution and restoring the purity of desire, the innocence of being and truth. Rather than create a lack or an absence, the castration returns man to wholeness, both of himself and of nature.

The lesson of Socrates, then, teaches that the outside must be kept in its place, excluded, quarantined to avoid contaminating man avid for knowledge and enticed by power and prestige. When he is drawn out beyond the natural into the dangerously supplementary, the mixing of self and other exacts what the essayist calls "a dear cost." Seeking remedy for his ignorance or status man infects himself with the untruth of writing (learning, books). Like the drug or medicine which enacts the mixture of cure and poison to make them indistinguishable, learning (and all that is not the self) operates the confusion of inside and outside, and obfuscates the distinctions between the true and the false, the good and the bad, the substantial and the empty. As the body politic suffers from its remedy, so the essayist suffers from his. How can things be kept in their place to avoid mixture and contamination?

V

Book learning and writing are thus opposed to true knowledge, a knowledge which one derives from the self, by oneself. Nature, the essayist claims, speaks within man and provides all that he need know to live at ease, that is, in the context of this essay, all that he need know about death: "Collect yourself: you will find in yourself Nature's arguments against death, true ones, and the fittest to serve you in case of necessity" (794).[29] The animals, peasants, and simple people whose attitudes toward death Montaigne cites (like those Socrates would cite), exemplify those untouched by doctrine and therefore innocent; their serenity in the face of death derives only from themselves and contrasts with the terror and apprehension of the philosophers who go beyond themselves seeking remedies, who read books, study, dispute. In the general contamination of nature by learning and art, the "rustic, unpolished mob" (803) may reveal the traces of her image but they cannot be models for the learned essayist. He cannot recover the "stupidity and lack of apprehension of the vulgar [which] gives them this endurance . . . and this profound nonchalance" (805); and although he calls ironically for the establishment of a "school of stupidity," he goes to school instead to learn *ignorance* with Socrates as his teacher (*regen*).[30] Assuming the position of Socrates and articulating the words of this supreme interpreter of the simplicity of Nature in his paraphrase of the speech before the judges, Montaigne achieves the desired *nonchallante* posture in a form proper to it: "it is a speech [*discours*] which in its naturalness ranks far behind and below common opinions. In an unstudied and artless boldness and a childlike assurance it represents the pure and primary impression and ignorance of Nature" (807).[31] In this overdetermined judgment, nature regains her proper place in discourse, or more precisely, *as* oral discourse, as natural language which speaks true.

Montaigne's effort to put things back in their place finds striking expression in the subject of physiognomy which he raises specifically toward the end of the essay. To this point, faces have been deceptive indicators of truth, elements of a general confusion of outside and inside, as we have seen. Beginning with a short discussion which insists on the commonplace coincidence of body and soul, beauty and virtue ("there is nothing more likely than the conformity and relation of the body to the spirit" [809]), the essayist claims that face and character can conform, that although the face is a weak guarantee, it nevertheless deserves some consideration.[32] The *Essays'* two most prominent exceptions prove the rule: although Socrates' ugliness appears to belie his divine wisdom, it faithfully reflects an earlier inclination to vice; la Boétie's ugliness was rather a superficial unattractiveness which "is less prejudicial to the state of the spirit and not very certain in its effect on men's opinion" (810).[33] But it is Montaigne's own face which returns nature to its rightful place, which overcomes opposition, discrepancy, confusion (of inside and outside) to set truth unequivocally in view, to fulfill "the promises which Nature had implanted on [his] brow": "I have a favorable bearing, both in itself and in others' interpretation" (811).[34] Montaigne's physiognomy uncovers the true face of nature, constant and universal. That which was outside, alien, excess, which contaminated and polluted has been expelled and excluded to recover the unity of surface and substance, and restore the integrity and wholeness of self: "As I have said elsewhere, I have simply and crudely adopted for my own sake this ancient precept: that we cannot go wrong by following Nature, that the sovereign precept is to conform to her. I have not, like Socrates, corrected my natural disposition by force of reason, and have not troubled my inclination at all by art. I let myself go as I have come. I combat nothing. My two ruling parts, of their own volition, live in peace and good accord" (811).[35] As the essayist earlier took for his own the posture and the words of Socrates, so here he takes his place altogether as the emblem of nature. The truth of that nature, first expressed in "Socrates' mouth," now becomes a function of "my lips" (*ma bouche*). Montaigne's own spoken words, consistent with his face and with what one reads in his eyes, are unequivocal, transparent signs of his intentions; he is never misjudged, he claims, as long as his freedom to speak his mind is heard "from my lips." Only when the words are repeated, mediated by a third party — either by a person or by print — do they betray that mind and reintroduce confusion: "Words when reported [*redictes*] have a different sense, as they have a different sound" (814).[36] By reaffirming the primacy of voice as the origin of truth, Montaigne guarantees nature's discourse and returns the dangerous supplements — learning, books, writing — to their proper place.

VI

This reading of "Of physiognomy" represents Montaigne's effort to secure the originary status of nature and to establish the authenticity of being and its discourse by rooting them in that nature, universal and constant. Like genuine virtue, "born in us from its own roots, from the seed of universal reason that is implanted in every man who is not denatured" (811),[37] self and its language emerge organically, from within themselves, to represent the presence and plenitude of the true and the real. It is the essence of truth that it is repeatable, stable, universal, identifiable as equal to itself, like the Platonic Idea. But Montaigne's text also demonstrates that if the disappearance or loss of truth as presence and origin is the condition for the possibility of its recovery, it is also, at the same time, the condition for its impossibility, for nontruth.[38] The project of the *Essays* derives from an overwhelming sense of diversity and alterity, fragmentation, absence, and confusion which cannot be finally overcome. The work returns always to acknowledge the consequences of *its* origin, indeed to disclose itself also as heterogeneity and indeterminacy, as the factitiousness of imitation and representation. The essayist would give voice to nature, but he must borrow an image of nature and naturalize it through rhetorical strategies and tropes, as we have seen with the organic metaphor. He must reinvent its interpreter, Socrates, as a figure of the text. When he seeks to articulate a discourse which is his own, and only itself, speaking, as Montaigne says, "absolutely all alone" (808), he must reappropriate the words of others (and most prominently of Socrates) and reinscribe them in its place. Presence and truth are always mediated through the writing, that very writing which is both the occasion for its repetition and, as Montaigne recognized, the necessity of its deformation.

Thus it might be said that Montaigne's text of "Of physiognomy" enacts the very opposite of the project it intended. Seeking to put things back in their proper place, to restore the distinctions between inside and outside, good and bad, by the absolute separation of learning and art from nature and their ultimate exclusion or suppression, the essay performs the inevitability of their interrelationship and the necessity of their mutual dependence. This was the lesson of "Of the power of the imagination" which affirmed the open boundaries between history and fiction, life and literature, text and context and illustrated that textual practice and its rhetorical instrumentation are inseparable from action and knowledge. But while the text posits mixture and interaction as benign in "Of the power of the imagination" ("There is no danger—as there is in a medicinal drug—in an old story being this way or that" [76]), it affirms in "Of physiognomy" that all confusion, commingling, overlap is potentially dangerous, that the drug itself as the very emblem of mixture is always "this way *and* that." The effort to recover the truth of nature, because it is lost in original presence and plenitude, requires that nature be represented, that the gap be filled by an image, an imitation, by writing. Its (absent) face must become a figure of rhetorical presentation, and thus be defaced by the very remedy introduced to restore it to presence. The bind is double here but the essayist also confirms as his closing words (in Plutarch's words) that *all* things have two faces, as Plutarch presented them, "variously and contrastingly" (814). The word and the alien word cannot help encountering each other in the living, tension-filled interaction which is the boundary itself.

NOTES

1. I have examined these various strategies in depth in *The Matter of My Book* (Berkeley: University of California Press, 1977).

2. Dominick LaCapra, *Rethinking Intellectual History: Texts, Contexts, Language* (Ithaca, N.Y.: Cornell University Press, 1983), chap. 1.

3. Quotations in English are from *The Complete Essays of Montaigne,* trans. Donald M. Frame (Stanford: Stanford University Press, 1958). French quotations are from *Les Essais de Michel de Montaigne,* ed. Pierre Villey and V. L. Saulnier (Paris: Presses Universitaires de France, 1965). "Les tesmoignages fabuleux, pourveu qu'ils soient possibles, y servent comme les vrais" (p. 105).

4. Nancy Streuver, *The Language of History* (Princeton, N.J.: Princeton University Press, 1970), p. 67.

5. "Plutarche nous diroit volontiers de ce qu'il en a faict, que c'est l'ouvrage d'autruy, que ses exemples soient en tout et par tout veritables; qu'ils soient utiles à la posterité, et presentez d'un lustre qui nous esclaire à la vertu, que c'est son ouvrage. Il n'est pas dangereux, comme en une drogue medicinale, en un compte ancien, qu'il soit ainsin ou ainsi" (p. 106).

6. "Par divers moyens on arrive à pareille fin"; "Le profit de l'un est dommage de l'autre"; "Divers evenemens de mesme conseil"; "De l'inconstance de nos actions."

7. Suzanne Gearhart analyzes the complex relationship between history and fiction in *The Open Boundary of History and Fiction* (Princeton, N.J.: Princeton University Press, 1984). She argues persuasively in her study of eighteenth-century literature and historiography that history and fiction are inextricably implicated in each other.

8. " . . . telles gens d'exquise et exacte conscience et prudence" (p. 106).

9. "C'est une foible garantie que la mine; toutesfois elle a quelque consideration" (p. 1059).

10. I have profited from Terence Cave's analysis of this issue and of Montaigne's relation to Socrates in his excellent pages on "De la phisionomie" in *The Cornucopian Text* (Oxford: Clarendon Press, 1979), pp. 302–12.

11. "... quasi toutes ces opinions que nous avons sont prinses par authorité et à credit" (p. 1037); "un siecle si foible."

12. "Nostre monde n'est formé qu'à l'ostentation: les hommes ne s'enflent que de vent, et se manient à bonds, comme les balons" (p. 1037).

13. "Certes j'ay donné à l'opinion publique que ces parements empruntez m'accompagnent. . . . Je m'en charge de plus fort tous les jours outre ma proposition et ma forme premiere, sur la fantasie du siecle et enhortemens d'autruy" (p. 1055).

14. "... presenté au monde pour exemple" (p. 1038).

15. "... la pure et premiere impression et ignorance de la nature" (p. 1054).

16. "Je me presche il y a si long temps de me tenir à moy, et separer des choses estrangeres; toutesfois je tourne encores tousjours les yeux à costé" (p. 1045).

17. "... pour se parer du fard des figures et feintes d'une oraison apprinse" (p. 1054).

18. "... interprete de la simplicité naturelle" (p. 1052).

19. "Et en ont faict les hommes comme les parfumiers de l'huile: ils l'ont sophistiquée de tant d'argumentations et de discours appelez du dehors, qu'elle en est devenue variable et particuliere à chacun, et a perdu son propre visage, constant et universel" (pp. 1049–50).

20. "... cette confusion où nous sommes" (p. 1046).

21. "... il n'y a jamais faute d'apparence en un meslange si confus" (p. 1044).

22. "Monstrueuse guerre: les autres agissent au dehors; cette-cy encore contre soy se ronge et se desfaict par son propre venin" (p. 1041).

23. "En ces maladies populaires, on peut distinguer sur le commencement les sains des malades; mais quand elles viennent à durer, comme la nostre, tout le corps s'en sent, et la teste et les talons; aucune partye n'est exempte de corruption" (p. 1041).

24. "Elle [war] vient guarir la sedition et en est pleine, veut chastier la desobeyssance et en montre l'exemple; et employée à la deffense des loix, faict sa part de rebellion à l'encontre des siennes propres. Où en sommes-nous? Nostre medecine porte infection" (p. 1041).

25. "Mais les sciences . . . Il y en a qui ne font que nous empecher et charger au lieu de nourrir, et telles encore qui, sous tiltre de nous guerir, nous empoisonnent" (p. 1039).

26. "Il ne nous faut guiere de doctrine pour vivre à nostre aise. Et Socrates nous aprend qu'elle est en nous. . . . Toute cette nostre suffisance, qui est au delà de la naturelle, est à peu pres vaine et superflue" (p. 1039).

27. "Le dangereux supplément rompt avec la nature." Jacques Derrida, *De la grammatologie* (Paris: Editions de Minuit, 1967), p. 217. Montaigne's text strikingly anticipates Derrida's analyses in Plato ("La pharmacie de Platon") and Rousseau (*De la grammatologie*) of the implications of writing as supplementary and the dangers it poses to the idea of originary Nature (Truth, Presence, Plenitude). The recent work of Terence Cave, Laurence Kritzman, Michel Beaujour, Antoine Compagnon, and my own, has illustrated the remarkable convergence of Renaissance concerns for reading and writing with those of modern Continental criticism.

28. "... chastier [les] appetits desordonnez" (p. 1039).

29. "Recueillez vous; vous trouverez en vous les arguments de la nature contre la mort, vrais, et les plus propres à vous servir à la necessité" (p. 1039).

30. " . . . la stupidité et faute d'apprehension du vulgaire [qui] luy donne cette patience . . . et cette profonde nonchalance" (p. 1052). Montaigne's vocabulary discloses the powerful traces of a conventional conceptual framework which identifies learning with school and teachers, even as the essayist claims the autonomy of nature and self. Like his learning, Montaigne's unlearning (of *doctrine*) must take place in a school, however untraditional. In this context, his claim of weak memory serves him well. See my "The Text of Memory" in *The Dialectic of Discovery* (Lexington, Ky.: French Forum, 1984).

31. " . . . c'est un discours en rang et en naifveté bien plus arriere et plus bas que les opinions communes; il represente en une hardiesse inartificielle et niaise, en une seureté puerile, la pure impression et ignorance de la nature" (p. 1054).

32. " . . . il n'est rien plus vraysemblable que la conformité et relation du corps à l'esprit" (p. 1057).

33. " . . . est de moindre prejudice à l'estat de l'esprit et a peu de certitude en l'opinion des hommes" (p. 1057). Socrates' status as "natural man" appears jeopardized by the *institution* (p. 1058) and *raison* (p. 1059) brought to the correction of the original defects of his character. Montaigne seeks to overcome this paradox by dismissing Socrates' claim to have changed himself ("Mais en le disant je tiens qu'il se mocquoit suivant son usage") and by overdetermining the naturalizing of his speech (see Cave, p. 311). The essayist's statement that he prefers that "virtue née en nous de ses propres racines par la semence de la raison universelle empreinte en tout homme non desnaturé" also touches on this question because it implies, by the repetition of *raison* and its association with that "raison universelle," that Socrates, "homme non desnaturé," changed himself not by artificial and untrue means but by nature itself. In any case, the essay blurs Socrates' recourse to the unnatural to secure his exemplary status.

34. " . . . les promesses que nature [leur] avait plantées au front"; "J'ay un port favorable et en forme et en interpretation" (p. 1059).

35. "J'ay pris, comme j'ay dict ailleurs, bien simplement et cruement pour mon regard ce precepte ancien: que nous ne sçaurions faillir à suivre nature, que le souverain precepte c'est de se conformer à elle. Je n'ay pas corrigé, comme Socrates, par force de la raison mes complexions naturelles, et n'ay aucunement troublé par art mon inclination. Je me laisse aller, comme je suis venu, je ne combats rien, mes deux maitresses pieces vivent de leur grace en pais et bon accord" (p. 1059).

36. "Les paroles redictes ont, comme autre son, autre sens" (p. 1063).

37. " . . . née en nous de ses propres racines par la semence de la raison universelle empreinte en tout homme non desnaturé" (p. 1059).

38. In the closing pages of "La pharmacie de Platon" (*La dissemination*, Paris: Editions du Seuil, 1972), Derrida demonstrates that truth and nontruth are both types of repetition and that repetition is only possible in what he calls "le graphique de la supplémentarité, ajoutant, au défaut d'une unité pleine, une autre unité qui vient la suppléer, étant à la fois la même et assez autre pour remplacer en ajoutant" (pp. 194–95). Montaigne's own effort to affirm the unity of nature takes place in that writing whose supplementarity he decries but to which he must have recourse if he is to attempt that recovery.

ELISE BICKFORD JORGENS

The Singer's Voice in Elizabethan Drama

In 1586, John Case, a musician, published a large and comprehensive defense tract entitled "The Praise of Musicke: Wherein besides the antiquitie, dignitie, delectation, & use thereof in civill matters, is also declared the sober and lawfull use of the same in the congregation and Church of God." Like the others of its kind, Case's work is a reaction to the attacks of critics like the Puritan Stephen Gosson, whose "Schoole of Abuse" (1579) blasted poetry, theater, and music—indeed, the whole milieu of art and entertainment—as incitements to wickedness. In defense of his art, Case has packed his book with the period's lore, calling up all the old stories about music's powers and beneficial effects and adding some conventional wisdom about when and where music can appropriately and judiciously be included in life's events.

But Case begins his seventh chapter, "The Particular Use of Musicke in Civill Matters," with a telling observation, indicating the limits to which he thinks he can go: "Now the civil use, to let pass all generalities which I touched before with a wet finger, may best be collected out of these solemn either actions or assemblies, which are frequented in al politique states, & may be listed for brevities sake within the compass of these four things, to wit, sacrifices, feasts, mariages and burials. For I dare not speak of dauncing or theatrall spectacles, least I pull whole swarmes of enimies upon me."[1] To modern sensibilities, the notion that a man apparently predisposed to think positively about theatrical music would find the subject literally too hot to handle seems ludicrous. Having heard an earnest rendition of the songs in *Twelfth Night*, say, we might well wonder what conceivable "swarmes of enimies" could be raised by discussing a tradition we now consider benignly pleasant.

Case, of course, is being cautious—or perhaps cagey. His purpose, after all, is to clear music of any bad name it had acquired, and he attempts to do so by hauling out all the old, venerable traditions, not by defending its actual use in the situations under attack—notably in the theater. And with good reason, at least within what we might reassemble as an Elizabethan context. Viewed against a backdrop of what people were saying about music and its use, both positive and negative, theater songs do begin to look provocative—or to use a stronger word than the fashionable "subversive," many songs seem downright pugnacious, as if to assert the Liberties' prerogative, flying in the face of critic and defender alike. Evidence from a variety of sources, including songs from the period's plays, suggests that while the so-called Puritan influence did not seriously disturb music's position as a favored pastime nor its roles in theatrical entertainment, the issues raised were not soon dead. The claims of the attackers and the counterclaims of the defenders are to be heard in the onstage singing in Elizabethan drama, carrying on the culture's debate about the practical value and moral efficacy of music.

The existence of the writings of critics and apologists has been of interest to scholars concerned with any of the arts in Elizabethan society; students of the theater in particular have paid heed to such critics as Gosson, and to his critics. Musicologists too have been alert to what these writers can tell us about music's status, and scholarly opinion has vacillated between the position—apparently initiated by pioneer music historian Charles Burney and perpetuated throughout the late eighteenth and nineteenth centuries—that Elizabethan Puritans were as dogmatically opposed to music as they were to the theater and therefore had a significant negative impact on Elizabethan musical life, and the more recent one that the influence of such critics had been greatly exaggerated.[2] The names of detractors other than Gosson are rarely mentioned by modern musicologists; some of music's critics, they note, were not Puritans; and even Gosson, they point out, did not openly object to suitable household music.[3] David Price, for instance, notes that "It was the 'incitements to whoredome' and the abuse of the powers of music for 'effeminate' ends which drew forth the most vitriolic expressions of Protestant opinion and thereby a continuing stream of tracts defending music as recreation,"[4] commenting on "the importance of private music-making, which the Reformation fostered almost unawares."[5] Modern musicology has thus promoted the idea that the practical, *musical* response to attack was to turn to private—and thereby acceptable—music-making, in effect defusing the critics. But while musical sources indicate a strong and growing tradition of household music, both devotional and recreational, the evidence from other, nonmusical sources suggests that the questions raised by the critics, whether Puritan or not, remained in the minds of many unresolved and perhaps unresolvable. Private music-making clearly did not supplant its objectionable public manifestations, and sources as diverse as statements by musicians like Case justifying their profession, pedagogical treatises by the schoolmasters and tutors of the period proclaiming music's value in the training of a schoolboy (or girl) and courtier, medical handbooks of the home-remedy variety insisting on music's therapeutic effects, and the tracts of religious men like Richard Hooker attesting its moral and spiritual benefits—all these suggest that attacks like Gosson's were, in fact, taken seriously.

In a culture with a love for categorizing, music was difficult to place. It is hard to imagine being genuinely concerned with the charge that music (especially Elizabethan music) could be an "incitement to whoredom" or guilty of some of the other charges we shall encounter below, and the very notion of *abuse*, which we shall see raised repeatedly, is, to me, incomprehensible. But to see the theatrical songs as a man like Gosson must have seen them, it is important to recognize that music, even more than the other arts, offers the potential for real dangers of the sort envisioned. For one thing, despite the efforts of the madrigalists to depict scenes and images and emotions with music, its fundamentally nonrepresentational nature made it fair game for almost any contentions as to its effects. Theorists spent considerable time and effort making their claims for its powers, but who could prove that music did or did not say anything at all? Or that the musical configurations one person found devotionally inspiring were not incitements to lust for another? Although this unfixed quality of musical expression was not acknowledged or discussed by either theorists or practitioners, music seems to have shared with eating and sex, in the Renaissance mind, the troublesome paradoxical position of having the potential for great good *and* great evil. Its defenders characteristically began by asserting its divine origins, referring to the heavenly harmony and the service to which the music had always been put in the worship of God. But because of its avowed capability of arousing the passions, music was also quite obviously open to the charge of fomenting excess and sinful behavior.

Gosson's attack may be taken as "typical" of the anti-music movement, not because we possess scores of others like it but because if we read backward from the counterstatements, and obliquely from the plays, we have to conclude either that Gosson was a much more powerful figure than seems likely, or that others echoed his sentiments. His charge, in characteristically hyperbolic prose, goes as follows:

Were the *Argiues* & *Pythagoras* nowe aliue, & saw how many frets, how many stringes, how many stops, how many keyes, how many cliffes, howe many moodes, how many flats, how many sharps, how many rules, how many spaces, how many noates, how many restes, how many querks, how many corners, what chopping, what changing, what tossing, what turning, what wresting & wringing is among our Musitions, I beleue verily that they would cry out with the countryman: *Heu quòd tam pingui macer est mihi taurus in arno.* Alas here is fat feeding, & leane beasts: or as one said at the shearing of hogs, great cry & litle wool, much adoe, & smal help. . . . When the *Sicilians,* and *Dores* forsooke the playn-song that they had learned of their auncestours in the Mountaynes, and practised long among theyr herdes, they founde out such descant in *Sybaris* instrumentes, that by daunsing and skipping they fell into lewdnesse of life. Neither staied these abuses in the compasse of that countrey: but like vnto yll weedes in time spread so far, that they choked the good grayne in euery place.

For as Poetrie & Piping are Cosen germans: so piping, and playing are of great affinity, and all three chayned in links of abuse.[6]

This is followed up by a lengthy diatribe against prostitutes, with reference both to their "working" the theaters and to their employment of music in the plying of their trade: "If their houses bee searched, some instrumente of Musicke is layde in sighte to dazell the eyes of euery Officer, and all that are lodged in the house by night, or frequente it by day, come thither as pupilles to be well schoolde."[7]

Gosson's concern seems to have focused largely on sex and on what he took to be music's role in inciting lewd and wanton sexual behavior. His views no doubt reflect a private obsession (indeed, Thomas Lodge implies as much in his response to Gosson, saying to his reader, "you heare open confession, these Abuses are disclaimed by our GOSSON, he is sory that hee hath so leudly liued, and spent the oyle of his perfection in vnsauery lampes").[8] But in the larger scheme, Gosson's views are not incompatible with the commonplace Renaissance (and of course much earlier) conviction that music could control the passions—a conviction that is *never* disputed by the defenders but is, instead, turned to positive account. Thus Richard Mulcaster says, "The science it selfe hath naturally a verie forcible strength to trie and to tuche the inclination of the minde, to this or that affection, thorough the propertie of number, wheron it consisteth, which made the *Pythagorian,* and not him alone to plat the soule out so much vpon number."[9] And Timothie Bright, in *A Treatise of Melancholie* (1586), writes, "that which reason worketh by a more evident way, that musicke as it were a magicall charme bringeth to passe in the mindes of men, which being forseene of wise law givers in times past, they have made choice of certaine kindes thereof, and have rejected the other, as hurtfull to their common wealthes; which agreement betwixt concent of musicke, and affection of the minde, when Aristophenes perceaved, he therby was moved to thinke, that the mind was nothing else but a kind of harmonie."[10]

Granting music's power "to tuche the inclination of the minde," the defenders turn to how that power can be used to good effect. Mulcaster encourages training in music for the young student "for the soule, by the name of learning, and for the body, by waye of exercise," claiming too that it is "verie comfortable to the wearyed minde: a preparatiue to perswasion."[11] Bright recommends it as a cure for melancholy: "as pleasant pictures, and lively colours delight the melancholicke eye, and in their measure satisfie the heart, so not onely cheerefull musicke in a generalitie, but such of that kinde as most rejoyceth is to be sounded in the melancholicke eare: of which kinde for the most part is such as carieth an odde measure, and easie to be discerned."[12] Thomas Cogan, in *The Haven of Health Chiefly made for the comfort of Students* (1612) advocates music as a restorative for "a mind wearied with studie," asserting that every student ought to learn music "not onely for solace and recreation, but also because it mooveth men to vertue and good manners, and prevaileth greatly to wisedome, quietnesse of minde and contemplation."[13] Thomas Elyot, in *The Castle of Health* (1541), gives an early prescription of music for the condition of melancholy: "The first counsaile is, that duryng the tyme of that passion, eschewe to be angrie, studiouse, or solitarie, and rejoice thee with melodie."[14] He also urges singing — loud singing — as exercise for the lungs and playing on shawms, sackbutts, "and other lyke instruments" for the entrails.[15] John Case provides the most eloquent plea for music's use in recreation and entertainment, marshaling all the evidence of precedent, from history and legend, although the defense itself — that music is important in recreation — predates the attack by many years, appearing in Castiglione and many of the other sixteenth-century tutors.

What is interesting in the claims for music's efficacy is a common note of caution, already evident in the passage I quoted from Bright. Sometimes the caution is politic: one must not seem too skilled at music lest one be lumped with its professional practitioners — a position detrimental to the desirable image of both social and moral standing or suggestive of too many hours spent at a pleasurable pursuit rather than in study of more serious business — the latter, of course, of more concern to men than to women. The more interesting caution, however, is personal rather than social: Repeatedly the reader is covertly warned that music is only beneficial if it be not *abused*. Thus, to return to Bright, the reader is cautioned, "That contrarilie, which is solemne, and still: as dumpes, and fancies, and sette musicke, are hurtfull in this case, and serve rather for a disordered rage, and intemperate mirth, to reclaime within mediocritie, then to allowe the spirites, to stirre the bloud, and to attenuate the humours, which is (if the harmony be wisely applyed) effectuallie wrought by musicke."[16] Or from Mulcaster, who typically seeks out a concrete reason for the advice he gives, "In curing diseases, which rise vpon some distemperature of the minde, the temperature of time iudically applyed, hath been found both a straunge and a strong remedie. Always prouided, that whether ye say loud, or sing loud, ye neither say to long, nor sing to much, for feare of worse turne, if any entrail teare, with to much straining."[17]

Implicit in such statements is the very fear that infuses Gosson's thinking. If music can control the passions, it can also arouse them, as Bright quite openly acknowledges in warning against music that stirs up "disordered rage and intemperate mirth," and in an age that viewed temperance and moderation as the roots not only of virtue but of health and well-being, both personal and social, *abuse* of music would understandably be perceived as dangerous.

These lines of thought are all brought to realization on the Elizabethan stage in the numerous instances in which music—and especially singing since the texts help us where the music is lost[18]—is called for within the dramatic context. The situations in which characters in the drama request the playing or singing of music—or indulge in such activities themselves—reflect precisely the "uses" of music referred to by the various documents that discuss it. And more often than not—particularly in the work of playwrights other than Shakespeare—they represent not the wholesome *uses* but what must have been deemed the *abuses*.

The three most common situations in which music is called for on stage, as part of the drama rather than as atmosphere, involve (1) the experience of melancholy or grief, brought on by the death of a loved one or, more commonly, by loss or rejection in love;[19] (2) convivial moments of recreation, usually involving eating and drinking as well; and (3) wooing. In the first, the medical advisors and pedagogues would recommend a sprightly tune and cheery lyrics. This we never see in the plays; the cautionary notes of real-life advisors are systematically ignored by fictional characters in the drama. The grief-stricken, whatever the cause of their grief, always sing—or cause to be sung to them—doleful songs intended to *nurture* rather than relieve their melancholy condition.

In George Peele's *The Arraignment of Paris,* for example, the forsaken Oenone "singeth as she sits":

> Melpomene, the Muse of tragic songs,
> With mournful tunes, in stole of dismal hue,
> Assist a silly nymph to wail her woe,
> And leave thy lusty company behind.
>
> Thou luckless wreath! becomes not me to wear
> The poplar-tree for triumph of my love:
> Then, as my joy, my pride of love, is left,
> Be thou unclothed of thy lovely green;
>
> And in thy leaves my fortune written be.
> And them some gentle wind let blow abroad,
> That all the world may see how false of love
> False Paris hath to his Oenone been.[20]

A well-known example is this lament from Richard Edward's *Damon and Pithias:*

> Awake, ye woful wights,
> That long have wept in woe:
> Resign to me your plaints and tears
> My hapless hap to show.
> My woe no tongue can tell,
> No pen can well descry:
> O, what a death is this to hear,
> Damon my friend must die!
>
> The loss of worldly wealth
> Man's wisdom may restore,
> And physic hath provided too
> A salve for every sore:
> But my true friend once lost,
> No art can well supply:
> Then, what a death is this to hear,
> Damon my friend must die!
>
> My mouth, refuse the food,
> That should my limbs sustain:
> Let sorrow sink into my breast,
> And ransack every vein:
> Ye Furies, all at once
> On me your torments try:
> Why should I live, since that I hear
> Damon my friend should die!
>
> Gripe me, you greedy grief
> And present pangs of death,
> You sisters three, with cruel hands
> With speed now stop my breath:
> Shrine me in clay alive,
> Some good man stop mine eye:
> O death, come now, seeing I hear
> Damon my friend must die![21]

Examples of singing to nurture sadness are plentiful in Shakespeare: Mariana in *Measure for Measure,* Desdemona in *Othello,* and—the purest example of all—Jaques in *As You Like It,* all call for songs to feed their melancholy.

In all fairness, I should add here that John Case, whose interest is in justifying rather than prescribing, comments on music's utility for those who desire the melancholy state: "For we know that life is as it were put into the dreadest sorrows by inflexion & modulation of voice. And they whose heartes even yearne for very greefe sometimes fall on singing not to seeke comfort therein (for the best seeming comfort in such cases is to

be comfortles) but rather to set the more on flote that pensivenes where-
with they are perplexed."²² Melancholy was, of course, a fashionable pose
as well as an apparently common medical problem. Jaques, as a character,
clearly fancies himself as the melancholic sort, and given the convention,
can readily call upon music to foster that image. The other sad souls, on
the other hand, would not, presumably, *want* to foster melancholy as an
image; their turn to music is portrayed as a normal component of their
genuine feelings.

For the second set of circumstances, the recreative use of music, proper
or suitable use is not so easily defined, but misuse, in accordance with
what we read, would clearly consist of fostering "intemperate mirth" or
overindulgence in eating or drinking. Dramatic songs in convivial situations regularly have to do with such overindulgence, with the not-
uncommon inclusion of amorous debauchery as well.

The anonymous *Timon* contains two songs of conviviality that make
these points clearly. In the first, Eutrapelus, a "dissolute young man"
who has just borrowed money to pay off his debt to a Usurer, calls for a
celebration:

> Bring me hither a cupp of wyne filld to the bryms
> Let'ts always drinck all upp
> I loue a cupp that swyms
> God Bacchus, God Bacchus
> Thee wee adore
> Thee wee ymplore
> Oh most sweete Iacchus.

In the second, Timon has just made the innocent Lollio thoroughly
drunk and convinced him he (Lollio) is a prince. They sing the following
"Three'man's song" (which could as well go in my next category but for
the context):

> There liues a lasse in the next towne
> Call'd Sophrony, call'd Sophrony
> Smiles sweetely when I lay her downe
> Blithe & bonny, blithe & bonny
> She is not like some foolishe elfe
> Shee will take vp her clothes herselfe.
> Ha ha he, ha ha he
> Ha ha ha ha ha ha he.
> She alone is amiable
> My Sophrony, my Sophrony
> Shee shee alone is tractable
> ffeele her cony, feele her cony
> Shee is not angry; touche her lippes
> Or els descende betweene her hippes

Ha ha he &c.
She weares a smocke downe to her waste
My Sophrony, my Sophrony
She hath but one & that is lac'd
Giue her mony, giue her mony
Shee weares a gowne downe to her small
She hath but one & that is all.
Ha ha he &c.[23]

In John Lyly's *Alexander and Campaspe,* three servants "on leave" having a good time sing the following song:

O For a Bowle of fatt Canary,
Rich Palermo, sparkling Sherry,
Some Nectar else, from *Iuno's Daiery,*
O these draughts would make vs merry.

O for a wench, (I deale in faces,
and in other dayntier things,)
Tickled am I with her Embraces,
Fine dancing in such Fairy Ringes.

O for a plump fat leg of Mutton,
Veale, Lambe, Capon, Pigge, & Conney,
None is happy but a Glutton.
None an Asse but who wants money.

Wines (indeed,) & Girles are good,
But braue victuals feast the bloud,
For wenches, wine, and Lusty cheere,
Ioue would leape down to surfet heere.[24]

In Peele's *The Old Wives' Tale,* the following song is sung as "sport" to pass the time away by characters named Antic, Frolic, Fantastic, and Clunch. The implications in the song are surely clear.

Whenas the rye reach to the chin,
And chopcherry, chopcherry ripe within,
Strawberries swimming in the cream,
And school-boys playing in the stream;
Then, O, then, O, then, O, my true-love said,
Till that time come again
She could not live a maid.[25]

The third type, the songs associated with wooing, presents a somewhat different relation to the popular wisdom concerning music. As we have seen, Gosson's concern had mainly to do with prostitution, the flip side, so to speak, of wooing. Nowhere in the eclectic group of documents I have explored does any writer come to music's defense on this matter: music is never proposed as a suitable or effective agent in courtship, nor does anyone attempt to deny its association with wanton sexuality. The plays, however, do give us both sides, but frequently with an unusual twist.

Musical associations with wenching, whoring, and illicit seduction are plentiful. In *Alexander and Campaspe,* at the end of V.3, Phrygius, a soldier of Alexander's troop, says to Lais, the courtesan, "Come sweete Lays, let vs goe to some place, and possesse peace. But first let us sing, there is more pleasure in tuning of a voyce, then in a vollye of shotte." No song text is provided, but the association is clear.

A marvelous example of the association of music and seduction appears in Peele's *The Arraignment of Paris.* The three goddesses, trying to sway Paris's selection, present "shows" to exhibit what they will give him in return for his choice. Venus promises him Helen of Troy, who appears before him singing *in Italian* — an obvious reference to the supposed wantonness of Italians since the language hardly suits Helen any other way.

> Se Diana nel cielo e una stella
> Chiara e lucente, piena di splendore,
> Che porge luc' all' affanato cuore;
> Se Diana nel ferno e una dea,
> Che da conforto all' anime dannate,
> Che per amor son morte desperate;
> Se Diana, ch' in terra e delle nimphe
> Reina imperativa di dolci fiori,
> Tra bosch' e selve da morte a pastori;
> Io son un Diana dolce e rara,
> Che con liguardi io posso far guerra
> A Dian' infern', in cielo, e in terra.[26]

Later in the same play (p. 37), the betrayed Oenone accuses the shepherds of an abuse of music:

> Ah, shepherds, you bin full of wiles,
>   and whet your wits on books,
> And rape poor maids with pipes and songs,
>   and sweet alluring looks.

When courtship with presumably honorable intentions is accompanied by song, the wooer—who may be male or female—customarily appears as pathetic or foolish or both. The best example of the foolish singing lover is Ralph Roister-Doister who, in his obviously ill-fated courtship of Mistress Custance, cries, "let us sing, to win my dear love Custance," and then sings,

> I mun be married a Sunday;
> I mun be married a Sunday;

> Whoever shall come that way,
> I mun be married a Sunday.
>
> Roister Doister is my name;
> Roister Doister is my name;
> A lusty brute I am the same;
> I mun be married a Sunday.
>
> Christian Custance have I found;
> Christian Custance have I found;
> A widow worth a thousand pound;
> I mun be married a Sunday.
>
> Custance is as sweet as honey;
> Custance is as sweet as honey;
> I her lamb, and she my coney;
> I mun be married a Sunday.
>
> When we shall make our wedding feast,
> When we shall make our wedding feast,
> There shall be cheer for man and beast;
> I mun be married a Sunday.[27]

Custance, coming to find out what all the racket is about, says (most unromantically), "What gauding and fooling is this afore my door?" The anonymous *Timon* contains a wonderful spoof of the singing wooer. The lying traveler, Pseudocheus, teaches Gelasimus (the vain young "heir of the city") to use as a love potion a song he claims to have learned on his world travels.

> *Fa, la, la, la, sol, la,* how i'st my doue
> *Fa, la, la, sol, fa, la,* my marrow, my holy day
> *Fa, la, la, sol, la, me, re,* I loue thee by *Ioue*
> *La, fa, la, sol, me, re, la,* yors not his owne *Gelasimus* from the goulden hill
> *La, la, la, la, la, sol, me, la, me, re, la, la, sol, fa.*[28]

Gelasimus learns the song, and when the time comes to use it, he repeats it dutifully—solmization syllables and all. Needless to say, his suit is not successful.

The pathetic is well represented by Thyestilis in *The Arraignment of Paris*. Through trickery, she is made to fall in love with an old churl and tries to win his love with an "old love song" (p. 46). Never does the serious wooer have much chance of success using songs; music *not* abused seems merely ineffectual.

It should be obvious that in the great majority of these instances, the abuse associated with music has to do with sex, whether it goes by the honorable name of love or the dishonorable one of lust. Second comes excess in eating and drinking, which has its own pattern of association with sexuality in Renaissance thinking. All other instances of onstage music-making form but a small proportion of the total, and even those we might place in another category are frequently accompanied by allusions to sex.

As an instance of another type, here is one announced as a "song of mowing" from Peele's *The Old Wives' Tale,* exemplifying the old tradition of songs of labor referred to by Case and others in defending music's place. By the second stanza (which appears several scenes later), the sexual innuendoes in the first are reinforced by the stage direction which reads "Enter the Harvest-men singing, with women in their hands."

> All ye that lovely lovers be,
> Pray you for me:
> Lo, here we come a-sowing, a-sowing,
> And sow sweet fruits of love;
> In your sweet hearts well may it prove!
>
> Lo, here we come a-reaping, a-reaping,
> To reap our harvest-fruit!
> And thus we pass the year so long,
> And never be we mute.[29]

The only songs appearing with any regularity that do not fit into any of the three contexts I have outlined and never turn to the bawdy are the paeons to Elizabeth contrived to conclude a number of the plays from her reign. In one instance—Peele's *The Arraignment of Paris* (where Elizabeth ends up winning the prize!)—the playwright has taken pains to dissociate that hymn from the other songs by providing it with a Latin text as though to assert its quasi-religious tone and to forestall any lubricious thoughts that might be generated by the music.[30] The picture that emerges, then, presents us with a decided—if one-sided—image of music as the regular companion of the dreaded sins of concupiscence: gluttony and especially lechery. The innocent household music hailed by modern musicologists, where it does appear, has been subverted by man's baser nature. To judge from these plays, Gosson's claim—whatever we, or the Elizabethans for that matter, may make of the severity of its consequences— was right.

A common explanation for the inclusion of song and dance in Elizabethan drama is the simple statement that audiences liked it. No doubt they did. But one must then ask whether they liked too the repeated evidence that music was indeed the inducement to sinful pleasure that Gosson and his like claimed it was and the defenders vociferously insisted it need not be. Dramatically, of course, characters who misuse, or abuse, *any* convention provide more interest, more potential for tension or conflict. We cannot know how many members of an Elizabethan audience would have been aware of or concerned about the controversy,[31] but whatever dramatic interest lies in the phenomenon of so many culturally provocative songs must come, it would seem, from an audience's cognizance of the ongoing debate. The playwrights, on the other hand, *cannot* have been oblivious of the issue since Gosson's attack was directed even more specifically at the theaters as dens of iniquity—a charge that the inclusion of some of the songs I have cited seems likely to have fueled.

In these songs, then, the singer's voice provides us with many voices, carrying on, at several levels, the period's cultural debate about the physical, spiritual, emotional, and moral efficacy of music. The voice of the dramatic character, for whom the turn to song is a conventionally accepted response to a predictable situation, reflects if not actual daily practice, at least the common wisdom about *when* and *where* music should be present. The voice of the playwright, for whom the singing represents a bid for success (since Elizabethans apparently *did* like music in their theaters), gives us, less obviously, a rejection or denial of the positions of detractor and defender alike in his presentation of *how* music is used. And beneath these a multitude of other voices from the culture sing out: the Gossons and the Cases, the Mulcasters and the Elyots and the Lodges and the Brights, and the members of the audience who—whatever their private responses to the songs they heard from the stage—were all in some way party to the debate. Whether they left the theater feeling self-righteous in the knowledge that *they* would never abuse music like that, or with their own puritanical fears for music's potential aroused by what they had just witnessed, or perhaps with the secret satisfaction of wish fulfillment in seeing enacted what they would never dare in real life, the audience must have enjoyed these songs not merely for the oft-touted pleasure inherent in music itself, nor for the strictly dramatic possibilities, but because they kept the debate alive, because the singer's voice spoke *to* them and *for* them about a subject which—perhaps more than any other—raised apparently insoluble questions. The plays seem to assert that for all the claims to holiness and the cautionary advice about its salutary effects, Elizabethans clung to the possibility that music might also be deliciously unwholesome. Orsino's "If music be the food of love, play on" has behind it a Neoplatonic tradition and a wealth of lofty ideals built up around the heavenly harmony and its symbolic representation of virtuous love. But it also speaks the unspeakable, asserting in the rapid succession of its nouns—music, food, love—the marvelously fickle nature of music, the divine and the carnal ambiguously latent in sound.

NOTES

1. John Case, *The Praise of Musicke: Wherein besides the antiquitie, dignitie, delectation, & use thereof in civill matters, is also declared the sober and lawful use of the same in the congregation and Church of God* (Printed at Oxenford by Joseph Barnes, Printer to the Universitie, Anno 1586), p. 79.

2. See, for example, Percy A. Scholes, *The Puritans and Music in England and New England* (1934; reprint, Oxford: Oxford University Press, 1969) and Walter L. Woodfill, *Musicians in English Society from Elizabeth to Charles I* (1953; reprint, New York: Da Capo Press, 1969).

3. See David C. Price, *Patrons and Musicians of the English Renaissance* (Cambridge: Cambridge University Press, 1981).

4. Price, p. 154.

5. Price, p. 154.

6. Stephen Gosson, *The Schoole of Abuse* (1579); quoted from *Markets of Bawdrie: The Dramatic Criticism of Stephen Gosson,* ed. Arthur F. Kinney, Salzburg Studies in English Literature, Elizabethan Studies, ed. Dr. James Hogg, No. 4 (Salzburg: Institut für englische Sprache und Literatur, 1974), pp. 84–85.

7. Gosson, p. 93.

8. Thomas Lodge, *A Defence of Poetry, Music and Stage-Plays* (1579), p. 22.

9. Richard Mulcaster, *Positions* (reprint, London: Longmans, Green, and Co., 1888), p. 37.

10. Timothie Bright, *A Treatise of Melancholie. Containing the Causes thereof, & reasons of the strange effects it worketh in our minds and bodies: with the phisicke cure, and spirituall consolation . . .* (Imprinted at London by Thomas Vautrollier, dwelling in the Black-Friers, 1586), p. 247.

11. Mulcaster, p. 37.

12. Bright, p. 247.

13. Thomas Cogan, *The Haven of Health, Chiefly made for the comfort of Students, and consequently for all those that have a care of their health, amplified upon five words of Hippocrates, written Epid.6.: Labour, Meat, Drinke, Sleep, Venus* (London: Printed by Melch. Bradwood for John Norton, 1612), p. 20.

14. Thomas Elyot, *The Castell of Health* (1541), p. 69.

15. Elyot, p. 51.

16. Bright, p. 247.

17. Mulcaster, p. 60.

18. I might point out here that although the music for most of these songs does not survive, given the emphasis placed on careful representation of text in Renaissance musical theory and practice, we can justifiably infer from the words to a song something of what the musical style and its connotations in the situation would be. It is in any case difficult to imagine—with twentieth-century ears at least—anyone being wrought to "intemperate mirth" or a libidinous frenzy by much Elizabethan music, as delightful as it is.

19. Or, in one instance at least, when a character has lost his fortune. See Gelasius's hymn to Melpomene in the anonymous *Timon.* It should be noted, however, that throughout this farce, love or lust for wealth is substituted for, or made the condition for, the same feelings for people. *Timon,* ed. J. C. Bulman and

J. M. Nosworthy, Malone Society Reprints (Oxford: Oxford University Press, 1980), V.4.2387–99 (p. 79).

20. *The Works of George Peele*, ed. A. H. Bullen (1888; reprint, Port Washington, N.Y.: Kennikat Press, Inc., 1966), I, 39.

21. *The Dramatic Writings of Richard Edwards, Thomas Norton, and Thomas Sackville*, ed. John S. Farmer, Early English Dramatists (1906; reprint, Guildford, Eng.: Charles W. Traylen, 1966), pp. 30–31.

22. Case, p. 34.

23. *Timon*, I.2.140–47 (p. 7) and II.5.1071–92 (p. 37) respectively.

24. John Lyly, *Alexander and Campaspe*, ed. W. W. Greg, Malone Society Reprints (Oxford: Oxford University Press, 1933), I.2. This song, like the others from *Alexander and Campaspe*, appears only in the 1632 edition (appended at the conclusion of the present edition). I quote it, however, because even if it is not the song actually called for in the original 1584 edition, it is fully in keeping with songs that are printed in earlier editions of other plays and illustrates—perhaps even more firmly—the conventional expectation that this kind of song is appropriate to this situation.

25. *Works of George Peele*, I, 306–7. To offer one counterbalancing example, here is a song from Thomas Heywood's *King Edward the Fourth*, sung for the disguised king and his humble friend Hobson over food and drink.

> Agencourt, Agencourt! know ye not Agencourt?
> Where the English slew and hurt
> All the French foemen:
> With our Guns and bills brown,
> O, the French were beaten downe,
> Morris-pikes and bowmen.
> &c.

The Works of Thomas Heywood (1874; reprint, New York: Russell and Russell, Inc., 1964), I, 52.

It should be noted, however, that songs are much less frequent in histories and tragedies than in comedies or pastorals, and when they do appear, they are less likely to project the "abuses."

26. *Works of George Peele*, I, 31–32.

27. *The Dramatic Writings of Nicholas Udall*, ed. John S. Farmer, Early English Dramatists (1906; reprint, Guildford, Eng.: Charles W. Traylen, 1966), p. 59.

28. *Timon*, I.4.390–95 (p. 15) and II.1.594–98 (p. 22).

29. *Works of George Peele*, I, 314 and 326.

30. See *Works of George Peele*, I, 71.

31. The kinds of writings in which the defensive stances appear do seem, however, to have been widely read. Paul Slack, for instance, notes that of the medical treatises, 153 vernacular titles were printed before 1605 and many were reprinted several times. See his "Mirrors of Health and Treasures of Poor Men: The Uses of the Vernacular Medical Literature of Tudor England," in *Health, Medicine and Mortality in the Sixteenth Century*, ed. Charles Webster (Cambridge: Cambridge University Press, 1979), pp. 238–39.

II

INTERTEXTUALITY:
Modes of Imitation

ARTHUR M. LESLEY

Jewish Adaptation of Humanist Concepts in Fifteenth- and Sixteenth-Century Italy

During the fifteenth and sixteenth centuries, there appeared in Hebrew, addressed to a specifically Jewish audience, a number of entirely unprecedented works in genres that the Italian humanists cultivated, such as history, rhetoric, biography, and comedy.[1] At the same time, existing genres of Hebrew writing, such as sermons, letters, poetry, and grammar study, were revised in form, style, and content, so that they conformed more closely to distinctive humanist standards. The humanist features of these Hebrew texts have commonly been treated as "superficial" adornments that their authors "borrowed" from international fashion. One important historian of the Jews in the Renaissance, for example, readily explained such phenomena as illustrations of the Yiddish proverb, *Vi es Kristelt sich, azoi yidlt sich* ("As the Gentile does, so does the Jew").[2] This is an inadequate methodological assumption. To assume that a minority culture that has long survived, such as that of the Jews, automatically imitates whatever it encounters in the surrounding society both ignores the internal dynamics of Jewish life and reduces intercultural relations to simplistic alternatives of borrowing or complete originality. Such schematism betrays its origins in outmoded cultural apologetics.[3] Ample evidence from fifteenth- and sixteenth-century Hebrew literature suggests that this was not reflexive imitation: Hebrew writers carefully selected what they adapted and appropriated from humanist practice and values. The ways in which Jewish scholars selected certain humanist activities and adapted and integrated them into Hebrew discourse are serious topics for the history of Hebrew literature.

Jewish interest in humanist scholarship was anything but automatic. Indeed, Jews could well have been expected to disregard or resist Italian humanism. Aside from the Arabic transmission of Aristotle, Plato, and some scientific writings, Jewish learning simply had no traces of classical antiquity to revive. Furthermore, Rome, which was both the destroyer of the second Temple and the capital of western Christendom, was far from being the object of Jewish nostalgia. Most specifically, relatively few Jews read or wrote Latin, and almost none knew Greek. The most important characteristics of Italian humanism, then, seem at first glance to have been remote from Jewish interest.

Nevertheless, Jews in Italy did not resist or ignore humanism. Instead, they could choose to take advantage of what interested them and disregard the rest, because they felt confident that they possessed a language and literature that was more ancient and perfect than those of the Greeks and Romans. Isaac Abravanel (1437–1508), the leader of the Jewish exiles from Spain in 1492, explained the conception of the transmission of learning that claimed precedence for Hebrew over classical learning in all the arts and sciences:

> Our rabbis of blessed memory long ago investigated the transmission of learning from the school of Shem to the school of Eber, and from there to our father Abraham. From Abraham the art of magic and occult natures came to the sons of Ishmael and of Keturah, as well as astrology and the rest of the investigative sciences. . . . Indeed, it was the sons of Esau who brought the sciences to the Romans and the Greeks, sons of Japheth, when Zepho, son of Eliphas, ruled over them. . . . And this is why the sciences are not found among the other nations descended from Japheth besides these two, the Greeks and the Romans, who at that time were one nation, with a common language. And the wisdom of the children of Israel was as far above them as the heaven is above the earth.[4]

This account of the transmission of learning, formulated by Jewish apologists already in Hellenistic times, defended the priority, perfection, and sufficiency of Hebrew revelation against claims that Greek wisdom, attained through reason, was first and most complete. Christian apologists later adopted the Jewish position, so that Origen could assert, "It seems to me that all the sages of the Greeks borrowed these ideas from Solomon, who had learnt them from the Spirit of God at an age and time long before their own, and that they then put them forward as their own invention."[5] Renaissance Christian thinkers who sought to recover the "ancient theology" also frequently assumed that any similarity between revealed truth and human truth resulted from a garbled pagan account of an original revelation to the Hebrews. In the fifteenth and sixteenth centuries, then, Jews could expect universal assent to their assertion that "On that awesome day at Mount Sinai, [God] crowned us with the whole Torah, which includes all sciences, natural, logical, theological, judicial and political, from which the whole world has drunk."[6] In consequence, Jews believed that they did not automatically need to adopt derivative, though ancient, foreign models for what was already to be found in their own ancient texts.

When, however, Jews first encountered Italian humanist learning, they recognized that, in some areas, their own scholarship was inferior to that of their Christian contemporaries. To overcome this inferiority, they resorted to a strategy for justifying cultural innovation which Jews in earlier periods had used repeatedly: Assuming that all learning was already contained in the Bible, they considered their attempts to remedy current deficiencies to be, not imitation of foreign nations, but rather recovery from the nations of those traces of biblical wisdom — Adamic, Mosaic, or Solomonic — that had been preserved among the nations when the Jews themselves lost it. Faced with their inferiority in certain fields, the Jews looked for evidence that the prophets or the rabbis already knew these fields and then, justified by these precedents, they integrated the new fields into Jewish discourse.

The Jews who first encountered Italian humanism in the fifteenth century were in a social and political situation to benefit from humanist learning, and some of them were already elaborating a grammar-based educational program that made humanism pertinent to their own studies. Between the fourteenth and the seventeenth centuries, Jewish settlements reappeared in Italy north of Rome and disappeared everywhere south of Rome, as well as from Europe west of the Rhine. During the fourteenth and fifteenth centuries, fragile new Jewish communities, created by the terms of *condotte* between communes and loan-bankers, came to be scattered over central and northern Italy. Some lasted only as long as the term of one *condotta*, and, before the sixteenth century, even the largest included no more than two hundred persons.[7] The organization of these new communities was complicated by the continual arrival of refugees from southern Italy, France, Germany, Provence, Spain, and Portugal. The diverse legal, educational, and social practices of the mixed populace were difficult to harmonize, and the authority of leaders was subject to challenge.[8]

The writings of northern Italian Jews from the fifteenth and sixteenth centuries show them to have been responding to their situation by adapting two earlier programs for cultural reform, both of which are based upon study of Hebrew: one program is found in the *Kuzari*, by Yehuda Halevi (1075–1141),[9] and the other in *Sefer Ma'aseh Efod* (1403), by the Aragonese scholar Profiat Duran, known as Efodi.[10] During the fifteenth and sixteenth centuries, Halevi is frequently mentioned and several commentaries on the *Kuzari* were written, clearly signs of a desire to displace the long-dominant Aristotelianism in Jewish philosophy. Efodi's book, an up-to-date grammar even by Latin standards, proposes an educational solution to the political and ethical flaws that crippled

Jewish communities in Spain and contributed to their collapse during and following the outbreaks of violence against them in 1391. Efodi diagnoses the flaws of the Jewish communities in Spain to be factionalism, mutual hostility among leaders of the factions, and the personal limitations of leaders, whom he calls "boorish men who were inept in the art of leadership." Efodi continues, "All three of these causes have been responsible for much of our affliction in exile, especially the choice of the private good, each of us being concerned for himself alone, and not knowing or understanding that, in the long run, the security of the parts depends upon the security of the whole."[11] Efodi's critique of Jewish communal leadership in exile focuses on the moral and educational deficiencies of the leaders. To reform leadership, Efodi invokes as models the ancient national rulers, King David and King Solomon, whose wise, just, and effective reigns resulted from their perfect understanding of the Hebrew language, which made all wisdom available to them.

In contrast with these exemplary ancient rulers, contemporary Jewish leaders—Talmudists, philosophers, and kabbalists—neglect the Hebrew of the biblical revelation that is the common source of their rival disciplines. To enable all Jewish factions to understand the Hebrew Bible and derive from it the interpretations useful for communal welfare in their time, Efodi presents a new grammar of biblical Hebrew. Armed with this necessary linguistic education, the factions will no longer be satisfied merely to allegorize the biblical text, like the philosophers; to disregard it, like the Talmudists; or to reduce it to occult meanings, like the kabbalists. They will rather search in the Hebrew Bible for solutions to contemporary problems and, in addition, effectively dispute the biblically based polemics of Christians. A Jewish community united in understanding its ancient texts will withstand all external threats and will repair its faults, to deserve speedy messianic redemption.

Efodi's ambitious claims for the art of Hebrew grammar include the assertion that, by remedying their faulty knowledge of Hebrew, Jews will begin to regain the virtues of pre-exilic Israel and thereby become more worthy of messianic salvation and the return from exile: "I think that my composition, this treatise, is a proof and demonstration that the salvation of the Lord is coming near, His kindness is to be revealed, and though He may delay, he will not be late. . . . 'For there is yet a prophecy for a set term, / A truthful witness for a time that will come. / Even if it tarries, wait for it still; / For it will surely come, without delay'" (Habakkuk 2:3).[12] The closing verse was frequently invoked during the early fifteenth century in Jewish calculations of the imminent coming of the Messiah. The original perfection of Hebrew, as revealed in the Bible, is still available to the Jews, in spite of their own current debasement and their corruption of the language. By dedicated study of Hebrew grammar, as exemplified in the Bible, Jews can revive their studies, their behavior, and their community, to repair the faults that prolong their exile.

Efodi's program, which may be characterized as biblicist hebraism, was readily adaptable to the task of integrating the diverse elements of the new northern Italian Jewish communities. To create a Jewish public discourse where none had existed, the learned leadership in Italy combined an educational program based on grammatical and political study of the Hebrew Bible with some linguistic and political features of Italian humanism. The result was a new and distinct Italian Jewish culture, which innovated several genres of Hebrew composition, notably rhetorical and ethical, and everywhere was recognized as supreme in every kind of Hebrew prose. The program of biblicist hebraism that the Italian Jews established had an affinity to Italian humanist moral and literary studies, but subordinated them to Jewish educational, moral, and political renewal.

Between the middle of the fifteenth century and the middle of the seventeenth century, Jews in Italy adapted each discipline of the *studia humanitatis*—grammar, rhetoric, poetry, history, and political philosophy —to the terms and forms of Hebrew expression. They did this by substituting biblical models for the Greco-Roman models that the humanists imitated.[13] In this way, the Jews made *reductio artium ad sacram scripturam,* the derivation of all arts from the Bible, serve the same function as Cicero's application of Terence's line: "homo sum; nil humani a me alienum puto."

II

By making the biblical canon, rather than rabbinic and medieval usage, normative for Hebrew style and grammar, Efodi took the decisive step for treating the Bible as the Jewish equivalent of classical literature. Although this decision was necessary for making available the disciplinary traditions of Hebrew grammar study and the practice of Hebrew poetry from Spain, it was by no means a natural or inevitable choice. Also, by stating that "The science of language is a science that includes grammar, rhetoric and poetry," Efodi both dignified grammar as a science and made the language arts in Hebrew congruent for the first time with the Latin trivium.[14] Previously, in Jewish scholasticism, following scholasticism in Arabic, grammar was a lowly propaedeutic to the logical arts.[15] Efodi's reclassification of grammar assisted the transference of Jewish scholarship from the Arabic and Islamic cultural background to the Latin and Christian background of Europe.

The achievements of Hebrew grammatical studies in Italy have still been investigated only in part, and their theoretical achievement appears to have been modest. The importance of grammar was its new function, at the beginning and center of Jewish education. Several grammars were composed, and dictionaries of Hebrew and foreign languages were compiled. Serving a new historical perspective, Elijah Levita's examination of the text of the Bible led to the conclusion that the vowels and diacritical marks of the Masoretic text were more recent than the consonants.[16]

Comparative study of Hebrew and the European languages developed to an unprecedented extent during the sixteenth century. Several centuries earlier, in the Arabic cultural setting, comparative study of Hebrew and the cognate languages of Aramaic and Arabic resulted in the first systematic Hebrew grammars. In the sixteenth century, comparison of Hebrew with Latin, Greek, and Italian served mainly to confirm the priority of Hebrew as the language of Adam which only the Jews preserved after the dispersion from the Tower of Babel. Comparison involved the juxtaposition of Italian, Greek, or Latin words with Hebrew words or phrases that had plausibly similar sounds and meanings. For example, the name of the Muse Kalliope could be derived from the Hebrew phrase *Kol Yafeh*, which means "beautiful voice," or "beautiful sound." Latin *uxor* was thought to resemble Hebrew *Ezer*, "helpmate," the term applied to Eve in Genesis. *Hospidale* was connected with *Osef Dalim*, "gathering of poor people," and *accademia* with *Bet Eked*, "house of assembly." The Mantuan scholar, David Provenzal, compiled over two thousand such similaries, to argue that these foreign languages preserved confused traces of the original Hebrew. Such an argument reinforced similar assertions that Jews and some Christian contemporaries made in other fields of learning. It harmonized as well with the kabbalistic ascription of special divine and divinatory power to the Hebrew language.[17]

III

Efodi's formulation of biblicist hebraism from the early fifteenth century became most fruitful for Italian Jews when they combined it with humanist rhetoric. That adaptation became possible once Jews accepted the Latin trivium as the definition of the linguistic arts, so that they could extend the biblical basis of grammar and poetry, the two linguistic arts that Jews studied within Arabic culture, to the third art, rhetoric. Efodi's definitions of the three arts prepared for the Italians' application of biblicist hebraism to the art of rhetoric: "When speech agrees with the elements and laws of the language, without particular sweetness, beauty, dignity or ornament, either in its simple or its complex statements, and is neither deliberately copious nor concise, such an utterance may be called grammatical. . . . When this utterance has sweetness, beauty, dignity and ornament, in both its simple and complex statements, it may be called eloquence [*MeLiTSah*], from the verse, 'How sweet [*NiMLeTSu*] are thy words unto my taste.' (Ps. 119:103) . . . When to these meter is added, the utterance is poetry."[18]

The biblicism that had long characterized Hebrew poetry and grammatical study could now be applied to a hitherto unpracticed linguistic art, rhetoric. Assisted by the power and the variety of applications that rhetoric demonstrated in humanist literature, Hebrew prose compositions could now be written according to humanist norms, but based on biblical models. All that was needed was a methodical analysis of the biblical text according to humanist rhetorical concepts. This was accomplished by Yehuda ben Yehiel, Messer Leon (ca. 1420–ca. 1490), a physician and teacher who was active in Padua, Mantua, and Naples. In *The Book of the Honeycomb's Flow*, printed in Mantua in 1475 but possibly written in Padua in the 1450s, Messer Leon puts the art of rhetoric at the disposal of Hebrew composition by combining a commentary on the *Rhetorica ad Herennium* with a commentary on Averroes' middle commentary on Aristotle's *Rhetoric*, and illustrating their definitions with passages from the Hebrew Bible.[19]

Messer Leon testifies to the process by which he has "recovered" the art of rhetoric for Hebrew: first he learned it from the nations, then he discovered its foundations in the Hebrew Bible: "When I studied the words of the Torah in the way now common amongst most people, I had no idea that the science of Rhetoric was included therein. But once I had studied and investigated Rhetoric . . . out of the treatises written by men of nations other than our own, and afterwards came back to see what is said of her in the Torah and the Holy Scriptures, . . . I saw that it is the Torah which was the giver."[20] Messer Leon goes on to demonstrate in detail the ways that the Hebrew Bible exemplifies all the teachings of rhetoric. Since the Bible contains all of rhetoric and is older than other sources of the art, Messer Leon does not doubt that it is the source of rhetoric. For example, he illustrates all the figures of speech from biblical passages and discovers several uniquely biblical figures: "For most of what we shall say herein, we shall draw upon Book IV of the *Rhetoric* [*ad Herennium*] written by Tully, and upon the account given by the Philosopher in Book III of his *Rhetoric*. The examples of the figures, however, I have taken from . . . the words of prophecy and the divinely inspired narratives."[21]

Messer Leon also derives the three kinds of rhetoric from biblical practice. Psalm 45, for example, illustrates the norms of epideictic rhetoric and even alludes to the classical prescriptions for this kind. The title of the psalm is, "In the mode of the *SHoSHaNiM*," a term resembling the number six, *SHeSH*, meaning, Messer Leon says, that the psalmist intended to present "a complete discourse . . . with all its parts—which are six, namely, introduction, statement of facts, partition, proof, refutation, and conclusion. . . . You will find many epideictic discourses of censure in Ezekiel, Jeremiah, and in some parts of Isaiah."[22] After careful analysis of psalm 45, Messer Leon concludes: "This psalm, composed through the instrumentality of the Holy Spirit, deals with the Messiah, with his deeds, and with the qualities for which one should praise him — physical attributes, qualities of character, and external circumstances. . . . This discourse, then, belongs in the class of Epideictic and, within this class, in the division of praise."[23]

An example of judicial rhetoric is the speech of the woman of Tekoa to David (2 Samuel 14:1–20). Many passages exemplify deliberative rhetoric. "Much, indeed, of what one finds in the Bible, and nearly all that is said to us in the form of commandments, admonitions, and reproofs . . . are in the category of deliberative oratory." In a similar manner, Messer Leon systematically turns the Hebrew Bible, which was already considered to be the ultimate source of truth and wisdom, into the supreme model of eloquence: "The sum and substance of all that we have said is that the speaker who is a son of our people should adopt his premises from what is found written in these books of Torah; his words will thus be most completely persuasive. . . . In this, as in all matters, our books of Torah rank first."[24] When rhetorical exemplarity is added to the other acknowledged excellences of the Hebrew Bible, it may be analyzed through rhetorical commentary and become the model for various kinds of Hebrew compositions. Hebrew writers in various genres were indebted to this achievement. Although *The Book of the Honeycomb's Flow* was printed only once before the nineteenth century, it had long-lasting influence on Hebrew education in Italy. It enabled other Hebrew writers to apply rhetorical concepts to compositions for which no Hebrew precedents existed, and modified established practice of commentary, composition, and oral address.

IV

Hebrew poetry since the eleventh century, in Spain, Provence, and Italy, had been written according to a set of biblicist hebraic norms, and it was not difficult to find biblical precedent for the writing of Hebrew poetry. Poetry obviously was present in the Bible, although scholars defined it in different ways: by fixed numbers of metrical feet, by distinctive cantillation marks, by transcription in columns, or by introduction with the terms *SHiR* or *SHiRah*.[25] There was, however, substantial difficulty in claiming biblical precedent for writing the kind of Hebrew poetry that was current in Spain, Provence, and Italy from the eleventh through the sixteenth centuries.

The sixteenth-century historian, Azariah de Rossi (ca. 1520–78), proposes solutions to these problems. He refers to a tombstone inscription found in Spain, which was written in the medieval Hebrew poetic style, but which also mentioned a prince, "Amatziah," whom de Rossi takes to be the biblical figure.[26] De Rossi concludes that medieval-style Hebrew poetry was indeed written as early as the biblical period, but that such poetry was not included in the biblical text because it was used only for occasional genres, such as funereal inscriptions, rather than for revealed, prophetic utterance. De Rossi takes the inscription to confirm that contemporary Hebrew poetry continues Hebrew poetic practice from biblical times, although it is excused from attempting to emulate the incompletely understood forms of prophetic poetry that appear in the Bible. Both kinds of poetry, sharing as they do the same vocabulary, exemplify the most perfect forms of the Hebrew language, as it was employed in different genres.

Hebrew writers more easily could claim biblical precedent for a kind of composition that was not previously practiced in Hebrew, drama. Yehuda Sommo Portaleone (1527–92), who was active in Mantua, like Provenzal and de Rossi, wrote a Hebrew "regular" comedy, several Italian comedies and pastorals, and four dialogues in Italian on the art of drama. In the dialogues he argues that the biblical book of Job is the original tragedy: "The sublime genius of the holy legislator Moses, the famous leader of the Jews, after he had written his five books of divine law as delivered to him by oracle—nay, from the lips of Almighty God Himself—in 5550 verses, produced, as is demonstrated in the literature of the Jews, the magnificent and philosophical tragedy of Job, introducing therein just five human characters."[27] Sommo acknowledges that Job was not meant to be presented on stage, "but it was cast in the form of a dialogue or discussion in which various characters took part—that is to say, in the form assumed by every poem suited for dramatic presentation." Sommo is not claiming a Hebrew precedent for every form of drama, or even for those in which he wrote, but only for the highest kind, for tragedy. He readily concedes the novelty of a Hebrew comedy, in the prologue to his *Comedy of Betrothal:* "What the other languages made a crown for their heads, this holy language made the heel of her shoes."[28] He decided to introduce the genre to Hebrew because: "Those sages thought it a flaw and corruption of the Hebrews that such pleasure and usefulness was absent from our stories. . . . I have therefore decided today to show all the people of the land that the Hebrew language is in no way inferior to any artistry in any foreign language." Given the availability of Job as the original drama, the absence of Hebrew comedy became a challenge to the dignity of Hebrew only when the genre could claim moral utility, through a combination of Horatian and Aristotelian arguments. In response, Sommo says he decided "to compose words which could be told before lords and nobles of the land, words in which pleasure and usefulness would be mingled, and in smooth words ... condemn individuals who rashly indulge in every vice and, in contrast to such people, ... praise and draw admiration to those who do good and justice."[29]

The plot of Sommo's comedy is taken from ancient rabbinic *midrash,* so that the matter of the comedy, like its purpose and its efficient cause, the author, are native to Hebrew. Only the comedic form is immediately taken from foreign practice; but since, according to Sommo, Job is the first drama, the form is one more item of ancient Hebrew wisdom now recovered from the nations.

V

Between Flavius Josephus and the sixteenth century, Jewish historiography was a desultory enterprise.[30] Like rhetoric, history had long been neglected in Hebrew, at least in part because the Jewish philosophical tradition disparaged it. According to Jewish philosophers, even the divinely inspired historical narratives of the Bible deserved attention only because they alluded to the eternal truths of physics and metaphysics. The outstanding Jewish philosopher, Maimonides (1135–1204), discouraged the reading of books "as are found among the Arabs describing past events, the governments of kings and Arab genealogy, ... which neither possess wisdom nor yield profit for the body, but are a sheer waste of time."[31] Like philosophers, Talmudists, kabbalists, and the simple pious recognized no need to study history.

Against this background, the dozen historical works that Jews wrote during the sixteenth century, most of them in Italy, indicate a substantial change in Jewish intellectual life. These historical compositions include a couple of biographies and autobiographies, works which trace the authoritative line of rabbis, a history of the Turkish and Frankish empires, and several accounts of Jewish suffering and salvation, as well as a Portuguese pastoral dialogue on this theme. In addition, earlier Hebrew histories were printed, notably *Sefer Yosippon,* a medieval book that included, with other material, sections translated from a Latin version of Josephus.

The unprecedented, sustained Jewish interest in history resulted when moral and political concerns were combined with the new capabilities of rhetorical composition. Rhetoric guided the formulation of historical material to provide the Hebrew-reading audience with examples of moral and political actions to emulate or avoid. It was, of course, the same motive that led Italian humanist educators to include histories among their studies, as recommended by classical rhetoricians and the historians themselves. Livy had declared: "What chiefly makes the study of history wholesome and profitable is this, that you behold the lessons of every kind of experience set forth as on a conspicuous monument; from these you may choose for yourself and for your own state what to imitate, from these, mark for avoidance what is shameful in the conception and shameful in the result."[32]

Exactly the same didactive motive for studying history is invoked for Hebrew readers in the preface to the second printing of *Yosippon,* in Constantinople, in 1510. The author of the preface, Tam Ibn Yaḥya, was a Jewish physician to the Turkish sultan, an authoritative figure in Jewish law, and a spokesman for the learned elite of the Iberian exiles. His preface conforms to the established formula of the *accessus ad auctores* and illustrates the way that humanist historiography could be adapted to the values of a Hebrew audience.[33] "Although chronicles regularly exaggerate about things that never were realized, and even invent things that never happened; this book, although it belongs to the same genre, is as different from them as truth is from falsehood. . . . The sign of this is that this book is the closest to prophecy of all those that were written after the holy scriptures. It was written before the Mishnah and Talmud, and God's hand was likely on this man while he was writing this book, so that his words were almost prophetic." The assertion that one's own book of history differs from the mass of lying histories can be found throughout sixteenth-century prefaces to histories.

Following the topics of the *accessus,* Ibn Yaḥya explains the purpose of histories in general, and of this particular book of history: "Like all histories, this book gives evidence from the past about the future. . . . Contemporaries may learn lessons, each according to his capacity: kings may learn how to win battles and counsellors, to conduct their affairs, 'for there is nothing new [under the sun],' and 'what is with us now was there in earlier times.' Like the histories of other nations, that teach about their origins, the origin of their race, and how they wandered and came to their country, so do we learn from this book about the place from which we were exiled, what it was like, and how we were driven out of our land."[34] There is no contradiction between the humanist form and values of Ibn Yaḥya's introduction and his purpose in addressing *Yosippon* to a Jewish audience that was composed, to a large extent, of exiles from Spain. He declares that the reading of this postbiblical, but almost inspired, Jewish history will "strengthen us in our worship of God; and the individual stories, such as those about Daniel, Ahasuerus, and Hannah's sons will sustain our strength to serve God." The Jewish histories that were written in the sixteenth century can all be seen to fulfill the same overall purpose, of providing moral and practical instruction, as well as encouragement for Jewish morale, through presentation of historical examples.

VI

Writings on moral philosophy, which Jewish writers tended to call political philosophy, have always been part of Jewish teaching, so that the most obvious innovation during our period was the use of new literary forms, often narratives, to present the goods and virtues. As in the other fields that correspond to the *studia humanitatis,* Hebrew writers tried to derive their compositions from the most ancient Hebrew texts in the discipline. The biblical book of Proverbs, attributed to King Solomon, fulfilled this function for moral philosophy. Further, Solomon himself was made an exemplary human being and complete sage and ruler, in a voluminous biography. Yoḥanan Alemanno (1433/34–c. 1504), a teacher and rabbi who received his medical degree from Messer Leon, wrote this book, *The Song of Solomon's Ascents,* between 1488 and 1492, at the request of Giovanni Pico della Mirandola.[35] Alemanno makes Solomon the Jewish model of the perfect sage and ruler, whose wisdom includes the complete curriculum of studies. Within the biography, Alemanno combines a chronological narrative with a topical arrangement of a wide, eclectic list of goods, arts, sciences, and virtues, taken from philosophy, kabbalah, magic, Jewish law and theology, and humanist sources, to define a *uomo universale,* in Hebrew, a *Ḥakham Shalem.* The classification of goods, virtues, and sciences most closely conforms to al-Ghazzali's *Criterion of Action,* and the narrative that illustrates it comes from the biblical books of Kings and Chronicles, as well as postbiblical material from varied sources.[36]

Biography had not been cultivated in Hebrew since biblical antiquity, and in Judaism since Philo, as the rabbis avoided turning Moses, Abraham, or David into competitors with the Christian image of Jesus. Alemanno, however, seems to be making Solomon into a Jewish countermodel to Ficino's claim for Jesus: "What else was Christ but a certain living book of moral and divine philosophy, sent from heaven and manifesting the divine idea itself of the virtues to human eyes. . . . Christ is the idea and exemplar of the virtues."[37] Whether Ficino's Christ, Xenophon's Cyrus, or Suetonius's *Divus Augustus* and *Divus Iulius* were his targets, Alemanno announces that he introduced biography to Hebrew in response to the practice of the nations:

> I am very well aware, my son, that you are a wise and understanding man, a Jew who is not used to such long stories telling of a man and his deeds, and who might say that listening to the bleating of this flock of Solomon's virtues wearies the mind. . . . Listen, then, to my two replies to anyone who would seal his ears from hearing more. First, I greatly envied those among all the nations who praise their idols and compose about a single man whole hosts of books, as long as the chronicles of Israel and Judea combined; while we, the community of Jews, do not know how to give two or three particles of

praise to one of the holy men of our people. I have therefore opened my mouth to glorify and praise King Solomon, may he rest in peace, with many praises. I undertook to put them into a book in an arrangement that will make it apparent to all the nations that we have as much heart as they.... I wrote this book of mine in order ... to teach the lesson of the wise man who taught in his book [the Song of Songs] that all the virtues and achievements with which he was crowned were vanity compared to the felicity of desire for, and attachment to, the Lord.[38]

Like other Hebrew writers who made innovations in the disciplines that correspond to the *studia humanitatis*, Alemanno establishes a Hebrew original for the genre — in this case, the exemplary life — and then treats that original through distinctive humanist methods. Biblicist hebraism and humanist classicism, although they are distinct, and often opposed, programs of cultural renewal, share enough strategies and values to benefit from each other's methods. Here, Solomon is made an ancient Hebrew exemplar of a system of virtues and sciences that competes with those that Ficino and Pico were proposing.

VII

Already forty years ago, Cecil Roth formulated the essential insight into the way that Hebrew writers appropriated elements of Italian humanism: "The Italian Jews became famous in the Jewish world for their flawless style and composition, in striking contrast to the studied inelegance of their northern European contemporaries.... In the same way as the humanistic scholars modelled their prose style on Cicero and Livy, abandoning the barbarous traditions of medieval Church Latin, so their Jewish contemporaries went back to the Bible."[39] It is this essential insight that I have tried to explain and confirm from the texts. Roth did not turn this insight into a guide for further investigation because, as his triumphal prohumanist tone indicates, he wanted only to show that both Jews and Christians were engaged in a clear struggle of Renaissance enlightenment against medieval obscurantism. To show that the Jews belonged to the enlightened camp, Roth adduced an impressive number of Jewish similarities to "Renaissance" traits: individualism, secularism, classicism, and so on. Starting as it did from a polemical caricature of the medieval, and ignoring the inner dynamics of Jewish communities, this argument paradoxically admitted Jews into "the Renaissance" to exactly the degree that they were not behaving as Jews. Our survey here shows, however, that it was not unreflective imitation of a foreign fashion that produced the admired Hebrew of Italian Jews. Instead, the Italian Jews were pursuing a resolutely independent religious and learned program, which they articulated by selectively adapting to their own intellectual heritage the literary, linguistic, and political arts that they could appropriate from humanism. It was in this way that the Jews in fifteenth- and sixteenth-century Italy, a marginal community, succeeded in opening themselves to the world without being assimilated by the world.

NOTES

Research for this paper was supported by the Social Sciences and Humanities Research Council of Canada, to which I express my thanks.

1. There is no adequate survey of Hebrew and other Jewish literature from fifteenth- and sixteenth-century Italy. The most helpful in English is Israel Zinberg, *A History of Jewish Literature,* trans. Bernard Martin (Cincinnati: Hebrew Union College Press and Ktav, 1974), IV.

2. Cecil Roth, *The Jews in the Renaissance* (1959; reprint, New York: Harper and Row, 1965), p. 21.

3. Robert (Reuven) Bonfil. "The Historians' Perception of the Jews in the Italian Renaissance: Towards a Reappraisal," *Revue des Etudes Juives* 143 (Jan.–June 1984), 59–89.

4. Isaac Abravanel, *Commentary on the Pentateuch* [Hebrew] (1862; reprint, Israel: Torah Vada'at, 1956), fol. 33r–v.

5. Origen, Prologue to the Commentary on the Song of Songs. Cited from James L. Kugel, *The Idea of Biblical Poetry* (New Haven, Conn.: Yale University Press, 1981), p. 143, n. 22. On this apologetic strategy, see Harry A. Wolfson, *Philo* (Cambridge, Mass.: Harvard University Press, 1947), I, 20–22, 141–63.

6. Abraham Farissol, *Magen Avraham.* Cited from David B. Ruderman, *The World of a Renaissance Jew: The Life and Thought of Abraham ben Mordecai Farissol,* Monographs of the Hebrew Union College, 6 (Cincinnati: Hebrew Union College Press, 1981), p. 77, n. 44.

7. Umberto Cassuto, *Gli Ebrei a Firenze nell'età del rinascimento* (1918; reprint, Firenze: Olschki, 1965), p. 212; Shlomo Simonsohn, *History of the Jews in the Duchy of Mantua,* I [Hebrew] (Jerusalem: Kiryat-Sefer, 1962), 140; Moses A. Shulvass, *The Jews in the World of the Renaissance,* trans. Elvin I. Kose (Leiden: Brill, 1973), pp. 1–28.

8. Cecil Roth, "Jewish Society in the Renaissance Environment," in *Jewish Society through the Ages,* ed. Hayim Hillel Ben-Sasson and S. Ettinger (New York: Schocken, 1971), pp. 240–41.

9. Judah Halevi, *The Kuzari: An Argument for the Faith of Israel,* trans. Hartwig Hirschfeld (New York: Schocken, 1964).

10. Profiat Duran, *Sefer Ma'aseh Efod* (1865; reprint, Jerusalem: Makor, 1970). On the historical context, see Yitzhak F. Baer, *A History of the Jews in Christian Spain,* II (Philadelphia: Jewish Publication Society, 1961), 150–60.

11. Baer, pp. 20, 157; Duran, pp. 191ff.

12. Duran, pp. 177–78; Baer, pp. 159–60.

13. On humanism, see Paul Oskar Kristeller, "Humanist Learning in the Italian Renaissance," in *Renaissance Thought,* II (New York: Harper, 1965), 3.

14. Duran, p. 42. See Yosef B. Sermoneta, "The Study of the Liberal Arts in

Italian Jewish Society in the Fourteenth Century" [Hebrew], in *The City and the Community* (Jerusalem: Historical Society of Israel, 1968), pp. 249–58.

15. The logical arts were classified as "Categoriae, Perihermenias, Analytica priora, Analytica posteriora, Topica, Sophistica, Rhetorica, Poetica." See Abu-Nasr Al-Farabi, *Catálogo de las Ciencias*, ed. and trans. Ángel González Palencia, 2d ed. (Madrid: n.p., 1953), p. 95.

16. Roth, *Jews in the Renaissance*, pp. 127, 145; Giuseppe (Yosef) B. Sermoneta, *Un Glossario filosofico ebraico-italiano del XIII secolo* (Rome: Edizioni dell'Ateneo, 1969).

17. Roth, *Jews in the Renaissance*, p. 331; Alexander Altmann, *"Ars Rhetorica* as Reflected in Some Jewish Figures of the Italian Renaissance," in *Jewish Thought in the Sixteenth Century*, ed. Bernard Dov Cooperman (Cambridge, Mass.: Harvard University Press, 1983), p. 20; Gershom G. Scholem, *Kabbalah* (New York: Quadrangle, 1974), pp. 169–74.

18. Duran, pp. 42–43.

19. Judah Messer Leon, *The Book of the Honeycomb's Flow*, ed. and trans. Isaac Rabinowitz (Ithaca, N.Y.: Cornell University Press, 1983). Cf. Robert Bonfil, Introduction to Judah Messer Leon, *Nofet Ẓufim, on Hebrew Rhetoric* [Hebrew] (Jerusalem: Magnes Press, 1981), pp. 7–69, v–xii.

20. Messer Leon, p. 145.

21. Messer Leon, pp. 416–17.

22. Messer Leon, pp. 190–91.

23. Messer Leon, pp. 172–75.

24. Messer Leon, pp. 316–17.

25. Kugel, pp. 69–70, 96–134.

26. Kugel, pp. 200–202; Kugel, "The Influence of Moses Ibn Ḥabib's *Darkhei No'am*," in *Jewish Thought in the Sixteenth Century*, pp. 308–25.

27. Allardyce Nicoll, *The Development of the Theatre*, 5th ed., rev. (New York: Harcourt Brace Jovanovich, 1967), pp. 252–78; Leone de' Sommi, *Quattro dialoghi in materia di rappresentazioni sceniche*, ed. Ferruccio Marotti (Milano: Il Polifilo, 1968), pp. 13–14.

28. Yehuda Sommo mi-Sha'ar Aryeh, *The Comedy of Betrothal* [Hebrew], ed. Hayim Schirmann (Jerusalem: Dvir-Tarshish, 1965), p. 30.

29. Sommo, p. 29.

30. Yosef Hayim Yerushalmi, *Zakhor: Jewish History and Jewish Memory* (Seattle: University of Washington Press, 1982), pp. 31–34; Yerushalmi, "Clio and the Jews," in *American Academy for Jewish Research Jubilee Volume*, 2 (1980), 615.

31. Moses Maimonides, *Commentary on the Mishnah, Sanhedrin* X, 1. Cited from Salo W. Baron, *A Social and Religious History of the Jews*, 2d ed., rev., (Philadelphia: Jewish Publication Society, 1958), VI, 198–99, n. 59.

32. Titus Livius, *Ab urbe condita*, praefatio 10. Cited from A. D. Leeman, *Orationis ratio: The Stylistic Theories and Practice of the Roman Orators, Historians and Philosophers*, 2 vols. (Amsterdam: n.p., 1963), I, 194.

33. Yerushalmi, *Zakhor*, pp. 35–36. See Edwin A. Quain, "The Medieval *accessus ad auctores*," *Traditio* 3 (1945), 215–64; Sermoneta, "Study of the Liberal Arts"; *Sefer Yosippon*, ed. A. Hominer (Tel Aviv: Sifriati, 1965), pp. 41–44.

34. *Yosippon*, p. 43.

35. Arthur Lesley, " 'The Song of Solomon's Ascents,' by Yohanan Alemanno: Love and Human Perfection according to a Jewish Associate of Giovanni Pico della Mirandola" (Diss., University of California, Berkeley, 1976), pp. 4–5.

36. Abu Hamid al-Ghazzali, *Sefer Moznei Tsedek,* ed. J. Goldenthal (1839; reprint, Jerusalem: Rare Judaica Publishing House, 1975). See Mohamed Ahmed Sherif, *Ghazali's Theory of Virtue* (Albany: State University Press of New York, 1975).

37. Marsilio Ficino, *De religione christiana,* XXIII (Basel, 1576), ff. 42r–43v. Cited from Charles B. Trinkaus, *In Our Image and Likeness,* 2 vols. (Chicago: University of Chicago Press, 1970), II, 741.

38. Lesley, pp. 55, 472–74.

39. Cecil Roth, *A History of the Jews of Italy* (Philadelphia: Jewish Publication Society, 1946), p. 216.

FRANÇOIS RIGOLOT

Between Homer and Virgil: Mimesis and Imitatio in Ronsard's Epic Theory

Between Homer and Virgil, just like a demigod, / Surrounded by spirits,
I have my place in their midst.

(Ronsard, 1560)

It seems unquestionable that Ronsard's greatest ambition from youth was
to exalt the French language and make it "illustrious." Along with other
Pléiade poets like Du Bellay and Peletier, he believed that the best way to
accomplish such a task was to write an epic poem in French in the
manner of Homer and Virgil.[1] Critics have long debated the question of
Ronsard's motivations in writing *La Franciade,* his self-proclaimed as well
as his unwritten poetics, and his desire to choose Virgil over Homer as a
model in spite of his statement to the contrary.[2] From Paul Laumonier to
Daniel Ménager and from Paul Lange to Bruce R. Leslie, every Ronsard
scholar seems to agree that the principal model for *La Franciade* must
have been the *Aeneid.*[3] "The *Franciade* owes more to Virgil than to any
other poet," wrote Walter H. Storer in 1923, basing his judgment on a
comparative count of figures in the two poems.[4] And Isidore Silver has
attributed the French poet's epic failure mainly to his Virgilian prejudice:
"It was under the influence of Virgil that Ronsard adopted the great
vitiating premise of the *Franciade:* its motivation in dynastic pride."[5]

Ronsard's unqualified admiration for the *Aeneid* is evidenced by many
of his own pronouncements. As early as 1572, in the first preface to his
heroic poem, he makes passing reference to the *Iliad* but dwells with
much fervor on the Latin epic: "Virgil . . . conceived of this divine *Aeneid*
which we continue to this day to hold with all reverence in our hands."[6]
With even greater emphasis, in the posthumous preface of 1587, he lists

some twenty-two quotations from the *Aeneid* with laudatory comments, and strongly advises his "apprentice reader" to imitate Virgil in the "composition and structure" of future epic poems: "Follow Virgil who is past master of the composition and structure of poems. Consider a moment the sound made by these two lines at the end of the eighth book of the *Aeneid* [ll. 689–90]. Why don't you try to compose in your own language as many of these as you can."[7]

Various explanations have been proposed for Ronsard's avowed predilection for the Latin model. One of the most convincing ones is that he may have followed Jacques Peletier du Mans's unambiguous recommendation. In his *Art poëtique* of 1555, Peletier had made a comparative study of the *Iliad* and the *Aeneid,* and had concluded that Virgil's epic was a far superior poem.[8] Whether Peletier's "idolatry for Virgil" was an *idée fixe* or not (he was himself a translator of the *Odyssey*), Ronsard may have been seduced by his friend's ingenious arguments. The main reason for Virgil's superiority, according to Peletier, was that while Virgil had imitated all the real beauties he had found in Homer, he had also carefully avoided Homer's own weaknesses: "Virgil imitated whatever he considered admirable in Homer. But he corrected him in several places. And I will list here a number of things which he left aside."[9] For instance, Virgil had eliminated Homer's superfluous epithets (Il "a bien sù euiter la superfluité d'Epithetes qui et an Homere") and numerous unwarranted repetitions ("Il s'et gardè des redites qui sont an Homere").[10]

To be sure, according to Peletier, Virgil had an excellent critical mind. He agreed with Horace that occasionally good old Homer would fall asleep ("Horace n'a pas dit hors de propos qu' aucunes fois dort le bonhomme Homere")—a reference to the famous line of the *Ars poetica.*[11] A nd therefore it was quite natural to expect greater perfection in the *Aeneid* than in the *Iliad.* Peletier was quite clear on this issue. According to him, poeticians had strangely confused Homer's so-called superiority with his temporal seniority. "Homere n'et an rien plus eureus [in no way more felicitous] sinon que pour auuoer précédé an temps."[12] Let us forget for a moment that the *Iliad* came first and let us imagine that the *Aeneid* was the original poem; there is little doubt that we would prefer Virgil's masterpiece over Homer's: "If the *Aeneid* had been composed before the *Iliad,* just think what people would have to say about it."[13]

Another way to produce an aesthetically valid judgment is to forget about the question of antecedents and base our appreciation solely on a synchronic comparison. After all, does it really matter to know who wrote first? Homer himself may not have been the "first epic poet" poeticians so self-confidently claim him to be. Imitation must be removed from its second-class category; it is not necessarily inferior to invention, rather the contrary. We know for sure that Virgil was an imitator; but we can only guess that Homer was an inventor: "Let us say from evidence that Virgil was an imitator and from judgment and opinion that Homer was an inventor."[14]

One of the obvious consequences of Peletier's meliorative theory is that, under appropriate circumstances, Virgil himself can be improved upon; and that it should be the duty of modern poets to take up that extraordinary challenge. Contrary to common belief among men of letters, Virgil is not an untouchable model, removed from history to be revered endlessly, like Homer, by future generations. In spite of all his consecrated merits, he did make mistakes ("fautes poétiques") which his best imitators will be able to correct. Contradiction, lack of credibility, which marred some passages of the *Iliad*, were repeated, sometimes verbatim, in the *Aeneid*: "And yet I find that Virgil fell into a similar error."[15] No work of art, no matter how great, can claim to be flawless.[16] Therefore the golden rule for future epic poets is to know what should be imitated and what should be left out of the imitation: "Let him know what he should imitate and what he should not."[17] There is an optimistic corollary to this: poets to come will confidently follow Virgil's example: they will imitate him imitating Homer, and will write epics that may surpass their classical model in excellence.

Peletier's theory, which is not unique in his time, may very well have appealed to Ronsard, as it seemed to give reality to his limitless ambitions. Nothing could please more the leader of the Pléiade than the idea of an "improved succession" of the great classical writers. If the *Aeneid* was indeed better than the *Iliad*, then the *Franciade* had a fair chance to outdo the *Aeneid*. Even though Ronsard never refers to it in his various prefaces, Peletier's theory of imitation confirmed, on the poetic plane, Ronsard's dominant political premise: namely that the French rulers were meant by destiny to be greater than their Roman predecessors. As Jupiter solemnly predicts it at the beginning of *La Franciade*:

> From Merove, from conquering peoples,
> Many princes and many great emperors will come;
> They will be elevated in supreme dignity.
> Among them a king, Charles the Ninth,
> (Ninth in name but first in virtue)
> Will be born to see the world conquered
> Under his feet—that world where the sun sets
> And where its rays shine on earth,
> Rising from the high seas
> And bringing light to men and gods.[18]

In other words, the French king will achieve what the Roman emperor never managed to complete, except in dreams: he will eventually dominate both the Orient and the Occident, and of his kingdom there will be no end ("Cujus regni non erit finis"). Similarly, in the poem that celebrates the king's deeds, Ronsard will exceed his Latin model. With the complicity of the Olympian god of gods, he will be to Virgil what Charles is to Augustus: an improved version of the greatest preceding exemplar.

Strange as it may seem, Ronsard himself gives us quite another explanation for his almost exclusive interest in the *Aeneid*. In the *Préface sur la Franciade* of 1587, in which he quotes some fifty-two lines from Virgil's epic and paraphrases many others, Ronsard seems to be unduly self-conscious about the weight he gives to the *Aeneid* in his own imitation theory. As a way to deflect possible criticism he writes: "I am sure that the envious will babble because I quoted Virgil more often than Homer who was his master and his model. But *I did it on purpose,* knowing well that the French have more familiarity with Virgil than with Homer and other Greek authors."[19] By concentrating on Virgil's style Ronsard had a better chance to reach his pedagogical goal: namely, to teach his "apprentice reader" ("Lecteur apprentif" [p. 331]) how to write the best possible imitation of a classical epic.

Therefore let us not be confused about Ronsard's motivations. His admiration for Virgil does not preclude an equal fervor for Homer; it simply means that he was considerate enough of his readers to use examples that could be easily understood. Communication is more important to him than self-indulgent pedantry; or, at least, that is what he would like to have us believe. Rhetorically speaking, this argument sells well. Ronsard is eager to proclaim his desire to reach out and identify with the largest number of readers in a common search for national origins. We find here, in his imitation theory, echoes of what Daniel Ménager called his "unanimisme."[20] Yet we know that this is mere wishful thinking: *La Franciade* stems from a purely aristocratic vision of art which has nothing to do, despite Ronsard's efforts, with the real aspirations of an actual community of readers and, therefore, is doomed to failure.

The question we have now before us is not which models Ronsard did actually follow in his *Franciade* (he borrowed copiously from Homer, Virgil, Apollonius, and many others); nor is it to what extent "the *Aeneid* furnished him the context and general lines of the story";[21] nor even what Ronsard specifically said about each of his possible models. The question is rather *how* it is he said what he said. In other words, it is a question of intentionality; and this question can only find an answer, it seems, through a close reading of the poet's prefaces and by reference to contemporary theories of imitation.

Ronsard wrote three prefaces for his *Franciade;* they can be found in the 1572, 1573, and the posthumous 1587 editions. In the first preface (1572), he defines his epic poem as "un Roman comme l'*Iliade* et l'*Aeneide*" (p. 5). From the outset, Homer and Virgil are designated as the two chief models he had in mind. Ronsard makes it clear that he wants to emulate their poetics, which is founded—to use Aristotelian language—on verisimilitude ("vraisemblance" [p. 5]) rather than truth ("vérité" [p. 5]): "Yet, whenever possible, I imitated both authors' artificial plots which are based more on verisimilitude than on truth. Following these two great characters, I did as they did."[22] The same language will be used again in the preface of 1587, with perhaps some confusion between the verisimilar and the possible: "Imitating these two luminaries of Poetry, and basing myself and relying on our old Annals, I built my *Franciade* without worrying about whether or not it was true, . . . making use of the possible and not of the true."[23]

Yet this self-conscious effort to present his two classical exemplars on an equal footing in theory becomes somewhat suspicious when we are confronted with Ronsard's actual practice. In the 1572 preface, for instance, he begins by pointing out Virgil's advantage over himself in dealing with dynastic matters: "If I talk about our kings more at length than Virgil's art allows, you must know, Reader, that Virgil in this respect (as in all others) was luckier than I am: since he lived under Augustus, the second emperor, he had few Kings and Caesars to account for and needed not lengthen much his paper, whereas I carry the burden of sixty-three kings."[24] Hyante's vision of the kings of France in the Underworld (*Franciade,* Book IV) is obviously patterned after Anchises's long lecture on Roman history (*Aeneid,* Book VI). Yet Ronsard's intention is to dramatize the difference between "l'art Virgilien" and "l'art Ronsardien."

The reason for this is given in the next paragraph in which Ronsard shifts emphasis and declares that he has indeed patterned his work on Homer rather than Virgil: "Besides, I have patterned my work (of which these first four books are samples) rather after Homer's *natural facility* than after Virgil's *careful diligence.*"[25]

In this very important statement, the contrast between Homer's "natural facility" and Virgil's "careful diligence" can be traced back to Quintilian. In Book X of the *Institutio Oratoria,* one reads: "In truth, although we must needs bow before the immortal and *superhuman genius* of Homer, there is *greater diligence* and exactness in the work of Virgil, just because his task was harder. And perhaps the superior uniformity of Virgil's excellence balances Homer's pre-eminence in his outstanding passages."[26]

To be sure, Ronsard parts with Quintilian by deliberately choosing genius over work, *natura* over *cura et diligentia.* Obviously this self-proclaimed preference for a naturally inspired poetry ("naïve facilité") clashes with the textual evidence that he gave much thought to Virgil's ornate style. Ronsard was never alien to an aesthetic of solid learning and skill. *Ars, studium, doctrina, exercitatio* were key notions in the theoretical background of the Pléiade poets. Of course "le naturel" (natural endowment) was an absolute prerequisite: poets had to be born poets. Yet, as Grahame Castor has remarked, the Neoplatonic theories of inspiration were so prevalent in the 1550s that Du Bellay felt he should tip the balance again in favor of art and work. In his *Deffence et Illustration de la Langue Françoise,* Ronsard's friend wrote a whole chapter to argue that "le naturel n'est suffisant à celuy qui en Poesie veult faire oeuvre digne de l'immortalité."[27]

Before suggesting an explanation for Ronsard's preference for Homer's "naïve facilité," let us turn to the second preface of the *Franciade,* i.e., the 1573 "Avertissement au lecteur." In this very short piece of prose, Ronsard talks exclusively about the corrections he decided to make in order to give a "more perfect" style to his poem: "Following the advice of my most learned friends, I have changed, moved, shortened, lengthened many passages of my *Franciade* to make it more perfect and put it in its final form. And I wish, indeed very dearly, that all our French writers deigned do the same. If they did, we would not see as many aborted works which, for lack of filing and polishing over time, bring only shame to their authors and bad reputation to France."[28] In this rewritten preface it is no longer a question of Homer's divinely inspired poetry. The emphasis is exclusively placed on patient, long-enduring workmanship ("changer, muer, abreger, alonger"). "Cura et diligentia" have replaced the inborn "immortal and superhuman genius"; the poet is now cast in the role of an "ouvrier," painfully correcting Nature's errors through systematic practical *exercitatio* ("la lime and parfaicte polissure requise par temps"). Boileau's famous dictum will not be very different:

> Twenty times return your work to the loom;
> Polish it all the time, and polish it again;
> Add sometimes, but erase frequently.[29]

There seems to be an insoluble contradiction in imitation theory between the 1572 and 1573–87 statements. Ronsard would like to have it both ways. On the one hand, true to contemporary attitudes and especially Peletier's, he welcomes the idea of "improved imitation" and lectures at length on the unequaled value of craftsmanship. The *Aeneid* will be his chief model. On the other hand, he emphatically declares that he has patterned his *Franciade* on the naturalness and spontaneousness associated with the *Iliad* rather than the artificiality typified by the *Aeneid.* Even in the last preface, in which Virgil is quoted so copiously, he fervently clings to his ideal of a "naifve & naturelle poesie": "You will enrich your Poem by using a varied style taken from Nature, without the frenzy of a madman. For, if you are too keen on avoiding or banishing the vernacular and never gaining fame by making grotesque and fanciful monsters, you will imitate Ixion who begot phantoms instead of legitimate and natural children."[30]

It is true that, in his chapter devoted to the epic poem, Du Bellay had recommended keeping a fair balance between *ars* and *natura*, work and inspiration. The successful poet had to be "gifted with an excellent felicity of nature" as well as "instructed in all good Arts and Sciences."[31]

Yet Ronsard's self-proclaimed set of double standards cannot be explained solely in terms of Du Bellay's theoretical compromise. I would like to suggest that the apparent contradiction between the various prefaces to the *Franciade* can be at least partly solved if we first manage to clear up a problem of semantics. After all what exactly did Ronsard mean by "imitation"? Do the French verbs "patronner" (p. 5), "suyvre" (p. 347), "imiter" (passim) always mean the same thing when they apply to Homer and Virgil? As we shall see, Ronsard's statements may not be as contradictory as one thinks: they may refer to two different kinds of realities, vaguely subsumed by the term "imitation" but actually corresponding to the distinct classical notions of mimesis and imitatio.

There is little doubt that for Ronsard, as for Peletier and Du Bellay, Homer stands as the one recognized source of epic inspiration. Regardless of the question of technical superiority, the *Iliad* is anterior to all other imitations, including the *Aeneid,* which it generates. Ronsard says so specifically in the first preface to his poem: "The Trojan War was created by Homer, as several serious authors have firmly established. The stories which came out of it since are all drawn from *the source which is Homer. . . .* The same could be said of Virgil who, having read in Homer that Aeneas did not die in the Trojan War . . . , conceived his divine *Aeneid.* "[32]

There seems to be a definite sense here that Homer stands as a "divine original" as opposed to all his successors, no matter how great, how "divine" even they may have been or will be. Ronsard does not simply acknowledge a distance separating his own poem from a timeless, unchanging source, removed from the vicissitudes of history. In fact, by introducing a major difference between the *Iliad* and the *Aeneid,* he problematizes the conception of the classical text as an undifferentiated font of eternal truth.

In his wide-ranging study of the source topos in Renaissance literature, David Quint has focused on the debate between alternative methods of reading, allegorical versus historicist, and shown how the Renaissance literary text became an instrument of epistemological criticism.[33] As this reading of Ronsard's theoretical statements seems to suggest, the *Aeneid* cannot make the same claims to transcendent truth as the *Iliad.* In other words, the awareness of textual historicity is not limited to Renaissance authors with respect to their own texts; it also extends to some of the greatest classical exemplars.

According to Ronsard, both Homer and Virgil are "two luminaries of Poetry" ("deux lumieres de Poësie" [p. 340]), even more: "two great demigods, each worthy of a temple" ("deux grands Demy-dieux dignes chascun d'un temple" [p. 354, l. 12]). Yet, in contrast to the *Iliad*'s timelessness, the *Aeneid* is placed within a specific history, the Augustan Age with its dynastic premise and its emphasis on change over time. This is in complete agreement with the French theoreticians of the 1550s who generally considered Virgil as a "political" poet. His name was commonly associated with Augustus in the context of Rome's imperialist claims. In his *Art poëtique,* for instance, Peletier exclaimed: "Oh, if only there could be another Augustus, that we might see if there could be another Virgil!"[34] And Du Bellay, in *La Deffence et Illustration,* made a similar comment: "Certainly if we had a new Maecenas and Augustus, Heaven and earth are not so hostile that they would prevent us from having other Virgils!"[35]

Mostly because of this historical factor, Ronsard probably felt drawn closer to the Roman epic which could offer him the guarantee of an illustrious political precedent. Yet, at the same time, France had to establish a direct link with Greek civilization, unmediated by the Latin experience. The foundations of a national mystique could only be built upon the solid rock of an original "primal scene." Since the Fall of Troy ("la guerre Troyenne") had been the founding myth of the *Aeneid,* it had to play a similar role within the French poem to give credence to its mythical claims. In other words, Ronsard implicitly rejected Virgil's modeling effect. Both Aeneas and Francus had successfully escaped from Troy's inferno and both had set out to found a "new Troy" ("Pour y fonder une nouvelle Troye" [p. 43, l. 302]). Therefore both poets were to be considered as equal. They had the same degree of kinship: their common *source* was Homer.

This may come to us as a surprise, but for Ronsard the ultimate significance of the *Aeneid* and the *Franciade* lies in the same critical gesture: the "allegorical reading" of an all-powerful source of fullness which is identified with Homer's *Urtext.* Once this is accepted, Virgil certainly appears to be an ideal means to transpose into French the best possible rules of structure and composition for an epic poem: "Follow Virgil who is past master of the composition and structure of poems."[36] This holds true even though, at times, Virgil may have lapsed into regrettable mistakes. As we have seen earlier, Peletier had followed Horace's identical reproach about Homer. Ronsard's remarks on Virgil's failure to respect the unity of time (in *Aeneid* V, ll. 46–48) may stem from his desire to distance the Latin poet from his Greek source, thereby bringing himself closer to the original locus of transcendent truth.

Ronsard's ambivalent motivation was undoubtedly to be both a Homer and a Virgil at the same time, that is, to be able to combine—in spite of his statement to the contrary—a Homeric claim for origins and a Virgilian perfection of style. In fact, this is precisely what he had suggested in his poem *L'Hylas,* published three years before *La Franciade.* In the oft-quoted closing lines he addressed Jean Passerat, a professor at the Collège Royal, and exposed his imitation theory in a most straightforward way:

> Dear Passerat, I resemble the Bee
> Who goes picking flowers, sometimes bright red,
> Sometimes yellow. Wandering in the fields,
> It flies to the places which are most to its liking
> Mustering many supplies before Winter comes.
> . . . .
> Thus running and leaping through my books,
> I gather, sort and select the finest motif
> Which I colorfully depict in one type of painting
> Or in another. Then becoming master painter,
> Without forcing myself, I imitate Nature.[37]

Here Ronsard clearly brings together two types of imitation which profoundly disturbed Renaissance theoreticians. As Grahame Castor has remarked, "the poet takes his 'colours' from others, and yet at the same time he claims to be representing Nature."[38] In fact, Ronsard never makes us believe that he intends to conflate the imitation of model authors and the representation of Nature. On the contrary, he needs to keep the two quite separate, just as in the 1572 preface to *La Franciade* he will make a distinction between "natural facility" and "careful diligence" (p. 5). In *L'Hylas,* first Ronsard says that he needs to imitate the bee's work ("Je ressemble à l'Abeille") and gather material from various authors; then, and only then, will he be able to dominate his art (to become "maistre en ma peinture") and give his own work the seal of originality.

When he writes: "Without forcing myself, I imitate Nature," Ronsard implicitly recognizes within himself the power to reach a god-given, original source of inspiration. It is the equivalent of saying: "I have patterned my work . . . after Homer's natural facility."[39]

Therefore true representation of Nature (mimesis) can only be achieved through the conscious and conscientious imitation of previous art (imitatio). This is no less than the reversal of the normal theoretical order. First comes a necessary rhetorical stage: borrowing arguments, composition, and style, according to the rules of inventio, dispositio, elocutio. Then the really creative process can take place: it is meant to reoriginate the new text and give it an autonomy that somehow makes it participate in a timeless source of truth.

In the opening statement of "Les Argumens . . . de la *Franciade,*" Amadis Jamyn, Ronsard's secretary and a poet in his own right, made a similar kind of commentary—again using the classical bee metaphor—on Ronsard's double theory of imitation: "In this laborious work, the *Franciade,* the Author intended to write like the Ancients, and above all like the divine Homer."[40] Divine Homer is thus singled out as the original source of inspiration. Jamyn, who was to give the first complete translation of the *Iliad* into French (thirty-four books in 1577), probably had good personal reasons for promoting Homer. Yet he continues his commentary as follows: "Although in this first book he mainly imitated Homer and Virgil, Francus's departure however is imitated from Apollonius of Rhodes."[41] In other words, whereas the general conception of Ronsard's poem is "patterned after Homer," the actual "imitation" of specific episodes can be traced to a variety of classical models (and Homer is one of them). In fact, Apollonius of Rhodes is the primary model for this kind of practical imitation. And Jamyn concludes: "He resembles the bee who takes advantage of all flowers to make its honey. This is why, without preferring one Ancient above the others, he considers what is best in each and uses it to enrich (always in a felicitous way) our French language."[42]

We seem to have here another version of Ronsard's "divided aspirations." Whether he expresses it himself or has his secretary come forth as his spokesman, the poet acknowledges his borrowings as being the necessary ingredients of a consciously crafted work of art. At the same time he strives "to ground his verse in an authorized source and to establish his own individuality as a literary creator."[43]

In their liminary poems in homage to the *Franciade,* Jean Passerat, the addressee of *L'Hylas,* and Amadis Jamyn, the author of "Les Argumens," claimed, in both Latin and French, that Ronsard had moved beyond the quarrel between Homer's and Virgil's supporters (pp. 22–23). The point was well taken indeed. Ronsard could afford to welcome both Homer and Virgil into his own epic because they appeared at two very different levels of functionality. Homer was virtually untouchable and served as an allegorical reference to a higher level of truth. Virgil was closer to him, geographically, linguistically, pedagogically, and politically. The *Aeneid* was so close indeed that one of its lines became an object of parody in the last preface to *La Franciade:*

To what literary heights will French glory soar![44]

Ronsard exclaimed, alluding to the many great poems that would elevate the glory of France if French writers would write their works in the vernacular. Paradoxically Ronsard expressed in Latin his fervent plea for French greatness: probably because he wished to show the limits of *imitatio* and invite his "apprentice reader" to reproduce mimetically the plenitude regained of lost origins.

NOTES

1. "La plus chère ambition de Ronsard était précisément de doter la France d'une épopée, qui, jetant une belle lumière sur notre poésie, ne manquerait pas d'en immortaliser l'auteur." P. Laumonier in his Introduction to Ronsard's *Œuvres complètes* (Paris: Nizet, 1983), XVI, v. All subsequent references to *La Franciade* are to this volume. On the epic poem in French Renaissance theory, see Thomas Sebillet, *Art Poëtique Françoys*, ed. by F. Gaiffe (Paris: STFM, 1910), II, xiv; Joachim Du Bellay, *La Deffence et Illustration de la langue françoise*, ed. H. Chamard (Paris: Didier, 1948), Book II, chap. V, pp. 127ff.; Jacques Peletier du Mans, *Art poétique*, ed. A. Boulanger (Paris: Belles-Lettres, 1930), pp. 194–210.

2. "J'ay patronné mon oeuvre . . . plustost sur . . . Homere que sur Virgile," "Epistre au Lecteur" (1572), *Franciade*, p. 5. This statement will be analyzed in detail in the following pages.

3. See D. Ménager, *Ronsard: Le Roi, le Poète et les Hommes* (Geneva: Droz, 1979), chap. IV, "La Tentative épique," 65, n. 1; and Bruce R. Leslie, *Ronsard's Successful Epic Venture: The Epyllion* (Lexington, Ky: French Forum, 1979), p. 111.

4. Walter H. Storer, *Virgil and Ronsard* (Paris: Champion, 1923), p. 99. Storer's belabored point is of course biased by the very onus of his thesis, which forces him to find as many parallels as possible between the two poets.

5. Isidore Silver, *Ronsard and the Hellenic Renaissance in France*, I, *Ronsard and the Greek Epic* (St. Louis: Washington University Press, 1961), 433.

6. "Virgile . . . conceut ceste divine Æneide qu'aveq toute reverence nous tenons encores aujourd'huy entre les mains." *Franciade*, p. 7. All references in parenthesis in the text will be to this volume.

7. "Suy Virgile qui est maistre passé en composition et structure des carmes: regarde un peu quel bruit font ces deux icy sur la fin du huictiesme [chant] de l'*Aeneide*. [*Ae.* VIII, 689–90]. Tu en pourras faire en ta langue autant que tu pourras" (*Franciade*, p. 347).

8. Peletier, *Art Poétique*, pp. 95–104.

9. "Virgile à imité ce qu'il à vu d'admirable en Homere. Mes il l'à chatiè an plusieurs androetz. E ici metrè quelque nombre de poinz, léquez Virgile n'a pas trouuèz bons an Homere, e dont il s'et gardè." Peletier, *Art Poétique*, p. 98.

10. Peletier, *Art Poétique*, pp. 98–99.

11. Peletier, *Art Poétique*, p. 102. "Quandoque bonus dormitat Homerus." *Ars poetica*, l. 359.

12. Peletier, *Art Poétique*, p. 98.

13. "Considere, si l'Eneide út etè fete auant l'Iliade, que c'et qu'il an faudroet dire." Peletier, *Art Poétique*, p. 98.

14. "Disons Virgile imitateur par euuidance: e Homere invanteur, par jugemant e opinion." Peletier, *Art Poétique*, p. 98.

15. "Si et-ce que je trouve Virgile etre tombè an samblable faute." Peletier, *Art Poétique,* p. 99.

16. "Il n'et si grand, qui ne tombe an faute." Peletier, *Art Poétique,* p. 102.

17. "Qu'il sache que c'et qu'il doèt imiter e quoe non." Peletier, *Art Poétique,* p. 98.

18. "De Merové, des peuples conquereur, / Viendra meint prince, & meint grand empereur / Hault eslevez en dignité supresme: / Entre lesquels un Roy CHARLES neufiesme, / Neufiesme en nom & premier en vertu, / Naistra pour voir le monde combatu / Desous ses pieds, d'où le soleil se plonge, / Et d'où ses rais sur la terre il allonge, / Et s'eslançant de l'humide sejour / Aporte aux Dieux & aux hommes le jour." *Franciade,* p. 41, ll. 247–56.

19. "Je m'asseure que les envieux caqueteront, dequoy j'allegue Virgile plus souvent qu'Homere qui estoit son maistre, & son patron: mais je l'ay fait tout expres, sçachant bien que nos François ont plus de congnoissance de Virgile, que d'Homere & d'autres Autheurs Grecs." *Franciade,* p. 342.

20. *Franciade,* p. 292.

21. Leslie, p. 111.

22. "Imitant toutefois a mon possible de l'un & de l'autre, l'artifice & l'argument plus basty sur la vraysemblance que sur la verité." "Suivant ces deux grands personnages, j'ay fait le semblable." *Franciade,* pp. 5, 7.

23. "Imitant ces deux lumieres de Poësie, fondé & appuyé sur nos vieilles Annales, j'ay basti ma *Franciade,* sans me soucier si cela est vray ou non, . . . me servant du possible, & non de la verité." *Franciade,* p. 340.

24. "Si je parle de nos Monarques plus longuement que l'art Virgilien ne le permet, tu dois sçavoir, Lecteur, que Virgile (comme en toutes autres choses) en ceste-cy est plus heureux que moy, qui vivoit sous Auguste, second Empereur, tellement que n'estant chargé que de peu de Rois & de Cesars, ne devoit beaucoup allonger le papier, où j'ay le faix de soixante & trois Rois sur les bras." *Franciade,* p. 5.

25. "Au reste j'ay patronné mon oeuvre (dont ces quatre premiers livres te serviront d'échantillon) plustost sur la *naïve facilité* d'Homere que sur la *curieuse diligence* de Virgile." *Franciade,* p. 5.

26. "Et hercule ut illi [Homero] *naturae caelesti* atque immortali cesserimus, ita *curae et diligentiae* vel ideo in hoc [Virgilio] plus est, quod ei fuit magis laborandum, et quantum eminentibus vincimur, fortasse aequalitate pensamus." *Institutio oratoria,* X.I.86. Translation by H. E. Butler (Cambridge, Mass.: Harvard University Press, 1936), IV, 49.

27. Du Bellay, *Deffence,* pp. 103–5. Cf. Grahame Castor, *Pléiade Poetics* (Cambridge: Cambridge University Press, 1964), p. 44.

28. "Par le conseil de mes plus doctes amis j'ay changé, mué, abregé, alongé beaucoup de lieux de ma *Franciade* pour rendre plus parfaite, & luy donner sa derniere main. Et voudrois de toute affection que noz François daignassent faire le semblable: nous ne verrions tant d'ouvrages avortez, lesquels, pour n'oser endurer la lime & parfaite polissure requise par temps, n'aportent que deshonneur à l'ouvrier, et à nostre France tres mauvaise reputation." *Franciade,* p. 3.

29. "Vingt fois sur le métier remettez votre ouvrage; / Polissez-le sans cesse et

le repolissez; / Ajoutez, quelquefois, et souvent effacez." Boileau, *Art Poétique* (1669–74), ll. 172–74, *Œuvres poétiques,* ed. F. Brunetière (Paris: Hachette, 1914), p. 196.

30. "Tu enrichiras ton Poëme par varietez *prises de la Nature,* sans extravaguer comme un frenetique. Car pour vouloir trop eviter, & du tout te bannir du parler vulgaire, si tu veux voler sans consideration par le travers des nues, & faire des grotesques, Chimeres & monstres, & non une *naifve & naturelle poesie,* tu seras imitateur d'Ixion, qui engendra des Phantosmes au lieu de *legitimes & naturels enfans."* *Franciade,* p. 334.

31. Du Bellay, *Deffence,* II, 5 "Du Long Poëme Françoys," p. 127.

32. "La guerre Troyenne a esté feinte par Homere, comme quelques graves auteurs ont fermement assuré: les fables qui en sont sorties depuis sont toutes puisées de *la source de cest Homere.* . . . Autant en faut estimer de Virgile, lequel lisant en Homere, qu'Ænée ne devoit mourir à la guerre Troyenne . . . , conceut ceste divine Æneide." *Franciade,* pp. 6–7.

33. D. Quint, *Origin and Originality in Renaissance Literature: Versions of the Source* (New Haven, Conn.: Yale University Press, 1983), pp. 23ff.

34. "O qu'il i ùt ancore un Auguste pour voèr s'il se pourroèt ancore trouver un Virgile!" Peletier, *Art Poétique,* p. 210.

35. "Certainement si nous avions des Mecenes & des Augustes, les Cieux & la Nature ne sont point si ennemis de nostre siecle, que n'eussions encores des Virgiles!" Du Bellay, *Deffence,* pp. 132–33.

36. "Suy Virgile qui est passé maistre en composition & structure des carmes." *Franciade,* p. 347.

37. "Mon Passerat, je ressemble à l'Abeille / Qui va cueillant tantost la fleur vermeille, / Tantost la jaune: errant de pré en pré / Volle en la part qui plus luy vient à gré, / Contre l'Hyver amassant force vivres. / . . . Ainsy courant & feuilletant mes livres, / J'amasse, trie & choisis le plus beau, / Qu'en cent couleurs je peints en un tableau, / Tantost en l'autre: & maistre en ma peinture, / Sans me forcer j'imite la Nature." Ronsard, *Œuvres completes,* XV, 252.

38. Castor, p. 72.

39. "J'ai patronné mon oeuvre . . . sur la naïve facilité d'Homere." *Franciade,* p. 347.

40. "En ce laborieux ouvrage de la *Franciade,* l'Autheur s'est proposé la façon d'escrire des Anciens, & sur tous du divin Homere." *Franciade,* p. 14.

41. "Combien qu'en ce premier livre il ait principalement imité Homere et Virgile, si est-ce que l'embarquement de Francus est à l'imitation d'Apolloine Rhodien." *Franciade,* p. 14.

42. "Il ressemble à l'abeille, laquelle tire son proffit de toutes fleurs pour en faire son miel: aussi sans jurer en l'imitation d'un des Anciens plus que des autres, il considere ce qui est en eux de meilleur, dequoy il enrichist (comme toujours il a été heureux) nostre langue françoise." *Franciade,* p. 14.

43. Quint, p. 30.

44. *"Gallica se quantis attollet gloria verbis!"* Here one recognizes a line from *Aeneid* IV, 1. 49: "Punica se quantis attollet gloria rebus." To what heights will Punic glory soar!

ANNE J. CRUZ

Spanish Petrarchism and the Poetics of Appropriation: Boscán and Garcilaso de la Vega

Andrea Navagiero's suggestion to Juan Boscán in 1526 that he imitate the Italian style of poetry based on Petrarchan models has long been acknowledged as the impetus behind the revolutionary poetics of the Spanish Golden Age.[1] That Boscán not only heeded Navagiero's advice but encouraged his young protégé Garcilaso de la Vega to do likewise indeed resulted in the formation of a new literary current, one that remains to this day Spain's highest poetic achievement. While imitation is thus central to the development of Renaissance poetry in Spain, many Hispanists have viewed this crucial process in a perfunctory manner as mere copy or reelaboration of motifs. In an apparent dismissal of his own efforts, Boscán speaks of his poetry as "a kind of invention, if such one wishes to call it," adding that he wrote it "not giving a thought to its remaining in the world."[2] His attitude, then, while reflecting the requisite poetic virtue of *humilitas,* would seem to underscore the poet's artlessness in his task.

Yet the very fact that Boscán applies the term "invention" to describe his endeavor belies his disparaging remarks and reveals a more profound knowledge of the imitative process than has previously been credited to him. The specific reference discloses Boscán's awareness of the rhetorical term of *inventio* as a productive-creative process that, in accordance with the Ciceronian rhetorical tradition, extracts meaning from things.[3] As the first of three phases of the triple rhetorical scheme of *inventio/dispositio/elocutio* which structures Renaissance literary theory, *inventio* singles out the elements to be culled from model texts. These elements are then ordered internally by the second phase, *dispositio,* and the correct vocabulary chosen through the process of *elocutio.* In particular, the first phase of the rhetorical scheme is analogous to imitation —

the "invention" of a new literary movement which subsumes both originality and dependence.

In effect, the new Italianate versification could only have been accomplished by a thorough understanding of imitation as a dynamic force
which engages the poet in an active collaboration with his predecessors.
Exemplifying Arthur Terry's statement that "sixteenth-century poetry
and poetic theory form such a coherent unity that any poem written in
the Italianate tradition is a concrete embodiment of the theory which lies
behind it,"[4] Boscán's imitation does not limit itself to the somewhat
vague and automatic choices of literary influences, but delineates clearly
its intertextual references.

In applying the concept of *imitatio,* Boscán and Garcilaso initiate in
Spain a new poetics based on Petrarch's *Canzoniere* as textual model
which appropriates the Petrarchan themes and the Italian forms of the
sonnet and *canzone.* Their poetic practice manifests further their cognizance of the various modes of imitation current at the time. Thus, by
emphasizing their particular preference for opposing modes, Boscán's
and Garcilaso's poetics reveal as well their keen awareness of the sixteenth-
century quarrels of imitation that were raging in Italy among such
eminent theoreticians as Gianfrancesco Pico, Pietro Bembo, and Erasmus.

As Thomas Greene has recently pointed out, the controversy over
imitation in Italy during the Cinquecento renewed the previous Quattrocento polemics between Cortesi and Poliziano, intensifying and extending
the debates over models and modes of appropriation.[5] The correspon-
dence exchanged between Pico and Bembo signals their differences, as
Bembo adheres to the Ciceronian imitation of the optimum model in his
de Imitatione. The four phases that Bembo's own poetic development
undergoes are noted by Pietro Floriani: "A first moment which we would
call eclectic ... without a criterion of choice other than the exact approval
of the classical *loci* imitated ... a second phase of complete linguistic
freedom. . . . After having defined the principle of imitation, it was not
clear whether to proceed to imitate the minor or major poets ... henceforth, Bembo affirms having attempted both imitative methods ... having
finally verified the dangers and risks involved, Bembo arrives at the
imitation of the 'optimus.' "[6]

Pico, on the other hand, recommends the more eclectic approach of
omnes bonos. As Greene indicates, although Pico in no way opposes the
study of the ancients, he believes that "the superstitious mimicry of a
single author induces excessive attention to 'dispositio' and 'elocutio,'
whereas the highest value in all serious writing lies in its 'inventio.' "[7] In
contrast, Bembo is concerned more with the quest for a formal resemblance,
offering Virgil and Cicero as optimum models for Latin poetry and
prose, and Petrarch and Boccaccio for the vernacular. A historical basis

for the debate may be found in Bembo's increasing disquiet over Italy's loss of political and cultural hegemony. His imitation of the optimum model may therefore be perceived as a defensive tactic which rejects the historical trend of foreign cultural invasion. Pico's eclecticism fully acknowledges the historical discontinuities between cultures, all the while retaining in its freedom to choose from different sources a poetic individualism and flexibility relinquished in the strict formalism proposed by Bembo.

In his own poetry, Bembo stresses the return to a Petrarchism devoid of the hyperbolic excesses common to the Quattrocentisti poets such as il Cariteo and Serafino di'Ciminelli dall'Aquila. Instead, in his *Rime,* he imitates the *Canzoniere* directly, assuming the same *imitatio vitae* of its biographical sequence. The Petrarchan *Canzoniere* corresponds to a poetic discourse that delineates in its form the historical temporality of the poet. Each poem of the *Canzoniere* symbolizes a day of Petrarch's life, with the final *canzone* 366 as formal closure. This linear "year," assembled in discrete spatial elements, serves as paradigm for the poet's life, in turn divided by Laura's death into two separate periods formalized by the poems written *in vita,* and those *in morte.* Yet the cyclical movement of the *Canzoniere,* centered as it is on Petrarch's first encounter with Laura, returns the reader always to its point of origin. Moreover, the circular movement of the *Canzoniere* is inscribed over the liturgical calendar of the Church: Petrarch meets Laura on Good Friday; her death occurs on an Easter Sunday. While traditional criticism has viewed these dates as a sign of Petrarch's repentance and Laura's salvation, the *Canzoniere*'s palinodic ending is not entirely convincing. Despite its apparent religiosity, *canzone* 366 recalls in its courtly discourse Petrarch's previous invocations to Laura:

> Vergine sola al mondo, senza esempio,
> che'l Ciel di tue bellezze innamorasti,
> . . . .
> Per te po la mia vita esser ioconda,
> s'a' tuoi preghi, o Maria,
> Vergine dolce et pia,
> ove 'l fallo abondò la grazia abonda.
> Con le ginocchia de la mente inchine
> prego che sia mia scorta
> et la mia torta via drizzi a buon fine. (366:53–65)[8]

> (Virgin unique in the world, unexampled,
> who made heaven in love with your beauties;
> whom none ever surpassed or even approached;
> . . . .
> Through you my life can be joyous,
> if at your prayers, O Mary,

Sweet and merciful virgin,
where sin abounded grace abounds.
With the knees of my mind bent,
I beg you to be my guide
and to direct my twisted path to a good end.)

Sonnet 213 offers just one example where Petrarch addresses Laura in analogous terms:

Grazie ch' a pochi il Ciel largo destina,
rara vertù non già d'umana gente,
sotto biondi capei canuta mente
e 'n umil donna alta beltà divina . . . (ll. 1–4)

(Graces that generous Heaven allots to few,
virtues rare beyond the custom of men
beneath blond hair the wisdom of gray age,
and in a humble lady high divine beauty . . .)

In the *Canzone,* the allusion to Heaven's being enamored of the Virgin's beauty calls to mind Laura's hold on the poet; in similar fashion, the line in the previous stanza, "donna del Re che' nostri lacci a sciolti" ("Lady of that King who has loosed our bonds") replicates the language of the *Canzoniere* in its inversion of the emblem of the lady who binds the lover with her loveliness, usually symbolized by Laura's tresses. The line "Con le ginocchia de la mente inchine" develops besides a concept in *rime aspre* ("scorta—torta") that pointedly alludes to the *vera beatrice* of the previous stanza ("prego ch'appaghe il cor, vera beatrice"—"I pray you to quiet my heart, O true bringer of happiness"). Since this allusion can only be understood in relation to Dante's Beatrice, it involves more than a substitution of Laura by the Virgin—it implicates both Laura and the absent figure of Beatrice in an uncommon trinity. The implicit comparison between the ladies of the two greatest Italian poets actualizes their literary rivalry and ultimately places the univocal invocation to the Virgin in doubt. The ambiguity of the *Canzoniere* precludes a privileged interpretation, since it challenges the ideal image of Petrarch as repentant sinner by revealing his worldly concern about his literary fame. Ernest Hatch Wilkins's remarks noting Petrarch's desire for coronation in the *canzone* "Nel dolce tempo" are further confirmed by John Freccero, who extends Petrarch's anxiety to the whole of his poetic achievement: "Petrarch makes no claim to reality or to moral witness. . . . The moral struggle and the spiritual torment described in the *Canzoniere* are . . . part of a poetic strategy. When the spiritual struggle is demystified, its poetic mechanism is revealed: the petrified idolatrous lover is an immutable monument to Petrarch, his creator and namesake."[9] The last *canzone*'s ambiguous language thus creates and maintains an idolatrous double reference—the Virgin and Laura are both figures that stand for Petrarch's poetry, whose intranscendent circularity replaces the *Logos* with the laurel.

In their formal imitation of the *Canzoniere,* Bembo's *Rime* consciously create a life history of the poet, from the amorous experiences of his youth and middle years to his election as cardinal. Unlike Petrarch, however, whose last *canzone* may be interpreted, not as a palinode, but as an idolatrously ambivalent analogy between the Virgin and Laura, Bembo's *Rime* assure the reader of his repentance. Eliminating the self-reflexiveness and ambiguity structurally marked in the reiterative Petrarchan language that ultimately converges upon itself, Bembo posits instead a linear trajectory that extends toward the future to reach a formal closure in the palinode of his last three sonnets and *ballata,* which critics have labeled "di pentimento et di preghiera." The biographical authenticity of Bembo's poetry, however, is disproved by the fact that his last *ballata* was most probably written in 1510, twenty-nine years before his appointment as cardinal. While the *ballata* thus duplicates the *Canzoniere*'s last *canzone* as palinode, rejecting an idolatrous or even ambivalent reading, the *Rime* acknowledge the last poem's strategic importance as poetic closure.[10] Moreover, in retaining in his edition of the *Canzoniere* Bernardino Daniello's annotation that classical lyric poets customarily ended their poetry with a laudatory hymn to a deity, Bembo implicitly corroborates the last poem's function as an imitative strategy that puts into question the sincerity of its repentance.[11]

In Spain, Boscán's Petrarchism follows the formalism recommended by Bembo. His Italianate verses, collected in the second of his four books of poetry (the fourth constituting his edition of Garcilaso's poems), reflect the structure of Petrarch's *Canzoniere* as imitated by Bembo, but limited to ninety-two sonnets and ten *canciones.* By patterning his poetry on Petrarch and Bembo, he alternates his poetic lament between the sonnets and *canciones,* and assembles his own Spanish version of a *Canzoniere.* Although Boscán's sonnets are never quite free of the conceptual wordplay and paronomasia that typify the medieval Spanish songbook convention in which he was schooled, the *canciones* demonstrate his ability to accommodate the Italian form to the Spanish language and to appropriate the Petrarchan thematics of the *Canzoniere.* His first *canción* develops the theme of the previous eighteen sonnets in its vacillating desire to express the suffering caused by love. It establishes the same confessional tone of conversion underlying Petrarch's first sonnet in his *Canzoniere,* as well as the same intimate and collusive relationship between reader and poet in their shared experiences. Paradoxically, although he is deterred by his fear that this will unleash a never-ending torrent of laments, thus prolonging his pain, he feels compelled to express his suffering as cautionary tale to other lovers. Once the poet has revealed his sentiments, his only recourse is to continue the poetic lament beyond the confines of the *canción*, repaying his poetic debt to the *Canzoniere* in the self-generating continuity of his imitation.

Although Boscán adheres to Petrarchan form, he, like Bembo, avoids all idolatrous references to the lady. His *canción* LII takes Petrarch's "Gentil mia Donna, i'veggio," as its model:

> Gentil mia Donna, i'veggio
> nel mover de' vostr'occhi un dolce lume
> che mi mostra la via ch'al ciel conduce;
> . . . .
> Io penso: se là suso,
> onde 'l motor eterno de le stelle
> degnò mostrar del suo lavoro in terra. (72:1–3, 16–18)
>
> (My noble Lady, I see
> in the moving of your eyes a sweet light
> that shows me the way that leads to Heaven
> . . . .
> I think: if up there,
> whence the eternal Mover of the stars
> deigned to show forth this work on earth.)

While the *canción* amplifies Petrarch's poem and incorporates in its thematics the constant paradox of love, it eliminates the juxtaposition of the power of salvation attributed to Laura's eyes and the reference to God as Supreme Mover, averting any ambiguity between secular love and religious expression in its use of the rhetorical strategy of *reticentia* by repeating the Spanish phrase "un no sé qué":

> Gentil señora mía,
> yo hallo en el mover de vuestros ojos
> un no sé qué—no sé cómo nombrallo. (LII, 1–3)[12]
>
> (My gentle lady,
> I find in the movement of your eyes
> something inexplicable—I know not what to call it.)

Following Bembo as its optimum model, Boscán's *Second Book* is also structured as an *imitatio vitae*. In its linear construct of Petrarchan laments, it traces a history of unrequited love and arrives at formal and temporal closure in the last poem's final recantation of that love. Indeed, the last *canción*'s allusion to the lover as a wanderer who had lost his way under the false protection of love, recalls both the Petrarchan topos of *vago errore* as well as his youthful *errare:*

Gran tiempo Amor me tuvo de su mano,
el bien con el dolor en mí templando,
traiéndome con gusto y con tormento;
. . . .
Duraron largo tiempo estos errores,
y oxalái pues tan grande fue'l errarse,
no comenzaran ni duraran tanto! (CXXX:1–3, 46–48)

(So long a time Love had me by the hand,
tempering in me the good with the pain,
bringing me along with pleasure and with torment
. . . .
These errors lasted such a long time,
and since so great was the error of my ways,
I wish they had never begun nor lasted so long!)

Yet Boscan's *canción* ends unequivocally on a religious note — the lover is delivered from his past errors by the intervention of Christ in the guise of Good Samaritan. Like Bembo's last *ballata*, the palinode should not be taken as an autobiographical rejection of secular love, but rather as a literary device of poetic closure. However, the *canción*'s overtly Christian stance discloses Boscán's strong attachment to medieval scholasticism, stressing the Thomistic idea of love as a sickness to be cured by divine grace.[13] The resultant conflictive poetic attitudes of Neoplatonic love and Christian repentance exemplify Boscán's inability to delimit fully the historical and philosophical differences between the medieval Spanish convention and the novel Renaissance poetry he so willingly undertook to imitate. In this, he again approximates Bembo, whose poetic reform serves as transition between the Italian Quattrocento and the Cinquecento. Boscán finds himself, as Luigi Baldacci has said of Bembo, "a cavallo tra i due secoli."

What Boscán carries out only partially in his acclimation of Italian models to Spanish poetics, Garcilaso de la Vega accomplishes in full. While Boscán's Italianate verses ensure fidelity to a single model, Garcilaso's poetry resists categorization as yet another imitation of a Petrarchan *Canzoniere*. Boscán's efforts to arrange his recently deceased friend's poetry in his *Fourth Book* following the linear narrative form of the *imitatio vitae* ultimately meet with failure. With the one exception of the first *canción*, Boscán finally groups Garcilaso's poetry by form: first the sonnets, then five *canciones*, two elegies, and the final three eclogues. In its syncretism, Garcilaso's poetry reflects his choice of imitation as that of *omnes bonos* as recommended by Pico. Besides the classical authors, Garcilaso reaches out to the various Italian poets he meets in Naples. Sannazaro's *Arcadia* was an especially influential text, as well as the poetry of his Italian colleagues Luigi Tansillo, Bernardo Tasso, and Giulio Cesare Caracciolo. Instead of arriving at narrative closure, his emphasis on *inventio* as creative process brings together three separate literary currents—classical literature, the more recent Italian influences, and the Spanish songbook tradition—transforming them into a seamless poetic garment of his own making.

Garcilaso effects a conscious misreading of the Petrarchan model which distances and historicizes his poetry from the *Canzoniere*. His five *canciones* do not constitute a poetic narrative with a final palinode, but individually address the Petrarchan problematics of unrequited love. His sonnets reflect their elaboration of Petrarchan themes, all the while signaling the differences between them and Petrarch as textual model. Instead of the solitary lover ever present in the melancholy Petrarchan landscape, Garcilaso populates his poetic world with a variety of narrative voices that assume a number of poetic personae—shepherds, soldiers, and lovers. Garcilaso's Petrarchism is thus a mimetic process by which he approaches his various sources, combining and reworking them in the different poetic forms.

His eclogues in particular illustrate the degree to which he transforms his sources in his own. The second eclogue's problematic structure illustrates the complex intertextuality of its influences. Following the pastoral tradition, the poem narrates the unhappy love of the shepherd Albanio who, after going mad and attempting suicide, is finally cured of his lovesickness by the Neoplatonic powers of the magus, Severo. The implicit condemnation of courtly love, symbolized in the early rejection of the myth of Narcissus, does not negate Petrarchism as a mode of imitation, however. The eclogue explores a multiplicity of poetic discourses, from the lyric forms of the ode and elegy, to the dramatic and narrative forms of dialogue, panegyric, and pastoral.[14] The eclogue's thematic resolution marks its poetic consciousness. Its final solution is not contained in the narrative, but in the poem's internal structure, in the Renaissance ideal of *discordia concors,* which underlies both its form and content.

Due to its problematic structure and narrative, critics have tended to view the second eclogue as poetic experiment, in contrast to the polished artifice of the first and third eclogues. Both these eclogues owe their formal precision to Garcilaso's constant reworking of his sources and, as in the second poem, reveal his constant concern over imitation as a self-generating force. The first eclogue stresses self-referentiality as a poetic strategy:

> El dulce lamentar de dos pastores
> Salicio juntamente y Nemoroso
> é de cantar, sus quexas imitando. (I:1–3)[15]

> (The sweet lament of two shepherds,
> Salicio together with Nemoroso,
> I shall relate in song, imitating their complaints.)

In the same way it incorporates its classical and Italian sources, the eclogue itself becomes another poetic source. The Virgilian lamentations of the two shepherds—Salicio over his lover's betrayal, Nemoroso over the death of his lover—echo the poet's previous lamentations on the loss of his lover. Traditionally, the *dédoublement* of the poetic voice into separate pastoral laments has been accepted as representing two versions of the poet's historical relationship with the Portuguese lady-in-waiting, Isabel Freyre, expressing his suffering over her disdain and her later death. The biographical reference, however, is subsumed in the fictional narrative. The structural and thematic parallels between Salicio's complaint and Nemoroso's lament blur the temporal and historical distinctions between the fictional lovers and the real-life characters. In an exchange of attributes, Salicio's Galatea, who shares the mythical qualities of her Greek namesake, is transformed into a Renaissance lady of the Spanish court, while Elisa, an anagram of Isabel, becomes mythified as Nemoroso's shepherdess. Both lovers, however, are absent from the poem, and the poetic desire to recuperate their loss through the Petrarchan lament informs the double structure of the eclogue.

Similarly, Garcilaso imitates classical and Italian tradition by converting the Petrarchan landscape to a Spanish one, singling out the river Tagus, the Extremaduran pastures, and the hills near Cuenca as the natural surroundings where he experiences his loss. He follows Petrarch, however, in that the subjectivized description of nature creates an internal landscape that fails to re-member the lady or recreate her presence:

> y en este mismo valle, donde agora
> me entristezco y me canso en el reposo,
> estuve ya contento y descansado. (I:253–55)

> (And in this same vale, where today
> I am saddened and weary in repose,
> I was then happy and rested.)

The poet's psychological state, his nostalgic longing, is reified in the barrenness of the landscape. Nature is modified by the lady's absence, its qualities transferred to the absent lover in codified Petrarchan epithets:

> por ti la verde yerva, el fresco viento,
> el blanco lirio y colorada rosa
> y dulce primavera deseava. (I:103–5)

> (Because of you, I desired the green grass,
> the cool breeze, the white lily and red rose,
> and sweet spring.)

The references to the natural elements—the ivy, the clear streams—unite the two laments, which are further integrated by the Petrarchan metaphor of tears as poetic discourse in the medieval Spanish songbook refrain repeated throughout Salicio's lament ("salid sin duelo, lagrimas, corriendo" — "flow forth unrestrained, tears, streaming").

The Orphic tension between Garcilaso's appropriation of Petrarchan poetics and his willing exclusion from the fold of Petrarchist imitators — between origin and originality — is evidenced in the opposing endings of the two shepherds' laments. Salicio offers to abandon the *locus amoenus* so Galatea may remain. His complaisance portends the poet's renunciation of his own poetry, since his departure would silence the poetic voice:

> no dexes el lugar que tanto amaste
> que bien podrás venir de mí segura.
> Yo dexaré el lugar do me dexaste;
> ven si por solo aquesto te detienes.
> Ves aquí un prado lleno de verdura,
> . . . .
> quiçá aquí hallarás, pues yo m'alexo,
> al que todo mi bien quitar me puede. (I:212–22)

> (Don't leave the place you loved so much,
> you may come forward safe from me.
> I'll leave the place where you left me;
> Come, if only this deters you.
> You see here a verdant meadow.
> . . . .
> maybe here you'll find, since I'll depart,
> the one who may take away all my treasure.)

Nemoroso's lament, on the other hand, ends with the desire to create a new landscape, one where the poet will be forever reunited with Elisa:

> y en la tercera rueda,
> contigo mano a mano,
> busquemos otro llano,
> busquemos otros montes y otros ríos. (I:400–403)

> (And in the third sphere,
> with you hand in hand,
> let us find another meadow,
> let us find other hills and other rivers.)

The *other* here is clearly Garcilaso's own version of Petrarchism, through which Nemoroso aspires to create a new world, where desire disappears before the eternal presence of love, and suffering is transformed into the aesthetic permanence of art.

Garcilaso's intent to follow Pico's mode of eclectic imitation while adhering to a Petrarchan poetics is best demonstrated in his third eclogue. This last poem is an ekphrastic representation of the tapestries woven by river nymphs depicting the three Ovidian myths of Orpheus and Eurydice, Venus and Adonis, and Apollo and Daphne, and incorporating the first eclogue's ill-starred pastoral couple, Elisa and Nemoroso, in the same mythological terms of the preceding lovers. The different levels of narration sustain a series of mediations between the reader and the biographical incident of Isabel Freyre's death traditionally considered the poem's motivating factor, illustrating the eclogue's self-referentiality in its marked choice of myths involving narratives of love, desire, and death.

In contrast to the *Metamorphoses,* the poem's Ovidian myths act as paradigms of desire — of unattainable love that leads inevitably to death as its final transformation. Through the myths, Garcilaso questions his own artistic power to transform the ineluctable moment of death and the immediacy of its pain into a universal aesthetic experience by structuring a poetic order according to the semiotic value of each myth. The first three myths anticipate the novel Spanish myth of Elisa and Nemoroso, who are elevated by their context to the pastoral tradition and classical mythology, and infused with the emotional psychology of the weeping Petrarchan lover. The fourth myth thus emblematizes the mimetic function of art as interpreted by Garcilaso. By positing the three Ovidian myths as precedents of his own original myth, he maintains the temporal difference between them, yet all the myths are metonymically linked to each other, creating a chain of correspondences which foregrounds the eclogue's self-creative process.

The three Ovidian myths chosen by Garcilaso disavow any transcendence of death. The first myth of Orpheus and Eurydice functions as a paradigm of the subsequent myths and of the poetic experience of love, death, and desire. Its scenes are related in three stanzas: the death of the loved one, bitten by a serpent; the poetic lament originated by this loss; and the uselessness of the lament, addressed to a landscape devoid of content and reflecting the psychological state of the poet. Motivated by his desire for Eurydice, Orpheus assumes the role of the originator of poetry in his lament over her untimely death, regarded in the eclogue as a disruption of the natural order:

> descolorida estava como rosa
> que ha sido fuera de sazón cogida. (III:133–34)

> (She was as drained of color as a rose
> that has been plucked before its prime.)

The second myth describes Apollo's pursuit of Daphne, all the while underscoring its futility in the distance observed and maintained between the lover and the object of his desire:

> que Apollo en la pintura parecía
> que, porque'lla templasse el movimiento
> con menos ligereza la seguía. (III:156–58)

> (in order to temper her swiftness,
> Apollo in the painting seemed
> to follow her with less speed.)

The myth stresses in turn the impossibility of attaining the object of desire through poetic intent. Apollo, the god of poetry, is impotent to halt Daphne's transformation. And although the laurel comes to symbolize Daphne, it does not contain her, as her essence escapes through her metamorphosis. Her transformation into the natural element impedes the fulfillment of desire; yet, like Daphne's metamorphosis itself, the second myth transforms the amorous accident into substance, reifying desire into poetry.

The third myth repeats the previous hunting imagery of the pursuit of love. Venus and Adonis, both personifications of physical beauty and desire, are tragically separated when the latter is gored to death by a boar. Yet the hunt of the boar is traditionally associated with the rejection of erotic love.[16] Adonis hunts his prey so as not to be captivated by love, since his death assures him the impossibility of obtaining his same desire. The final depiction of a mortally wounded Adonis prefigures the image of the dead Elisa in the fourth myth:

> y el moço en tierra estava ya tendido
> . . . .
> con el cabello d'oro desparzido
> . . . .
> las rosas blancas por allí sembradas
> tornavan con su sangre coloradas. (III:179–84)

> (and the youth now lay lifeless on the ground
> . . . .
> with his golden hair spread out
> . . . .
> the white roses planted nearby
> were reddening with his blood.)

While the first myth of Orpheus and Eurydice centers on poetic self-creation, the two following myths recall the tension previously noted between the differing resolutions of the two shepherds' laments in the first eclogue. Just as Nemoroso wished to unite with Elisa in death, so Apollo desires to obtain the unobtainable Daphne; and as Salicio previously acquiesced to abandon the poetic landscape, leaving his poetry in his stead, so Adonis accepts the impossibility of his love in the sacrifice of the hunt.

The fourth myth's narrative length—nine stanzas compared to three for each of the previous myths—indicates its importance within the sequence. In its specific mention of the Tagus River, the myth returns the reader to the historical present, distancing it from the classical past. Yet Garcilaso subtly interweaves the poetic polyvalence of the three previous myths in the presentation of the modern Spanish myth in his depiction of the nymphs grieving over Elisa's beheaded corpse:

> Todas, con el cabello desparzido,
> lloravan una nympha delicada
> cuya vida mostrava que avia sido
> antes de tiempo y casi en flor cortada;
> cerca del agua, en un lugar florido,
> estava entre las yervas degollada
> qual queda el blanco cisne cuando pierde
> la dulce vida entre la yerva verde. (III:225–32)

> (All, with their long hair flowing,
> wept for a delicate nymph
> whose life had been clearly shorn before its flowering;
> Near the water, in a meadow of flowers,
> she lay beheaded amid the grasses
> as the white swan lies when he has lost
> his sweet life midst the green grass.)

The classical myths which anticipate and contribute to the fourth are subsumed by the linear reading of the text into the final myth, effectively calling to mind Harold Bloom's sixth revisionary ratio of *apophrades*—the return of the dead, but clothed in the new poet's colors and speaking in his voice.[17] Yet the resonances of the three previous myths enhance the significance of the fourth: both Adonis and Orpheus are evoked in the violent description of the nymph's lifeless body; her premature death compared in almost the same terms to Eurydice's; while the jarring juxtaposition of Elisa's inanimate body lying amid a meadow of flowers recalls the unnatural transformation of a fleeing Daphne into a rooted and gnarled tree. The white swan, which is also a symbol of Venus, reduplicates in its form the nymph's slackened figure, but it also brings to mind the poet's song of love for the dead Elisa. Carved on the bark of a tree by one of the river nymphs, Elisa's epitaph is the final transformation of the eclogue, as it is narrated in the first person by Elisa herself, collapsing the fiction of the poet, the lover, and the narrator into a single voice of absence:

> "Elissa soy, en cuyo nombre suena
> y se lamenta el monte cavernoso
> testigo del dolor y grave pena
> en que por mí se aflige Nemoroso

y llama 'Elissa'; 'Elissa' a boca llena
responde el Tajo, y lleva pressuroso
al mar de Lusitania el nombre mío,
donde será escuchado, yo lo fío." (III:241–48)

("I am Elissa, in whose name the cavernous mountain
reverberates and laments
witnessing the pain and profound grief
that Nemoroso suffers for me
and calls out 'Elissa'; 'Elissa' responds the Tagus
in full force and rushes
my name to the Lusitanian sea
where I am certain it will be heard.")

The three Ovidian myths thus function semiotically as Garcilaso's poetics, appropriated and transformed from Petrarch's: from the myth as poetic creation (Orpheus as the first poet and Apollo as god of poetry); to the impossibility of desire (the deaths of Eurydice and Adonis, the flight of Daphne); and to the metamorphosis of desire into poetry (Daphne in her final transformation into the laurel, Adonis into the anemone). Through the imitative process of *inventio*, then, Garcilaso orders the three classical myths that will supply the poetic material for the elaboration of the final myth, eloquently expressed in the Spanish vernacular. Each myth is therefore dependent upon the reading of the following, and the three combine their multiple meanings of creativity, metamorphosis, and desire in the ekphrastic presentation of the fourth. By following Pico's dictum to imitate, not one *optimus*, but many *omnes bonos*, Garcilaso's imitation results not only in the transformation of his various models into his own poetic work, but in the historical subversion of their influence.

NOTES

The ideas expressed in this essay have been developed further in my study on Petrarchism in Spain, *Imitación y transformación: el petrarquismo en la poesía de Boscán y Garcilaso de la Vega,* Purdue University Monographs in the Romance Languages (Amsterdam: John Benjamins, 1987).

1. While some Hispanists attribute the innovation of Italianate versification in Spain to the marqués de Santillana, the majority agree with Rafael Lapesa, who considers his sonnets an isolated literary instance in the fifteenth century, and blames the historical moment for the difference between what was proposed by Santillana and what he actually achieved. See *La obra literaria del marqués de Santillana* (Madrid: Insula, 1957), pp. 200–201. Boscán himself is certainly aware of his role as innovator when he states "he querido ser el primero que ha juntado la lengua castellana con el modo de escribir italiano." *Obras poéticas de Juan Boscán,* ed. Martín de Riquer et al. (Barcelona: Universidad de Barcelona, 1957), p. 89. (Hereafter cited as Boscán.)

2. "Assí también en este modo de invención (si assí quieren llamalla) nunca pensé que inventava ni hazia cosa que huviesse de quedar en el mundo, sino que entré en ello descuydadamente como en cosa que iva tan poco en hazella que no havia para qué dexalla de hazer haviéndola gana" (Boscán, p. 89).

3. Arthur Terry, Introduction, *An Anthology of Spanish Poetry, 1500-1700* (Oxford, N.Y.: Pergamon Press, 1965), pp. xv–xxv.

4. The *Rhetorica ad Herennium*, I.ii.3, defines *inventio* as "excogitatio rerum verarum aut veri similium quae causam probabilem reddant." (Cambridge, Mass.: Loeb Classical Library, Harvard University Press, 1963), p. 6.

5. See Thomas M. Greene, "Sixteenth-Century Quarrels: Classicism and the Scandal of History," in *The Light in Troy: Imitation and Discovery in Renaissance Poetry* (New Haven, Conn.: Yale University Press, 1982).

6. "Un primo momento che diremmo eclettico . . . senza criterio di scelta che non sia nell'approvazione puntuale dei *loci* classici imitati . . . una seconda fase di assoluta libertà linguistica. . . . Una volta poi definito il principio d'imitazione, restava in dubbio se preceder all' imitazione dei minori . . . o dei massimi; e di seguito, il Bembo afferma di aver tentato le due vie . . . verificati infine danni e rischi di questa posizione, il Bembo pervenne all'imitazione dell' 'optimus.' " Piero Floriani, *Bembo e Castiglione: Studi sul Classicismo del Cinquecento* (Rome: Bulzoni Editore, 1976), p. 56 (my translation).

7. Greene, p. 173.

8. For all translations of the *Canzoniere*, I have relied on Robert M. Durling's bilingual edition, *Petrarch's Lyric Poems: The "Rime sparse" and Other Lyrics* (Cambridge, Mass.: Harvard University Press, 1976).

9. John Freccero, "The Fig Tree and the Laurel: Petrarch's Poetics," *Diacritics* 5, no. 1 (1975), 34–40. Ernest Hatch Wilkins, in *The Making of the "Canzoniere" and Other Petrarchan Studies* (Rome: Edizioni di Storia e Letteratura, 1951), states that in the *canzone* "Nel dolce tempo," lines 38–49, the "first of the metamorphoses undergone by the poet . . . is metamorphosis into a laurel tree; and within the account of this experience there is placed a frank statement of Petrarch's desire for coronation" (p. 25).

10. See Carlo Dionisotti, *Prose e Rime di Pietro Bembo*, Classici Italiani, Collezione fondata da Ferdinando Neri, diretta da Mario Fubini (Torino: Editrice Torinese, 1960), p. 649.

11. "Fù antico costume de Poeti & spezialmente de Lirici, così Greci, come Latini, di chiuder sempre i Poemi loro, con alcun 'Hinno in laude d'alcuna Deità composto, come si vede che fece Pindaro nella Greca, & nella Romana lingua Horazio nell'vltima delle sue Caz." Francesco Petrarcha, *Sonetti e Canzone in vita...*, ed. Pietro Bembo (Lyone, 1558), p. 463. However, in lines 22–23 of the *canzone* 366, where Petrarch imitates Virgil ("Vergine que' belli occhi / che vider tristi la spietata stampa / ne' dolci membri del tuo caro figlio"), Bembo leaves out Daniello's gloss ("Così Virgilio in persona di Venere, parlando col figliuolo di Sicheo: 'Crudeleis aras, traiecta qī; pectora ferro nudauit' ") perhaps to avoid a possible comparison between Venus and the Virgin. See *Sonetti, canzoni e triomphi di messer Francesco Petrarcha con la spositione di Bernardino Daniello da Lucca...* (Venice, 1541), p. 213.

12. For Boscán's poetry, I have utilized the Riquer edition mentioned above. All translations are my own.

13. David H. Darst, *Juan Boscán* (Boston: Twayne Publishers, 1978), p. 80.

14. See Inés Azar, *Discurso retórico y mundo pastoral en la "Egloga segunda" de Garcilaso,* Purdue University Monographs in Romance Languages (Amsterdam: John Benjamins, 1981), p. 36.

15. I have utilized Elias L. Rivers's edition, *Garcilaso de la Vega: obras completas con comentario* (Madrid: Editorial Castalia; Columbus: Ohio State University Press, 1974), for quotations. All translations are my own.

16. See Marcelle Thiébaux, *The Stag of Love: The Chase in Medieval Literature* (Ithaca, N.Y.: Cornell University Press, 1974), p. 96.

17. Harold Bloom, *The Anxiety of Influence: A Theory of Poetry* (London: Oxford University Press, 1973), p. 141.

MARÍA CRISTINA QUINTERO

Translation and Imitation in the Development of Tragedy during the Spanish Renaissance

The role of translation in the development of literary genres during the Renaissance is a topic which has not received adequate attention, particularly in Hispanic studies. Although there are several important works on the linguistic and cultural implications of translation, there has been a tendency, from a literary perspective, to dismiss translation as an inferior, parasitical practice and consecrate the original texts as superior products.[1] As a result, translations are seldom included in histories of literature and their contribution to the evolution of national literatures is ignored. In Renaissance studies, the history and theory of translation have been overshadowed by critical attention to the intrinsically related activity of *imitatio*.[2] This neglect, all the more glaring in Spanish criticism, may be due in part to the scarcity of Renaissance treatises on the question of translation. In spite of the fact that fifteenth- and sixteenth-century Spain witnessed a proliferation of translations from both classical and other Romance languages, there were few attempts to formulate theoretical models for translation. Aside from prefaces to actual translations, e.g., the introduction to Fray Luis de León's *Cantar de los cantares,* and allusions to the topic within broader treatises on poetics by a López Pinciano or a Cascales, we are hard pressed to find a systematic guide to the theoretical foundations governing this activity. The only notable exception to this silence on translation in Spain can be found in the works of the great humanist Juan Vives.[3] Given the small body of Renaissance theories of translation, it has been difficult for modern scholars to form a clear conception of the procedure. In addition, problems arise from the inadequate classification of certain Renaissance texts. Works that were categorized as translations were frequently so divergent from the original texts as to constitute new works altogether, and texts that were in fact translations were not acknowledged as such. Because there were no unequivocal standards to designate the degree of faithfulness to an original source text, a considerable problem facing scholars today is precisely the determination of the practice of translation as opposed to that of imitation during the Renaissance.

Writers and theoreticians in the fifteenth and sixteenth centuries were equally ambivalent about the relationship between the two endeavors, but many tended to view translation as another form of imitation. In fact, *translatio* seems to have become a type of pragmatic *imitatio* cultivated by many Renaissance authors. Translation was the necessary first step toward an ideal imitation of the classical masters, and this imitation became in turn the prerequisite for creativity and originality. This process was perhaps best expressed in the seventeenth century by John Dryden. In his "Preface to the Translation of Ovid's Epistles," Dryden identifies three stages in translation: first, *metaphrase,* representing a literal transfer from a source language into another; second, *paraphrase,* which represents a free translation or what Dryden calls "translation with latitude"; and finally, *imitation,* where, in Dryden's words, "the translator (if now he has not lost that name) assumes the liberty, not only to vary from the words and sense, but to forsake them both as he sees occasion; and taking only some general hints from the original, to run division on the groundwork, as he pleases."[4] This evolutionary process, from transmission to interpretation to creative imitation, can be seen reflected in the development of Renaissance drama in Spain. Before the spectacular flourishing in the seventeenth century of the *comedia nueva,* the most important manifestations of Spanish drama were the result of diffusion of treatises and dramatic texts translated from classical and Italian sources. In many ways, the *comedia nueva* itself was the culmination of tendencies that began with these translations during the sixteenth century. The present study will deal in particular with the impact of translation of Renaissance tragedy in Spain.

While it is true that most Renaissance authors neglected the comprehensive study of translation, we can nevertheless turn to classical authorities and discover there a basis for the discussion of the problem. Antiquity provided implicit theoretical models for the practice of translation, and it would be useful at this point to provide a brief overview of those authorities who doubtless influenced Renaissance conceptions in this area. Greek treatises on the subject were unknown and neither Aristotle nor Plato mentions translation directly. Translation as a cultural program became prevalent with the Romans precisely as a manifestation of their cultural rivalry with the Greeks. Although the bilingualism of the educated Roman class precluded the need for prolific translation of Greek texts into Latin, writers such as Cicero, Horace, and Quintilian were very conscious of the activity and wrote on its implications. Consequently, the texts that were to influence medieval and Renaissance attitudes toward translation were written in Latin. For both Horace in his *Ars Poetica* and Cicero in *de Inventione,* the art of the translator consisted in the judicious interpretation of the original text. Horace warned against slavish translations and Cicero clearly voiced the intrinsic problem implied in any translation: "If I render word for word, the result will sound uncouth, and if compelled by necessity, I alter anything in the order or wording, I shall seem to have departed from the function of the translator."[5] Cicero recognized the necessity of modifying the original text in order to take into account the needs of contemporary readers. The Ciceronian approach, later echoed by St. Jerome in his often-quoted "non verbum de verbo, sed sensum exprimere de sensu," that is, rendering not word-by-word but sense for sense became an ideal for Renaissance translators.[6] Quintilian, in his *Institutionis oratoriae,* approached translation from a pragmatic and didactic point of view. In his exercises for developing oratory, he stressed the usefulness of paraphrasing a given text as a means of assisting the student both to analyze the structure of the text and to experiment with forms of embellishment or abridgment. In paraphrasing, Quintilian recommended first a straightforward closeness to the original text, to be followed by a second and more complex stage where the translator begins to incorporate his own style within the framework provided by the original.

As mentioned in my introduction, in addition to these three classical authorities on translation, Renaissance Spain also benefited from the writings of Juan Vives. Vives's theories were based on the same Latin sources but offer some innovations to the theory of translation. Given his prestige among humanist circles, he probably contributed to the development of an ideology of translation in Renaissance and post-Renaissance Spain.[7] His definition of translation as "versio est a lingua in luguam verborum traductio sensu servato" corresponds to the classical emphasis on sense over style. Vives, however, was less interested in establishing a rigid set of rules and procedures than in offering a descriptive analysis of different types of translation. He states that translation is basically a reflective activity, and theory should be based on the individual practice of each translator. Different types of translations are determined by the demands of the text being translated and the function the translator assigns to language. The Spanish humanist isolated three modes of translation which correspond to three different types of texts. First of all, he identifies translations which concentrate only on the meaning or sense of the original work: "solus spectatur sensus." These correspond to texts in which what is said (*ratio sensorum*) is more important than the manner in which it is said (*figurae et conformationes*). Although Vives does not mention specific texts, the first type of translation would seem to be most appropriate for informative works of a scientific or didactic nature. In this type, the translator has a great deal of freedom. He can omit what is superfluous to the content and even add elements that may contribute to the understanding of the work. The second type of translation takes into account only the form, the expression. Vives dismisses this type as too difficult and undesirable given the linguistic peculiarities and specificity of each language. It is virtually impossible to reproduce in a second language (*posterior lingua*) the idioms and turns of phrase of the first (*prior lingua*).

This attitude is striking in its modernity and is reminiscent of Roman Jakobson's assertion that absolute translation, especially in poetry, is unattainable and only "creative transposition" is possible.[8] In his linguistic theories, Vives consistently emphasized the diversity of languages which made translating word-by-word nearly impossible. The third type of translation takes into account both the *ratio sensorum* and the *figurae*. Again, although he does not specify which texts would fall in this category, it seems clear that this type of translation was, in his opinion, the most appropriate for literary texts in which the relationship of form and content comprises their basic characteristic.

From this brief exposition of some of the underlying theories governing translation, we turn to its role in the production of tragedies during the Spanish Renaissance. Tragedy in general has had an uneven history in Spanish letters, and translations of classical tragedies into *castellano* have been virtually ignored. Most Hispanists have dismissed these translations as mere academic exercises with little if any influence in the evolution of a national dramatic form. Others, most prominently Alfredo Hermenegildo, have wisely recognized that the reduced influence these translated texts had on popular theater does not in any way deny their importance in the development of a Renaissance conception of tragedy.[9] Unfortunately, we do not have a complete picture of the role of translation in the production of tragedies in Spain because translations of Greek tragedies by Renaissance luminaries such as El Brocense and Boscán have been lost to us and we have only fragments of Fray Luis de León's translation of Euripides' *Andromache*.[10] Given the precarious conditions in which many humanists worked, particularly their uneasy relationship with the Inquisition, we are fortunate that translations of Greek and Latin tragedies by lesser known writers did, in fact, survive. Of particular interest and perhaps paradigmatic of translations that have been lost to us, are those by the humanist Fernán Pérez de Oliva, a rector at the University of Salamanca. His versions in Spanish of Sophocles' *Electra* and Euripides' *Hecuba* illustrate both the importance of translation for dramatic activity in Spain at the time and the imprecise nature of the task.

Pérez de Oliva's *La venganza de Agamenón* and *Hecuba triste* have been classified by Hermenegildo as examples of "tragedia de círculo cerrado," that is, tragedies produced for a closed circle or reduced audience. The Spanish critic applies the term to tragedies written in the universities and to those belonging to the scholastic tradition in the *colegios* run by the Jesuits. This drama written in the cloistered environment of the universities and secondary schools began as the type of exercise described by Quintilian, that is, one designed to develop knowledge of Latin and to a lesser extent, Greek.[11] Translation since the Middle Ages had formed part of the typical curriculum at the universities and was intended to lead students to a second and more important activity: the imitation *in Latin* of the translated text. The version in *castellano* was used initially only as a mediating text in the development of Latin rhetoric and grammar. The use of translation by Pérez de Oliva, however, is indicative of the new trend among many humanists in the Renaissance: to transcend the reverential attachment to Latin and use translations for different but equally didactic purposes.

Although Pérez de Oliva probably had at least some knowledge of Greek, it is not known whether his translations were done directly from the Greek or via Latin translations. One thing is certain: his *La venganza de Agamenón* and *Hecuba triste* remain the first known Spanish versions of Greek tragedies.[12] Before the appearance of these texts between 1525 and 1528, the only example of Greek tragedy in a modern language was Giovanbattista Gelli's Italian translation of Euripides' *Hecuba*, edited around 1519. Along with Gelli's translation, Pérez de Oliva's texts represent the first attempts to mold classical tragedy in the vernacular as a means of enhancing the status of Romance languages. Turning to the models provided by antiquity in order to increase the prestige of the vernacular was a characteristic tendency of all the emerging Romance literatures, which still had little written tradition of their own. The sixteenth century, as we know, represents one of the most important periods in the evolution of the European vernaculars. Translation, like imitation, played a crucial role in this process. Pérez de Oliva's intention was to give new respectability to *castellano* by proving it capable of the noblest expression. Like his contemporary, Juan de Valdés, Pérez de Oliva became a self-appointed champion of *castellano* at a time when the Romance languages were forbidden in the universities and avoided in literary circles. His intention is made clear in many of his nondramatic works and in the prologue to his translation of Plautus's *Amphitruo*, where he states that the play was written "como muestra de la lengua castellana," as a sample of the Castilian tongue.

Pérez de Oliva's texts are exemplary of the type of creative translation which becomes more than the automatic rendering of one text into a language other than the original. All translations provide a way of presenting at least two texts superimposed as one: the original source text, which is present regardless of the switching from one linguistic code to another, and the translator's interpretation of the original. In the process, the translator reveals his own intention and conception of translation. We are reminded again of the modernity of Vives's emphasis on the pragmatic determination of any theory of translation. His assertion that translation represents a reflective process is the equivalent of saying that a translator always engages the source text in a critical polemic through the choices he makes. These choices can be of a formal, external nature such as the elimination or the addition of certain scenes; or linguistic, in the choice of lexicon, syntax, and meter. In the case of Pérez de Oliva, the critical choices he made became didactic and ideological.

As stated above, Pérez de Oliva's intention was to elevate the prestige of *castellano* by proving it capable of communicating the grandiose tone of the Greek originals. At the same time, he wanted to provide concrete paradigms for the correct use of *castellano*. Recently, George Peale has convincingly argued that Pérez de Oliva was less interested in the dramatic or literary implications of his translations than in the opportunity they provided to illustrate rhetorical and linguistic decorum.[13] Following the classical precepts, particularly Quintilian's, the liberties the Spanish humanist took corresponded to a manifest didactic intention. This explains, first of all, why he transformed the difficult Greek meter into elegant Spanish prose, worthy of imitation by students of rhetoric. From a dramatic standpoint, the result was uneven. Pérez de Oliva virtually eliminated all the lyrical passages of the Greek original and diminished the role of the chorus. One possible explanation for this change may have been a desire on his part to speed up the action of the tragedies, thus anticipating the emphasis on action that was to characterize the *comedia nueva* in the following century. On the other hand, by reducing the lyrical content, he inevitably robbed the play of a poetic dimension important to the source texts. At times, however, his prose achieves its own poetic originality in *castellano*. *Hecuba triste* contains moments of great lyrical impact which owe little to the Greek original. When Polidor's lifeless body is discovered floating in the river, for example, Hecuba's attendants exclaim:

Ves lo aquí Senora limpio y lauado con las aguas que lo trayan.... ¡Qué lindos pechos, qué braços tan lindos, qué piernas, qué pies! ¡O qué cabello de oro! ¡Qué frente, qué boca, qué hermosura tan grande, que aun la muerte no pudo quitarla!... Nosotras agora pongamos este corpezito en este lienço más limpio. Los pies assí juntos, las manos en el pecho, y bien compuesto su cabellico. Parece flor cortada a la mañana, que está desmayada con el sol de medio día.... Assí esta muy bien. Cojamos agora de aquestas yervas mas

verdes, de que le hagamos una camita, y la cabecera sembremos de flores."
(scene 4, p. 641)

(See him here, my lady, cleansed and washed by the waters that brought him.
... What beautiful breast, what beautiful arms, legs, feet. Oh golden hair.
His forehead, his mouth, what lasting beauty that not even death could rob.
... Let us now place this small body on the whitest of linens. His feet just so,
his hands on his breast, and his hair well-combed. He looks like a flower
freshly cut in the morning but fainting with the noon sun. . . . Let us gather
the greenest fronds to make his bed, and let us seed his pillow with flowers.)

The colloquial use of the Spanish diminutive (corpezito, cabellico, carnezicas, camita), together with more sophisticated rhetorical constructs such as the anaphoric repetition of "¡qué!" are indicative of Pérez de Oliva's success in forging an authentic poetic voice in the vernacular.

Other liberties that Pérez de Oliva took were more of an ideological nature. He avoided the "paganism" of the Greek texts by inserting into the plays a Christian moral ambiance that would have made the plays more palatable to his Spanish audience. The changes in linguistic style and genre, i.e., poetry to prose, are parallel to the cultural alterations he incorporated into his text. Although the *argumentos* and episodes in his tragedies are exactly the same as those in the original, the Spanish author managed to eliminate all allusions to Greek myths. In *La venganza de Agamenón*, he found it necessary to attenuate Electra's joy at the death of her mother, Clytemnestra. Whereas vengeance for a crime against blood relations was in keeping with the ethos of Greek tragedies, in Renaissance Spain the idea of filial vengeance was morally reprehensible. As a result, at the end of the play, Electra (called Elecha in the Spanish play) expresses what could be interpreted as regret:

No lloro yo porque huuo Clitemnestra tal muerte, sino porque la meresció.
Quisiera yo que ella no oviera sido tal, que sus hijos dessearamos su vida,
con aquel ansia que procuráuamos su muerte. Pero pues ella tuuo la causa,
nosotros no ternemos la culpa. (scene 7, p. 620)

(I do not weep because Clytemnestra met this death, but because she deserved
it. How I wish that she had been different, and that we her children had
longed for her life with the same intensity with which we sought her death.
But because she was the cause, we are not guilty.)

At other times, in his eagerness to improve on the original morally, he simplified the depiction of most of his characters, making them either completely good or completely evil. As a result, he reduced the ambivalence that made the Greek originals richer in the psychological portrayal of the characters. The transformation of the Greek text and his desire to find culturally acceptable expressions and situations manifest themselves even at the level of insignificant details of plot. The virgins of the temple in Euripides' play become *dueñas* or servants in the Spanish version, in another attempt to "domesticate" the pagan setting of the source texts. In *La venganza,* Orestes is anachronically buried in a coffin instead of being cremated as was the Greek custom, and in *Hecuba triste* Polidor is interred in a hole in the ground. While all these alterations have the effect of Hispanizing the Greek original, it can be argued that the changes also corresponded to the artistic demands of his craft. Conscious of the fact that he was translating a tragedy and perhaps recognizing that intelligibility is the essence of dramatic communication, he may have wanted to adhere to the essence of tragedy as a genre at the expense of certain details. In order to move his Christian audience to experience the emotions of pity and fear, he needed to change the context without betraying the dramatic integrity of the original. He found a way of adhering to the tragic spirit of the original text by translating the majestic tone into Hispano-Christian terms. This accounts for the curious biblical echoes noticeable in some passages, as in the following example: "Envía, Señor, tu yra sobre ellos, y parezca sobre la tierra tu gran poderío, por que los hombres no se olviden que solo tú eres el que la gobierna" (*La venganza,* scene 6, p. 603). (Send, oh Lord, thy wrath upon them, and let thy power be known on earth, so that men may not forget that only thou are Lord.) Even within the space of comedy, Pérez de Oliva felt it necessary to change situations which might be uncomfortable for a Spanish audience. While in Plautus's *Amphitruo,* the eponymous hero good-naturedly accepts his cuckoldry because it was Zeus who seduced his wife, the Spanish Amphitrion allows himself to express anger at this treachery.

The anachronisms were of course in keeping with the trend among some humanists to Christianize classical sources. At the same time, the tension created by what some critics would deem "mistranslations" dramatized the historical and cultural distance between the source texts and their modern versions. Gianfranco Folena, a modern theorist of translation, divides translations into two types: vertical and horizontal.[14] Horizontal translations are those in which both the source language and the arrival language are considered to have similar cultural value or prestige, as for example a translation from one Romance language into another. A vertical translation, on the other hand, is the translation into the vernacular from a source language that has special authority and prestige. The translation from Latin or Greek into any of the vernacular tongues would be considered a vertical translation. Pérez de Oliva's works would belong to this second category. In the vertical type, there is a wide cultural gulf between the source text and the so-called target language and this distance liberates the translator to interpret the source text at will. It was precisely this distance which permitted the liberties taken by Pérez de Oliva in his *La venganza de Agamenón* and *Hecuba triste.* Although the ideal according to Vives's theories, for example, would have been to attempt to reproduce both the sense and the style, in these tragedies, both form and content necessarily undergo changes due to the pressure of a new cultural context.

The contradictions presented by Pérez de Oliva's works illustrate the problems inherent in any approach to Renaissance translations. Given the conscious formal and thematic changes, can his works be considered true translations? When does a translation acquire independence from the original work and become an adaptation or imitation instead? Or, to approach the polemic from the opposite perspective, are not imitations also forms of translation, creative examples of mistranslation? The process of selection and elimination in Pérez de Oliva's tragedies, while explained somewhat by the concept of vertical translation and the conflict of cultures and moral styles it dramatized, is still clearly very similar to the process implied in any imitation. *Imitatio* involves the same dialectic present in translation: the production or writing of a new text and the critical contemplation or reading of an earlier one. Just as a translation continuously refers back to the original, so does an imitation privilege a progenitor text or texts. Implicit in both activities is the dual task of, on the one hand, patterning after a subtext and, on the other, the free play of originality. Pérez de Oliva participated in this dialectical process and created tragedies which were both classical and modern at the same time. Critical attitudes about Pérez de Oliva reflect the ambiguity present in his works. Some critics have dismissed his works because he is a "mere translator" or "mistranslator" of classical texts. Others lavish praise on the humanist for being one of the first playwrights in Europe to "nationalize" Greek and Latin plays. While many have questioned the classification of his *Hecuba triste* and *La venganza de Agamenón* as translations, literary histories still list them as such.[15] These tragedies demonstrate how the boundaries between translation and imitation became blurred during the Renaissance, and how the designation of translation does not do justice to their complexity.

As we have seen, Pérez de Oliva attempts to render tragedy in Spanish by basing his work on Greek texts. Later, in the second half of the sixteenth century, a new generation of playwrights cultivated tragedy based not on Greek but Latin models, particularly Seneca. The tragedies produced at this time illustrate yet another way in which the activity of translation influenced the development of Spanish tragedy. These plays, representative of an intermediary phase in the evolution of a national dramatic form, were written outside the closed circle of the universities and *colegios,* as their authors sought recognition with a wider audience. Hispanists are in agreement that the influence of Senecan tragedy in the sixteenth century came about not through a direct translation of the original texts, but rather through the imitation of Italian translations and versions of the Latin. Throughout the Renaissance, Spain and Italy were closely linked both politically and culturally, and it is not surprising that the abundance of translations from Italian works into *castellano* during this time has never been proportionally equaled.[16] The influence of Italian letters on the development of Spanish literary genres, particularly poetry, has been well documented. The Italians were perceived as being more advanced in literature because, by the sixteenth century, they could already boast an illustrious tradition headed by modern classics such as Boccaccio, Dante, and Petrarch. Spain, on the other hand, could not claim a comparable tradition and there seems to have been a widespread feeling of inferiority vis-à-vis the Italians. The following exchange, taken from Juan de Valdés's *Diálogo de la lengua,* eloquently expresses this sense of inadequacy:

> MARCIO: No tenéis por tan elegante la lengua castellana como la lengua toscana?
> VALDES: Sí que la tengo, pero también la tengo por mas vulgar, por que veo que la toscana sta ilustrada y enriquecida por un Bocacio y un Petrarca, los quales, siendo buenos letrados, no solamente se preciaron de scrivir buenas cosas, pero procuraron escrivirlas con estilo muy propio y muy elegante; y como sabéis, la lengua castellana nunca ha tenido quien escriva en ella con tanto cuidado y miramiento quanto sería menester para que hombre, quiriendo o dar cuenta de lo que scrive diferente de los otros, o reformar los abusos que ay oy en ella, se pudiesse aprovechar de su autoridad.[17]

> (M: Do you not consider the Castilian tongue as elegant as the Tuscan speech?
> VALDES: Yes I do consider it so, but at the same time, it is more vulgar, because I see that the Tuscan tongue has been honored and enriched by a Boccaccio or a Petrarch, who, as good scholars, not only prided themselves on writing worthy texts but also endeavored to write them in a style that was both proper and elegant. As you know, Castilian has never had anyone [like Boccaccio et alia] who wrote with as much care and attention to all that is necessary so that a person who wants to write differently from the others or to correct the abuses we see today, could turn to them and benefit from their example and authority.)

Italy had also anticipated Spain by at least fifty years in the formulation of classicist poetics dealing with tragedy. The translation into Spanish of treatises by Robortello and Scaliger, among others, awakened Spanish consciousness to the tragic genre at a theoretical level. The appearance of prescriptive works on tragedy had also motivated early experimentation with the genre in Italy. Spanish playwrights celebrated the Italian imitators of Seneca in particular, and a substantial debt to the Italians is apparent in the work of Lupercio Leonardo de Argensola, Cristóbal de

Virués, and Pedro Bermúdez, the so-called "generación trágica de España."
The Spanish plays were frequently adaptations or imitations of tragedies
written by playwrights such as Trissino, Ludovico Dolce, and Giraldi
Cinthio. Interestingly, these imitations of Italian texts often incorporated
direct horizontal translations from the Italian. Translation, then, played
a crucial role, at both the theoretical and practical levels, in the development of drama in Spain during the second half of the sixteenth century.
Senecan tragedy as practiced by the Spanish authors incorporates a
complex layering of influences which underlines how translation and
imitation became fused and confused in the creation of new texts during
the Renaissance.

    As an example, we can take Cristóbal de Virués's most successful
tragedy, *Elisa Dido.* This play has been generally considered one of the
most purely classical in conception. The work also represents a complex
tapestry of influence, imitation, and translation.[18] *Elisa Dido* seems to
have been directly inspired by the works of the Italian Trissino, particularly *Sofonisba,* written in 1515. Both Trissino and Virués based the stories
of their tragic heroines on classical historians, particularly Justin and his
Historiae Philippicae. There are many parallels in the plots of *Elisa Dido*
and *Sofonisba:* the fortitude and suicide of the heroine, the devotion on the
part of the maid to her lady, among others. Stylistically, Virués adopted
the hendecasyllabic blank verse which Trissino had established as the
most appropriate for tragedy and combined it with Spanish *versos cortos.*
At the same time, the moralizing tone of the Spanish play can be ultimately traced to Seneca, but a Seneca filtered through the works of yet
another influential Italian playwright and critic, Giraldi Cinthio, who
also wrote a play about Dido (1547). The complications of plot derive
mostly from this Italian writer, as do the division into acts and the
secondary plot, and, like Giraldi Cinthio, Virués breaks with purely
classical traditions, abandoning the three unities. Other Italian versions
of the Dido story which may have been familiar to Virués are Alessandro
Pozzi de Medici's *Dido en Carthagine* (1524) and Ludovico Dolce's *Didone*
(1547). Virués's play is then a selective imitation of elements borrowed
from various sources. The play, however, goes beyond being an imitation
in that it contains verbal passages that seem directly translated from the
Italian models. Episodes such as the dialogue between Delbora and the
general in Virués's play and Sofonisba's appeal to Masinissa in Trissino's
work, clearly show a relationship between the two texts that approaches
paraphrase and translation. To limit this play to the classification of
imitation alone simplifies the elaborate modes of borrowing present in
the Spanish work.

    A similar case of translation in the guise of imitation can be found in
the work of Lupercio Leonardo de Argensola, who is considered, along

with Cervantes, one of the most important practitioners of the so-called *teatro antiguo*. Leonardo de Argensola borrowed the plot for his *Alejandra* from Ludovico Dolce's *Marianna* and much of the language of the play is taken from Giraldi Cinthio's *Orbecche*.[19] Critics have frequently commented on this influence. More than influence is at work here as imitation at times becomes a direct translation, erasing the differences between what Dryden called paraphrase (free translation) and metaphrase (literal translation). Instead of translating entire plays, Leonardo de Argensola translated passages from previous Italian texts and placed them in the new context of his own plays. Often, the changes amount to little more than the substitution of the proper names of the characters or the names of the cities where the action takes place. As a brief example, we can mention the parallel passages that begin Giraldi Cinthio's *Orbecche* and Leonardo de Argensola's *Alejandra*. The earlier Italian text begins with:

> Forse pensarete
> In Ferrara trovarvi, Città piena
> D'ogni virtù.

The Spanish *Alejandra* duplicates the Italian in the following "Hispanized" context:

> Imagináis quizás que estáis ahora
> contentos en la noble y fuerte España
> en la insigne ciudad de Zaragoza.

The facile substitution of Zaragoza for the Italian Ferrara is typical of passages which abound in Leonardo de Argensola's plays. Again, the so-called influence or borrowing becomes more akin to a word-by-word technique of translation, far more literal than the sense-for-sense recommended by Cicero and Vives, among others. Just as Pérez de Oliva's translations were really interpretations bordering on imitation, within these Senecan trage-dies recognized as imitations we can identify a process that is really a form of literal translation. In addition, Leonardo de Argensola translates entire passages from the *Aeneid*. Thus, in Argensola's works, we find a process we can recognize as translation from both Italian and Latin within the larger imitative text. In the practice of Spanish tragedians such as Virués and Argensola, layers of translation, imitation, adaptation, and borrowings coexist simultaneously. Spanish Senecan tragedy, therefore, represents a multiplicity of texts: the Spanish version which simultaneously imitates and translates an Italian text that is, in turn, an imitation of plays written by Seneca in Latin. Furthermore, we can safely assume that the Latin texts were themselves ultimately based on Greek models.

Translation and imitation as practiced during the Renaissance involved a complex dialectic between a text and its assimilation of a progenitor text or texts. This dialectic invites polemics not only on the specificity of each practice, i.e., how they differ from each other, but also on the broader questions of originality and the diachronic relationship between cultures and literary styles. Both practices permit us to view the Renaissance in terms of what Thomas Greene has called "the interplay between the intuition of rupture and the intuition of continuity."[20] The tragedies studied in these pages eloquently dramatize the imprecise nature of these classifications and the indiscriminate manner in which they have been applied to a wide-ranging scale of related activities. The first task of scholars approaching texts like these is to take into account the dichotomies and ambivalence embodied by the two practices. There must also be a concerted effort to avoid privileging imitation over translation since, as we have seen, the boundaries between the two are difficult to delineate. While the problem of *imitatio* will no doubt continue to play a central role in the study of Renaissance letters, no history of the literature of this time will be truly complete without a consideration of the practice and theory of translation. The importance of the tragedians studied here has been underestimated because of the classification of their works as translations/mistranslations of classical texts on the one hand, and eclectic imitation of Italian models on the other. Fernán Pérez de Oliva's texts, while still bound to classical sources, contributed to the evolution of Spanish as a rhetorical tool capable of the highest literary expression. Although his works had no direct repercussions in the development of drama, they formed part of a cultural program whose aim was the enrichment of the language. Later in the sixteenth century, the dramatic works of Lupercio Leonardo de Argensola and Cristóbal de Virués, with their syncretism of imitation and translation, represent an important transitional stage in the development of a national dramatic form in Spain. Translation, for these writers, was nothing less than another form of literary creation which, like imitation, profoundly influenced the emergence and evolution of Spanish literature during the Renaissance.

NOTES

1. Two useful recent books on translation are Louis G. Kelly's *The True Interpreter: A History of Translation, Theory and Practice in the West* (New York: St. Martin's Press, 1979); and Valentín García Yebra's *En torno a la traducción* (Madrid: Gredos, 1983). See also Georges Mounin, *Les problèmes theoriques de la traduction* (Paris: Gallimard, 1963) and George Steiner, *After Babel* (London: Oxford University Press, 1975). An excellent study on early theories of translation is Gianfranco Folena's "'Volgarizzare' et 'tradurre.' Idea e terminologia della traduzione dal Medio Evo italiano e romano all'Umanesimo europeo" in *La traduzione. Saggi e Studi* (Trieste: Lint, 1974), pp. 59–120.

2. The bibliography on *imitatio* during the Renaissance is abundant. The most recent study is Thomas Greene's *The Light in Troy: Imitation and Discovery in Renaissance Poetry* (New Haven, Conn.: Yale University Press, 1982). See also Bernard Weinberg, *A History of Literary Criticism in the Italian Renaissance*, 2 vols. (Chicago: University of Chicago Press, 1961) and for French literature, Terence Cave, *The Cornucopian Text: Problems of Writing in the French Renaissance* (Oxford: Clarendon Press, 1979). There is no equivalent comprehensive work on imitation in Spanish literature. The one that comes closest is Antonio García Berrio's *Formación de la teoría literaria moderna*, I (Madrid: Cuspa, 1977).

3. See Eugenio Coseriu, "Vives y el problema de la traducción," in *Tradición y novedad en la ciencia del lenguaje* (Madrid: Gredos, 1977), pp. 86–102.

4. W. P. Ker, ed., *Essays of John Dryden* (Oxford: Clarendon Press, 1900), I, 237–43.

5. Cicero, *De optimo genere oratorum*, Loeb Classical Library, trans. H. M. Hubbell (London: Heinemann, 1959).

6. St. Jerome's famous phrase is found in "Ad Pammachium de optimo genere interpretandi." I have used the text found in volume I of *Cartas de San Jeronimo*, a bilingual, Spanish-Latin edition, edited by Daniel Ruiz Bueno (Madrid: Biblioteca de Autores Cristianos, 1962). Jerome based his theories of translation on Cicero's *De optimo genere oratorum*.

7. Vives's theories on translation can be found throughout several of his works but the most important text is "Versiones seu interpretationes" in *De ratione dicendi*. Quotations used here are taken from Coseriu, *Tradición y novedad*. Coseriu bemoans the fact that Vives's linguistic theories, among which we find his views on translation, have been ignored by linguists and Hispanists alike. The most recent manifestation of this neglect is García Yebra's otherwise excellent book (*En torno a la traducción*), published six years after Coseriu's article, which still does not mention Vives's contribution to Renaissance theories of translation.

8. Roman Jakobson, "On Linguistic Aspects of Translation," in *On Translation*, ed. Reuben A. Brower (New York: Oxford University Press, 1966), p. 238.

9. For the best study of tragedy in Renaissance Spain, see Alfredo Hermenegildo, *La tragedia en el renacimiento español* (Barcelona: Planeta, 1973).

10. See Hermenegildo's chapter 6, "Tragedias no conservadas" for an account of what we know about these lost translations. He also reproduces the surviving fragments of Fray Luis de León's *Andromache*.

11. For an informative account of the drama produced in the universities and Jesuit schools, see Justo García Soriano's *El teatro universitario en España* (Toledo: Talleres Tipográficos de D. Rafael Gómez Menor, 1945). For the importance of translation in their curricula, see also Raymond Leonard Grismer, *The Influence of Plautus in Spain before Lope de Vega* (New York: 1944).

12. There are several studies on the theater of Pérez de Oliva, most recently, George Peale's *Fernán Pérez de Oliva. Teatro. Estudio crítico y edición* (Córdoba: Real Academia de Córdoba, 1984). The quotes in this article are taken from William C. Atkinson's edition of the tragedies, *Hernán Pérez de Oliva. Teatro. A Critical Edition* in *Revue Hispanique* 64 (1927), 521–659.

13. See George Peale's introduction.

14. Folena, pp. 65–66.

15. See, for example, Theodore Beardsley's *Hispano-Classical Translations Printed between 1482 and 1699* (Pittsburgh: Duquesne University Press, 1970). Beardsley acknowledges the problems presented by Pérez de Oliva's so-called translations but still catalogues them as such.

16. See García Yebra, p. 324.

17. Juan de Valdés, *Diálogo de la lengua* (Madrid: Cátedra, 1982), p. 123.

18. The most complete study of Cristóbal de Virués's dramatic production is Cecilia Vennard Sargent's *A Study of the Dramatic Works of Cristóbal de Virués* (New York: Instituto de las Españas, 1930). See also Hermenegildo, pp. 207–78.

19. Works on Lupercio Leonardo de Argensola include J. P. W. Crawford's "Notes on the Tragedies of Lupercio Leonardo de Argensola" in *Romanic Review* 5 (1914), 31–44. Also, Otis H. Green's *The Life and Works of Lupercio Leonardo de Argensola*, Studies in Romanic Languages and Literatures, 21 (Philadelphia: Pennsylvania University Press, 1927).

20. Greene, p. 175.

III

INTERTEXTUALITY:
Interdisciplinary Relations

PAUL F. WATSON

To Paint Poetry:
Raphael on Parnassus

To the memory of Rennselaer W. Lee:

Historia luget, eloquentia muta est,
Ferturque musas tum graecas tum
latinas lacrimas tenere non potuisse.

Let us suppose that Raphael of Urbino paints himself into his *Parnassus*, itself painted toward 1511 to complete the decorations of the Vatican's Stanza della Segnatura (Pl. 1). A tradition going back to 1695 and Giovanni Pietro Bellori maintains that the painter appears on the summit of Parnassus, to the right of a group formed by Dante, Homer, and Virgil, and just to the left of the Muses who frame Apollo (Pl. 2). What Bellori first suggested finds encouragement in this particular laureate's resemblance to Raphael as he appears in self-portrayals from this time: fashionably long of hair, slender-necked, smooth and gentle of feature.[1] Encouragement is by no means proof positive but, for the sake of argument and the value of insight, accept its promptings and let Raphael stand there. The painter's presence suggests many things, such as pride in his performance. It is also evident that Raphael himself here performs, to play a part in a figural mime, or as he might have called it, an *istoria*, whose theme is poetry. *Parnassus*, then, can be considered as a mimesis, whose forms, patterns, and significance become this essay's chief concern.

Commissioned by Pope Julius II and occupying a windowed wall in the Stanza della Segnatura, Parnassus is a landscape, mountainous and multileveled, arboreal and, thanks to a rustic spring, verdant. Apollo crowns its summit and marks its center, there to make music in company with the Muses, who form his court. Nature is further crowded by poets, crowned all with laurel, who assemble on the lower stages of Mount Parnassus at the left, move across its summit and then disperse at the right, where some indicate the very space the viewer inhabits. So involved, the spectator sees and recognizes authors of time long past, such as Homer or Sappho; writers of more recent times, such as Dante; and even persons of the artist's present day, among them the painter himself. Mortals join with the gods of poetry to make a company essentially ideal.

The poets on Parnassus are matched by other companies, equally ideal, assembled in this room. To the visitor's left are theologians and saints, representing the Old Law and the New, the participants of the *Disputà,* so-called. To the right is the equally misnamed *School of Athens,* where Plato and Aristotle captain the philosophers of ancient and more recent times. Above these companies, each deployed upon lunettes defined by a proscenium arch rendered in perspective, rises the Stanza's vault, transformed by Raphael into a harmonious configuration, the faculties of human learning opposed and contrasted yet balanced and reconciled (Pl. 3). These faculties—Poetry, Theology, Jurisprudence, and Philosophy as you read them clockwise from the bottom of Plate 3—are each embodied by noble, comely young women armed with appropriate attributes and accompanied by putti who bear tablets carved with identifying inscriptions. So personified in the ceiling, each faculty is further exemplified by the assemblies depicted below. Hence Raphael's Poetry (Pl. 4) sits enthroned in her roundel holding the implements of her particular art, a book and a musical instrument—objects multiplied below where poets and their muses display them in Raphael's landscape.[2]

The words that accompany poetry are these: NUMINE AFFLATUR. "Suffused by the divine will," these can be rendered, or more generally, stirred by some divine spirit. Some savant from the court of Julius II framed that Latin phrase for Raphael to paint. His words define poetry as an art of inspiration and they serve also as a rubric for Parnassus below. Raphael's task, insofar as the commission can be reconstructed, was nothing less than to show through figures set in a landscape the nature of poetry as given by the epigram: spiritual creation, an airy nothing.

As an epigram, NUMINE AFFLATUR also evokes a venerable tradition, that of literature on literature in the form of poetics. Cicero, by way of example, speaks of poetry as an infusion, almost, of the divine spirit; but what he says echoes an idea developed centuries before by Plato and his followers, and enjoys an extended alternative in the writings of his younger contemporary Horace, the author of antiquity's most poetic expression of poetics, the *Ars poetica.* Classical poetics found Renaissance renewal in the writings of Petrarch, as in his "Coronation Oration" of 1341, and Boccaccio, who concludes his *Genealogy of the Gods* with an extended defense of poetry. Poetics was also a concern of Quattrocento humanists, such as Cristoforo Landino who prefaces his edition of Dante's *Divine Comedy,* printed in Florence during 1481, with a long essay on the nature of poetry and its historic origins. In Raphael's own time the court of Julius II was graced by a youthful poet of great promise, Marco Girolamo Vida, whose *De arte poetica,* although written during the pontificate of Leo X, provides an eloquent summation of classical poetics and a spirited reworking of Horace. What Raphael was given to inscribe, "numine afflatur," touches upon a literary and theoretical tradition not only venerable but vast.[3]

Poetry's particular epigram also follows from poetic diction. Its phrasing echoes Virgil, whom Raphael paints below, and who characterizes the fine frenzy of the Cumaean Sibyl, Aeneas's guide to the Underworld, as *enthusiasm* in the archaic sense of the word: the god drew nearer and the breath of his power was upon her, or as Virgil says, "adflata est numine quando / iam propriore dei."[4] The making of poetry—NUMINE AFFLATUR—implies a state like that possessing the Sibyl, the unseen inspiration of some unnamed god.

Poetry provides another, more visual, metaphor of poetic creation. It figures in invocation, where poets from Homer to Virgil to Vida and beyond call upon gods whom they name, the Muses and Apollo, who dwell upon the summit of Mount Parnassus, steep-sided, twin-peaked, thickly forested and watered by a spring, sometimes Pierian, sometimes Castalian. So Dante, to cite another poet whom Raphael portrays, invokes the Muses as he descends into Hell, summons the aid of Calliope their chief as he ascends Mount Purgatory and then, at the threshold of Paradise, turns to Apollo far away upon his mountain to ask for his grace, renewed inspiration: "Enter into my heart and breathe there."[5] So invoked, poetic inspiration takes the form of figures in a landscape, whose general topography Raphael recreates in his Parnassus.

There are also pictorial precedents for Raphael's poets in landscape. Mount Parnassus itself is the subject of a cryptic work by Mantegna, the most famous painter of Italy when Raphael was a boy, and it figures in several minatures and a panel from the late Quattrocento. Ancient and more recent art also presents the gods of Parnassus, Apollo and the Muses, the theme of a chapel in the ducal palace of Raphael's Urbino decorated in part by his own father, Giovanni Santi. Nearby in that same palace Justus van Ghent painted a *studiolo* with portraits of famous men, among them poets such as Homer, whose blindness and whose touching gesture Raphael would remember in Rome. Renaissance art sometimes alludes to poetic inspiration or poetic reward, as in a medal cast around 1462 by Sperandio of Mantua to honor Lodovico Carbone (Pl. 5); on its obverse Carbone appears as a gentleman of the Ferrarese court; on the reverse he receives his poet's laurels from the Muse Calliope, seated upon a rocky mesa and before an ornate fountain, the Pierian spring.[6] The medal puts an old image, the poet inspired by his muse, into

Renaissance dress as well as setting both in a Parnassian landscape, or at least one by implication. Sperandio's medal may also epitomize the artistic possibilities of Parnassus before Raphael—images in some plenty, and many of great ingenuity, a series of precedents but none of them a comprehensive model.

To the task of painting poetry Raphael brought other and more personal resources. He himself wrote poetry or, more precisely, essayed verse. Among his drawings for the Stanza della Segnatura, and especially for the *Disputà* which he began in 1509, are several sheets where Raphael marks down words as well as figures, to try his hand at sonnets, wrestle with the complexities of a rhyme scheme and grope for the most telling phrase (Pl. 6). For the painter's brush we remember Raphael, not the poet's pen. Yet his verses demonstrate that he was familiar enough with the forms, imagery, and sentiment of poetry essentially Petrarchan. As the physical evidence for his rhymes also indicates, some topics of Renaissance poetics may have struck him as familiar; penned lines, lines scratched out, and lists of alternative words show Raphael's own experience of the distance between first thoughts, the *divin furore* of poetic jargon, and final offering in the form of exquisite discourse.

Raphael's private struggles with poetry are also recalled in the public commemoration of poetry that is *Parnassus*. At the lower left poets group themselves around a tree to make a visual introduction, leading the viewer into their world (Pl. 7). That is one role Raphael gives Sappho, the author closest to us, who turns inwards to regard her male companions. The scroll she upholds, inscribed to identify her, contrasts with the bound codices other poets carry to make a little essay on the history of the book, poetry's artifact, from ancient to more recent times. One book-bearing poet, dressed in yellow and set at the extreme left, also clasps a small sheet of paper neatly inscribed with letters whose paucity suggests an epigram. His paper touches a colleague, also burdened with a codex, who holds in his left hand what was once a crumpled page; its white surface has disappeared but the outlines still remain. A pictorial equivalent to Raphael's own messy lines jotted down on convenient scraps of paper (Pl. 6), this frescoed detail suggests that *Parnassus* begins with the aftermath of some poetic competition whose loser concedes defeat by suppressing the evidence of his art. As such, Raphael's byplay recalls at once the occasional competitions that poets undertook during the Renaissance; the advice authors of poetics give to aspiring bards: "try your hand at poetic contests"; and the conventions of earlier painting in which poets argue with one another, as in the ducal *studiolo* of Raphael's Urbino.[7] But here the competition is over and its loser brings no rancor to Parnassus.

Raphael's introductory passage takes the form of a mimesis. Those observed by Sappho, for example, make their chief activity a conversation, dominated by a youthful poet with the most bewitching smile, to whom the rest give heed. That unvoiced conversation is truly introductory, for it appears elsewhere on Parnassus as a mimed motif, especially at the right where the conversation of two poets, one seated as the other stands, brings the fresco to a forceful conclusion. With conversation goes exhortation — most evident again at the right where the seated poet points out the viewer's world, but present too at the introduction where the smiling youth gestures, and nearby at the summit of Parnassus where Virgil points Dante to the circle of the Muses. Exhortation and conversation are varied by the solitude of contemplation. At the upper right and in the distance stands a poet gazing as if entranced upon a vista that we cannot see. Another man, leaner and more vigorous, poses in the right foreground to stare fixedly, one bony finger pressed to his lips, leftwards at those poets conversing under a tree. Two others, painted at the right but separated from one another, look outwards to this room and its occupants (Pl. 8). The solitude of contemplation finds a match in the isolation of inspiration. Set apart by his blindness, Homer thrusts back his head in speech as verses overwhelm him, verses he must dictate to a boyish scribe seated nearby who neglects his stenographic duty to drink in what we cannot hear.[8]

What Raphael makes his poets do corresponds to forms of poetic activity that poets themselves describe. Homer's utterings offer a transparent case in point. He dramatizes a familiar theme from poetic theory, platonizing either directly from Plato himself or from a more general tradition, that true poetry flows from divine possession — as the painted rubric NUMINE AFFLATUR indicates, as Landino says when he writes in praise of the poet's *furore divino,* or as Vida demonstrates by verbal pyrotechnics what it is to feel the presence of the muse.[9] Raphael's technics to the same end follow from visual art, for he endows his Homer with an impassioned intensity derived from the *Laocoön,* installed nearby at the Vatican early in 1506. The adaptation from classical sculpture is itself inspired; the perfect instance of heroic agony, Laocoön undergoes transformation to become the vessel of poetic inspiration.

Raphael also paints poets who contemplate, among them the admirer of nature at the right (Pl. 8) whom Bellori identified as Giovanni Boccaccio. Iconographic tradition bears him out, as demonstrated by several early author portraits, his tomb effigy of 1503, and a Florentine medal cast around that time, all of which show Boccaccio as Raphael does: plumpcheeked, serene, amply girthed. What Raphael makes his Boccaccio undertake and where he stands are equally apposite, for in the *Genealogy of the Gods* that author defends the rustic solitude poets are said to seek, claiming that the pleasures nature gives soothe the poet's soul, refresh his mind, and renew his *ingenium;* those pleasures are aural and visual; to see is to meditate.[10] Raphael modulates contemplation in the person of the poet who presses a finger to his lip, a striking pose that follows from another sculptural model, one of the prophets that Donatello carved for the campanile of Florence's cathedral some eight decades before this (Pl. 9), who occupies a lofty niche to meditate upon the world below. Remembering that marble figure in Rome, Raphael adapts it to make contemplation energetic.

On Parnassus most of Raphael's poets become collegial, grouping to converse. That activity is defined and defended by the poet of solitary contemplation, Boccaccio, who maintains that poetry arises from colloquy and that poets gather to confabulate.[11] His historical argument is fanciful but perhaps his phrase, *confabulatio,* may serve here to characterize what Raphael repeatedly depicts. Confabulation becomes an activity that bridges generations, especially at the right (Pl. 8) where an elderly poet directs a young laureate to the viewer's world, a combination repeated in the distance where another greybeard urges a proud youth to Parnassus's heights. Such colloquies recall the avuncular tone of poeticized poetics, such as the *Ars poetica* where Horace offers urbane advice to would-be poets of a younger generation. Similarly, Vida casts himself into the role of an aged mentor (although he was no older than Raphael) to narrate *De arte poetica,* encouraging mere boys to make their way up the slopes of Mount Parnassus.[12]

Confabulation, contemplation, and the chanting of inspired verse all contribute to a more general poetic mime, movement through the landscape. There is the general movement of Raphael's composition, taking shape at the left and marshaled by the massive yet graceful person of Sappho, cresting with Homer, descending and then rising through the enchanting group of poetry's gods, faltering slightly at the right and then resumed to conclude with the final outward-turning colloquy between youth and age. Movement is encouraged by figures who seem in motion, most notably Virgil and Dante, masked by Homer but wayfaring nevertheless, just as they voyage through Renaissance illustrations of the *Divine Comedy.* Another pilgrimage finds room at the right where an old poet presses his young colleague to press on and not rest there on his laurels (Pl. 8). Raphael's smiling poet (Pl. 7) poses with one foot set tiptoe, an act of figural grace but perhaps one that indicates that he interrupts his journey to confabulate with those around him. For Parnassus is there to be traversed and scaled. Untracked are its heights, so Virgil claims, and difficult are its pathways, as Vida was to observe.[13] But it is characteristic of this particular Parnassus that its paths are crowded and that the painter makes the rough ways smooth.

At the summit of Parnassus are Apollo and his court. All differ from the poets, ancient or modern, as poetic traditions and visual custom insist they must. Dress or its lack, attributes unmistakably ancient in form if capricious in detail, and a self-contained and gently semicircular composition all distinguish gods from mortals. Sperandio's medal makes the same point (Pl. 5), contrasting Quattrocento dress with antique undress. Here Raphael himself acts to underline that distinction, placing himself between Virgil and the Muses. And yet the Muses make a gentle, almost dreaming mime that echoes what the poets around them do. Some Muses contemplate; one exhorts; several embrace to make a feminine and loving counterpart to masculine *confabulatio*. Indeed, the Muses' particular manner of conversation is such that specifying objects, like the mask of comedy, are shared by embracing goddesses so that no one can pinpoint whom Raphael designates as Thalia. The painter covers his tracks or, as poets are said to do, he veils his utterance.

Pictorial veiling works to serve another purpose, more general and fittingly poetic. It is suggested by Sappho (Pl. 7), who varies the pose of the Muse seated above, clad in a luminously white gown. Such repetition serves the particular purposes of painting, for Raphael's is an art of classic simplicity content to investigate the possibilities of a motif by its sustained reappearance. It also reflects his particular investigation of a sculptural model, a famous antique *Ariadne* housed in the Vatican. Art, however, combines with details of costume to liken Sappho to the goddess seated behind her so that, as Roger Jones and Nicholas Penny recently observe, the poetess might almost pass for a stray tenth Muse were it not for her inscribed scroll.[14] Similarly, Raphael's ninth Muse turns her back to reveal a modern costume and an equally modern headdress, like those worn by fashionable ladies of the early Cinquecento who are the subjects of Raphael's portraits. The color of her dress, a saffronlike yellow, and her standing pose also cause this Muse to echo Raphael's very first poet, the victor in a presumed epigrammatic competition (Pl. 7). Raphael draws a pictorial veil, then, to ease the distinctions others make between the gods of poetry and those who write it.

There are other veilings, further blurrings. The masculine counterpart to Sappho, as an instance, is the vigorous poet seated at the right who also resembles Homer—but younger, as well as sighted—just as Homer's cast of feature resembles the eyeless mask of tragedy carried by a Muse just to his left. Similarly, Dante has his double in the poet who fiercely contemplates: hawklike features, pinkish mantle. And yet this Dantean author wears modern dress beneath his cloak: the black tunic, fine linen, and golden chain of a Cinquecento gentleman. Similarly, the young poet standing just behind him, a prim cousin of the youth who smiles at the left to introduce Parnassus, wears shoes quite modern even though his costume remains classical. These are anachronisms. Their effect is to undermine what initially seems immutable and obvious: historical distinctions. If a poet such as Dante's double may attire himself in antiquity's toga to cover fashion's latest doublet, or if a Muse on Parnassus can dress as a grand lady of papal Rome, then the art that links them, poetry, can be sensed as a perennial activity founded in remote antiquity but continuing into the Roman present—an idea forcefully seconded by the Homerian poet who points out a new Parnassus, this room.

One way that such a continuity through time becomes possible is by imitation. Dante models his epic, to cite an obvious instance, on Virgil's verses, especially those devoted to the Underworld, in turn a Latin counterpart to Homer's odyssey through Greek realms of the dead. Hence Raphael's Dante follows the lead of Virgil, who brushes against Homer (Pl. 2). Imitative continuity may be suggested here in a subtler and more pervading way, by the pictorial veiling that Raphael devises. One of its consequences is that his poets resemble one another. Discussing imitation as a poetic device, Petrarch lights upon a similar metaphor to argue that poems resemble their models, other poems, but the resemblance should be like that of sons to fathers, "a certain suggestion, what our painters call an 'air,' most noticeable in the face and eyes," and one that indicates true kinship even though each individual retains his particular identity.[15] In Raphael's time Vida advises aspiring poets to imitate only the best of authors, urging his charges always to strive to resemble him, forming themselves upon his habits and manner while at the same time taking care to give their imitative creations a new face and form.[16] As poets characterize it, imitation implies metaphors that are pictorial and biological. So too here: Dante has his progeny just as Homer enjoys his.

In similar fashion the Muses gain a sister, Sappho of Lesbos. That is a point made not only by Raphael but also by a late antique poet, Ausonius, who by so praising Sappho follows the lead of Plato, who makes her the tenth Muse in an epigram much admired and imitated by Renaissance authors, including Marullo, Poliziano, and Sir Thomas More.[17] Although none of Raphael's male poets can be said to be the Muses' brother, some do enjoy the company of one of those goddesses. She is Raphael's modern Muse, who turns from her companions to contemplate the group of poets centered upon Boccaccio and by so doing seems almost to share their confabulation (Pl. 8). Her relationship with these authors repeats that of Sappho and Raphael's introductory group (Pl. 7). Both configurations present a subtle variation on an old theme in letters and art: that a loving bond joins poets with their muses, a point well understood by Sperandio who makes his Calliope smile upon her protégé Carbone (Pl. 5). Masquerading as a muse, Sappho joins poets in their deliberations, just as a true Muse eavesdrops upon other colloquies. By these pictorial suggestions, Raphael makes of poets and Muses one company.

Gathered into a semicircle on the summit of Parnassus, the Muses frame poetry's god, Apollo. He too alludes to a fabled past and a glorious present: undressed *all'antica,* the god plays a modern viol. Like the poets, but unlike the Muses, Apollo wears a laurel crown. That wreath and his instrument are enough to suggest that here Raphael plays another veiling game to depict not the lordly Apollo of ancient art and Renaissance painting, including Raphael's own art, but some musician of antiquity, such as Orpheus.[18] But Raphael offers clarification in the ceiling above where, in a panel to the left of Poetry, Apollo witnesses the flaying of Marsyas (Pl. 3). That divine victor and Parnassus's violinist are one and the same. The twofold appearance of laureated Apollo takes on significance because what he ordains above, the flaying of Marsyas, became a metaphor of the poet's inspiration. So Dante calls upon Apollo, lord of Parnassus, entreating him to inspirit his art "just as you drew Marsyas from the sheath of his flesh."[19] Inspiration is also mimed here by the god's upturned gaze and its consequence, the inattentive bowing of his instrument. A divine spirit directs his hand and his art just as it guides Homer in his blindness.

Upwards to Poetry Apollo looks but through a natural veil, the foliage of laurel trees that form a demi-tholos above him. To these same trees the Muse seated at the god's proper left lifts her eyes. And to that grove another goddess, in possession of comedy's mask, directs the attention of Raphael's modern Muse. Two more Muses, embracing one another at the left, direct their dreamy gaze toward this particular exhortation.

Raphael's gesturing Muse indicates a landscape which is shaped, as is everything else here, by Raphael's fanciful reading of poetic direction. Mountainous this arboreal platform may be, but hardly as precipitous as poets usually claim. Poets, among them Dante, sometimes insist that Apollo's home has two summits, one for the Muses, the other for the god himself. To that topography the painter responds by giving his Parnassus two peaks, or rather peaklets, one appropriated by Homer's scribe, the second serving as Apollo's throne.[20] On these slopes Raphael plants three stands of trees whose trunks appear to number seven and thereby encourage giddy prospects of quantifying symbolism. But the painter contrives to veil numeration. Just behind Apollo, for example, are two slender trunks that frame his bow as it moves across the viol. Trace these downwards and they become one, a single tree bifurcating to reduce the grove's grand total to six. Perhaps what reads as a tree trunk is a stray fold of Apollo's robe; bark and cloth are painted with like colors, like tones. The matter can be interpreted either way, or perhaps even both.[21]

On one botanical point Raphael is both clear and consistent. All the trees he paints are laurels, whose organic life is splendidly observed. They grow here because on these very slopes Apollo first caught sight of

Daphne, fated to become the very first laurel tree, whose foliage her lover still wears. There are other reasons for this plantation, summed up by Petrarch on the occasion of his own coronation as a laureate: abundantly leafed, laurels shade poets as they compose; always green and immune even from lightning they represent that undying fame poets earn as their reward; laurels even suggest that great mystery, inspiration, because those poets who dream beneath them find that their dreams are true. To Petrarch's botany attention must be given because that poet stands on Parnassus, squeezed in at the left to hear the first confabulation (Pl. 2). As a medal cast in Florence around 1500 and reflecting the traditional iconography of Petrarch indicates (Pl. 10), he is the man wearing a hood who stands in the shadow of a single laurel tree, as Petrarch also does figuratively, in his verses. Beside him smiles Raphael's enchanting poet, who gestures to make Parnassus's first exhortation. Upwards he points his hand, no doubt to indicate the mountain's summit, but also to draw attention to the laurel which Raphael then contrives, and at some expense to spatial logic, to support the idle hand of Homer's enraptured scribe. That youth contributes to a formal configuration—a descent from Homer leftwards and in opposition to the fresco's prevailing movement—that suggests that the laurel buttressing him serves as a metaphor of poetic inspiration. As the topic of the introductory confabulation, the tree is also explained by the grove of laurels depicted in Petrarch's medal (Pl. 10), where the poet's Poetry plucks their foliage to make her garland and suggest laurel's inspiriting role.[22]

A second compositional play helps unveil the meaning of Raphael's landscape. To the right of Virgil stands Raphael's first Muse, in possession of tragedy's mask and probably, then, Melpomene. She moves, to be exact, as if dancing to Apollo's music. Yet her energy hardly accounts for the billowing of her gown, which flutters as if stirred by some breeze. Strategically placed to support the linking of Homer, scribe, and laurel, her garment's movement also evokes a beautiful notion about Parnassus, articulated by Martianus Capella, that the winds playing round its summit and through its laureled groves make musical harmonies for Apollo to imitate.[23] Thus Apollo here makes his music as the wind blows, stirring Melpomene's gown into glorious motion and ruffling, perhaps, the dress of her fellow-sentinel, Raphael's most modern Muse. Above them sits Poetry, the only one of Raphael's personifications to bear wings—and wings that still beat, as if they were the source, or rather the efficient cause, of that breeze playing through Parnassus (Pl. 4).[24]

NUMINE AFFLATUR are the words accompanying and defining that winged art, Poetry. They apply equally well to her landscape below. Inspiration as suggested by the motto and its sources finds embodiment in the forms and foliage of the landscape, the songs of Apollo and the chanting of Homer, and the more diffused activities of the Muses and poets gathered around them, conversation and contemplation. Inspiration finds visualization in another, seemingly negative, way. No one here writes—not even Homer's scribe. The manual idleness of poets becomes even more evident in the Stanza della Segnatura, where the frescoes flanking *Parnassus,* the *Disputà,* and the *School of Athens* display the act of writing in full measure as a scribe takes down sacerdotal dictation or disciples record the thoughts of philosophers. But on this wall writers fail to write. That poets are idle no poet denies. Those who write poetics also make a distinction between mere writing, something any notary does, and literary composing, the inward creation of the true *poeta* who like the divine creator himself makes something out of nothing.

For that reason, Raphael makes very little of the physical monuments of poetry, books, apart from the byplay of his initial confabulation and two scenes, probably added long after he finished the fresco, showing the good works of princes who preserve the relics of Homer and Virgil (Pl. 1). Only a few writers bring books to Parnassus, votive offerings as it were to the genius of this place dedicated to creating; making must happen elsewhere. Of Raphael's seventeen poets, only one laureate carries a book to the highest reaches of Parnassus, where its god sings. He is Dante. Also the last poet with a book, as the mime continues rightwards, he clasps it to his breast with a dignity almost sacramental. But then his is a comedy truly divine. Dante's offering, a Christian epic, helps orient the general notion of poetry as inspired utterance toward inspiration that is divine in a contemporary Christian sense.[25] The religious cast of poetry, only implied by Dante's mimesis on Parnassus, finds more overt expression above in the centralized plan that is the vault (Pl. 3), where Poetry joins with Philosophy to contemplate the true source of all art and wisdom, Theology, the revelation of things divine.

Near Dante stands Raphael (Pl. 2). Wearing a poet's crown, he may also assume a particular poet's identity. Formally, he contributes to his own compositional movement as well as rounding out a subgroup—Dante, Homer, Virgil—to four, making it match the quartet of poets grouped round a tree below. Raphael's role here suggests that he plays the part of a poet like those he accompanies, a writer of epic such as Statius, who also joins Virgil and Dante as they ascend Mount Purgatory. Statius himself concludes his epic, the *Thebaid,* by sending it on its way to fame and to a reflected glory, for it must follow in the footsteps of the *Aeneid.* So here, where Raphael adopts the poet's crown to follow in Virgil's path as Dante also does.[26]

Raphael plays another role, muted but significant. Behind Melpomene he stands to gaze as she does in her bemused way at the first Muse, who sits to display an instrument much like a trumpet. It and her position, closest to Virgil, suggest that she is epic's patron, Calliope. To further the writing of heroic verse, first Virgil then Statius and finally Dante call upon Calliope, whom Raphael's father, Giovanni Santi, endows with a great trumpet as her particular attribute in his chapel of the Muses at Urbino.[27] Here Calliope's trumpet takes on a particular prominence. She displays it as if it were some heroic trophy, and to it she directs her meditations. Its flaring lip further coincides with the contour of Melpomene's inflated robe. On that visual byplay Raphael fixes his gaze. What he singles out is not only Calliope's particular attribute—for the trumpet's loud clangor that incites us to arms helps inspire those who sing of arms and the man—but also the instrument peculiar to Fame.[28] With gravity Raphael gazes upon the man-made equivalent of those laurels, ever green as fame is, that he and his fellow-poets wear. The poet's true reward is also his.

So painting himself, Raphael seems to presume too much. His own verses (Pl. 6) hardly win him the same rank as Virgil or Dante; a strict poetic justice, in fact, would bar him from Parnassus and even exile him far away from Greece. To Parnassus Raphael does make his way in disguise to act out the part of Statius, a tactic also consistent with what his patrons so much admired in him, discretion and gentle manners. In a larger sense, however, Raphael has every right to award himself the poet's bays. Even the most cursory skimming of Renaissance poetics, such as Landino's introduction to Dante or Vida's advice to young writers, reveals ideas—inspiration, *furore,* creating something out of nothing—matched by as well as contributing to the language of art evolved during the Renaissance. Raphael's own drawings, including those filled by his verses, and their role in shaping this fresco are enough to suggest the validity, for his time, of analogies between the painter's *furia* and the poet's *furor.* NUMINE AFFLATUR, Raphael seems to say, are words that painters as well as poets live by.

There is also a proprietary and utterly appropriate reason why Raphael should place himself upon Parnassus. Nothing quite like this painting existed before Raphael assembled his drawings and picked up his brush to fresco this windowed wall. Visual precedents for motifs, figures, and scattered details existed in some abundance, as this and other studies show, but for Parnassus in all its fullness the painter had no sure guide. From scattered sources, art's version of *rime sparse,* Raphael fashioned a poetics. Hence his presence among the poets, the counterpart in flesh and blood of a signature, *Raphael pinxit.*[29] If he does join them on their mountain, no one will begrudge him his self-honoring. Painting here, Raphael takes on a contradiction: the depiction of an art defined as beyond depiction, the unseen presence of a numen. But what Raphael left for all to see, the landscape of Parnassus, is numinous.

Plates

1. Raphael, *Parnassus*. Rome, Vatican, Stanza della Segnatura (photo: Vatican Museums).

2. Raphael, *Parnassus*, detail (photo: Vatican Museums).

3. Raphael, Ceiling, Stanza della Segnatura (photo: Vatican Museums).

4. Raphael, *Poetry* (photo: Vatican Museums).

5. Sperandio, *Lodovico Carbone,* medal,
obverse and reverse. Washington, National
Gallery of Art, Samuel H. Kress Collection
(photo: museum).

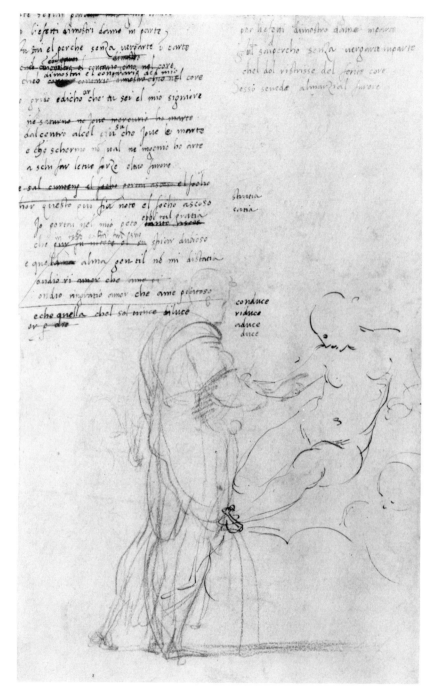

6. Raphael, drawing for *Disputà*. Oxford, Ashmolean Museum (photo: museum).

7. Raphael, *Parnassus*, detail (photo: Vatican Museums).

8. Raphael, *Parnassus*, detail (photo: Vatican Museums).

9. Donatello, *Prophet.* Florence, Museo dell'Opera del Duomo (photo: Alinari).

10. Florentine, *Petrarch,* medal, obverse
and reverse. Washington, National Gallery
of Art, Samuel H. Kress Collection (photo:
museum).

NOTES

1. Raphael's self-portrayal on Parnassus was first noted by G. P. Bellori, *Descrizzione delle imagine dipinte da Raffaelle d'Urbino* (Rome, 1695; reprint, Farnborough: Gregg International Publishers, 1968), p. 24. Although Bellori's identification has been denied by L. Dussler, *Raphael* (London: Phaidon, 1971), p. 74, who prefers to see this poet as Statius (a matter considered below in note 26), it has been revived by R. Jones and N. Penny, *Raphael* (New Haven, Conn.: Yale University Press, 1983), p. 74. The self-portraits by which this figure must be judged have been assembled by H. Wagner, *Raffael im Bildnis* (Bern: Benteli, 1969); see in particular pp. 51–57 and Abb. 3 for Raphael's self-portrait in the adjacent *School of Athens,* a likeness that when reversed, as in Wagner's Abb. 44, bears a close resemblance to the face Bellori saw as Raphael's.

2. Scholarship on the fresco, the room, and its painter is vast and continues to grow: see *Raphael: A Bibliography 1972-1982* (Williamstown, Mass.: RILA, 1984). Older studies are summarized by Dussler, *Raphael,* pp. 74–76. More recent accounts include K. Oberhuber, *Raffaello* (Milan: Arnaldo Mondadori, 1982), pp. 67–69, and Jones and Penny, *Raphael,* pp. 68–74, whose concise but informative treatment depends upon the work of, among others, J. Shearman, *The Vatican Stanze: Functions and Decoration* (London: Oxford University Press, 1971), pp. 15–17. The imagery of the fresco and its iconographic sources are the topics of E. Schrötter, "Raffaels *Parnass:* eine ikonographische Untersuchung," in *Actas del XXIII Congreso internacional de historia del arte,* III (Granada, 1973), 593–605; "Raffaels *Parnass,*" *Kunstchronik* 30 (1977), 75–77; and her monumental "Die Ikonographie des Themas Parnass *vor* Raffael" (Diss., Friedrich-Wilhelms-Universität, Bonn; Hildesheim: Georg Olms, 1977). Raphael's first thought for this fresco, an engraving by Marcantonio Raimondi whose iconography deserves separate study as an alternative to the final work, is treated by those just cited as well as I. H. Shoemaker and E. Brown, *The Engravings of Marcantonio Raimondi* (Lawrence, Kans.: Spencer Museum of Art, 1981), pp. 155–57 and pl. 45b. Drawings are studied by E. Knab, E. Mitsch, and K. Oberhuber, *Raphael: Die Zeichnungen* (Stuttgart: Urachhaus, 1983) and by P. Joannides, *The Drawings of Raphael* (Oxford: Oxford University Press, 1983).

3. Cicero's phrase is "et quasi divino quondam spiritu inflari," from *Pro Archia poeta,* VIII, 18, a passage whose importance for Renaissance poetics is signaled by Schrötter, "Ikonographie," pp. 75–79. In addition the editorial commentary enveloping C. Landino, *Scritti critici e teorici,* ed. R. Cardini, 2 vols. (Rome: Bulzoni, 1974), makes this a major summary on the state of poetics in the late Quattrocento; particularly important is I, 97–164, Landino's introduction to Dante, and II, 97–224, Cardini's commentary. The same helpfulness characterizes R. G. Williams, trans. and ed., *The De Arte Poetica of Marco Girolamo Vida* (New York: Columbia University Press, 1976).

4. *Aeneid,* VI, 50–51, cited by P. Fehl, "Poetry and the Art of Raphael," in *Raphael and the Ruins of Rome* (Urbana-Champaign: Krannert Art Museum, 1983), pp. 12–13 and by Dussler, *Raphael,* p. 70.

5. *Paradiso,* I, 19: "Entra nel petto mio, e spira tue." See further I, 11–33 as well as *Inferno,* II, 7–9 and *Purgatorio,* I, 7–12. In his commentary to Dante,

published first in 1481, Landino makes it clear that the poet's invocation is the same as his inspiration; see *Comedia di Danthe* [*sic*] *Alighieri* (Venice, 1529), fols. CCI^v, CCXX^v–CCXXI. Consult also the helpful survey on invocations in Schrötter, "Ikonographie," pp. 2–45 and for Dante, pp. 91–99.

6. G. F. Hill, rev. by G. Pollard, *Renaissance Medals from the Samuel H. Kress Collection at the National Gallery of Art* (London: Phaidon, 1967), p. 26, no. 114. The reverse's inscription reads: HANC TIBI CALLIOPE SERVAT LODOVICE CORONAM. For this poet, see W. Gundersheimer, *Ferrara: The Style of a Renaissance Despotism* (Princeton, N.J.: Princeton University Press, 1973), pp. 165–66.

7. Poetic competition is touched on by Horace, *Ars poetica*, 220–21, and Raphael's contemporary Vida in *De arte poetica*, I, 320–31 (ed. Williams). For a famous poetic competition of 1441 see G. Holmes, *The Florentine Enlightenment 1400–50* (New York: Pegasus, 1969), pp. 103–5. Raphael's pictorial metaphor for such a *certame coronario,* the crumpled sheet, can still be traced in outline on the spot as well as in a good color photograph; see Jones and Penny, *Raphael,* pl. 80 on p. 67. It is a last-minute addition for which there is no counterpart in the preliminary drawing for this passage, illustrated by E. Knab, E. Mitsch, and K. Oberhuber, *Raphael,* Abb. 372 and p. 590. The motif that Raphael invents is analogous to that shown in another competition where the Virgin's rejected suitors break their staffs but Joseph keeps his entire, as in Raphael's own *Sposalizio* of 1504 (Jones and Penny, *Raphael,* p. 18, pl. 18). As such, Raphael's motif tones down the quarrelsome aspect of poets in colloquy evident at Urbino.

8. The youth seated beside Homer has frequently been identified as a poet, Ennius, who dreamed that he was a second Homer: see D. Redig de Campos, "Il ritratto del poeta Ennio," *Roma* 13 (1935), 193–200; Dussler, *Raphael,* p. 75; and Jones and Penny, *Raphael,* p. 72 who, however, note that he might just as plausibly be a scribe. On this point there seems to be little room for doubt or reservation because Raphael is consistent in distributing laurels to everyone here except the Muses and this youth. Since poets receive laurels (as in my Pl. 5), it follows that the seated boy is no poet and hence no Ennius.

9. See Landino, *Scritti,* I, 142–43 and Cardini's notes in II, 209 with further references; also Vida, *De arte poetica,* II, 394–454.

10. G. Boccaccio, *Genealogia deorum gentilium,* ed. V. Romano, II (Bari: Laterza 1951), 712–13; also C. G. Osgood, trans. and ed., *Boccaccio on Poetry,* 2d ed. (Indianapolis: Bobbs-Merrill, 1956), pp. 54–58, together with the notes which document that here Boccaccio gives eloquent form to a commonplace in his writings and in those of all poets. Similar sentiments are voiced in Raphael's time by Vida, *De arte poetica,* I, 486–515. Pictorial analogies to this passage are suggested by the medal reproduced here as Pl. 10 and by Simone Martini's frontispiece to Petrarch's copy of Virgil, where the poet sits to contemplate in nature, as if inspired: see G. Contini and M. C. Gozzoli, *L'opera completa di Simone Martini* (Milan: Rizzoli, 1970), pp. 100–101 and Tav. LXII.

11. Boccaccio, *Genealogia,* II, pp. 705–6; also Osgood, *Boccaccio on Poetry,* p. 47 and the attendant notes.

12. Horace, *Ars poetica,* pp. 366–69 and 385–90; also Vida, *De arte poetica,* I, 1–10, as well as III, 542–53.

13. Virgil, *Georgics,* III, 291–93 and Vide, *De arte poetica,* II, 2–8 and III, 533–38, among innumerable instances.

14. Jones and Penny, *Raphael,* p. 69; they are preceded by J. Richardson, *An Essay on the Theory of Painting* (London: A. Bettesworth, 1725; 1st ed. 1722), p. 112: "The Name of *Sappho* is written to shew 'twas She, and not one of the Muses intended in the *Parnassus.*"

15. Petrarch, *Fam.,* 23, 19: "Umbra quaedam et quem pictores nostri aerem vocant, qui in vultu inque oculis maxime cernitur, similitudinem illam facit," cited and trans. by T. M. Greene, "Petrarch and the Humanist Hermeneutic," in *Italian Literature: Roots and Branches,* ed. G. Rimanelli and K. J. Atchity (New Haven, Conn.: Yale University Press, 1976), p. 211. Greene further notes that Petrarch takes his metaphor from Seneca, *Epistulae morales,* LXXXIV, 7: "Etiam si cuius in te comparebit similitudo, quem admiratio tibi altius fixerit, similem esse te volo quomodo filium, non quomodo imaginem," a passage then transposed by Macrobius to introduce his *Saturnalia.*

16. Vida, *De arte poetica,* III, 190–91: "Cui contendas te reddere semper / Assimilem, atque habitus gressusque effingere euntis," and III, 220: "Nova sit facies, nova prorsus imago."

17. Ausonius, *Opuscula,* ed. S. Prete (Leipzig: Teubner 1978), p. 308: "Lesbia Pieriis Sappho soror addita Musis" (*Ep.* 51). Plato's epigram is in the *Greek Anthology,* IX, 506: "Some say the Muses are nine but how carelessly! Look at the tenth, Sappho from Lesbos," from W. R. Paton, trans. and ed., *The Greek Anthology,* III (London: Loeb Classical Library, 1917), 280–81. Renaissance imitations of Plato's epigram are summarized by J. Hutton, *The Greek Anthology in Italy to the Year 1800* (Ithaca, N.Y.: Cornell University Press, 1935), pp. 559–60. Other depictions of Sappho are considered by E. R. Spencer, "The Tenth Muse in the Baltimore Museum of Art," *The Baltimore Museum of Art Annual,* III (1968), 4–7, and by J. E. Stein, "The Iconography of Sappho, 1775–1875" (Diss., University of Pennsylvania, Philadelphia, 1981), pp. 9–24. See also H. Rüdiger, *Sappho: ihr Ruf und Ruhm bei der Nachwelt* (Leipzig: Dieterich, 1933).

18. Raphael's Apollo with a fiddle also resembles Orpheus as depicted by Marcantonio Raimondi, as in Shoemaker and Brown, *Raimondi,* pp. 86–87, no. 17. See further G. Scavizzi, "The Myth of Orpheus in Italian Renaissance Art, 1400–1600," in *Orpheus: The Metamorphoses of a Myth,* ed. J. Warden (Toronto: University of Toronto Press, 1982), pp. 111–62, esp. figs. 4, 11, 17–21. Raphael depicts Apollo in his proper classical guise in his engraved *Parnassus* (Shoemaker and Brown, *Raimondi,* pp. 155–57) and, as a colossal statue, at the left in the *School of Athens* just adjacent to this fresco: see Jones and Penny, *Raphael,* pl. 87.

19. "Spira tre / si come quando Marsia traesti / de la vagina de le membre sue' (*Par.,* I, 19–20). Landino, *Comedia,* fol. CCXXI, paraphrases this as "spira in me tal canto quale usasti quando vincesti Marsia." And, indeed, Apollo receives the victor's crown in Raphael's fresco as Marsyas, the loser, loses his flesh. The scene becomes thereby the mythical counterpart and a gruesome one to the poetic competition implied just below it (my Pl. 7). For its significance as a metaphor of poetic inspiration, see also E. Wind, *Pagan Mysteries in the Renaissance,* rev. ed. (Harmondsworth, Eng.: Peregrine Books, 1967), pp. 171–76.

20. The topography of twin-peaked Parnassus, as it existed and as Renaissance authors reported it, is discussed at length by Schrötter in her published articles and her dissertation, observing that Raphael fails to show two quite distinct summits as other artists sometimes do. Indeed, Dante as he invokes Apollo dwells upon the same landscape, claiming that he has scaled one peak and now needs the god's aid to ascend another: "Infino a qui l'un giogo di Parnaso / assai mi fu; ma or con due amendue/m'e uopo intrar ne l'aringo rimaso" (*Par.*, I, 16–18), a tercet glossed by Landino, *Comedia*, fol. CCXXI, to mean one peak for Bacchus according to some authorities, the other reserved for Apollo and his troop. From these remarks and the fresco Schrötter concludes that there is a problem, which she resolves by invoking another peak, the Vatican's hill, as an implied second Parnassian summit. This is appropriate enough but Raphael does depict two eminences, where Dante himself makes his way past one to another, distinguished by the rustic spring that waters lower stretches of the landscape. As in the attributes of the Muses and the dress of the poets, Raphael is playful. He is also serious.

21. The visual ambiguity and what I take to be a bifurcating tree are evident also in good color photographs, such as the detail of Apollo in G. L. Mellini, *Raffaello: le stanze vaticane* (Florence: Fratelli Fabbri, 1965), tav. 1. The question becomes important because the presumed number of painted trees has led many to erect a symbolic scaffold for Raphael to paint upon. See in particular H. B. Gutman "Zur Ikonologie der Fresken Raffaels in der Stanza della Segnatura," *Zeitschrift für Kunstgeschichte* 21 (1958), 32–34, who reads the landscape of Parnassus as Dante's Earthly Paradise (cf. *Purg.* XXXIX, 44–51), an interpretation accepted by J. Pope-Hennessy, *Raphael* (New York: Phaidon, 1970), p. 139. It is not confirmed, however, by the fresco even though many Dantean elements and the presence of Dante himself cannot be denied. As in the note preceding: Raphael paints as he paints.

22. Petrarch's juxtaposition to the laurel tree is suggested not only by his portraitlike medal but also by a manuscript of ca. 1480 (Baltimore, Walters Art Gallery), where he stands behind a verdant laurel; see M. Jasenas, *Petrarch in America* (New York: Pierpont Morgan Library, 1974), pl. 15. Raphael and his predecessors all refer to Petrarch's own verses in celebration of laurels and Laura, imagery further explicated by R. Durling, "Petrarch's 'Giovene donna sotto un verde lauro,'" *MLN* 86 (1971), 1–20.

23. Martianus Capella, *De nuptiis Philologiae et Mercurii*, I, 11–13, cited by Schrötter, "Ikonographie," pp. 53, 129, who notes that Martianus bases himself on Virgil, *Eclogue* VI, 29, where the poet's music makes the trees sing, and has a follower in Dante, *Purg.*, XXVIII, 16–21, on the arboreal music of the Earthly Paradise. What Martianus says requires further study, particularly in connection with Apollo as the musician who transforms the harmonies of Parnassus into the harmonies of the spheres, an image present in the ceiling to the right of Poetry (Pl. 3) where Urania, the Muse of the Heavens, sets her sphere into motion; see further Jones and Penny, *Raphael*, pp. 52–57, as well as N. Rash-Fabbri, "A Note on the Stanza della Segnatura," *Gazette des beaux arts* 94 (1979), 97–104.

24. The wings of Poetry are also a novelty in earlier Renaissance depictions of the art, treated by P. Egan, "*Poesia* and the *Fête champêtre*," *Art Bulletin* 41 (1959),

303–13. Landino, *Scritti,* I, 143–44, provides a nearly scholastic explanation for Poetry as winged: her appendages represent that *scientia* which enables those who write poetry, as learned men, to attain the highest summits of inspiration. As Judith Dundas has reminded me, poetry may also possess wings because verse itself is light, airy, and swift of flight, for which there is chapter and verse in Vida, *De arte Poetica,* III, 373–74: "Hic melior motuque pedum, et pernicibus alis / Molle viam tacito lapsu per levia radit," among many poets who can be cited.

25. See further Wind, *Pagan Mysteries,* p. 174, and the engraving where it is Virgil who displays a book, not Dante.

26. See Statius, *Thebaid,* XII, 816–17: " 'nec tu divinam Aeneida temptu, / sed longe sequere et vestigia semper adora," a deferential attitude acted out in person by Statius as he reverences Virgil in Dante, *Purg.,* XXI; see also XXIV, 119–20 where he, Virgil, and Dante make their way up Mount Purgatory: "Virgilo e Stazio e io, ristretti, / oltre anadavam." See also K. Clark, *The Drawings by Sandro Botticelli for Dante's Divine Comedy* (London: Thames and Hudson, 1976), pp. 129, 131, 143, illustrating *Purg.,* XXI–XXVII and showing Statius with his fellow poets; in this case Statius is costumed *all'antica* to distinguish him from other souls purged in this place, who wear nothing, and to link him with Dante and Virgil.

27. See R. Dubos, *Giovanni Santi* (Bordeaux: Samie, 1971), pl. XLII, where the panel is inscribed "Carmina Calliope libris haeroica mandat." This and other trumpet-bearing Calliopes need to be stressed because there is little consensus about the identity of the Muse whom Raphael gives a trumpetlike instrument to; from Bellori onwards she has been labeled Calliope or Clio or Euterpe. Her spatial position, however, occupying the place of honor on Apollo's proper right, makes her the foremost of the Muses, as Calliope is and as Landino notes (*Comedia,* fols. X[v] and CXXXIII). In the latter case he comments on Dante's invocation of Calliope in *Purg.,* I, 7, noting there an echo of *Aeneid,* IX, 525–28, another call upon her services that is echoed in a more general way by Statius, *Thebaid,* I, 13.

28. FAMA blows her own horn, and thereby looks much like Calliope in the instance just cited, in a beautiful woodcut accompanying a text of Petrarch's *Trionfi* printed at Venice during 1488 and reproduced by E. Callman, *Beyond Nobility* (Allentown, Pa.: Allentown Art Museum, 1980), p. 30, to cite just one instance of Fame's trumpet. As a poet contemplating that instrument, Raphael acts out what other authors put into words, modestly sometimes as in the case of Statius (as in n. 26), but more customarily as a claim on immortality; see, for example, Ovid, *Metamorphoses,* XV, 878–79: "I shall live on in fame through all the ages," *perque omnia seacula fama... vivam.*

29. Such words accompany the engraved *Parnassus,* itself an autonomous essay in poetics meriting further study, where Raphael fails to appear. Here in the fresco I maintain he does, as note 1 indicates. Nor is he the only painter to appropriate the poet's bays; Mantegna wears them in his self-portraying tomb effigy, discussed by A. Radcliffe in *Splendours of the Gonzaga,* ed. D. Chambers and J. Martineau (London: Victoria and Albert Museum, 1981), pp. 30–31.

WYMAN H. HERENDEEN

Wanton Discourse and the Engines of Time: William Camden — Historian among Poets-Historical

Historical writing in its varied forms, and particularly historical verse, appears to have been ubiquitous during the European Renaissance, from the Danube to the Dee, but its popularity and esteem should not be taken for granted. Apparently not everybody could agree with George Puttenham's opinion that "Poesie historical is of all other next the divine most honourable and worthy."[1] Edward Hoby, translating Matthieu Coignet, hissed at those lascivious rhymers, corrupters of truth who meddled with the simple verity of history and coupled it with fable: "Through their lying and wanton discourses they corrupt the manners of youth. . . . And the principal ornament of their verses are tales made at pleasure, and foolish and disorderly subjects, cleane disguising the trueth and historye, to the end they might the more delight."[2] The views voiced in these passages represent two extreme positions in the war of the disciplines during the Renaissance. The rivalry is but one front in the ongoing battle waged for the hand of Dame Rhetoric, and its implications challenge the most fundamental aspects of epistemology in the Renaissance—the relation between language and reality (or *verba* and *res*). Speaking from practical rather than theoretical points of view, these authors remind us that the lofty issues addressed by figures such as Mazzoni, Scaliger, and Sidney, about whether history, philosophy, or poetry can approach nearest to Truth, actually involved writers having immediate concerns about their craft.

The rivalry between poetry and history is nothing new to Renaissance scholars, but it is rare that we allow that it has anything to do with the writing of either history or poetry; there is little sense that writers themselves were drawn into the debate and attempted to understand the relationship between poetic and historical discourse. But in fact, if we think of the prolific experimentation with new combinations of historical and poetic genres, we see that writers spent a good deal of time questioning all aspects of their craft. Indeed, Thomas Nashe, always in the thick of literary controversies, mocked those who belabored the proper relation between the increasingly divided disciplines: "I can but pittie their folly, who are so curious in fables, and excruciate themselves about impertinent questions as ... whether *Lucan* is to be reckoned amongst the Poets or Historiographers."[3]

Thus, although we recognize the existence of the controversy while we work safely within the fortress of our own disciplines, we rarely get the sense that poets and historians were ever seen together, or ask what their numerous and often collaborative experiments in one another's forms had to do with these broader theoretical issues. Nashe reminds us that his contemporaries were less well disciplined than we are, and that poets and historians not only spoke with one another, but often fraternized with the enemy.

This is not to deny the existence of what was an ever-increasing gap between the disciplines. However, we generally overlook the serious efforts to bridge that gap, and I want to look at the career of William Camden as an illustration of and main force behind them. The influence of the man and his work tells us much about the vitality and importance of the dialogue between poets and historians in the sixteenth and seventeenth centuries, particularly in England. As I want to suggest, he succeeded in bridging that gap, and how far he was stretched in the process is indicated by these passages from his contemporaries. While he served as a liaison for writers working in different forms, he also contributed to the redefining of generic barriers, and in so doing, altered the course of various kinds of writing, including historical prose and verse.

In Camden, a man known to us now almost solely as an historian, we see, in fact, a person whose contemporary influence was divided equally between poets and historians. His case illustrates how the debate actually served to bring authors together, and to intensify interest in the epistemological and generic questions raised by the growing rift between the disciplines. No man in England was more welcome in both camps than Camden. His influence extended not only to major poets (such as Spenser and Jonson) and historians, but, of more importance, to the *relation* between the two groups as they met together in forums such as the Society of Antiquaries and the College of Arms. In his impact on his contemporaries we see the dynamics of a struggle between two kinds of knowledge—empirical and mythical—and in it we see how the debate, shaped largely by him, affected the work of major figures of the period who are now locked into our modern academic disciplines.

Camden's primary place among historians has been proclaimed with hardly a dissenting voice. Smith Fussner's view is largely that of F. J. Levy, Hugh Trevor-Roper, and many others: "By the time of Camden's death the whole character of English historiography had changed. The medieval chronicle had been superseded by modern history. Original research, especially in the public records, had become the hallmark of good historical writing."[4] Among his contemporaries as well, Camden enjoyed nearly universal popularity and esteem based on the recognition of his contribution to learning, not only in the field of history — in his reformation of the College of Arms, his role in establishing the Society of Antiquaries, and in endowing the first lectureship in history at Oxford, for example — but also in his contribution to the life and fabric of Westminster School, and through his writings in various forms. So pervasive was his influence on his generation that Thomas Kendrick has described it as the "age of Camden."[5]

There has been similar agreement about the nature of Camden's contribution. Notwithstanding the extraordinary diversity of his activities and friendships, scholars have consistently identified him with the development of modern empirical historical methods in England. "The steady concentration of Camden's thought was toward a secular, empirical explanation of history," says Fussner, and it was this quality that made him the quiet leader of the historical revolution.[6] Indeed, it is striking that a man of such importance has been received with so little diversity of critical opinion.

Accurate as these assessments are, though, they do not address the man's equally remarkable impact on the larger community of writers, and particularly contemporary poets. Their interest in Camden's experiments in genre cannot simply be explained away as the general Renaissance concern for history, since developments in historical methodology would seem to run counter to the tenets behind sixteenth- and seventeenth-century poetics. By the end of the sixteenth century, the patriotic impulse that led authors to the "Renaissance discovery of England" also led them into generic and theoretical problems when they tried to integrate historical material into their verse. If the *Britannia* was popular because of its appeal to nationalistic feelings, its attacks on such poetic fluff as the legend of Brutus would seem to undermine this appeal. Thus, Camden's empiricism, as defined by Fussner, for example, would seem to be incompatible with the more or less Platonic view of historical truth that we see in such poets as Sidney, Spenser, and their followers. At the end of the sixteenth century, poets (historical or otherwise) had to reconcile Tudor myth to the generic requirements of history, and in the process had to make specific decisions about genre, and larger ones about the nature of poetry and writing. Notwithstanding the popularity of historical verse forms, poets could not ignore current developments in historical writing, and this cross-disciplinary influence has been ignored by literary critics who have been content to point to the mythical element in historical verse.

Thus, more important than its patriotism is the *Britannia*'s challenge to the form and content of historical writing in prose and verse. The attraction of an historicist like Camden for poets essentially Neoplatonic in orientation is complex at best, and paradoxical in any case, and it is safe to say that it is partly because of this challenge, which seemed to offer the possibility of bringing poetry closer to the requirements of historical truth, that Camden was so highly esteemed among the poets of the age. Camden's contemporaries, and perhaps most significantly the poets, thought of him in terms of the two disciplines. Edmund Spenser's praise of Camden in *The Ruines of Time* is more than a simple expression of admiration for a contemporary:

> *Cambden* the nourice of antiquitie,
> And lanterne unto late succeeding age,
> To see the light of simple veritie,
> Buried in ruines, through the great outrage
> Of her owne people, led with warlike rage;
> *Cambden,* though Time all moniments obscure,
> Yet thy just labours ever shall endure.[7]

Camden is presented not just as the preserver of the British past, but as a link between historians and poets. The lines specifically redefine the opposition between fact and fiction that is central to the poem. Camden's "simple veritie" stands in sharp contrast to the obscurity and ignorance that characterizes Verulam's past and the nymph's muddled thoughts. Spenser adds an element of strategic irony to his poem by using Camden the historian to praise Sidney the critic of historians. In so doing, he achieves a kind of literary reconciliation of friends, and makes his elegy (part encomium, part dream vision, part historical verse) an interesting study in mixed genres. Camden's historicism and Sidney's poetic invention are both antidotes to obscurity and ignorance in the poem, and in this, Spenser's elegy on Sidney is also a corrective comment on his *Defence.*

In much the same way, Ben Jonson's sonnet on Camden (Epigram XIV) raises questions about the relations between disciplines and literary genres:

> CAMDEN, most reverend head, to whom I owe
>   All that I am in arts, all that I know,
> (How nothing's that?) to whom my countrey owes
>   The great renowne, and name wherewith shee goes.

Then thee the age sees not that thing more grave,
　　More high, more holy, that shee more would crave.
What name, what skill, what faith hast thou in things!
　　What sight in searching the most antique springs![8]

The poet's praise of Camden here and in other encomia is not mere rhetoric, but constitutes a coherent expression of an intellectual ideal. Like Spenser's lines, it too presents Camden as a link between the historian's knowledge and the poet's, and indeed, sees him as both historian and poet ("Many of thine, this better could than I").

There is something in these and other encomia of equal intensity by Drayton, Daniel, Campion, Hall, and others, that suggests that Camden spoke to poets with the same immediacy that he did to the new breed of historian; that his penchant for demythologizing fictions dear to poets was not regarded as antagonistic to poetry; and that he was able to defy the barriers that had grown up between poets and historians and were reinforced by men like Sidney. Camden was a herald in more ways than one, for in his relations with poets and historians he acted as mediator and as interpreter of their forms; as such, his importance reached beyond historiography to broader concerns for epistemology and genre reform.

Although Camden exists for us exclusively as the father of modern British history, for his contemporaries he was linked specifically with Spenser and Sidney and the problems of historical writing raised by them. They recognized that the two great historical epics of the sixteenth century—*The Faerie Queene* and the *Britannia*—were responses to the generic and intellectual debate that, in England, first found expression in Sidney's *Defence of Poesie*. Indeed, both Spenser and Camden express their debts to Sidney. Spenser's affinity with the soft Platonism of the *Defence* is generally accepted, and we see his explicit interest in the problems raised by Sidney in his letter to Raleigh, where he explains how he has obliterated the historical coherence of *The Faerie Queene*: "For the Methode of a Poet historical is not such, as of an Historiographer. For an Historiographer discourseth of affayres orderly as they were donne . . . but a Poet thrusteth into the middest, even as it most concerneth him . . . recoursing to thinges forepaste, and divining of thinges to come, [he] maketh a pleasing Analysis of all."[9] Significantly, Spenser is as intensely interested in the nature of historical writing as he is in his Platonic idealism or the Aristotelian virtues, and the passage demonstrates his desire to deal with the problems posed by the *Defence*. In relating the paradoxical quality of his poetry, which is at once historical and ahistorical, he makes a methodological distinction between "poets historical" and "historiographers," and tells us how he combines the roles of poet and historian. His emphasis here is on the *relation* between the two—on the methods that join the historian and poet; he presents history as discourse, and in this he succeeds in reconciling the forms that Sidney sets in opposition. Significantly, Sidney does not speak of "poets historical": he is doggedly determined to keep the two apart. Spenser, however, finds a middle way through his use of the neologism, and thus demonstrates one poet's attempt to deal with theoretical problems.

Camden too admits a strong personal and professional debt to Sidney which dates from the 1560s, when the two lived together in Dr. Thornton's household during their years at Oxford.[10] The *Britannia,* like the *Defence,* grew out of the reading of those years, and it stands as an explicit answer to the questions raised in the *Defence.* Both works deal overtly with the epistemological problems and possibilities of poetry and history. In attacking the chosen literary form of his schoolmate, Sidney reveals his understanding of contemporary historiography by developing two separate critiques, each leveled at one of the methods current in historical writing at the end of the sixteenth century. He first goes after the rather vulnerable rhetorical, humanist historian, satirizing his manner and exposing the fallibility of his method: "[he] scarcely giveth leysure to the Moralist to say so much, but that he, loden with old Mouse-eaten records, authorising himselfe . . . upon other histories, whose greater authorities are built upon the notable foundation of Heare-say, having much a-doe to accord differing Writers and to pick trueth out of partiality."[11] If the humanist historian (such as Hall) is more interested in myth and moral *exempla* than in facts, the new historian, such as Guicciardini or Bodin, with his empirical emphasis, "is . . . tyed, not to what shoulde bee but to what is, to the particular truth of things." The empirical historian's concern for the accuracy and authenticity of his sources rectifies the shortcoming of the humanist, but in so doing undermines his ability to formulate moral precepts from history, and thus becomes morally dangerous: "the Historian, beeing captived to the trueth of a foolish world, is many times a terror from well dooing and an incouragement to unbridled wickedness."[12]

For Sidney, the true historian, "bound to tell things as things were," is one who is faithful to historical fact. On the other hand, to be "liberall" in one's treatment of history, and to use myth or fictional forms to transform events into moral *exempla* is to abandon the role of historian and assume the mantle of the poet.[13] In turning the Puritan's arguments against poetry (that it is false and immoral) against history, Sidney creates an impasse between the poet and the historian. Thus, when the empiricism of the historian fails him and he must go beyond the facts to explain events, he ceases to be an historian: "manie times he must tell events whereof he can yeelde no cause: or if hee doe, it must be poeticall."[14] The argument of Sidney's *Defence* reveals a cunning familiarity with the questions current among historians; his twofold attack is meant to separate and undermine both the medieval and the modern historian, and to prevent any form of coalition between them and the poet. Intellectually intolerant, he allows no compromise, no yoking together of incompatible words to form "poet-historian."

Throughout the *Britannia* and the *Remains* Camden demonstrates an acute sensitivity to both sides of Sidney's critique, although he does not explicitly link them with the author of the *Defence;* his "modern" methods are clearly efforts to avoid the charges of foolish credulousness and insidious factitiousness, but his strategy is positive rather than evasive. Thus, although he is concerned to raze the "notable foundation of Hearsay" and construct his narrative on the more solid material of fact, he is no less determined that the historian should not be cut off from the wisdom of poetry. Camden avoids both pitfalls identified by Sidney without allowing himself to be fettered by theoretical restraints; for him, the historian should be slave to neither myth nor fact. This *via media* converts Sidney's criticisms into strengths. Although not a theoretician, Camden is a very self-conscious writer, repeatedly questioning the methods and forms that he works in. When reading the *Britannia* we can observe his efforts to navigate a course between Sidney's Scylla and Charybdis and still arrive at some kind of historical truth. On the one hand, his scholarly use of authenticated primary sources and accurate texts vindicates him of one of Sidney's charges, and constitutes one of his greatest methodological contributions. In his preface, he explains his empirical method of rediscovering pre-Roman Britain by following the thread of primarily Roman sources: "I have travell'd almost all over England, and have Perused our own writers, as well as the Greek and Latin. . . . I have examined the publick Records of the Kingdom, Ecclesiastical Registers and Libraries, and the Acts, Monuments, and Memorials of Cities. . . . I have searched out ancient Rolls, and cited them in their stile."[15]

Camden's aim is expressed modestly enough: he hopes that this use of data and authentic sources will do justice to Truth. He makes no extravagant claims for his empiricism. In his preface, and throughout the narrative, he emphasizes his frequent need to resort to conjecture and judgment—in Sidney's phrase, to treat history "liberally"—thereby calling attention to the limits of his methods. More than just an attempt to disarm his critics, this is an expression of Camden's view of the epistemology of history, and it is a view that is more far-reaching than that expressed in Sidney's derivative polemic. He is careful to make us aware of the relation between fact and fiction, or interpretation, and to refute those who insist that historians must be content with facts alone: those (he says) who "will utterly exclude conjecture [from] history, I fear will exclude the greatest part of polite Learning, and, in that, of human knowledge. . . . And since

Conjectures are the signs and tokens of somewhat that lies hid, and are . . . the directors of reason to find the truth, I always accounted them a kind of Engine with which Time draws up Truth from the bottom of Democritus's well."[16] Far from making great claims for the veracity of his method, Camden stresses the need to resort to another kind of knowing when interpreting history, and his frequent use of the words "understanding," "judgment," and "conjecture" (his Latin words are "interpretari," "intellegere," and "suscipio") remind us of his influence on Jonson, for whom these are key words. This acceptance of nonrational, nonempirical insights as essential to the quest for truth is part of Camden's recognition that (to paraphrase Sidney) at times historians must be like poets. For Camden this is part of the historian's task, while for Sidney it is very particularly not so.

What was important for Camden's contemporaries (and ultimately for the development of historical study) was that he did not pass off poetry or fable as history. He clearly identifies their point of separation from each other, as when he introduces some "antique" lines on Arthur with the ingenuous explanation that "because they seem to flow from a good vein, I will venture to insert [them]."[17] His refreshing bluntness in dismissing some of the old saws of Tudor mythology is of interest less for its historical content than for the clarity of its judgment, the directness of its style, and honesty of its method—as we see when he prefaces some verses on the etymology of the name Marlborough with the comment that "the derivation of this place from *Merlin's* Tomb, which *Alexander Necham* . . . hammer'd out in this Distich, is ridiculous."[18]

But the demythologizing should not blind us to the fact that all the myths and falsehoods of the rhetorical tradition are preserved as part of the instruction and delight of the *Britannia*. Thus, Camden seems to be doing two things at once, things which, for Sidney and others of his camp, were mutually exclusive. His respect for poetry and poets is obviously great, and they have an important place in his work. The *Britannia* is the first such work to include literature as part of our cultural history: it is presented rather like an "histoire des mentalités" and not as narratives pretending to truth. The work is among other things a repository of poetry dealing with the historical landscape. Virtually every page includes poetic fragments filling out the no less fragmentary historical scene. Similarly, the *Remains* embodies an anthology of primarily post-Conquest poetry arranged in chronological order, and collected to convey a sense of the "dark mist" of that "middle age." Between 1586 and 1604, Camden's work develops an archaeology of myth and history; in its clearly delineated strata of fact and fiction it gives us a view of the cultural, intellectual, as well as political growth of Britain, and effectively develops (especially in the *Remains*) a history of English literature long before Bacon advances the idea.[19]

Significantly, Camden was himself a poet-historical, and he interlaced his poem, *de Connubio Tamae et Isis,* throughout the *Britannia.* In form very close to its exact contemporary, Spenser's marriage of the Thames and the Medway in Book IV, canto xi of *The Faerie Queene,* it too presents us with historical and legendary heroes of the British past, and in this it would at first seem to run counter to the historical method of the *Britannia* as a whole. The verses are essential to the larger design of the work: as in Spenser, the mythic landscape is used to release us from the past, to stress the present and inspire noble thoughts and patriotic action. The poetic fragments are set off in contrast with the prose narrative: "The poetical description of ... [Isis's] head or fountain, taken out of *the Marriage of Tame and Isis,* I have here added; which you may read or omit, as you please."[20] The poem addresses history but does not pose as history; poetic myth serves as the subtext to the historical narrative. Thus, in the poem he is able to make clear what is likely to be lost in the work as a whole: that Britain, not her history, is the subject of the *Britannia.* Camden the historian uses poetry here in just the way that Sidney says he must, but ironically in doing so he makes poetry serve history. The poetry becomes a tool for critical understanding, a means of analysis, as we see when the personified Thames puts the moral ambiguities of history into proper perspective when he eulogizes Elizabeth:

> *Windsor,* no more thy ancient glories tell,
> No more relate the wonders of thy hill,
> Thy Forts, thy Fenns, thy Chapel's stately pile.
> Forget the knights thy noble stalls adorn ...
> These glories now are all eclips'd by one,
> One honour vies with all thy old renown ...
> *Elizabeth,* whom we with wonder stile
> The Queen, the Saint, the Goddess of our Isle.[21]

Not likely to replace *The Faerie Queene* in our curriculum, the poem is nonetheless important as an example of an historian assuming the role of poet-historical in order to advance his historical analysis by transcending empirical considerations.

In the *Britannia* Camden separates poetry from history and past from present as Spenser's work does not. In Spenser, the focus is on a mythic past which adumbrates the future; "history" is the subtext clarifying poetic myth and the imagination: Arthur, Verulam, and Gloriana are parts of the mythic fabric of the poem whose meanings are sharpened by their status as "history." In Camden's work, on the other hand, this relationship is reversed: it focuses on the historical world, and uses the poetry as a commentary on the history. It achieves its rhetorical and moral effect by unraveling the strands of myth and history, and in so doing it offers an alternative kind of historical poem—one that found fuller development in the work of Daniel and Drayton, and, indeed, one that was emulated more assiduously than was Spenser's model.

Thus, while usually considered Spenserian in inspiration, Drayton's *Poly Olbion* and Daniel's *Civile Wares,* as historical poems, are closer to the *de Connubio* than to *The Faerie Queene:* both poets are troubled by the proper assimilation of the historical material as Spenser was not, and ultimately they both weave the threads of history and poetic invention together in ways very different from Spenser, so that generically their debt to Camden the historian is greater than it is to Spenser the poet. This reevaluation of historical and poetic modes can be seen in virtually all the poets-historical after 1600, and can be traced to Camden's influence. In the *Britannia* and the *Remains,* then, we see the sort of work that galvanized the imagination of a generation and contributed to new attitudes toward the rhetoric of history, and the decorum of prose and verse. In Camden's response to Sidney's very Ciceronian *Defence,* there are intellectual, stylistic, and methodological features which go beyond questions of historiography and become characteristic of the thought and modes of the next several generations. For example, Camden's explicit rejection of Ciceronian eloquence for the more taciturn style of Tacitus is one of the first expressions of the anti-Ciceronian intellectual reform that will shape the prose and verse of the period. Camden was a stylist, and his emphasis on plainness, directness, and judgment is precisely that ideal associated with the later English Renaissance and articulated most clearly by his protégé, Ben Jonson, and illustrated in the work of unproclaimed followers such as Bacon, Browne, and Fuller.

Likewise, the seventeenth-century effort to shake the yoke of antiquity found its first fully developed expression in the demythologizing methods of the *Britannia*—that is, twenty years before Bacon's *Advancement of Learning* and sixty years before Browne's *Pseudodoxia Epidemica.* Bacon's attempt to destroy the "idols of the cave," and Browne's exposure of the "vulgar errours" of the ancients both had their less flamboyant antecedents in Camden's embracing reassessment of untested historical and cultural *idées reçues.* His warning—"let Antiquity herein be pardoned, if she sometime disguise truth with the mixture of a fable," and that the "authority [of ancient poetry] seems weak"—becomes the refrain of the next century.[22] In submitting ancient, medieval, and modern texts to the logic of the landscape, Camden not only revises the form and content of British history, but he also contributes to the reform of rhetoric in seventeenth-century England. There are more specific, and I think less important, "firsts" that can be traced to Camden, but all of them work together to make him a far greater influence than his works might now suggest. When readers opened the quarto editions of the *Bri-*

tannia, from 1586 to 1594, they actually saw something they had not seen before: they saw history subjected to method; they saw history and poetry unraveled, the worlds of fact and fable divided, commented upon, and given styles and importance proper to themselves. His influence is first of all on the minds and perceptions of his and the next generation, not on academic disciplines or genres. It enabled poets and historians especially to see the generic conventions of their forms more clearly, and in this he generated activity and experimentation in historical writing in prose and verse.

Thus, if both *The Faerie Queene* and the *Britannia* are responses to Sidney's *Defence,* we see in Camden's work an augury of what is to come in the intellectual history of the next century, while in Spenser we see a culmination of what had come before. Never again do we have the marriage of poetic myth and history that we do in Spenser. Poets who were clearly influenced by both Camden and Spenser self-consciously call attention to the different strands of fact and fiction in their historical verse; as they did not before, historical poets have to consciously decide to write history — or not to. Drayton does this explicitly when he invites Selden to write prose "additions" to his *Poly Olbion* which separate historical truth from the "intollerable Antichronismes, incredible reports . . . and Bardish impostures . . . in our Ancients." Not content with a historical poem in the manner of Spenser, Drayton points to the differences between his poetical and historical material, and as Selden makes clear, this results in more sharply defined generic criteria for historical poetry: "Yet so, that, to explaine the Author, carrying himselfe in this part, an *Historicall,* as in the other, a *Chorographicall* Poet, I insert oft, out of the *British* story, what I importune you not to credit."[23] The point is not that Drayton has greater respect for either poetry or history, but that the two are irrevocably split. Writers can bring the two forms nearer together, or set them in contrast with each other, but they cannot fuse them as Leland, Spenser, and Sackville were able to do.

Similarly, for Samuel Daniel, the clash of history and poetry is a genuinely troubling literary dilemma. In the revisions of *The Civile Wares* between 1594 and 1609, he purifies its historical content, and develops an increasingly rigid conception of historical verse. By 1596 his ideal of a historical poem is one which would suppress poetic invention. Inadvertently anticipating Jonson's charge that he was more historian than poet, Daniel tells his readers that historical accuracy rather than poetical ornament is his first concern: "setting-aside those ornaments proper to this kinde of Writing [e.g., verse], I have faithfully observed the Historie. . . . Nor have I sworne Fealty only to rhyme, but that I may serve in any other state of invention" — and this comes from the author of the *Defence of Rhyme*.[24] Increasingly, Daniel distinguishes between history and poetry, and makes history his focal point. His austere aesthetic looks logically toward the abandonment of verse forms of history, and indeed, he finally deserts his lyric muse for Clio, and turns from verse to write (in the manner and method of Camden) a prose *History of Britain* after the Conquest. Thus, he begins his career as a poet-historical, and ends it as an historian.

What we see in Drayton and Daniel we also see in many other poets of the period including, for example, Jonson and Milton: an aggravated awareness of the problematic relationship between history and poetry, and an intensified interest in combining the forms in different ways. In them we see a new kind of poet-historical, one for whom the distinctions between poetry and history have become inescapable—as they had not been for Spenser. They are, if you will, poets-historical writing under the influence of the new history. Earlier poets could ignore the theoretical problems posed by Sidney as long as history remained a jumble of myth and fact, imperfectly combined in antiquated texts. Camden's model, however, could not be ignored. Never again could the casual approach to the material be taken; and for the next two generations, amid the flurry of renewed interest in the form, simple verity either deadened historical verse, or eventually drove poets to other forms. We can see that Spenser's response to Sidney offers no answer for the poet in an age of empiricism: Platonic poets-historical are an endangered species after 1586, and extinct after Spenser's death in 1599. The *Britannia,* on the other hand, nurtured the poetic fashion of demythologizing and historicizing. For a time it encouraged poets without giving them a successful poetic model: it seemed to carry Spenserian ideals to the next logical step, but finally proved poetically impracticable. *The Faerie Queene* is the last great historical poem in the classical and humanist tradition, and seen in the context of Camden, it is clear that it could not have been written even a decade later than it was. The *Britannia,* on the other hand, a historical poem in prose and verse, is the first great history. Although less inspired, it looks forward to new forms (the biblical epic, for example) in ways that Spenser's work does not, and their contemporaries recognized this: they idealized Spenser as an Elizabethan poet whom they could never rival, but they identified with Camden and learned new techniques from him. In helping to redefine our notion of history, Camden has married us to history, and now, far down the line, his descendants live on in works such as *In Cold Blood* and *Armies of the Night.* As Joseph Hall suggests, the *Defence of Poesie, The Faerie Queene,* and the *Britannia* stand as a triptych indicating different moments in the development of Renaissance historical thought and verse:

One fayre Par-royall hath our Iland bred
Wherof one is a live and 2 are dead
Sidney ye Prince of prose & sweet conceit
Spenser of numbers & Heroick Ryme
Iniurious Fate did both their lives defeate . . .
 Camden thou livest alone of all ye three
 For Roman stile & English historye;
Englande made them thou makest Englande knowen
So well art thou ye prince of all ye payre
Sithence thou hast an Englande of thine owne. . . . [25]

Each of them offers a window facing in a different direction in the history of literary form and offering a different cultural view of the past.

NOTES

1. George Puttenham, *The Arte of Englishe Poesie* (London, 1589), p. 31; see also pp. 5–7 and 31–37 for discussion of the different kinds of poetry and the subject matter appropriate to them. Puttenham's volume is something of a beginner's guide to poetics and contains little that would seem to be controversial.

2. Edward Hoby, trans., Matthieu Coignet, *Politique Discourse Upon Trueth and Lying* (London, 1586), Introduction. The debate took various forms, and it is useful to recognize that while Hoby's is typical of Puritan attacks on poetry, it is embedded in the broader context of the relation between poetry and history and the treatment of historical "truth" in literature; Sidney's *Defence* uses the same framing argument to answer Stephen Gosson's charges.

3. Thomas Nashe, *The Anatomie of Absurditie* (1589), ed. Ronald B. McKerrow, in *The Works of Thomas Nashe*, 5 vols. (Oxford: Oxford University Press, 1958), I, 46–47. Most scholars dealing with these subjects are more interested in the author's rhetorical strategies than in the subject of the debate itself, as in the recent study by Margaret W. Ferguson, *Trials of Desire* (New Haven, Conn.: Yale University Press, 1984), pp. 142–46. Although he is not primarily concerned with the Renaissance, Hayden White looks at the philosophical implications of the rhetorical strategies of the historian and the poet in his important paper, "Historicism, History, and the Figurative Imagination," in *Essays in Cultural Criticism* (Baltimore: The Johns Hopkins University Press, 1978), especially pp. 100–116.

4. F. S. Fussner, *The Historical Revolution: English Historical Writing and Thought, 1580–1640* (London: Routledge & Kegan Paul, 1962), p. 230. See also F. J. Levy, *Tudor Historical Thought* (San Marino: Huntington Library, 1967), and Hugh Trevor-Roper, *Queen Elizabeth's First Historian* (London: British Library, 1971). Each identifies Camden as the first in England to make significant use of the new historical methods being developed in Italy and France.

5. T. D. Kendrick, *British Antiquity* (London: Methuen & Co., 1950), p. 167; documents in the Muniment Room of Westminster Abbey record Camden's frequent monetary gifts to the school after his departure in 1597; his *Greek*

Grammar became the standard text for the study of Greek for the next century and a half; his influence as an educator is attested to by the support he received from Queen Elizabeth and Lord Burghley, and by the lasting affection of students such as Ben Jonson and Robert Cotton.

6. Fussner, *Historical Revolution,* p. 231. It should be stressed that Camden's contemporaries also perceived his methodological originality—authors were aware of the "historical revolution" that was taking place.

7. Edmund Spenser, *The Ruines of Time,* ll. 169–75, published in *Complaints* (London, 1591). Passages from Spenser are from the variorum edition of the *Works of Edmund Spenser,* edited by Edwin Greenlaw, Charles Grosvenor Osgood, Frederick Morgan Padelford, and Ray Heffner (Baltimore: The Johns Hopkins University Press, 1932–49). In "Spenserian Specifics: Spenser's Appropriation of a Renaissance *Topos,*" *Medievalia et Humanistica* n.s. 10 (1981), 159–88, I discuss the nymph of Verulam's confusion and how it relates to the landscape of the poem. In the elegy, Camden and Sidney, historian and poet, provide the ideal that contrasts with the misplaced nymph.

8. Ben Jonson, Epigram XIV, first published in the 1616 folio of Jonson's *Works,* here cited from the edition of C. H. Herford, Percy Simpson, and Evelyn Simpson, *Ben Jonson,* 11 vols (Oxford: Oxford University Press, 1925–52), VIII, 31.

9. Spenser, *Works,* I, 168–69. While Spenser makes clear how he alters the historian's method, a large portion of his letter is concerned to stress the close link between the two. He speaks of history in both senses of the word, as "narrative" and as a record of past events, using the word itself to bridge the gap made by Sidney. Thus, using many of the same models and much the same critical vocabulary that Sidney uses, he explains that the allegory of *The Faerie Queene* teaches by example (as does history) although it works toward precepts, or *exempla.* In thus being historical (or ethical) before being philosophical, his poetry works to overcome the barriers set up by theoreticians like Sidney without sacrificing the idealized status of the poet.

10. In the Preface to the *Britannia,* Camden speaks of Sidney's encouragement; he contributed to the 1587 Oxford collection of elegies on Sidney, *Exequiae Illustrissimi Equitis, D. Phillipi Sidnaei....*

11. *Sidney's Apologie for Poetrie,* ed. J. Churton Collins (Oxford: Oxford University Press, 1907), p. 15. For the trends in historical method current at this time, see Eric Cochrane, *Historians and Historiography in the Italian Renaissance* (Chicago: University of Chicago Press, 1981), pp. x–xvi; Sidney's debt to Italian writers reflects the extent of English indebtedness by the last quarter of the sixteenth century. See also Fussner, *Historical Revolution,* pp. 250–53.

12. *Sidney's Apologie,* pp. 16–17, 23. For the Renaissance origins of empiricist and historicist thought, see B. C. Hurst, "The Myth of Historical Evidence," *History and Theory* 20 (1981), 278–90, and George Huppert, "The Renaissance Background of Historicism," *History and Theory* 5 (1966), 46–60.

13. That is, he cannot establish precepts or moral patterns without dealing "liberally" with the facts—"without hee will be poeticall"; Sidney's strategy is to be very literalistic in his use of these labels—*Sidney's Apologie,* pp. 21, 23.

14. *Sidney's Apologie,* p. 21.

15. William Camden, *Britannia: or, a Chorographical Description*, trans. and ed. Edmund Gibson, 2 vols. (London, 1753), preface. Passages from the *Britannia* will be from this edition. Both Fussner's and Levy's assessments of Camden stress his empiricism without due recognition of his skepticism.

16. Camden, *Britannia.*

17. Camden, *Britannia*, p. 23.

18. Camden, *Britannia*, p. 129. Camden's Latin is no less blunt than the translation; there is also a strong ironic, even playful streak to some of Camden's prose.

19. Of course, Camden was among the first in England to examine archaeological material for its historical significance; see, for example, F. J. Levy's "The Making of Camden's *Britannia*," *Bibliothèque d'Humanisme et Renaissance* 26 (1964), 76–97. However, I am suggesting something rather different here—and that is, that the *Britannia* and the *Remains* themselves embody an archaeological quality that develops chronological strata as they move through different historical periods and landscapes.

20. Camden, *Britannia*, p. 286. Camden's poems, including the passages comprising *The Marriage of Tame and Isis*, have been conveniently collected by George Burke Johnson, in his "Poems by William Camden," *Studies in Philology* 72 (1975).

21. Camden, *Britannia*, p. 175.

22. Camden, *Britannia*, p. xi.

23. Drayton "From the Author of The Illustrations," in *Poly-Olbion, a Chorographicall Description of Great Britain* (London, 1612), sig. A3. As the title suggests, the landscape rather than the history is the overriding focus of Drayton's view of Britain; history is interpreted through nature. Selden makes frequent acknowledgment of Camden in his illustrations.

24. Samuel Daniel's *The Civile Wars* were first published serially in 1595, and here, in the dedication to the countess of Pembroke (pp. 6–7), he goes to great length to stress the importance of historical accuracy and the "impietie" of "introduc[ing] fictions of our owne imagination, in things of this nature" (p. 5).

25. Joseph Hall, "To Camden," in *The Collected Poems of Joseph Hall*, ed. A. Davenport (Liverpool: University Press, 1949), pp. 105–6.

IV

CONTEXTUALITY:
Relations of Power

JULIE A. SMITH

The Poet Laureate as University Master: John Skelton's Woodcut Portrait

In the late 1520s a woodcut appeared representing John Skelton (Fig. 1) in two books printed by John Rastell, Skelton's *Agaynste a Comely Coystrowne* and *Dyuers Balettys and Dyties Solacyous*.[1] The figure wears a laurel wreath and is a university master, for he sits in an elaborate cathedra. Depicting poet laureates as masters was a late medieval fashion, popular in the fifteenth century but in decline by the mid-sixteenth. The practice grew out of the long tradition of representing authors as schoolteachers; when the universities became important, these figures took on the look of university professors. Finally, they were given the laurel crown following Petrarch's 1341 laureation ceremony, which generated both actual and purely pictorial laureations. This is the background for the woodcuts of laureates in early English books, one of which is that of Skelton.

I

Authors often were depicted as schoolmasters, because the discipline of grammar quite thoroughly conflated the two roles. Authors in their use of language were understood to be grammarians, and their texts served as the basis for the formulation of grammatical rules. Furthermore, grammar included the study of authors: interpretation of literature was an important aspect of the curriculum.[2] This interchangeability of roles was embedded in the iconography of grammar, first devised in the fifth century by Martianus Capella when he gave the seven liberal arts their first pictorial representation.[3] Grammar was a schoolmistress, who symbolized all aspects of the discipline of grammar, including authors and their texts. In fact, in her person were conjoined what seem to us very disparate conceptual categories. She says, "I have four parts: letters, literature, the man of letters, and literary style. Letters are what I teach, literature is I who teach, the man of letters is the person whom I have taught, and literary style is the skill of a person whom I form. I claim to speak also about the nature and practice of poetry."[4] Grammar thus combined in one figure of a schoolteacher physical writing, that is, the alphabet and words; the author's text, which served as the schoolbook; the author (or commentator, or poet) who wrote the text and who was himself a student of grammar; and the grammatical and stylistic rules of language.

Being in one aspect a "man of letters," the schoolteacher Grammar came to serve as an author-portrait formula for grammarians: the teacher with pupils was used to represent the historical practitioner. Thus, for example, at the Ducal Palace in Venice, Priscian is shown as a schoolmaster teaching grammar to three youths.[5] Grammar also had a special relationship to another visual formula: the figure of the author seated at his desk, which derived from the image of seated philosophers or rhetoricians on late classical funerary monuments,[6] and became an author-portrait formula for all sorts of people: the Evangelists, church fathers, secular authors, and, by the twelfth century, scribes. Capella's Grammar is related to this figure through the iconographic practice of coupling emblems of the seven liberal arts with their most famous practitioners, depicted in this formula of working at their desks.

On the Royal Portal of Chartres Cathedral, for example, each of the seven liberal arts is depicted with the author whose work was primary to its study.[7] Grammar is shown as a woman with two children at her knee, holding a book and a whip. Below her is seated either Priscian or Donatus leaning over his desk. Called the "paradigmatic representative,"[8] the historical practitioner depicted in the portrait formula of the author seated at his desk often replaced the personification, so that, for example, Priscian writing at his desk served as a reference to grammar. What this means, simply, is that either the schoolmaster or the seated author (to be called henceforth the scholar) could personify grammar, although this is true of the scholar only when he appears on grammar books (being indistinguishable from other seated authors).

Both master and scholar appeared interchangeably for "grammarians" in a strict sense, those who wrote grammatical treatises, handbooks, or commentaries, and for authors whose literary texts were used as schoolbooks. As we will see, Italian woodcuts of laureates include either scholar or schoolmaster, and often the two formulas are combined. Behind both figures was an iconographic history which blended the author, grammar master, and textbook into one symbol. This coalescence explains many phenomena about the portraits otherwise attributable to printer indifference: the frequently ambiguous identity of the laureated scholar or schoolmaster, or the appearance of the laurel on mere grammar teachers.

II

With the growth of the universities, this grammar teacher began to take on the appearance of a university master: his whip was discarded; his cathedra looked grander; and the students, when they were included, seemed older. Of these innovations, it was the cathedra which became the conspicuous symbol of a revised identity. Difficult to interpret because it is long and varied, the history of this chair nevertheless suggests in broad outlines its new importance after the thirteenth century. As an attribute of the university, the cathedra expressed an intellectual authority sought by churchman, academic, and author alike.

In Greek and Roman iconography, the cathedra, a high-backed, armless chair, was traditionally the seat of philosophers, rhetoricians, and school-masters. In the paleo-Christian era, that is, from the first to the sixth centuries, Christ in cathedra appeared on sarcophagi and in cata-combs as the central figure of the "apostolic college." The iconography was influenced by classical council scenes, wherein the ruler sat facing full-front and flanked by attendants. The same composition was used to render the Last Judgment.[9]

By the sixth century, the medieval uses of the cathedra had come to include two additional variations: the thrones of bishops and the chairs of literary people. The bishops very early adopted this chair, as we see from Roman catacombs containing chairs carved out of bedrock, used by the bishop as his seat of authority when he taught converts and held services.[10] By the time of Constantine, the cathedra was the bishop's throne, fusing the two activities of Christ in cathedra: teaching and judging. In illustrations, the sense of a teaching place was rendered almost always by the presence of a book. The cathedra represented two roles, "the bishop's teaching authority and his relation to the apocalyptic throne of God,"[11] but the teaching role was often less emphasized. Further, the cathedra was not an especially important episcopal attribute. Bishops as often stand as sit; and when they sit, the chair is frequently the faldstool or not visible at all. Many styles replace the high-backed, low-armed chair.

Literary persons were depicted differently in their chairs. Often their cathedras retained the high back of the classical one, no doubt because in practice it provided back support. Even so, their seats were plainer in style, and the whole visual presentation was less prestigious. A compari-son between two chairs of similar design dramatizes the difference. In an illustration from a late thirteenth-century antiphoner, St. Peter as bishop of Rome sits in cathedra (Fig. 2). His authority is expressed by features persistent in the iconography of bishops, for example, the fully frontal disposition. Viewed from this perspective, the arms of the chair appear

splayed to create the impression of a throne. Elsewhere, episcopal authority might be expressed by the bishop's grand size, the presence of
subordinates, the addition to the chair of a canopy, dais, or baldachin. In
the illustration of Peter, his expression distances him from his subordinates,
thus enhancing his authority, while only a small book expresses his
teaching office. By contrast, the twelfth-century monk and author Laurence
of Durham is depicted in a volume of his poetry and prose in the more
retiring profile composition typical of literary people, like authors,
illuminators, scribes (Fig. 3). Alone with writing stand, pen, and scraping
knife, he expresses only literary occupation, diligence to his task. So
different are these two modes of representation that when a bishop is
depicted in a literary cathedra, he seems to have put aside his judicial
authority (Fig. 4).

Blurring the clear distinction between literary and episcopal chairs
are the cathedras of the Evangelists. As I have said, the first portraits of
Evangelists derived from images of classical philosophers in cathedra.
But because of the great prestige of the Evangelists and the continuation
of their portraits for centuries, they are depicted in a great variety of
cathedras, from the simple type described above for literary figures to
seats absolutely thronelike. No matter how grand, cathedras of Evangelists are usually distinguishable from bishops' thrones by the inclusion in
the illustration of writing paraphernalia. Thus, they communicate a
different kind of authority, that of the divine word. It may be from them
that Renaissance *literati* derived the precedent of authors in elaborate
literary chairs.

No doubt the growth of the universities enriched the meaning of the
cathedra. From the beginning a symbol of the graduate's authority to
teach, whose significance derived from the classical master's chair, the
cathedra was part of the ceremony of inception: the new master took his
place there following receipt of the insignia of his office.[12] Fourteenth-
and fifteenth-century depictions of masters suggest that the chair was
becoming more elaborate. In the north, the high back curved toward the
front to produce a canopy, a long-established symbol of religious authority.
The cathedra became larger; it might be placed on a dais and have a
baldachin. To some extent these features reflect the flamboyance of the
gothic style that affected bishops' thrones as well. But the result was that
often the only way to tell whether the chair was professorial or ecclesiastical was by the occupant (compare Figs. 5 and 6). A similar effect was
achieved in Italy, where high backs and elaborate classical decoration
replaced Gothic canopies. Author portraits often were modeled on those
of university professors, as we see from the use of similar kinds of
cathedras and the frequent presence of adult students in the illustrations.

Because many universities grew out of cathedral schools, the master's chair may have evolved to compete with the bishop's throne. At the same time, because of the growing prestige of the universities, the bishops were placing more emphasis on their thrones as symbols of the university. Perhaps related to this interchange is the fact that cathedra and pulpit were often indistinguishable. In front of the cathedra might be a structure to hold a book: desk, lectern, or pulpit. The use of such a bookstand without any chair was an alternative to the cathedra. In these cases, the viewer's impression is that the person speaks from a pulpit. A 1484 Lyon edition of Pierre Michault's *Le Doctrinal du Temps Présent* provides evidence of the interchangeability of cathedra and pulpit. The work is a moralized grammar organized around the teachings of two schools, Falseness and Virtue. The headmaster of each has twelve subalterns who deliver lessons in grammar illustrative of the individual vices and virtues. The masters of Vice are both religious and lay persons and stand in pulpits (Fig. 7). The mistresses of Virtue are nuns in cathedras (Fig. 8). It is clear that by the end of the fifteenth century, cathedra and pulpit were symbols easily shared by university and church. By the time of the Skelton woodcut in 1535, competition for the intellectual authority they represented may have been the case.[13]

III

Petrarch was crowned poet laureate in 1341, initiating the wide popularity of the honor. No single way of depicting the laureate followed. Coronation scenarios, groups of authors sitting in discussion, opening scenes with first-person narrators, any illustration containing an author might show him wearing the crown if he were a classical writer or one of Italy's own illustrious three: Dante, Petrarch, Boccaccio. One kind of picture incorporating the laurel was the emblem of grammar *qua* university professor (Fig. 9), found on schoolbooks and infolding into its signification the author and the book. The inclusion of the laurel on this composite figure occurred when it represented an "auctore," a respected classical author. This image of the laureated master was, no doubt, created by Petrarch's association of the poet laureate with the university in his coronation ceremony.

Petrarch's coronation, his oration on the occasion, and the diploma he helped devise testify to his deliberate attempt to graft the laurel onto the academy.[14] Petrarch actively sought and obtained a coronation invitation from two sources: the University of Paris and the Senate of Rome. Although he chose the latter because the ancient poets had been crowned in Rome, he designed the event as a university affair. Before going to Rome, he arranged a long preliminary examination by King Robert of Naples, one imitating that for university degree candidates. Petrarch was anxious that King Robert, whose sponsorship had produced the invitation, send his representative to Rome to crown him. Robert closely guarded his authority to confer degrees at the University of Naples, held by the Angevin kings since Frederick II created it in 1224 by imperial fiat.

The diploma or *Priviligium,* which Petrarch helped draft, bestowed on him three rewards which were clearly magisterial: the title of master; a license similar to the *ius ubique docendi* (the right upon inception to teach at any university without undergoing further examination); and the power to examine and license other candidates for the laurel. Petrarch's efforts to make his ceremony academic probably reflect, not only his hope for the revival of the classics within the discipline of grammar at the universities, but his own desire to legitimize his self-granted honor. Perhaps he expected the criticism he received for instigating his own laureation.

Upon Petrarch's coronation followed many unwelcome and increasingly numerous imitations. He himself had effectually produced them by encouraging nobility to crown laureates; by creating a link between the laureate and the university degree; by spreading the fame of his own coronation as an example; and by providing a rationale in his oration for self-sought glory: "Let this one truth suffice: that the desire for glory is innate . . . in greatest measure in those who are of some wisdom and some excellence."[15] Assuming that literary self-promotion served the cause of letters as well as their own, the many imitators of Petrarch and their sponsors broadcast the honor widely. This situation is reflected in the number of laureates in early Italian printed books: the not-so-great frequently appear with the laurel crown (or with some other foliage poorly executed or deliberately unidentifiable), and in many cases their only laureation was by the woodcarver.

The master and pupils was one kind of illustration affected by the vogue of laureation. Aesop, Ovid, Vergil, Seneca, Horace, any classical author already appearing as a professor with students on texts used by the universities for language and literary instruction could appear as a laureated professor (Fig. 9). By the end of the fifteenth century, this image came to serve contemporaries. Perhaps this occurred because the identity of the master was traditionally composite, representing grammar, the author, and the schoolbook itself. Because contemporaries helped create the text by serving as compilers, translators, commentators, they too might be represented as the master figure. Very often the title leaves ambiguous whether the figure is the original classical author or the contemporary contributor, citing one above the illustration, the other below, as on an undated *Aesop* in the British Library (c.56.b.6) containing an often-copied, black-paneled cathedra with white floral decoration. Above the illustration appears the title "La Uita de Esopo Hystoriata" and below it the name of the translator, Francesco del Tuppo. Whom does the figure in cathedra represent? Aesop? the translator? the life of Aesop (i.e., the book of his life)? It no doubt stands for all three, since the master figure as emblem of grammar traditionally symbolized these things. First represented in this collective way, contemporaries next began to assume unambiguously the identity of the laureated master. A version of the Aesop woodcut appears both as Thibaldeo da Ferrara (1463–1534) on his 1519 *Opere* (Fig. 10) and as Pamphilo Sasso (c. 1455–1527) on his 1519 *Sonetti, Capitoli, Egloge*.[16]

This displacement of the classical author can be seen most clearly when the master with pupils is used to represent the classical author and his commentators. In such cases, the contemporary enters the iconography as the pupil, the word "discipulus" meaning both student and disciple. A 1497 woodcut of Terence in a three-tiered cathedra shows his commentators below him as students.[17] A 1510 *Epistles* of Ovid shows Ovid's commentators represented by three disciples and one schoolmaster (Fig. 11). (Or perhaps the schoolmaster is another illustration of Ovid: in our copy someone has tinted the two masters, creating a link between them.) In any case, a version of the upper illustration of this title page is also used on an edition of Horace's *Opere* to depict only four commentators, one of whom thus becomes the laureated master.[18] Further, the lower illustration on the Ovid title page is later used alone for Francesco Maria Grapaldi (1465?–1515), designated laureate by the title, although not by a laurel crown.[19] In these examples we see the same woodcut used on different occasions for the classical master and a contemporary disciple. This transference of the laurel is more explicitly visualized in a 1494 *Historia* of Herodotus, which shows the classical author crowning his translator.[20] These woodcuts express not just the printer's indifferent granting of honors, but his exploitation of a particular notion of authorship: the "author" is the sum of all authorial enterprise producing the text.

The fifteenth- and sixteenth-century Italians who were presented as laureated masters included many grammarians. For example, Guarinus Veronensis (1374–1460), humanist, scholar, schoolmaster, and university professor, is depicted on the title page of his 1488 *Grammaticales regulae* in the opening initial, wearing a laurel and pointing to his text.[21] A more typical format is that of the portrait of Joannes Policarpus Severitanus (1470–1525?) on an edition of Donatus containing his commentary (Fig. 12), and that of Gasparino Barzizza (1370–1431) on the 1518 edition of his *Vocabolarium*.[22] Both illustrations conflate the scholar with the schoolmaster by adding a student to the scholar's study. A modern format is the bust composition, seen both on the 1519 *De syllabarum quantitate* of Joannes Quintianus (1484–1537)[23] and a 1516 *De partibus aedium* of Francesco Maria Grapaldi (Fig. 13). Both laureated authors hold pen and scraping knife, recalling the old scholar, although now they are shown half-length and full-face. Since not all of these individuals received the laurel in an official ceremony, we may assume printers are drawing on the connection between the discipline of grammar and the laurel created by Petrarch when he made his own ceremony academic.

Poets, too, were represented as laureated masters. The poet Pamphilo Sasso was mentioned, and another poet was Bernardo Accolti (1458–1535), who is shown on a 1515 edition of his *Sonetti* as a scholar in his study being crowned with a wreath by an angel, a reference perhaps to his appointment by Leo X as a writer in the Curia.[24] Another example is the lovely Venetian woodcut used first to represent the poet Francesco degli Stabili (1269–1327) on a 1501 edition of his astrological poem *Acerba* (Fig. 14).[25] Fra Robert Caracciolo (1425–95), famous for his theatrical interludes to the Mass written in Italian verse, appears as a laureated master in a 1524 edition of his sermons.[26] These poets might appear as professors because poet and teacher were historically identified within the discipline and iconography of grammar. The association was modernized when Petrarch, in his coronation ceremony, represented the poet laureate as a university master. One eventual result was that the meanings of this figure were narrowed. It once was a composite figure signifying the author, language, and the text. It was the visual counterpart to the anonymous voice of countless prefaces and prologues, wherein many sorts of authorial contributors from successive ages merged. Now the master became a factotum for specific individuals, a picture to accompany a contemporary name and a way to advertise its intellectual authority. The effect was to clarify that ambiguity about identity which had held suspended the figure's multiple meanings.

IV

In the 1480s, William Caxton introduced the figure of the master into English printed books, employing it as both an author portrait and an emblem of grammar. His *Myrrour of the worlde* (1481; STC 24762) contains four master and pupils scenes. For example, a master (instead of the more usual scholar) serves as an author portrait at the head of the prologue (Fig. 15). Three other masters in the text represent the arts of grammar, logic, and rhetoric, revealing some emblematic borrowing from grammar, although only the grammar master holds a whip. The second book, *Paruus Chato* (1481[?]; STC 4852), uses two masters from the *Myrrour,* one after the title, the other at the end.

The title cut of the *Paruus Chato* is that of the *Myrrour*'s grammar master (Fig. 16), used because this is a language book. The figure infolds into itself the meanings of author and textbook, just as the emblem of grammar traditionally did. On the one hand, the title, *Hic incipit paruus Chato* ("Here begins the little Cato" or "Here begins Cato's little book") represents the illustration as an author portrait, just like the one beginning the *Myrrour*. But the illustration also stands for the book itself, in the same way that the "Chato" of the title stands, metonymically, for the book written by Cato. This use of the author's name for his book has a special history in textbooks. By the thirteenth century, the scholastics had taken over the grammar curriculum, promoting rules of language discovered by logic rather than the study of literature. As a result, the word "auctore," French *autor* or *auctor,* Latin *auctor* or *actor,* which originally meant "ancient classical Latin poet," he who provided a model for the formulation of correct Latin, came to refer to the little reading books used as elementary school texts written by these authors: the *Cato, Aesopus, Avianus,* for example.[27] Thus, one word, "auctore," meant both the "author" and "schoolbook." The figure of the master is, I believe, a visual pun on the word "auctore," using a picture of the author to signify a schoolbook.

All three of these meanings for the illustration of the master—the master as image of the author, emblem of grammar, and sign that the book is a school text—come into play when Wynkyn de Worde used it to promote Robert Whittinton as poet laureate, one important precedent for the Skelton woodcut. In 1513, de Worde began advertising Robert Whittinton on the title pages of his grammar books as England's laureate: *Robert Whittintoni lichefeldiensis grāmatices magistri & prothouatis anglie, ī florentissima Oxoniensi academia laureati* ("Robert Whittinton of Lichfield, teacher of grammar and chief poet of England, laureate in the most flourishing academy at Oxford"). Thereafter, an illustration of a master sometimes accompanied the title. For example, de Worde's most-used master (he had three woodblocks of the design) was included in the 1516, 1517, and 1518 editions of Whittinton's *De concinnitates grāmatices* (Fig. 17). In 1518 he used a new cut, the so-called melancholy scholar, on a Whittinton school text (Fig. 18). Finally, in about 1519, de Worde acquired a new master, used only four times but each time for Whittinton (Fig. 19). All these books describe Whittinton as teacher of grammar, chief poet of England, and poet laureate, as part of a campaign to promote him and his books. The result was to further publicize the already existing relationship between the laureate and the grammarian.

A master on Charles Kyrfoth's *Compotus manualis ad vsū Oxoniēsiū* (1519; STC 5613; Fig. 20) is the second predecessor of the Skelton woodcut and perhaps provides a gloss on the Whittinton illustration. Combining instruction on the ecclesiastical calendar with basic Latin verses to be memorized, the work is a school text for young arts students at Oxford.[28] The inclusion of armillary, clock, and globe indicates that this illustration has some relation to woodblock planet books, to illustrations therein of Mercury as god of arts and crafts, whose various children are shown using the instruments of their trade.[29] The schoolmaster has a whip, the tool through which his craft is practiced. What the whip stands for, in addition to the use of corporeal punishment as a tool to learning, is, most likely, the "rules of language": the whip had replaced the file which, in the early iconography of grammar, was divided into eight sections signifying the eight parts of speech (the foundation for any approach to language instruction by precept). Perhaps the master came to represent on Whittinton's texts the study of language through rules rather than authors, one side of the grammarians' war going on at this time, and that for which Whittinton was the chief spokesman.

The de Worde and Kyrfoth masters reflect an existing relationship between the laureate and the university grammar degree. At Oxford, the laurel was sometimes given with the lesser degrees of grammar and rhetoric. Men who had been schoolmasters could get these degrees by petitioning the university and fulfilling some minor requirements, like verses in praise of the university or a public lecture. Robert Whittinton was one of two schoolmasters who received the laurel in this way. Several other graduates were not given it (one Thomas More included), although they fulfilled similar requirements.[30] Given this background, we must wonder what contemporaries made of the title, particularly what status it had. In "Agenst Garnesche," Skelton's response to Garnesche suggests that his opponent may have attacked the office not just the man: "I am a laureat, I am no Lorell."[31]

In John Skelton's life and poetry, the laureateship is associated with the grammar master. Although the records at Oxford for this period are lost, we know from Caxton[32] and from Skelton that he, like Whittinton, received the laurel with his degree at Oxford. Perhaps it was the grammar or rhetoric degree, for Skelton concludes a description of his laureation at Oxford

> A Kynge to me myn habyte[33] gave
> At Oxforth, the universyte,
> Avaunsid I was to that degre;
> By hole consent of theyr senate,
> I was made poete lawreate (*AG* v, ll. 80–84)

by alluding to himself as master to the prince:

> It plesyth that noble prince roiall
> Me as hys master for to calle
> In hys lernyng primordiall. (*AG* v, ll. 95–105)

Nine years later, however, the 1523 *Garland of Laurel* little recalled the origin of the laurel at Oxford. Skelton depicts himself as the servant of Pallas, and Pallas as "Madame Regent of the Seven Sciences" (l. 53), that is, a member of the arts faculty at the university. But Madame Regent has been transformed from university master into the mythological figure of Wisdom.

The image of the laureate found on Skelton's *Agaynste a Comely Coystrowne* and *Dyuers Balettys* belongs with the earlier English grammar masters. Like the Kyrfoth figure, he is at a desk; and the relation of his hands to the two books in front of him is nearly identical to that of the Kyrfoth teacher, both deriving from illustrations of scribes copying a book on a stand into another book on a desk. The figure representing Skelton, however, is a considerably revised version of the grammar master. He sits in an elaborate cathedra indistinguishable from a pulpit, one which includes a canopy of Gothic style from the north. Also, the schoolmaster's whip has been discarded to create the look of a university professor; the pupils have disappeared, giving place, presumably, to the readers; and the laureate's importance is asserted in a caption taken from the end of the *Garland of Laurel,* which translates: "All kinds of trees yield to the laurel."

The designer of this woodcut has understood the new laureate, the intellectual and religious claims that he asserted. What the history of woodcut laureates tells us is that both authors and printers went to considerable effort to promote an image supporting those claims.

Figures

Figure 1: Skelton, John, *Agaynste a comely Coystrowne*. N.p., n.d. Reproduced by permission of The Huntington Library, San Marino, California (HEH 59200).

Figure 2: Baltimore, The Walters Art Gallery, *Ms. W. 761*, f.196v.

Figure 3: Durham, University Library, *Cosin Ms. V. III. 1*, f.22v.

Figure 4: London, British Library, *Royal Ms. 10 A XIII*, f.2v.

Figure 5: *Reparationes lectionum et exercitiorum Novae logicae Aristotelis*. Cologne: H. Quentell, 1507. Bayerische Staatsbibliothek Munchen (Inc.c.a. 1825^g/1).

Figure 6: Braunschweig, Hieronymus, *Liber de arte distillandi*. Strassburg: J. Grüeninger, 1500. By permission of the British Library (IB.1495).

Figure 7: Michault, Pierre, *Le Doctrinal du Temps Présent*. Lyon: l'Abuzé en court, c. 1484. From the collections in the Rare Book and Special Collections Division, The Library of Congress.

Figure 8: Michault, Pierre, *Le Doctrinal du Temps Présent*. Lyon: l'Abuzé en court, c. 1484. From the collections in the Rare Book and Special Collections Division, The Library of Congress.

Figure 9: Aesopus, *Fabule hystoriate*. Trans. A. Zucco. Venice: A. de' Zanni, 1528. By permission of Houghton Library, Harvard University.

Figure 10: Thibaldeo da Ferrara, *Opere*. Venice: G. de Monteferrato, 1519. Biblioteca Universitaria di Napoli.

Figure 11: Ovidius Naso, Publius, *Epistolae Heroidum Ouidii*. Taurin: J. Angelum & B. Fratres de Sylva, 1517. From a copy in the Rare Book Collection, University of North Carolina Library, Chapel Hill.

Figure 12: Donatus, Aelius, *De octo orationis partibus libri octo*. Commentary by J. Severitanus. Perugia: C. Bianchino, 1517. By permission of Houghton Library, Harvard University.

Figure 13: Grapaldi, Francesco Maria. *De partibus aedium*. Parma: for A. Quintianus, 1516. By permission of Houghton Library, Harvard University.

Figure 14: Peckham, John, *Perspectiua communis*. Venice: for G. B. Sessa, 1504. By permission of Houghton Library, Harvard University.

Figure 15: Vincentius, Bellovancensis, *Here begynneth the book callid the myrrour of the worlde*. Trans. W. Caxton. Westminister: W. Caxton, 1481. Reproduced by permission of The Huntington Library, San Marino, California (HEH 69795).

Figure 16: Cato, Dionysius, *Paruus Chato.* Westminister: W. Caxton, c. 1481. John Rylands University Library of Manchester.

Figure 17: Whittinton, Robert. *Editio de concinnitate grammatices et constructione.* London: W. de Worde, 1517. Oxford University, Bodleian Library (Mason H.45, t.p.).

Figure 18: Whittinton, Robert. *Editio de concinnitate grammatices & cōstructione.* London: W. de Worde, 1517. Reproduced by permission of The Huntington Library, San Marino, California (HEH 59568).

Figure 19: Whittinton, Robert. *De heteroclitis nominibus.* London: W. de Worde, c. 1517. Reproduced by permission of The Huntington Library, San Marino, California (HEH 59566).

Figure 20: *Compotus manualis ad vsū Oxoniesiū.* Oxford: C. Kyrfoth, 1519. By permission of the Syndics of Cambridge University Library (Sel.5.42).

1

2

3

4

5

6

7

8

9

10

11

12

Francisci Marii Grapaldi:poetæ Laureati:de Partibus Aedium:Addita
modo:Verborum explicatione:Quæ in eodem libro:continen
tur:Opus Sane elegans:& eruditum:tum propter Mul
tiagant:Variarum rerum:Lectionem:cū propter
M.Vitruuii & Cornelii Celsi:emaculatas
dictiones:Quæ apud ipsos:Vel
Mēdosæ:Vel obscuræ:
Videbātur.

13

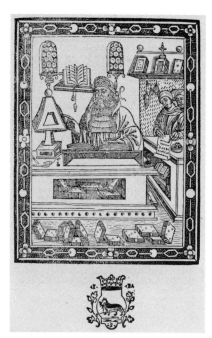

14

After this foloweth the Recapitulacion of the thinges
aforsaid capitulo   cxviij.
Hier endeth the table of the Rubrices of this
present book.

Prologue declaryng to whom this book apperteyneth

Consideryng
that wordes ben
perisshyng/vayne / ꝫ
forgetful/And Wri
tynges duelle'ꝫ abi
de permanēt/as I rede
Voy audita perit/lit
tera scripta manet /
Thise thinges haue
caused that the faites
and dedes of Ayncyent men ben sette by declaracion in
fair andy flourned volumes/to thende that science and
Artes lerned andy founden of thinges passedy myght be
hady in perpetuel memorye andy remembraunce/ffor the
hertes of nobles in eschewyng of ydlenes at suche tyme
as they haue none other vertuouse ocupacōn on hand ought
texercise them in redyng/studyng/ꝫ visytyng the noble
faytes andy dedes of the sage and wysemen somtyme tra
uaillyng in prouffytable vertues/of whom it hapeth ofte
that somen ben enclynedy to visyte the bookes treatyng
of sciences particuler/Andy other to rede ꝫ visyte bookes
spekyng of faytes of armes/of loue/or of other marueill:

a.4.

15

Hic incipit paruus Cato

Um sia aduertere quam hies grauiter errare
whan I aduerte in my remembraunce
And see how fele folkes erren greuously
In the Wey of vertuous gouernaunce
I haue supposedy in myn herte that I
Ought to supporte and counceyl prudently
Them to be vertuous in lyuyng
And how they shal them self in honour bryng
Igitur fili carissime doceo te quo pacto mores
Therfore my leue chyldy I shal now telle the
Herken me wel the maner and the guyse
How thy sowle inward shal acqueyntedy be
With thewes good and vertues in al wyse
Rede and conceyue for he is to dyspyse
That redyth ay and note not What it ment

a.ij.

16

CRoberti Whittintoni lichfeldiensis grā
matices magistri ⁊ prothouatis anglie in
florentissima Oxoniensi academia laure
ati. Editio de concinnitate grammatices
et constructione.

17

CRoberti Whittintoni lichfeldiensis grā
matices magistri ⁊ prothouatis Anglie in
florentiss ma Oxoniensi academia laurea
ti. Editio de concinnitate grammatices ⁊ cō
structione.

18

CDe heteroclitis nominibus
C Editio roberti whittintoni lichfeldien
sis Gramatice magistri ⁊ prothouatis An
glie in florentissima Oxoniensi academia
laureati de heteroclitis nominibus ⁊ gradi
bus comparationis

CTetrastichon eiusdē ad lectorem.

Protheos vt possis varios dinoscere vultus
Cyrelie sexus ambiguosqȝ senis
Salmacidos ne vndis coeant heteroclita mixta
Hoc whittintoni voluito lector opus

CDistichon eiusdem in zoilum.

Cornua rhinoceros/dentem ni zoile ponas
Sanguinolēta feret tela hecatebeletes

19

CCompotus manualis
a) b.ū Oxoniēsi.

20

NOTES

1. Both are undated and without the printer's name. For evidence that John Rastell printed them between 1524 and 1529, see Robert S. Kinsman, "The Printer and Date of Publication of Skelton's *Agaynste a Comely Coystrowne* and *Dyuers Balettys,*" *Huntington Library Quarterly* 16 (1953), 203–10. I do not mean to suggest that this woodcut is a likeness of Skelton or was made with him as the subject, only that it was used by the printer with the intention of referring to him. For a more complete statement of the way in which the woodcut "represents" Skelton, as well as for a discussion of its iconographical background, see Mary Erler, "Early Woodcuts of John Skelton: The Uses of Convention," *Bulletin of Research in the Humanities* 87 (1987 for 1986), forthcoming.

2. On the medieval grammar curriculum as, in part, the interpretation of authors, see, for example, Ernst R. Curtius, *European Literature in the Latin Middle Ages,* trans. Willard R. Trask (New York: Pantheon Books, 1953), pp. 88–89; and Louis J. Paetow, *The Arts Course at Medieval Universities with Special Reference to Grammar and Rhetoric,* University of Illinois Studies, 3, no. 7 (Urbana-Champaign, Ill.: University Press, 1910), pp. 12–13.

3. Martianus Capella, "The Marriage of Philology and Mercury," vol. II of *Martianus Capella and the Seven Liberal Arts,* trans. William Harris Stahl et al. (New York: Columbia University Press, 1977). Appendix A contains a bibliographical survey of the iconography of the seven liberal arts in the Middle Ages and Renaissance.

4. Martianus, "Marriage of Philology and Mercury," p. 68 (Book III, Section 231).

5. The figure is reproduced in Raimond Marle, *Iconographie de l'art profane au moyen-age et à la renaissance* (Le Haye: Matinus Nijhoff, 1931), II, Fig. 249.

6. See A. M. Friend, Jr., "The Portraits of the Evangelists in Greek and Latin Manuscripts," *Art Studies* 5 (1927), esp. pp. 143–46.

7. The figures are discussed in Adolf Katzenellenbogen, "The Representation of the Seven Liberal Arts," in *Twelfth Century Europe and the Foundations of Modern Society,* ed. Marshall Claggett, Gaines Post, and Robert Reynolds (Madison: University of Wisconsin Press, 1961), pp. 39–55.

8. Raymond Klibansky, Erwin Panofsky, and Fritz Saxl, *Saturn and Melancholy* (Cambridge: W. Heffer & Sons, 1964), p. 311.

9. See Christopher Walter, *Iconographie des Conciles dans la Tradition Byzantine* (Paris: Institut Français d'Etudes Byzantines, 1970), pp. 220–26. Other paleo-Christian examples of Christ in cathedra with the apostolic college can be found in *Die Malereien der Katakomben Roms,* ed. Joseph Wilpert (Freiburg: Herdersche Verlagshandlung, 1903), II, pls. 148, 155, 177, 193. The classical cathedra was also a chair for women; perhaps as a conflation of this usage with its pedagogical associations, it persists in the iconography of Mary and the Christ Child receiving the Three Wise Men.

Literature on the cathedra as episcopal throne is scarce but includes "Chaire," *Dictionnaire raisonné de l'architecture française du XIe au XVIe siècle* (1895); "Cathedra," *The Catholic Encyclopedia* (1908); F. E. Howard and F. H. Crossley, "Bishop's

Thrones," in *English Church Woodwork*, 2d ed. (New York: Charles Scribners' Sons; London: B. T. Batsford, 1927), pp. 191–95; Alexander Nesbitt, "Cathedrea, or Episcopal Chairs, and Benches for the Clergy," in "On the Churches of Rome Earlier than the Year 1150," *Archaeologia* 40 (1866), 215–16; C. A. Ralegh Radford, "The Bishop's Throne in Norwich Cathedral," *Archaeological Journal* 116 (1959), 15–34; J. Charles Cox and Alfred Harvey, "Thrones and Chairs," in their *English Church Furniture* (1907; Yorkshire: EP Publishing, 1973), pp. 248–55.

On the professorial chair, see Florens Deuchler, "Magister in Cathedra: Lehrer und Schuler im Mittelalter," in *Schülerfestgabe für Herbert von Einem* (Bonn: Kunsthistorisches Institut der Universität Bonn, 1965), pp. 63–69; and Emil Reicke, *Lehrer und Unterrichtswesen in der deutschen Vergangenheit* (Jena: Eugen Diederichs, 1924), and *Der Gelehrte in der deutschen Vergangenheit* (Jena: Eugen Diederichs, 1924).

10. "Chaire Episcopale," *Dictionnaire d'archéologie chrétienne et de liturgie* (1914).

11. Karl Baus et al., *The Imperial Church from Constantine to the Early Middle Ages*, trans. Anselm Biggs (London: Burns & Oates, 1980), II, 286.

12. Hastings Rashdall, *The Universities of Europe in the Middle Ages*, ed. F. M. Powicke and A. B. Emden, 2d ed. (London: Oxford University Press, 1936), pp. 228, 285.

13. On the claim of universities to have religious authority, see Guy Fitch Lytle, "Universities as Religious Authorities in the Later Middle Ages," in *Reform and Authority in the Medieval and Reformation Church*, ed. G. F. Lytle (Washington, D.C.: Catholic University of America Press, 1981), pp. 69–97.

14. On the coronation of Petrarch, see Ernest Hatch Wilkins, *The Making of the "Canzoniere" and Other Petrarchan Studies* (Rome: Edizioni di Storia e Letteratura, 1951), pp. 9–69. As Wilkins points out, Albertino Mussato's coronation, also an academic one, anticipated Petrarch's. Petrarch knew of it and was influenced by it when he devised and popularized his own. What relation, if any, existed between the laurel and the universities before Mussato remains obscure. Petrarch's oration is available in English translation in E. H. Wilkins, *Studies in the Life and Works of Petrarch* (Cambridge, Mass: Medieval Academy of America, 1955), pp. 300ff.

15. Wilkins, *Studies*, p. 305. On post-Petrarchan coronations, see J. B. Trapp, "The Owl's Ivy and the Poet's Bays," *JWCI* 21 (1958), esp. pp. 247–52, and J. B. Trapp, "The Poet Laureate: Rome, *Renovatio* and *Translatio Imperii*," in *Rome in the Renaissance: The City and the Myth*, ed. P. A. Ramsey (Binghamton, N.Y.: Center for Medieval and Early Renaissance Studies, 1982), pp. 93–130.

16. Both books were printed in Venice by G. de Monteferrato.

17. First cut for Lazzaro de' Soardi of Venice in 1497; see Harvard College Library, Dept. of Printing and Graphic Arts, *Catalogue of Books and Manuscripts. Part I: French Sixteenth Century Books*, comp. Ruth Mortimer (Cambridge, Mass.: Belknap Press of Harvard University Press, 1964), II, #495.

18. Horatius (Quintus) Flaccus, *Horatius cum quattuor commentariis* (Venice: Joannes Alvisius de Varisio, 1498), title page; reproduced in Prince d'Essling, *Les Livres à Figures Vénitiens de la Fin au XVe Siècle et du Commencement du XVIe* (Florence: Leo S. Olschki, Paris: Henri Leclerc, 1929), II, pt. 2, #1164.

19. On the title page of *Francisco Marii Grapaldi poetae laureati: de partibus Aedium* (Turin: Jo. Angelum & Berardinum de Sylua, 1517). The woodcut is

reproduced in Bersano Begey, *Le Cinquecentim Piemontesi* (Torino: Tipografia Torinese Editrice, 1961), I, 22.

20. Printed in Venice by F. & G. de Gregori; reproduced in Francesco Barberi, *Il Frontespizo nel Libro Italiano del Quattrocento e del Cinquecento* (Milano: Il Polifilo, 1969), Fig. 9.

21. Printed in Venice by Nicolaus dictus Castilia; reproduced in Essling, II, pt. 1, #315.

22. Printed in Perugia by Cosimo Bianchino Veronese; reproduced in Max Sander, *Le livre à figures italien depuis 1467 jusqu'à 1530* (New York: G. E. Stechert & Co., 1941), VI, no. 727. In this illustration the features of the laureated master are so undefined that he appears more a personification of grammar than a portrait.

23. Printed in Venice by G. de Monteferrato; reproduced in Essling, II, pt. 2, #2036.

24. Printed in Venice by N. Zoppino and V. de Polo; reproduced in Essling, II, pt. 2, #1833. The title describes Accolti as "scriptore apostolico & abreuiatore." Information on positions for writers in the Curia, including the offices of scriptor and abbreviator, can be found in John F. D'Amico, *Renaissance Humanism in Papal Rome* (Baltimore: The Johns Hopkins University Press, 1983), esp. pp. 21–26.

25. The woodcut is later used to represent the English Archbishop John Peckham in his *Perspectina communis* (Venice: for Giovanni Battista Sessa, 1504).

26. *Prediche* (Venice: Jo. Tacuino, 1524), title page; reproduced in Sander, V, #352. The same design was used earlier for Gasparinus Bergomensis [Gasparino Barzizza], *Vocabularium breve* (Venice: 1516), title page; and Albertus Magnus, *De virtutibus herbarum* (Venice: 1508), title page, reproduced in Essling, I. pt. 2, 267.

27. On the "auctores," see Paetow, *Arts Course,* pp. 53–54, and his *Two Medieval Satires on the University of Paris,* Memoirs of the University of California, 4, nos. 1–2, ed. Armin Leuschner (Berkeley: University of California Press, 1927), p. 37; Gérard Marie Paré, *Les Idées et les lettres au XIII siècle: Le Roman de la Rose* (Montreal: Centre de Psychologie et de Pédagogie, 1947), p. 16.

28. E. Bosanquet, *English Printed Almanacs and Prognostications: A Bibliographical History to 1600* (London: Bibliographical Society, 1917), p. 50.

29. See the Mercury woodcuts in F. Lippmann, trans. F. Courbin, *Les Sept Planètes* (Paris: Société Internationale Chalcographique, 1895), esp. pl. D6.

30. For the few facts about the relation of the laurel to these degrees and several possible interpretations, see E. K. Broadus, *The Laureateship* (1921; reprint, Freeport, N.Y.: Books for Libraries Press, 1969), pp. 12–23; William Nelson, *John Skelton, Laureate* (New York: Columbia University Press, 1939), pp. 40–47; H. L. R. Edwards, *Skelton* (London: Jonathan Cape, 1949), pp. 34–38. See Edwards, p. 260, for references to older discussions of this topic. Information on the status of grammar and rhetoric at the universities may be found in W. Keith Percival, "Grammar and Rhetoric in the Renaissance," in *Renaissance Eloquence,* ed. James J. Murphy (Berkeley: University of California Press, 1983), pp. 303–30. William Nelson, "Thomas More, Grammarian and Orator," *PMLA* 57 (1943), 337–52, argues that the Thomas More who received the grammar degree from Oxford was the humanist More and implies that the humanists held the university grammar degree in high regard.

31. "Agenst Garnesche," iii. Lines 96–100 read: "Yower termys ar to grose, / To far from the porpose, / To contaminate / And to violate / The dygnyte lauryate." All quotations from Skelton's poetry are from *John Skelton: The Complete English Poems*, ed. John Scattergood (New Haven, Conn.: Yale University Press, 1983).

32. In the prologue to his translation of the Eneydos, c. 1490, aii[r–v]. The reference, along with other contemporary comments on Skelton as laureate, may be found in Anthony S. G. Edwards, ed., *Skelton: The Critical Heritage* (London: Routledge & Kegan Paul, 1981).

33. The "habit" of these lines has been interpreted as an actual dress given to Skelton at this time by the king. Critics point to Skelton's earlier comment that he wears the king's colors (*AG*, ll. 137–41) and to his remark in "Calliope" that he wears the name of "calliope" ("Regent of poetes al") embroidered in letters of silk and gold (ll. 1–12). It seems also possible that "habit" may be a reference to a state of being, used by Skelton to link his own laureation to Petrarch's (Petrarch was given an actual robe by King Robert; see Wilkins, *Making of the "Canzoniere,"* pp. 49–50) or a dress that Skelton later devised for himself. Apparently the laureate costume worn by the Kyrfoth master is quite fanciful: see E. C. Clark, "College Caps and Doctors Hats," *Archaeological Journal* 61 (1904), esp. pp. 68–69.

PHILIPPE DESAN

The Tribulations of a Young Poet: Ronsard from 1547 to 1552

The poet has always been accorded a status well set off from that of other members of society. Poetic production and everyday necessities coexist only with difficulty, for the Muses' elect would seem to have other preoccupations than imagining themselves members of a civil and industrious society. The spirituality of poetry transcending material needs, the poet would subsist merely on rhymes and sparkling water, or even, as with Celadon in *L'Astrée,* on "cress and tears"; his always-gratuitous production would demand no real work. The image that we have of the poet is that of a demigod blackening pages of a book under the impulse of genius—no trace of monotonous labor. The poet simply grazes the surface of each page, pouring out illuminated visions; in the evening he falls asleep in peace and dreams of other poems, more beautiful still.

Clearly this is all a myth. Yet, as Claude Lévi-Strauss has effectively shown, we often organize our universe around myths which consequently become reality. One would then have to accept this nebulous idea of the poet. Nevertheless, the children of Calliope are also human beings, and must therefore pay their debts and feed themselves. Some among them even go so far as to consider their "art" a profession. It is this perception of poetry as *remunerable* work and the poet's self-recognition as a member of a market economy that interests me here.

Given the complete confusion of social stratification and the importance of poetry during the period, the sixteenth century would appear to be the privileged locus for the consideration of problems related to the mode of existence and the professional status of the poet in the midst of civil society. By poet, in this study, I mean male poet. There is some poetry written by women during the Renaissance, but it is a fact that the great majority of these women were already wealthy before they started writing. They belonged overwhelmingly to the aristocracy or the rising bourgeoisie, so for them poetry was never a way to make a living.

Marguerite de Navarre is one very typical example. Likewise, Louise Labé, the daughter of a rich rope-maker from Lyon, obviously did not need to write poetry to earn a living. The opportunity to overcome social stratification and to become professionally successful as a poet was limited to men in the sixteenth century. Poetry was first perceived as a profession by men, and it is not a coincidence that the Pléiade poets were all men.

I will therefore take the poets of the Pléiade as the point of departure of my analysis, and will more particularly analyze the case of the young Ronsard who, in 1550, presents himself on the employment market with the hope of living off his pen. The period I consider in this study extends from 1547 to 1552; these dates, although somewhat arbitrary, correspond to the years when Ronsard started writing his first poems (1547) and when he received his first real financial reward for his poetry and became curé of Marolles (1552). Yet, in order to understand the professional path of Ronsard and the other poets of the Pléiade, it is necessary first to discuss the social structure of France during the sixteenth century.

The social organization of the French Renaissance is marked by the structural prevalence of three orders: the clergy, the nobility—further divided into *noblesse d'épée* and *noblesse de robe* —and finally the Third Estate, which embraces the rest of the people. This static organization, however, suffered a crisis as a result of the decline of the *noblesse d'épée* and the rise of the city bourgeoisie, which aspired to the rank of nobility through the purchase of offices and charges. The members of this new class arising out of the Third Estate were most often educated in the best universities and occupied the key posts in the state bureaucratic apparatus. These *robins* thus became jurisconsults, lawyers, procurators, intendants, and city councillors. The sale of offices allowed them to rise rapidly within the social hierarchy and to entitle themselves *sieurs* and even *gentilshommes.*[1] In order to cover rising state expenditures caused by costly wars, the king was forced to multiply the number of offices which could be purchased. Under Henri II the sale of these offices increased with a rapidity that inflamed further the antagonism between the "old" nobility and the younger rising class.[2]

The social inertia which had prevented mobility within French society for centuries, and which had thus preserved the stability and fixity of that society, was abruptly shattered, and "passage" from one order to another suddenly appeared possible for the first time. Money transformed lifestyles, offered a means to success, and became the object of much coveting. If one possessed sufficient savings, for example, one could buy an office; financial security would then often be guaranteed. But this means of social assertion had an important disadvantage, for the obligations connected with the office had to be conducted in person and the delegation of duties was not permitted. Thus, the officer was constrained to reside continuously and permanently where his office was located. One can easily understand why this "mode of subsistence" never became popular among the poets, who could not accept the restriction of residence imposed by François I in 1535 and reaffirmed in 1539. The poet of the sixteenth century had to follow his patron and move about constantly according to the dictates of the market. Further, if we consider the Pléiade poets, we see that most of them could not aspire to the most profitable offices because they did not possess the necessary capital to buy the best charges. The military profession, needless to say, also did not give the freedom of movement required by the poet. Strategies of social mobility were consequently quite restricted for those who decided to embark on a literary occupation.

Looking more closely at the lifestyle of the sixteenth-century poets, we find that the majority of these poets received their revenues in the form of ecclesiastical benefices, prebends, and sinecures in abbeys, rectories, and priories. They thus depended on the ecclesiastical order for survival and surrendered themselves almost completely to what Henri Weber has judiciously called "the chase for benefices."[3] How is this at-first-glance-baffling "vocation" to be explained? The answer lies in the manner in which ecclesiastical benefices were distributed during the sixteenth century. After the Concordat of Bologne (1516) between François I and Leo X, the so-called simple benefices could be granted directly by the king without referring to Rome. The concordat had in fact suppressed the election imposed by the Pragmatic Sanction for the regular benefices. These benefices were now at the disposal of the French sovereign, who had the power to recompense whomever he wanted under the condition that the recipient of the ecclesiastical benefice receive the tonsure. Even though residency was required for these simple benefices, there existed nonetheless the possibility of "legitimate" excuses, which opened the path to nonresidency. Charles Loyseau, a jurist at the end of the sixteenth century who has left us a treatise on the right to offices and benefices during this period, tells us that "the Casuists presently hold that the inveterate practices and customs excuse the necessity of residence on the location of the simple benefices."[4] It was permitted as well to transfer the task associated with the benefice onto someone else while continuing to receive the revenue associated with this benefice. Loyseau explains the attraction of such an indulgence: "Thus, the exercise rendered separable from the title, the labor from the payment, the office from the benefice, in short the spiritual from the temporal, the majority of the beneficiaries have had little trouble retaining the title and revenue of their benefice while discharging on others the labor of serving the poor."[5]

Only these simple benefices exempted the beneficiary from living in residence. They were in fact revenues with no obligation; this explains why these "simple benefices . . . consist more of revenue than of personal function."[6] It should not surprise us then if rectories, priories, presbyteries, and abbeys were much sought after by the poets and artists of the sixteenth century. Loyseau remarks on this subject that, during this time, "there is a large company of almoners, chaplains and clerks"[7] and that "one no longer chooses whom to award the offices of the Church, rather one gives the benefices to the men one wants to gratify."[8] Many poets thus chose to receive the tonsure and remained celibate so as to secure revenue from the ecclesiastical benefices they were awarded for having praised the prince. Such is the case with Ronsard, Du Bellay, Baïf, Pontus de Thyard, and a large number of their contemporaries. For example, from 1553 to 1557 the Vendômois poet was accorded the benefices of four provincial rectories.[9]

These benefices, however, were not so easily procured, and the poet who wanted to gain the favors of highly placed persons had to compose all sorts of occasional poems and commissioned pieces. Regarding the function of "official poet," Raymond Lebègue counts no fewer than six important tasks demanded of the poet: (1) to eulogize the king, his family, and the highest civil servants, (2) to celebrate the events of the royal family, (3) to serve the royal politics in verse, (4) to contribute to court feasts, (5) to produce amorous poems on command, and (6) to provide occasional pieces.[10] It should also be noted that the pecuniary advantages of this post were far from being proportional to the prestige of such a function, and, despite the affirmations of Ronsard's first biographer, Claude Binet, our poet, though he received in 1554 the title of *poëte ordinaire du Roy*, was never fully paid for his services to Henri II.[11] It is only when Charles IX offered his patronage to the *Franciade* in 1560 that Ronsard was finally guaranteed shelter from material difficulties.

A substantial network of responsibilities and constraints, all bound to the profession of the poet, emerged in the sixteenth century and forces us to resituate poetic production within its larger socioeconomic context. The work of Ronsard attests to this constant awareness of and preoccupation with material security. In fact, Ronsard, who eventually became the greatest of the Pléiade poets, was compelled, at the beginning of his career, to establish himself among his fellow poets and to "make a living" laboriously before becoming the prince of poets. The competition was quite stiff at this time. If we take as a point of reference the number of poets who published their verses between 1545 and 1565 in the hope of attracting princely favors, we discover that the market for poetry was more than saturated. Of more than two thousand authors indexed by La Croix du Maine in his *Bibliothèque françoise*, approximately one-fourth are accorded the title of "poet." When Ronsard presented himself on the market as a poet in 1550 he not only had to attract the attention of the prince but also had to distinguish himself from the rest of his colleagues. While toying with the Muses, Ronsard had to seek the support of patrons who would allow him to devote himself entirely to his art without any pecuniary worries. The *Odes* demonstrate well this desire to overcome material problems. I now propose to read the *Odes* as a poetic paradigm in which the poet presents, in an academic fashion, all his knowledge of the art of rhymes according to the highest of models: Pindar and Horace. In this respect, the *Odes* also accompany the search for an occupation, and thus function as the young poet's request for employment.

In 1550, the poets attached to the king were François Habert—one of the last *rhétoriqueurs*—and Mellin de Saint-Gelais, a stubborn defender of Marotic poetry, who, as a result of the respect due his age and his white beard, controlled poetic production at the court. Ronsard was not even next at this time. Philibert Delorme—who, between 1547 and 1548, obtained three abbeys from the king in recompense for his poems, which were much appreciated at the Louvre, and who directly participated in the royal entry of Henri II into Paris in 1549—certainly preceded Ronsard. The Vendômois poet still seemed a novice and his poetic production remained somewhat meager.

In 1549, with the intention of attracting the favors of the princes, our poet published his *Epithalame d'Antoine de Bourbon et Jeanne de Navarre,* a celebration of their marriage the previous year. This enterprise sought to find a rich patron upon whom Ronsard could bestow his lyre. Apparently the effort achieved nothing, as Jeanne de Navarre remained deaf to Ronsard's eulogistic demand for employment. After this negative experience, the poet concentrated his effort directly on the royal person, as he probably began to realize that in the domain of the arts there can be no compromising: the first poet of France must be the poet of the king. All the same, the task was not so simple, and Ronsard suffered setback after setback. In 1549, for example, he saw himself refused the organization of the various festivities planned for the royal entry of Henri II into Paris. Jean Martin and Thomas Sebillet, the latter having published the previous year his *Art Poëtique François,*[12] were to be in charge of the ceremonies. Nonetheless, Ronsard published for the occasion an *Avantentrée du Roi treschrestien à Paris,* but, once more, the poem was not a success and did not receive the attention anticipated.

Ronsard always considered the production of occasional verses an indispensable activity, for as Daniel Ménager has noted, "even though the Court gives no official command, a poet of the Renaissance, since he depends on the Prince, cannot simply exempt himself from this task."[13] All the poets of that time had to devote a good part of their artistic production to this exercise, and the anecdotes of Ronsard and Du Bellay writing epitaphs for the dogs of Charles IX and the sparrow of Marguerite of Savoy are famous.

In 1549, Ronsard also had his *Hymne de France* printed by Michel Vascosan. He ends the poem with an appeal to the king, imitating Virgil's *Georgics:*

> As your poet, having first dared
> To have composed a rhyme to praise you,
> I beg that my lyre suits your pleasure.[14]

Once more the enterprise failed to attract the king's attention. The poet nevertheless did not despair; he would only be satisfied once he had gained the king's support:

> But my soul is only ravished
> By a burning desire
> To dare to attempt a work
> Which would content my great king
> So that the work's honey-sweetness
> Would so anoint his ear
> That I might find it facile
> To importune him for my well-being.[15]

Direct access to the monarch remaining for the moment impossible, Ronsard solicited protectors in the entourage of Henri II. Since it was not possible to flatter the king's ears directly, being still too accustomed to the "small Petrarchan sonnets or some delicacies of love"[16] from Mellin de Saint-Gelais and his disciples, the young poet therefore had to create a network of influential "friends" that would bring him closer to the royal person. It is a matter of strategy: because Henri II refused to hear the young poet, it had to be through the detour of his entourage that the latter would approach him. This might explain why Ronsard dedicated several poems to courtiers susceptible of appreciation in an attempt to make his poetry known to the royal family.

Ronsard was engaged in a search for friends, and by "friend" it is necessary to understand someone capable of speaking favorably of his poems at the court. Friendship is here defined in terms of belonging to a network of individuals who choose to aid each other, everyone being ready to intervene for the other if a reciprocal action could be expected. In a society where social mobility is still relatively slow, this system of mutual help was the only "rapid" way to success. It was therefore necessary to allure the patronage of men who had sufficient power at the court and to offer them the possibility of gain so that the relation might be mutually "profitable." It is important to note that what we now call the Pléiade poets originally grouped themselves under the name of *Brigade* —a word which evokes well the idea of military formation according to strict rules of membership. Organization into a group permitted the poets to "tighten ranks" and form a school in order to confront better the resistance of the poets "in place."

It is therefore not an accident if, among the great number of poets distributed all over France at this time, Ronsard, Du Bellay, Baïf, Belleau, Jodelle, and La Péruse all attended two small Parisian *collèges*, both located on the hill of Sainte-Geneviève. Baïf, Ronsard, and Du Bellay were students and friends of Dorat at the Collège de Coqueret, while Belleau, La Péruse, and Jodelle attended the courses of Muret at the Collège de Boncourt. These two institutions were not to be counted among the most prestigious *collèges* of the capital. We could ask ourselves at this point if the success of these poets did not come precisely from the fact that they knew how to organize themselves into a school and push to the extreme that esprit de corps necessary for their personal success, for the members of the Brigade were from 1547 to 1552 to follow the same road to poetic and social success and thus share the same interests.

Of course, schools and coteries disputed among themselves as to who occupied first place; such is the case, for example, with those who opposed the Marotic tradition, defended by Mellin, to the "new" poetry of the Pléiade poets. Yet, in all cases we have a comparable organization: the individual has power only insofar as he is recognized by the influential members of his profession and sustained by the rich members of the court. In the case of Ronsard, it suffices to count the odes dedicated to Baïf, Du Bellay, Belleau, Peletier, and other poets and friends from the Collège de Coqueret—Julien Peccate, Bertran Berger, and René d'Urvoy for example—in order to account for the cohesion that existed at that time among individuals of the same profession.[17]

On this point, the example of Pierre Paschal is illustrative. A Gascon poet and friend of the Pléiade authors until 1558, Paschal let it be known that he was preparing to draft a book inspired by Paul Emile's *Vies et eloges des hommes illustres* in order to laud the members of the Brigade. All the poets concerned regarded this plan with a favorable eye and rewarded Paschal *in advance* by inserting into their poems several flattering references to him. Ronsard even dedicated an entire ode to Paschal. However, this "payment" in advance revealed itself to be a bad investment, as Paschal quickly forgot his project when he gained the favor of Henri II and accepted the post of royal historiographer in 1558. The poets of the Pléiade who, through their praise of the Gascon poet, had directly participated in the establishment of his renown and thereby played an important part in his ascension to such a sought-after post demonstrated their fury when they discovered that they had been duped and that they would receive nothing in return for their investment. Ronsard, particularly infuriated by this lack of gratitude, composed a Latin invective against Paschal entitled *Petri Paschali Elogium.*[18]

But the case of Paschal must ultimately be considered an exception. Other "friends" of Ronsard kept the bargain, "tit for tat" (*troque pour troq*) as the poet tells us. These "other friends" were particularly numerous at the court. In fact, the nobility and the ecclesiastical authorities represented the second important group that Ronsard had to seduce as they were, after all, the ones who held the purse strings and could assure a comfortable future to the poet. Ronsard had therefore "to sweeten the famous ones"[19] and transform himself into "a trumpeter / Of one and the other glory."[20] At this time his "shop [was] stocked with nothing but the drugs of praise and honor."[21] From 1547 to 1552 there were more important things for Ronsard to do than painting nature in rhyme. This would come later, after employment had been secured.

In order to succeed, Ronsard had to fight on two fronts: first he had to acquire a certain credit as a poet and, second, he needed to make himself sufficiently visible to the king to become the official poet. As Michel Dassonville points out, it is in the Pindaric ode, which had been introduced to Ronsard by his master, Dorat, that Ronsard saw the possibility of "reconciling the two ambitions which drove him for many years to please at the same time both the learned and the public at large."[22] Ronsard thus took for his model the greatest of Panhellenic poets who had been so skillful at capturing glory while at the same time accumulating an immense fortune for having lauded the rich citizens of Syracuse, Agrigente, Thebes, Argos, Athens, and Rhodes. As he rhymed his verses, Ronsard probably dreamed of the author of the *Olympics*, who had received 10,000 Athenian drachmas for having composed a dithyramb in honor of the Greek city.

Ronsard's project, however, did not unfold as expected—at least not at the beginning of the poet's career. Glory does not necessarily accompany material success. In attempting to gain both at once, the poet found himself confronted by a paradox, for it is difficult to please the learned and the princes in the same manner. By producing dithyrambs designed to gain the patronage of men of high rank, Ronsard brought upon himself the criticism of his fellow poets. His contemporary and friend, Etienne Pasquier, in a letter dating from 1555, reproaches Ronsard for his "half-courtly servitude" and closes his letter with the wish "that it will not come to pass that the good work of your pen should be used to the end of highly praising several we know not worthy of it."[23]

There also existed a problem of quantity for Ronsard in 1549; he lacked a poetic corpus sufficient for a first publication. Although he had already published a few poems, Ronsard did not have a book on the market. He therefore arduously put himself to the task and collected his compositions together with new unpublished work celebrating the monarch, for, as the poet would later declare, "the glory of kings is a fertile subject."[24] Ronsard even envisaged placing himself totally in the service of Henri II in order to recount in verse the deeds of the king and his family:

> Nevertheless the desire which goads my heart
> To demonstrate how I am your servant.[25]

At the beginning of 1550, Ronsard finally published a small octavo volume containing the first four books of the *Odes*. At the time he was just twenty-six years old; nevertheless, in the preface "Au lecteur," he immediately proclaimed himself the first poet of France: "But when you will call me the first French lyrical poet, and the one who has guided the others onto the path of this so honest labor, then you will bestow upon me that which is my due, and I will strive to make you understand that it is not unjustly that I have received it."[26] Mellin de Saint-Gelais felt the blow and rose to defend his own employment and status. It was after all his own place which he defended. The *rhétoriqueur* violently attacked Ronsard's poems in front of the king, Marguerite de Navarre, and her chancellor, Michel de l'Hospital. The favorite poet of the king ridiculed the hermetism, obscurity, and pedantry of certain odes, and for a time successfully diverted the king's favor.

Ronsard was fortunate enough, however, to find in the person of Michel de l'Hospital an influential protector at the court against the accusations of Saint-Gelais. To express his thanks for the intervention of the future chancellor of France, Ronsard dedicated to him one of the most beautiful odes describing the birth of the Muses. The same strategy was used on Jacques Bouju, Maître des requettes of the queen, who had also defended Ronsard, and Jean Martin, who wrote an "exposition" of the most difficult passages of the *Odes* — this exposition accompanying the first edition of the *Odes* in 1550.

Notwithstanding the moderate success of the *Odes*, Ronsard still awaited the recognition of his talent and the favors that usually follow such recognition:

> As one often sees the ship at port
> Attending the conduct of the wind
> Before departing, its swelling sail rising up
> To the side that the wind blows the stern,
> So, Prince, without stirring, I await
> Your royal favor, which I hope one day
> Will command me to make an honorable voyage
> Favorable to the winds of your fortune.[27]

The king kept him waiting and the Vendômois poet became more impatient "to taste the manna of royal grandeur."[28] Nevertheless Ronsard did not despair and he continued to refine the academism of his Pindaric odes. He had little choice, for he knew that before becoming the king's poet, he had first to impose himself as the French Pindar. With this goal in mind he imitated the Greek bard to the best of his ability in strophe, antistrophe, and epode. The mastery of the ancient poets became part of Ronsard's intellectual maturation; he could not and did not really wish to avoid this necessary stage of his poetic maturation. His authority as a poet needed to rest on something solid and directly linked to the humanist movement; the student found a master in Antiquity and applied himself to equaling his effort in the medium provided by the French language. Ronsard proceeded to offer the proof of his standing as an academic poet but also seemed aware of the fastidious nature of his odes. In fact, the result is not always brilliant, and Ronsard himself appears conscious of his lack of originality:

> Thus, following the gods, I beseech you to take
> Favorably this little gift as interest, while awaiting
> A present more perfect and worthy of a king,
> And that my Calliope will bear within me.[29]

Should we begrudge Ronsard his striving after the security of a decently remunerated occupation? We have a tendency to place the poet above society and do not think of him or her as an intriguer. This vision which we create of the poets is part of the false view we have of artistic production in general. Consider the situation of Ronsard. Before putting words into rhyme, Ronsard had first to operate in a world that was already socially and economically organized. It is precisely these existing preconditions that Jean-Paul Sartre has brilliantly analyzed in his study of Tintoretto. In Venice, at the same time as Ronsard wrote his odes, Tintoretto also had to confront painters of greater renown in order to gain part of the market for Venetian painting. As with Ronsard, Tintoretto had to "astonish, hit hard and impose himself"[30] to survive. Sartre has systematically deconstructed the vision we have of the "sublime" and lofty painters of the Italian Renaissance and he has transformed Jacopo into a laborer always on the lookout for a new contract.

What Sartre has shown for Tintoretto applies equally to Ronsard. The poet often speaks of the physical and technical aspect of his art; expressions like "laboring hand,"[31] "art of my thumb,"[32] "labor of my fingers,"[33] recur frequently in the *Odes,* and we have the sentiment that wooing the Muses requires much more than mere imagination: it is also necessary to do *physical* work in the elaboration of the poem. Isidore Silver has underlined the "craftsman" side of Ronsard's poetry by highlighting the laborious aspect of an apprenticeship which possesses none of the celestial grace one would often think to find with the poet.[34] It is perhaps because the poet must submit to material exigencies before devoting himself to the Muses that Ronsard considered his art as a "trade" (or a *traffic* in French): "I am the trader of the Muses"[35]—that is to say a merchant—Ronsard tells us. For it is in fact "merchandise" that the poet wished to exchange on the market.

Ronsard considered his writing as *labor,* and it is therefore not a coincidence if the word "labor" recurs as a leitmotif in the *Odes.*[36] In the preface of the 1550 edition, for example, the noun appears seven times in the space of five pages, most often in a context which leaves no ambiguity concerning its economic connotation. Ronsard also describes how he has written "industriously"[37] this volume and, in the first version of the ode "La Victoire de François de Bourbon" written in 1545, the Vendômois poet even considers himself as an "ingenious craftsman."[38] This idea of poetry as a professional occupation was again to be defended fifteen years later when, in his *Art poëtique,* Ronsard gave the following advice to his disciple Alphonse Delbene: "so far as human artifice, experience and labor permit, let me give you here several rules so that one day you can be the first in the knowledge of this so agreeable trade."[39]

At this point it is important to distinguish between *work* and *labor.* The first word is a generic term that implies a physical or intellectual process, while the second expression places work within a socioeconomic structure with all of its implications and therefore suggests a remuneration. It is for this reason that Ronsard perceived his poetic production in terms of its exchange value rather than its use value. The idea of poetry as a thing in itself which would be unrelated to the market is totally absent in the *Odes.* For Ronsard, poetry is part of the economic circuit and is consequently dependent on the laws of the market. Our poet was always conscious of the exchange value of his poetry; from the start, his odes had to be converted into money or gifts.[40] Endlessly he attempted to convince a potential patron that his verses had a price, and it is precisely the sum to be paid for fame and posterity that instigated the sighs and lamentations of the Vendômois poet. Ronsard frequently complained of the insufficient value that was accorded to his poetry and even drafted an ode "Contre les avaricieus" to this effect. The poet declared that he would content himself with what the king might offer if the present seemed appropriate for the investment of his labor. For many years Ronsard waited for a proper price:

> Prince, I send you this Ode
> Trading my verses in the same way
> A merchant trades his goods,
> Tit for tat: you who are rich,
> You, king of wealth, do not hesitate
> To exchange your gift for mine.

Do not tire of offering,
And you will see how I will accord
The honor which I promise to sound
When a present adorns my lyre.[41]

Ronsard defined the price of his verse as a long-term investment for the prince who wished to see himself glorified for posterity. Poet of the powers in place, Ronsard enabled the monarch and princes to belong to a tradition that combined men and gods alongside one another. Mythical and real contemporary figures were united in the same discourse so that Apollo, Jupiter, Hercules, and Henri II became interchangeable. As critics have already noted, mythology was in fact the principal instrument of flattery at the court of Henri II.[42] Moreover, the written and thus "durable" form of his poems allowed Ronsard to offer the king eternal renown. As with Pindar, he praised his contemporaries as in the "Usure a luimesme,"[43] where he borrows the title given by Pindar to an ode to Agesidomas in the *Olympics:* Henri II here replaces the Greek hero. What Ronsard proposed to the king appears clearly in the following passage:

Therefore your renown
Will reach the heavens, animated
By the labor of my hands:
Such a durable treasure
Describing the royal grandeur
You should look upon favorably.[44]

Poetry possessed a functional aspect for Ronsard. The value of the poem is calculated in proportion to what it could yield to the person who becomes historically objectified in and by the verses. Much more than words artistically juxtaposed and beautifully arranged, poetry, in the sixteenth century, also served to establish differences between individuals and social classes. It contributed to the reinforcement of social order and instituted itself as a discipline designed to establish distinction. The beauty of the rhyme also served to define social classes and to distinguish between individuals:

For Kings and Emperors
Differ from laborors
Only if someone sings their glory.[45]

As the seventh ode of the first book of the *Odes* would have us understand, no monument could better preserve the memory of kings than the poems promised by Ronsard. These "would render your renown alive," and the rhyme "could perpetuate your name,"[46] since "without the Muses the kings cannot live twice."[47] It is not enough for the prince to win battles, subjugate peoples, and accumulate a fortune; it is equally necessary for him to think of his glory for future generations. This offer of an existence for posterity was precisely the object of Ronsard's work: the *Odes* attempt to demonstrate the poet's mastery of this sort of exercise and accentuate his knowledge of the poetic tradition. Not only do the *Odes* emphasize the competence of the author to glorify the prince, but they also give credibility to his search for employment. On this point Ronsard is explicit:

> On the banks of Acheron: this glory is only
> Conceded by God to those daughters which Memory
> Conceived by Jupiter, to bestow upon those
> Who attract the poets with their gifts.[48]

In order to convince the sovereign of the importance of poetry, the poet was therefore forced to transform himself into a courtier. Nobody escaped the game of the adulators and the flatterers at the court of Henri II. Ronsard solicited and begged more than ever; in his demands he often showed some insolence and effrontery and even developed a theory of impudence:

> Impudence nourishes honor and the State.
> Impudence nourishes the screeching lawyers,
> Nourishes the courtiers, sustains the gendarmes.
> Impudence is today the best weapon
> One can enlist, even for the one
> Who wishes to succeed at court. . . . [49]

If impudence can provide the poet with the expected considerations, he will eventually become "the most impudent" and, like a "leech," he will never leave the prince's footsteps until he receives "the bait of a sweet favor."[50]

Helped by friends in high position, Ronsard had to frequent the immediate entourage of the king and praise the nobility. He spent a good part of his youth at the Louvre. However, although he was a regular attendant of the Parisian salons, Ronsard never became a good courtier and was in fact often maladroit. He revealed on several occasions his ignorance of the subtleties of the court[51] and complained later of the time he had lost because of these activities. In the second book of the *Melanges,* published in 1559, the poet admits his error to one of the most illustrious courtiers of his epoch—the cardinal of Chatillon, Odet de Coligny:

> Suddenly abandoning the Muses, I conceived
> Bishoprics, priories and abbeys, amazed
> To see myself transformed from a schoolboy

> Into a new courtier and restless court-bidder.
> Oh! That ambition unwillingly clothes itself!
> Thus I learned to take the path to the Louvre,
> Against my nature I learned to attend to
> Both your rising and your retiring.[52]

Ronsard had nevertheless to play the game and comply with the decorum of the court. Intrigues, alliances, and manipulations were the price to be paid in order to obtain the ecclesiastic positions and other compensations that could assure the poet's financial security. With this perspective in mind, Ronsard endeavoured to organize a "lobby," since before labor can be rewarded, it is first necessary that one's work be recognized:

> But it is necessary to bid the great gods of the court,
> To follow them, serve them, attend their table,
> To deliver before them a delectable story,
> To court them, watch them, and often bid their favor,
> Otherwise your labor will amount to no more than wind,
> Otherwise your science and your esteemed lyre,
> For lack of these, will dissipate like smoke.[53]

Ronsard clearly wrote his *Odes* in this prospect and from 1550 worked out what has justly been called a "theory of mendicancy."[54]

Impudence and mendicancy form the intrinsic polarities inherent in every ambitious young person. On one hand, it is in fact necessary to accept the authority of the potential patron who wields the hiring power, but on the other hand, it is equally important to show to the latter a certain detachment and aloofness that can eventually extend to the point of insolence and therefore indicate a certain autonomy and creative independence of the poet, showing his desire to place himself above the rest of job seekers. The *Odes* offer many examples of the interactions between these two poles that perhaps appear contradictory but are nonetheless strategically desirable. Impudence and mendicancy enabled Ronsard to sustain two discourses simultaneously: the poet new to the market of poetry addressed the prince with a sweet, soft-spoken tone—it is here the young man seeking his first employment who speaks to us—and, finally, in attempting to prove himself the equal of Pindar and master of the Muses, Ronsard could behave boldly and impudently before the king; his authority in poetry assured him this possibility. Thus, if Ronsard wished to secure employment and be accepted as the first poet of France, he had to maneuver between these two discourses with subtlety. What Ronsard sought to reconcile in the end are the two dreams of every beginner: glory and fortune.

In total we have observed five or six years of continual pursuit of a decently remunerated position. As we have seen, the long road of such an apprentice poet as Ronsard in search of first employment was not without hurdles. A sociological reading of the first writings of the Vendômois poet effectively permits us to ponder the function of the male poet during the sixteenth century, and highlights problems concerning the physical and material existence of these professionals of rhyme. We have seen how, by placing poetry and the poet within their social context, it is possible to raise questions of a conjectural nature concerning the ambiguous situation of the poet within a network of political and economic constraints. I have underlined several difficulties encountered by the poet at the beginning of his career, a period when it was not a question of describing what he desired but rather of imposing himself on the market and obtaining a first employment.

NOTES

1. See the studies of Roger Doucet, *Les Institutions de la France au XVIe siècle*, 2 vols. (Paris: Editions A. et J. Picard, 1948); Roland Mousnier, *Les Hiérarchies sociales de 1450 à nos jours* (Paris: Presses Universitaires de France, 1969); and George Huppert, *Les Bourgeois Gentilshommes, An Essay on the Definition of Elites in Renaissance France* (Chicago: University of Chicago Press, 1977).

2. Roland Mousnier, *La Vénalité des offices sous Henri IV et Louis XIII* (Paris: Presses Universitaires de France, 1971); see the second chapter, "Les temps modernes: le XVIe siècle," pp. 35–92. See also Doucet, *Institutions de la France,* more particularly the chapter on "Le système bénéficial," pp. 693–718.

3. Henri Weber, *La Création poétique au XVIe siècle en France de Maurice Scève à Agrippa d'Aubigné* (Paris: Nizet, 1955); see the chapter on "La condition sociale des poètes et l'influence de la vie de cour," pp. 63–106.

4. Charles Loyseau, *Cinq Livres du Droict des Offices, suivis du Traitez des Seigneuries et de celui des Ordres* [1610]. I use here the edition of his *Œuvres complètes* published in Paris in 1666 by Alliot, p. 42 ("toutesfois les Casuistes tiennent qu'à present l'usage ou coustume inveterée excuse de resider aux Benefices simples" [my translation; all subsequent translations are mine]). On the legislation of ecclesiastical benefices during the sixteenth century, see Jean Gérardin, *Etude sur les bénéfices ecclésiastiques aux XVIe et XVIIe siècles* [1897] (Geneva: Slatkine Reprints, 1971).

5. Loyseau, *Cinq Livres du Droict des Offices,* p. 43 ("Ainsi donc l'exercice ayant esté fait separable du titre, le labeur du loyer, l'Office du Benefice: bref le spirituel du temporel, la pluspart des Beneficiers ont esté bien aises, en retenant le titre & revenu de leur Benefice, de se décharger de l'exercice & labeur des pauvres gens").

6. Loyseau, *Cinq Livres du Droict des Offices,* p. 460 ("les benefices simples . . . consist[ent] plus en revenu, qu'en fonction personelle").

7. Loyseau, *Cinq Livres du Droict des Offices,* p. 335 ("il y a une grande troupe d'Aumôniers, de Chappelains & de Clercs").

8. Loyseau, *Cinq Livres du Droict des Offices,* p. 460 ("on ne met plus par choix

les hommes aux Offices de l'Eglise, mais on baille les Benefices aux hommes qu'on veut gratifier").

9. See Paul Bonnefon, "Ronsard ecclésiastique," *Revue d'Histoire Littéraire de la France* 2 (1895), 244–48. Though he had already been curé at the vicarage of Marolles associated with the diocese of Meaux since 1552, Ronsard ceded this charge in 1554 in order to become curé of Chally, as this vicarage, granted by the cardinal Jean Du Bellay, had revenues superior to those at Marolles. The curé of Chally replaced Ronsard at Marolles; yet the poet reserved for himself an annual rent of 50 livres on the occasion of this succession. In 1556 Ronsard obtained the vicarage of Evaillé, near Le Mans, and added the rent from this vicarage to that from Marolles. In 1557 he accepted a third benefice—the vicarage of Champfleur—granted by his friend Pisseleu, bishop of Condom. Ronsard renounced this latter charge in 1561, since he had in the meantime obtained the archdeaconry of Château-du-Loir. However, these three appointments yielded relatively little, and it was only under Charles IX that Ronsard replaced Amyot as abbot of Bellozane (1564) and was granted the priories of Saint-Cosme-lès-Tours (1565), Saint-Guingalois de Château-du-Loir (1569), and Saint-Gilles-de-Montoire (1569). These last four priories and abbeys assured him good revenues. It is necessary to add that Ronsard received also the title of *aumonier ordinaire* (chaplain) of Charles IX and Henri III, a charge which guaranteed a pension of 1,200 livres per year. All those benefices acquired under the reign of Charles IX would not, however, increase after his death. Under Henri III the favors toward the poet became less frequent.

10. Raymond Lebègue, "Ronsard poète officiel," *Studi in onore di Vittorio Lugli e Diego Valeri* (Venise: Neri Pozza, 1961), pp. 373–87.

11. See the commentary of Paul Laumonier in *La Vie de P. de Ronsard* [1586], historical and critical introduction and commentary by Paul Laumonier (Geneva: Slatkine Reprints, 1969), p. 132.

12. On the royal entries during the sixteenth century, see Antoinette Huon, "Le thème du Prince dans les entrées parisiennes au XVIe siècle" and V. L. Saulnier, "L'entrée de Henri II à Paris et la révolution poétique de 1550," in Jean Jacquot, ed., *Les Fêtes de la Renaissance* (Paris: CNRS, 1956); and I. D. McFarlane, *The Entry of Henri II into Paris, 16 June 1549* (New York: Medieval & Renaissance Texts & Studies, 1982). See also the book of Josèphe Chartrou, *Les Entrées solennelles et triomphales à la Renaissance* (*1484-1551*) (Paris: Presses Universitaires de France, 1928).

13. Daniel Ménager, "Ronsard et le poème de circonstance," in Louis Terreaux, ed., *Culture et pouvoir au temps de l'Humanisme et de la Renaissance* (Geneva, Paris: Slatkine & Champion, 1978), p. 319. On occasion poetry, see Predrag Matvejévitch, *La Poésie de circonstance, étude des formes de l'engagement poétique* (Paris: Nizet, 1971).

14. Ronsard, *Hymne de France* (ll. 217–19), in Paul Laumonier, ed. *Œuvres complètes,* 18 vols. (Paris: Société des Textes Français Modernes, 1914–67), I, 35 ("Moy ton Poëte, ayant premier osé / Avoir ton loz en ryme composé, / Je te supply, qu'à gré soit ma lyre."). Unless otherwise indicated, all references to Ronsard are to this edition and appear in the text with the number of the book, ode, and lines in parentheses.

15. *Odes,* "A Bouju Angevin" (I, X, 17–24), I, 122–23 ("Mais mon ame n'est ravie / Que d'une brulante envie / D'oser un labeur tenter / Pour mon grand Roi

contenter, / Afin que le miel de l'euvre / Son oreille oigne si bien, / Que facile je la treuve / L'importunant pour mon bien.")

16. *Odes,* "Au lecteur," I, 47 ("petit sonnet petrarquizé, ou quelque mignardise d'amour").

17. With respect to this subject, it should be noted that Ronsard often deleted from new editions odes which no longer served a particular function.

18. This text is reproduced in Pierre de Nolhac, *Ronsard et l'humanisme* (Paris: Champion, 1921), pp. 262–70.

19. *Odes,* "A Jouachim Du Bellai Angevin" (I, IX, 16), I, 109 ("emmieller les renoms").

20. *Ode de la Paix* (499–500), III, 35 ("sonneur / De l'une & de l'autre gloire").

21. *Odes,* "Au lecteur," I, 48 ("ma boutique n'est chargée d'autres drogues que de louanges, & d'honneurs").

22. Michel Dassonville, *Ronsard: étude historique et littéraire,* II, *A la conquête de la toison d'or (1545-1550)* (Geneva: Droz, 1970), 16.

23. Etienne Pasquier, *Choix de lettres sur la Littérature, la Langue et la Traduction,* published and annotated by D. Thickett (Geneva: Droz, 1956), pp. 5–6 ("servitude a demy courtisane," "que ne fissiez si bon marché de vostre plume à hault-louer quelques-uns que nous sçavons notoirement n'en estre dignes"). The Protestants Antoine de La Roche-Chandier and Bernard de Montméja also reproached Ronsard for his flattery and servility directed toward those of high rank. Our poet defended himself against these accusations in 1563 by writing a "Responce de Pierre Ronsard, aux injures & calomnies de je ne sçay quels Predicantereaux & Ministreaux de Genéve," published in *Discours des Misères de ce temps.* On Ronsard's response, see Ullrich Langer, "A Courtier's Problematic Defense: Ronsard's 'Responce aux injures,' " *Bibliothèque d'Humanisme et Renaissance* 46, no. 2 (1984), 343–55.

24. *Second Livre des Meslanges,* "A Monsieur Du Thier" (7), X, 39 ("la gloire des Roys en suget est fertile").

25. *Odes,* "Au Roi Henri IIe de ce nom" (36–37), dedication of the third edition of the *Odes* appearing in 1555 and reproduced by Charles Guérin in his edition of the *Odes* (Paris: Editions du Cèdre, 1952), p. 4 ("Toutefois le desir qui le coeur m'aiguillonne / De te montrer combien je suis ton serviteur").

26. *Odes,* "Au lecteur," I, 43 ("Mais quand tu m'appelleras le premier auteur Lirique François, & celui qui a guidé les autres au chemin de si honneste labeur, lors tu me rendras ce que tu me dois, & je m'efforcerai te faire apprendre qu'en vain je ne l'aurai receu").

27. *Odes,* "Au Roi Henri II" (1–8); in Guérin, *Odes,* p. 145 ("Comme on voit le navire attendre bien souvent / Au premier front du port la conduite du vent / Afin de voyager, haussant la voile enflée / Du côté que le vent sa poupe aura soufflée, / Ainsi, Prince, je suis sans bouger, attendant / Que ta faveur royale aille un jour commandant / A ma nef d'entreprendre un chemin honorable / Du côté que ton vent lui sera favorable").

28. *Odes,* "Au lecteur," I, 50 ("gouter les mannes de la roialle grandeur").

29. *Odes,* "Au Roi Henri IIe de ce nom" (71–74); in Guérin, *Odes,* p. 5 ("Ainsi, suivant les dieux, je te suppli' de prendre / A gré ce petit don, pour l'usure

d'attendre / Un présent plus parfait et plus digne d'un roi / Que jà ma Calliope enfante dedans moi.").

30. Jean-Paul Sartre, "Le séquestré de Venise: les fourberies de Jacopo," *Les Temps Modernes* no. 141 (Nov. 1957); text reproduced in *Situations IV* (Paris: Gallimard, 1964), pp. 291–346.

31. *Odes*, "A Michel de l'Hospital" (V, VIII, 6), III, 119 ("main laborieuse"); and "A Jan de la Hurteloire" (II, XIV, 15), I, 215 ("laborieuse main").

32. *Odes*, "A Jouachim Du Bellai Angevin" (I, IX, 14), I, 109 ("art de mon pouce").

33. *Odes*, "Au Seigneur de Carnavalet" (I, VI, 37), I, 92 ("labeur de mes dois").

34. Isidore Silver, "Ronsard poète rusé," *Cahiers de l'Association Internationale des Etudes Françaises* no. 22 (1970), 41–52.

35. *Odes*, "A Bertran Berger de Poitiers" (I, XV, 11), I, 139 ("Je suis le trafiqueur des Muses").

36. Ronsard uses the word "labeur" 152 times in his work. If one compares the frequency of this word with the rest of Ronsard's vocabulary—which extends to more than 12,000 words—one sees that this noun occupies the 430th position. The verbs "être," "faire," "avoir," "voir," etc., as well as a large number of adverbs and prepositions, evidently monopolize the top of the list. For more details on Ronsard's word usage, see A. E. Creore, *A Word-Index to the Poetic Works of Ronsard* (Leeds: W. S. Maney & Son, 1972).

37. *Odes*, "Au lecteur," I, 48 ("industrieusement").

38. *Odes*, "La Victoire de François de Bourbon" (I, V, 10), I, 83 ("ouvrier ingenieux").

39. *Abbrégé de l'Art Poëtique François*, XIV, 3 ("d'autant que l'artifice humain, experience & labeur le peuvent permettre, j'ay bien voulu t'en donner quelques reigles icy, afin qu'un jour tu puisses estre des premiers en la connaissance d'un si agreable métier").

40. Daniel Ménager has shown that the notion of "value" also occupies a central place in the *Hymnes;* in *Ronsard: le Roi, le Poète et les Hommes,* Travaux d'Humanisme et Renaissance, no. CLXIX (Geneva: Droz, 1979), p. 55. The "suyte de l'hymne au cardinal de Lorraine" illustrates well the preponderant importance of value in the *Hymnes.* Ménager believes, however, that in the end Ronsard refuses to "assign a price to his writing."

41. *Ode de la Paix* (469–78), III, 33–34 ("Prince, je t'envoie cette Ode, / Trafiquant mes vers à la mode / Que le marchant baille son bien, / Troque pour troq': toi qui es riche, / Toi roi de biens, ne soi point chiche / De changer ton present au mien. / Ne te lasse point de donner, / Et tu verras comme j'acorde / L'honneur que je promai sonner / Quant un present dore ma corde").

42. Weber, *Création poétique,* p. 87.

43. *Odes*, "Usure a luimesme" (I, VII), I, 99–100.

44. *Odes*, "Au Seigneur de Carnavalet" (I, VI, 35–40), I, 92 ("Ores donq' ta renommée / Voira les cieus, animée / Par le labeur de mes dois: / Telle durable richesse / Sur la Roiale largesse / Heureuse estimer tu dois").

45. *Elegies, Mascarades et Bergerie,* "Ode à Monsieur de Verdun" (46–48), XIII, 258 ("Car les Rois & les Empereurs / Ne different aux laboureurs / Si quelcun ne

chante leur gloire"). This ode was first published in 1565 in the *Elegies* before appearing in the later editions of the *Odes.*

46. *Odes,* "Usure a luimesme" (I, VII, 6, 8), I, 99 ("Ne feront vivre ton renom, / Pourra perpetuer ton nom").

47. *Odes,* "Au Roi Henri II" (117); in Guérin, *Odes,* p. 148 ("Sans les Muses deux fois les rois ne vivent pas").

48. *Odes,* "Au Roi Henri II" (119–22); in Guérin, *Odes,* p. 149 ("Aux rives d'Achéron: seulement cette gloire / Est de Dieu concédée aux filles que Mémoire / Conçut de Jupiter, pour la donner à ceux / Qui attirent par dons les poètes chez eux").

49. *Second Livre des Meslanges,* "Complainte contre Fortune" (423–28), X, 36–37 ("L'impudence nourrist l'honneur & les estas. / L'impudence nourrist les criards avocas, / Nourrist les courtizans, entretient les gendarmes: / L'impudence aujourd'hui sont les meilleures armes / Dont lon se puisse ayder, mesme à celuy qui veut / Parvenir à la court . . . ").

50. *Second Livre des Meslanges* (431–41) ("le plus eshonté," "sangsue," "l'apast d'une douce faveur").

51. On the tactlessness of Ronsard before the court, see Michel Dassonville, *Ronsard: étude historique et littéraire,* and more particularly the third volume of his work, *Prince des poètes ou poète des Princes (1550-1556)* (Geneva: Droz, 1976), pp. 13–27.

52. *Second Livre des Meslanges,* "Complainte contre Fortune" (121–28), X, 22–23 ("Je conceu Eveschez, Prieurez, Abayes, / Soudain abandonnant les Muses, esbahyes / De me voir transformer d'un escolier contant / En nouveau courtizan, demandeur inconstant. / O que mal aisement l'ambition se couvre! / Lors j'apris le chemin d'aller souvent au Louvre, / Contre mon naturel j'apris de me trouver / Et a vostre coucher & à votre lever").

53. *Nouvelles Poésies,* "Compleinte a la Royne Mere du Roy" (296–302), XII, 186–87 ("Mais il te faut prier les grands dieux de la court, / Les suyvre, les servir, se trouver à leur table, / Discourir devant eux un conte delectable, / Les courtizer, les voir, & les presser souvent, / Autrement ton labeur ne seroit que du vent, / Autrement la science & ta lyre estimée / (Pour n'user de cet art) s'en iroit en fumée").

54. Isidore Silver, "Pierre de Ronsard: Panegyrist, Pensioner and Satirist of the French Court," *Romanic Review* 45 (1954), 92.

V

CONTEXTUALITY:
Cultural Representations

MARGARET L. KING

The Death of the Child
Valerio Marcello: Paternal Mourning
in Renaissance Venice

In the last dark days of December, 1460, not yet nine years old, Valerio Marcello lay dying. Surrounded by doctors, priest, teacher, friends, in the spare comfort of a Venetian palazzo, the boy grew pale and thin, and his father grew desperate with grief. The child's death and father's response have left an unusual literary record worthy of attention for the light it may shed on the family of the Italian Renaissance.

Valerio had first been struck ill the previous August when the family vacationed at their formidable suburban villa in Monselice: thorns in the garden, observed one writer who told the tale (Perleone, G, 245). Doctor Matteolo was summoned from nearby Padua, and bled the child. The incision festered; Valerio worsened. The boy's father—the Venetian nobleman Jacopo Antonio Marcello—summoned other doctors. His health regained, Valerio returned with the family to Venice, and there resumed the studies that his illness had interrupted. But the fever, defeated once, seized the child again. Facing an enemy he could not conquer, the now-frightened father called again for doctors. Among them came Gerardo Bolderio of Verona, the Aesculapius of the day, who employed all the available medical arts. Failing, Valerio still recognized the doctor who had once cured an older brother and whose earlier success encouraged Marcello to hope for another. The anxious Gerardo called in a colleague to consult on the case; then a Jewish doctor (who terrified the child) came to the bedside. More bleeding, more herbs and unguents, more inspection of urine; no improvement.

The Marcello household ceased to hope, and began to console not the child but the father. He now saw what would happen: the muscles of his face rigid, "like a rock," he stared at his son, stupefied (Perleone, G, 246). Valerio commended to him a beloved sister; then once-rosy cheeks white, coral lips turned ashen, nose and chin trembling, the whole of his tiny body possessed by fever, he fixed his eyes on heaven. Marcello stood by, helpless, wretched, weeping. "And do you cry, my father?" said the remarkable boy; "that is not worthy of a man" (Perleone, G, 246). Rebuked, the father collected himself and embraced the child, who soon afterwards lost hearing and power of speech. A priest rushed in; the child kissed the offered cross. Then he died, on the first day of the new year (in our calendar) of 1461. The father, "like a stone," seeing the inanimate body, made the sign of the cross over the boy, then fled from the light into darkness to grieve (Perleone, G, 247). The house was draped in mourning, Marcello dressed himself in black, and the small corpse was clothed in white. He entered heaven; those left on earth wept.

The foregoing is the account of an eyewitness to at least some of the events described: Pietro Perleone, of whom more later. The following are presented as the father's own words, but were actually written on his behalf by Giorgio Bevilacqua da Lazise, Marcello's aide:

> When I saw him, I scarcely thought that it would result in death, that my son would desert me, his father; unthinking me! it never entered my mind. At that time I believed that the beginning of his illness was a silly trifle, and I thought that his good health would soon return. But when I saw that the situation slipped into serious illness, oh me! what effort did I expend to save him! How I exhorted the doctors to cure him! how assiduously I urged them! what vows did I offer for his safety not only with tears but with rivers of tears! I called on the assistance of heaven, beseeched all the saints friendly to me. I called for the help of mortals and immortals; vainly I tried everything. . . . I approached all the monasteries of our city, and all the most religious men of the religious orders I wearied with my importunity. (Bevilacqua, V, fol. 96r–v)

But those weighty prayers, as Bevilacqua describes them, remained unanswered. Valerio's condition worsened, and so did Marcello's state: "Miserable, I was stabbed by sorrow on sorrow; I could not speak, nor respond to his sweetest words; I could bring forth only tears, and sobs" (Bevilacqua, V, fol. 158). Death came, and devastated the usually impassive Marcello. "And the rest of life has become for me a time of wretchedness; and when death won for him the eternal felicity and beatitude of heaven, it brought me enduring evil, and as long as life continues for me, I disintegrate in sorrow" (Bevilacqua, V, fol. 99).

The man thus convulsed by grief, according to these and other observers, was an unlikely candidate for tenderheartedness. But this veteran of twenty years of battle, this seasoned diplomat and statesman, this wealthy and proud aristocrat, grieved for his child publicly and defiantly. A year later, he was still lost in despair. More than two and a half years after the death, he defended, through the spokesman Bevilacqua, his immoderate grief. A year or two thereafter he died, perhaps still mourning the death of his youngest son.

He is not the only father to have lost a child. In that century such events were common. But he is one of the few whose grief is documented in a form that can be measured and weighed. For Valerio's death spurred a series of consolatory works by humanist professionals and amateurs addressed to a father who was himself a patron and amateur of *bonae litterae.* Marcello had previously sponsored several translations from the Greek, including the famous Strabo of Guarino Veronese. And he had more than once bundled such works in handsome manuscript books — two were illuminated by none less than Andrea Mantegna. These he sent with covering letters of his own composition to a former comrade-in-arms, a member of the highest French nobility and pretender to Italian dominions: René, duke of Anjou and count of Provence.

Now, enmeshed in his personal tragedy, Marcello found himself at the center of a flurry of humanist composition. The works composed to console him for the loss of a son include some of the most substantial and interesting of the genre of consolation to emerge from the Italian Quattrocento. The volume they comprise is a literary memorial deliberately constructed by a grief-stricken father to honor a lost child. True to pattern, Marcello bundled them up — most of them — in one remarkable manuscript, exquisitely written, beautifully illustrated, not quite finished, and never sent to René, here again the intended addressee. Three centuries later, Apostolo Zeno saw the manuscript in the Marcello palace. Then Jacopo Morelli spotted it in an old bookstore. On 18 March 1776, it was sold at auction in London from the collection of Caesar de Missy to Dr. William Hunter. It is now in Glasgow, in the library founded by that bibliophile.

Thirteen authors wrote seventeen works in consolation of Jacopo Antonio Marcello. In addition, two works by two authors can be grouped with these: a response to one of the consolers, and Bevilacqua's work purportedly by Marcello in defense of mourning against the consolers. And one work generated two original translations. In discussing this incident, in sum, reference must be made to twenty-one works by sixteen authors. Most but not all appear in the Glasgow codex. Those that do may also appear in other manuscript versions, some of which are superior to those in the Glasgow collection. Some have been printed. The names of these authors and their works, the dates of composition, and the location of alternate versions are summarized at the end of the appended Bibliographical Note.

Early in April, 1461, just three months after Valerio's death, the immigrant humanist George of Trebizond, then in Venice, wrote Marcello a consolatory letter (a substantial work, no hasty note). Probably at about

208 | MARGARET L. KING

the same time, another immigrant and humanist wrote a similar letter: the ducal secretary Niccolò Sagundino. These works were followed in August by another of comparable scale by perhaps the most remarkable woman humanist of the century, Isotta Nogarola. Francesco Filelfo dated his extensive *De obitu Valerii filii consolatio* from Milan on Christmas day of the same year, when Jacopo Antonio's grief had almost reached its first anniversary. Filelfo also wrote a Greek (later translated) and a Latin elegy (in the name of his patron Francesco Sforza, Marcello's former comrade-in-arms); these are undated. The Venetian citizen and learned cleric Michele Orsini, responding to Filelfo's long *consolatio*, wrote in 1462 (26 August) an elaborate letter disputing the historical sections of that work and celebrating both Venice and the still-heartbroken Marcello.

Other consolatory *opuscula* were offered at dates I cannot establish between Valerio's death and his father's by the humanists Giovanni Mario Filelfo, Battista Guarini, Montorio Mascarello, and Gregorio Tifernate. The soldier Carlo Fortebraccio da Montone wrote a similar work, probably in 1463. Two anonymous authors wrote brief consolatory works in July and October of that year. Ludovico Carbone, a regular composer of such celebratory works at the court of Borso d'Este of Ferrara, composed an elegy, probably also in 1463. On 1 November 1463, while Marcello was heading the Venetian siege of Trieste, Pietro Perleone (Riminese by birth, Venetian by adoption) wrote Marcello from Udine a long *Laudatio in Valerium eius filium puerum eximium*, revealing his close relationship with the child and the family. Two days later, the Veronese Giorgio Bevilacqua da Lazise (like Perleone, in Udine, and of Marcello's intimate circle) wrote to Marcello a letter introducing the last and most interesting work (dated 13 November) of this consolatory series: the *Excusatio adversus consolatores in obitu Valerii filii*, ghosted by Bevilacqua for his noble patron at the latter's request. For Marcello wished to address to King René a work defending his unstemmed grief for a beloved son. But he had not, it seems, the leisure or learning to do so himself. The true author is revealed by Bevilacqua's letter, extant in a Veronese manuscript, perhaps autograph: "So I have urged that the letter (written by me as though you had composed it)," the aide wrote his employer, "be sent by you, as I persuaded you, to the divine King René.... Now ... I give it to you" (V, fol. 6).

In the Glasgow codex, the *Laudatio* stands alone, the capstone work of the collection, without prefatory letter. There it seems indeed, to an innocent reader unacquainted with the original text, to have been written by Marcello. The other of the works named above stand in that codex in the order shown in the appended table: the letters of Sagundino and George of Trebizond; the *Consolatio* and Greek elegy (with translation of Ludovico Carbone) of Francesco Filelfo; Nogarola's letter and Fortebraccio's

Consolatio; a *Dialogus* with prefatory letter and additional consolatory letter by Mascarello; Battista Guarini's letter and Perleone's *Laudatio;* the two anonymous letters (henceforth Anon. A and B), but between them Orsini's *Epistola* to Filelfo; Bevilacqua's *Excusatio.* The order is roughly chronological. The *Excusatio* is probably the latest of these works and perhaps of all the consolatory literature associated with this episode. Outside the Glasgow collection stand only the short Perleone *epistola,* the Tifernate oration, the work of Giovanni Mario Filelfo, lost to view, and the Carbone consolation.

Who were the authors of the component works of the Glasgow codex, and what were their relations to Marcello? The noted humanist Francesco Filelfo does not require introduction. His *Consolatio* for Marcello is a rich, even a brilliant work, said by Filelfo's biographer to be among his best. Certainly Marcello was delighted; he may in fact have commissioned Filelfo (as he later did Bevilacqua) to compose this seemingly spontaneous work. He rewarded Filelfo with a lavishly expensive gift. Father of Giovanni Mario Filelfo, Francesco may have first become acquainted with the Venetian during his difficult offspring's brief career in Venice (in 1460) as first teacher of that city's public school of rhetoric. Mario had had prior contact with René d'Anjou—as *juge du palais* at the Frenchman's court around 1450—and was himself to write a *consolatio* to Marcello. During his unhappy sojourn in Venice, the younger Filelfo entered into fierce competition with George of Trebizond and Pietro Perleone, foreigners like himself resident in the city, for the position of public historiographer. Both his competitors, like both Filelfos, were later to console Marcello for the loss of Valerio. Both knew Marcello even before that unhappy death—as did, apparently, many of the commoners of Venice's *ordo litteratorum,* as they called themselves, ever in search of wealthy men who liked a little learning. Perleone, indeed, a teacher in Venice's public school of San Marco, had been Valerio's teacher (and Francesco Filelfo's pupil, whose friend he remained). Intricate links, therefore, connect these four consolers of the saddened nobleman and seekers of his favor.

Related to this group but more remotely are Sagundino and Orsini, the former a Greek long resident in Venice, the latter a Venetian citizen. Sagundino belonged to the circle of government secretaries who occupied a sociological niche in Venice similar to that of the teachers. Like them, he actively sought the patronage of wealthy noblemen; he would have reveled in Marcello's, if he did not in fact win it. Sagundino's close friendship with Perleone is witnessed by the lengthy consolation the latter wrote for the Greek-born secretary after a tragic shipwreck which destroyed half his family and all his books. Orsini was a cleric, for many years the abbot of San Antonio da Vienna in Venice, where Marcello and his family had taken refuge during an invasion of plague at some time during Valerio's brief lifetime; further association with the family is suggested by his words. And Orsini was related by marriage to Pasquale Malipiero, once Marcello's colleague in the field, and at the time of Valerio's death, doge of Venice.

In Verona, Marcello had met the Nogarola family (when Isotta, probably, was still small; can this meeting be assigned to 1439, when Marcello was present at the reconquest of Verona?). Perhaps at the same time he met Bevilacqua, who was in these years an admirer of both prodigious Nogarola sisters. Nogarola and Bevilacqua both belonged to the city's noble clans, collaborators in Venetian domination. Also Veronese by birth was Battista Guarini. His father Guarino Veronese had translated Strabo for Marcello and inaugurated a tradition of praise for that personage. And on that elder scholar's death on 4 December 1460, shortly before that of Valerio Marcello, Battista had acquired his post as resident pedagogue at the Ferrarese court. Not from Verona but nearby Vicenza came Montorio Mascarello. His relations otherwise with Marcello are not now known to me. Fortebraccio, a soldier and son of the notorious *condottiere* Braccio da Montone, had fought with Marcello during the wars with Milan and participated in the Trieste campaign of 1463 led by Marcello and his colleague Vitale Lando. The identity of Anon. A is unclear. Anon. B is perhaps a Paduan student, the acquaintance of some members of the circle of Udinese litterati whom Marcello knew in 1462–63.

This group of consolers, then, which includes some exceptionally obscure figures in the humanist movement, contains subgroups of related personages and is not really so disparate. The works they wrote to comfort the bereaved nobleman, similarly, though various in size and miscellaneous in genre, have strong family resemblances in content and theme. In the sum they deal with four main issues: the boy Valerio, the father Jacopo Antonio and his Marcello ancestors, the city of Venice which nurtured father and son alike, and the means of consolation. Bevilacqua's *Excusatio* presents a fifth issue: the legitimacy of grief and consequent rejection of consolatory arguments. Each of these issues merits close consideration both in terms of the Marcello incident itself and in relation to Venetian and humanist culture. What follows is a composite account of the portrayal of the boy Valerio in the Glasgow codex. Who was Valerio? and how was he perceived by father and friends?

Conceived when his fruitful mother possessed optimal good health, Valerio was born in Venice in 1452 when his father, then fifty-three or fifty-four, was abroad as governor of recently conquered Crema: the father's military role at the time was an omen, wrote Perleone, of the son's own destined military greatness, had he survived to realize that promise (Perleone, G, 211–13). Still in Crema, Marcello had visions of his son: "of a male child of most elegant form, replete with every kind of virtue" (Bevilacqua, V, fols. 34v–35). Returning to Venice when the infant was three months old, he found Valerio exactly resembled the child of his vision: him whom "quiet nights had shown me, whom in my sleep I had closely embraced," in the words presented as Marcello's (Bevilacqua, V, fol. 35v). The first meeting of father and son had other notable features, and is described by several of the Glasgow authors (Bevilacqua, V, fols. 35v–36; George, ed. Mon., 237; Filelfo, G, 42; Fortebraccio, G, 144; Mascarello, G, 176; Perleone, G, 212, 213, 215; Anon. A, G, 254). Marcello had entered the house quietly, wrote Filelfo in an early and lengthy account, without prior announcement that might have created a fuss in the household. As soon as Valerio saw the stranger enter, he pushed from his mouth his nurse's breast, which when aroused from sleep a few minutes before he had seized hungrily. He lifted his head and eyes and seemingly cocked his ears, as though some inner message had reached him that here was something especially worthwhile noting. He struggled from his nurse's arms and threw himself into his father's embrace, eyes wide, smiling sweetly, babbling "father," though he could not yet say the word. Marcello was surprised but delighted, and bent to kiss the child, who then kissed his father repeatedly, and would not stop, and peered deep into his parent's eyes. The nurse reached for the infant but he rejected her. Finally coaxed away by his mother, Valerio turned his head sharply to see his father again, babbling vigorously sounds no one could understand. Marcello gazed on the boy with wonder, saying nothing, but rejoicing within himself that his son would surely be a great man and a great citizen. The special relationship between father and son, of which more is said later, began at this moment.

Valerio thrived. He grew rapidly and engaged early in play, soon showing skill at bodily exercise. He was remarkably beautiful—a consequence, again, of his parents' condition at his conception. Beauty was not a merely incidental consideration. Beauty was admired by the ancients; Jesus Christ had been a beautiful child (Bevilacqua, V, fols. 36v, 39ff.; Orsini, M, fol. 19; George, ed. Mon, 238; Perleone, G, 220, 221). Valerio's exquisite eyes, nose, ears, hands, fingers, neck, mouth, tongue, were matched by the acuteness of the senses related to those organs: sight, hearing, touch, the beauty of his voice. That voice was slow to form words, and Marcello longed ardently to speak with the child. But then speech blossomed suddenly, not beginning (as with most children) with babbling and improving gradually, but from the first correct and eloquent: "For in him there was always the highest comeliness of words, and a certain flawless integrity of speech, a sweetness and smoothness of voice" (Bevilacqua, V, fol. 54). Health and beauty for these Renaissance writers are intrinsically related to acuity and expressiveness—and in closely related passages to moral and intellectual qualities (Bevilacqua, V, fols. 52ff.; Orsini, M, fols. 18vff.; Fortebraccio, G, 145; Perleone, G, 217, 221ff.).

These qualities are central elements in the description of the young Valerio. He is depicted as innately virtuous: temperate, magnanimous, a wise manager of time, respectful toward his teacher, pious (Bevilacqua, V, fols. 60ff.; Perleone, G, 218ff.; Anon. A, G, 261). An earnest desire for glory may be added to these virtues—a quality admired by these authors and linked to moral virtues more familiar to us (Bevilacqua, V, fols. 61, 64v; Perleone, G, 222). Orsini, Perleone, and Anon. A describe the time that Valerio gazed on the tomb of the Venetian naval hero Vettor Pisani and yearned to emulate his greatness (Orsini, M, fols. 19v–20; Perleone, G, 239; Anon. A, G, 255). Here is one eyewitness account:

> In Venice in the Church of the Blessed Antonio Vienensis . . . , committed to my care, there stands a marble monument of Vettore Pisani, the unvanquished naval leader and victor indeed of the Chioggian war with the Genoese, in pedestrian pose, with sword and helmet. Seeing this, as he sometimes used to, the boy Valerio, turning to me, often asked to which man among mortals was due this immortal monument; and heard that it was no common thing but the rare reward for virtue, not granted except for momentous service to the republic. With his eyes raised to heaven, he said, "Oh may the powers above allow that I might be numbered among such rare men." (Orsini, M, fols. 19v–20)

Striking amid the description of Valerio's virtues is mention of his precocity, a major theme for George of Trebizond (ed. Mon, esp. 238). From the earliest years he was drawn to serious pursuits, wrote Perleone; in ability and diligence he exceeded his years (G, 221, 231–32). He exceeded his years in all virtues, wrote the first anonymous authors (G, 254, 257). The power of his mind was such that daily he accomplished something beyond his age and beyond nature, wrote Filelfo (G, 43). He excelled his older siblings and relatives in learning, noted Fortebraccio (G, 144).

This precocity is the mark of a student, and the boy's preternatural maturity and vibrant spirit are linked with aptness for learning (Bevilacqua, V, fols. 52, 59v–60, 61r–v; George, ed. Mon., 238ff.; Filelfo, G, 43–44; Perleone, G, esp. 226–27). He seemed to guide himself, wrote Bevilacqua, gifted with superb memory—an essential in that age for all intellectual tasks, and thus noted by several authors (V, fols. 61v, 59v–60; also Orsini, M, fol. 20; Fortebraccio, G, 145; Perleone, G, 229–31; Anon. A., G, 255). Among other feats, especially conspicuous was Valerio's deathbed recognition of the doctor Gerardo, introduced at the outset. Valerio had met him only once, years earlier, when the physician came to Monselice to treat an older brother, Girolamo. Barely clinging to life, Valerio recalled in detail the circumstances of that event of his early childhood (Sagundino, G, 6; Fortebraccio, G, 145; Perleone, G, 229–31; Anon. A., G, 255). Valerio was also avidly curious, interested in everything, reported his teacher Perleone (G, 226, 232; also Bevilacqua, V, fol. 65r–v). His active mind turned to great and small matters alike, and he would seek explanations for the causes of things from his father or other elders. "And having often seen triremes and biremes and other diverse kinds of ships, he would eagerly seek to know what their names were, and the names of all their armaments and equipment, and what the arrangement of the sailors was, and the art of navigation, so much that frequently those knowledgeable in these things, admiring his intelligence, could not answer his questions" (G, 232). The business of terra firma life also aroused Valerio's interest: hounds and horses. How were they to be fed and cared for? how could one tell which would be fleetest? which suited for the battlefield? And when mainland guests, his father's friends, came to visit, Valerio would receive them properly—and then when the occasion presented itself, inquire as to "the size of their cities, the nature of the site, the population and its customs, and what manner of government made it worthy and great" (G, 232). Other Glasgow authors report encounters with paternal visitors. Filelfo described how when important men of the city would come to the palazzo to salute Marcello or transact business, Valerio would greet them, if his father were out, ask their business, promise to convey their messages, and dismiss them courteously. These matters he would communicate precisely to Marcello on the latter's return, to his stupefaction: "for they were all the words of a mature man, not a boy" (Filelfo, G, 44). In the presence of dark-robed senators, Marcello's colleagues in the government of Venice, Valerio gamely asked questions about the regime, according to Perleone, Anon. A, and Orsini (G, 224, 255, and M, fol. 20). When learned men came to visit, the latter further reports, Valerio inquired politely about the structure of the heavens (Orsini, M, fol. 20r–v).

Of his father's military exploits, Valerio asked often and could retell the tales (Bevilacqua, V, fols. 65v, 69; Perleone, G, 231): "So smoothly and beautifully did he describe cities besieged, mountains overpowered by ships, or assaults and victories in their proper order, that he seemed not to narrate the events but to perform them, not just to have heard of them but to have participated" (Perleone, G, 231). And Valerio yearned to know about the government and history of Venice. "He asked me to tell him by what means and by what persons the foundations of our city were built amid these waters and lagoons, and how, boldly, these piles of enormous houses and kingly temples [came to be] made and raised on these bars of sand; whether the governance of our republic had been from the beginning managed as it is now, and whether its regime had ever been interrupted" (Bevilacqua, V, fol. 69). In these subjects his father instructed him. For Marcello delighted in his child's vigorous mind, and early sought to educate him in the best tradition of the day.

In describing the education of Valerio Marcello, the gifted son of a wealthy and cultivated man, the humanist authors who wrote in consolation found an opportunity to encourage the new learning. Born with the necessary abilities, they said, a child must be well taught (Bevilacqua, V, fol. 56v; Perleone, G, pp. 223, 228–29). Early learning in liberal studies is important: the rudiments of language especially must be learned young (Bevilacqua, V, fol. 57r–v; Perleone, G, 226, 229). Even the character of the infant's nurse is important in intellectual development (Bevilacqua, V, fol. 55v; Perleone, G, 221). Soon a good teacher must be sought—the father's responsibility. Marcello cheerfully took on that burden, according to these words Bevilacqua wrote as though they were that nobleman's own. "When I considered how much men are aided in gaining honor and cultivating virtue through letters to which study they confer themselves, and how my son lacked nothing that might make him conspicuous in all virtues and in every regard perfect, it seemed best to hire the finest teachers, from whom he might be trained in the good arts from infancy. . . ." (Bevilacqua, V, fol. 56v). Perleone praises Marcello's diligence in seeking a skilled teacher, without whom the benefits of natural intelligence and industry might wither: "I must make it clear at this point that I can't help but admire the diligence and prudence of Jacopo Antonio Marcello as much as I despise the negligence . . . of those parents who, when it comes to growing crops, training horses, building houses, sailing ships, and other lowly pursuits, select and handsomely pay those who are considered most skilled in that art; but in this highest duty of educating a child, we find they are incautious and negligent and faulty, so that without reflection they commit the minds of their children to be shaped and formed by some ignorant fool or other. . . ." (Perleone, G, 228). Here speaks a professional educator! And he had good reason to commend Marcello's diligence in this regard. For the tutor the nobleman chose for Valerio was himself—Perleone. The child revered him, and the tutor claimed that his love for Valerio rivaled Marcello's (G, 228, 229; also Sagundino, G, 5).

Endowed with native ability, well taught by a true devotee of the new learning, Valerio flourished (as the Glasgow authors report) in the pursuit of the liberal studies (see Orsini, M, fol. 20; Perleone, G, 226–27, 233). "He so flamed with the desire to learn, he so bent himself to studies, he so grasped the rudiments of the good arts [*bonae litterae*], that there was no kind of knowledge that he did not yearn to master" (Bevilacqua, V, fol. 59v). These are Bevilacqua's words. And the pedagogue Guarini reported that Valerio, once he began his schooling, "desired nothing less than the military life, delighted in nothing more than the studies of the good arts..." (G, 181). He soon developed all the qualities of the consummate orator: "a pleasant and clear voice, sweetness of speech, charm of pronunciation combined with gravity, easy expression of any passage in either language [Greek or Latin] as though he had been born to it..." (G, 181).

Surely there is exaggeration in these accounts. But it is clear that Valerio had studied both Greek and Latin, according to witnesses guided not only by his teacher but by his father as well (Orsini, M, fols. 20; Guarini, G, 181; Perleone, G, 227, 229; Anon. A, G, 254, 255); and he had progressed enough before his death at age eight to gratify Marcello, an amateur in those same arts. "I rejoiced that my son, with my assistance and diligent effort," wrote Bevilacqua in the mask of Marcello "had emerged so virtuous, that I could foresee he would accumulate in himself by his acute mind the virtues of my ancestors, so that our whole posterity would be enriched by the glory of deeds well done" (Bevilacqua, V, fol. 58).

Not Marcello's words, but possibly expressive nonetheless of the thoughts of a father who valued learning as a worthy ingredient of patrician glory and who was besotted with his son. Clearly the relationship between Valerio and Marcello was unusually intense (Filelfo, G, 44; Fortebraccio, G, 144; Mascarello, G, 176; Perleone, G, 217). Apparently the child resembled the father, as several authors note (Fortebraccio, G, 145; Perleone, G, 218; Anon. A., G, 251; Anon. B, G, 198). Could that resemblance account in part for the firm tie between the two? or did their closeness persuade the consolers to assume a physical resemblance? If Valerio was the "image" of Marcello, that likeness might indeed have struck the gnarled soldier when he first greeted his infant son, and spurred a unique relationship. Certainly there is a mystery in that first meeting. The repeated (and slightly variant) accounts by different authors accentuate its importance in this story. It is as though the child was divorced abruptly from a female world of immaturity and play, of breasts and milk, and engrafted into the tough, stern world of his father: a world of business and sobriety, of war and government, of Greek and Latin. He flourished in that world, in his father's orbit; and never returned, as our authors describe these events, to the nursery. Valerio would accompany his father through the city, curious, questioning, Bevilacqua informs us (V, fol. 69). At home, he clung to his father, as Filelfo reports. "When you [Marcello] were at home, he was never very far from your side (to the extent that he thought it proper); he either stood next to you while you sat or followed you when you walked, observing whatever you did or said. He acutely inspected your face and every motion of your body in order to imitate them.... And if perhaps he noticed you from time to time wrapped in thought, as sometimes happened, silent he would attentively examine the motions of your eyes and of your whole body; then would ask his mother or the servants, 'Is there anything bothering father? What is he thinking about in that way?' " (G, 44).

The exceptional warmth of this father-son relationship is suggested also by other incidents. Once Valerio was confronted by neighborhood children—there were bullies then as now, and a Venetian nobleman's household was set in the midst of the city, adjacent to families of quite different social standing. Valerio stood firm, refusing to flee, in imitation of his soldier father who later chided him for foolhardiness: a soldier was not required to face overwhelming odds (Perleone, G, 233–34). And when, as Valerio lay dying, Marcello vowed to wear only coarse and dark clothes if God mercifully spared the child, Valerio said no, that if spared he would wear such clothes: for Marcello, a senator, needed to dress resplendently in fulfillment of his duty to class and city (Perleone, G, 246; Anon. A., p. 257).

But Valerio was not spared. Of his dying I have already spoken, and of his father's grief. There follows the business of consolation. Your son is now in heaven, the Glasgow authors chorus to Marcello (Nogarola, ed. Abel, 171; Sagundino, G, 24; Filelfo, G, 50, 107, 126; Fortebraccio, G, 154; Mascarello, G, 178; Perleone, G, 248; Anon. A, G, 259–60; Anon. B, G, 299ff.). He has gone to heaven, where—and not in Venice—is found the "true patriciate," eternally in the embrace of God (Bevilacqua, V, fol. 158; also Filelfo, G, 107). Innocent in life, he is assured of salvation, and is now one of God's angels (Mascarello, G, 178; Perleone, G, 248; Anon. B., G, 299ff.). How much better to have a worthy son in paradise than an unworthy one on earth! (Anon. A, G, 261, 268; also Fortebraccio, G, 153–54). We will join our sons soon, wrote Filelfo, Marcello's contemporary, who had just lost a son the same age as Valerio; they are not lost to us (Filelfo, G, 55). God, who wished to place the finest of children in the Marcello family, wrote Anon. A, gave you an extraordinary son, who now casts glory upon you (G, 261, 259).

Marcello, stubborn, was unconsoled (Bevilacqua, V, fols. 99ff., 102vff., 105ff., 156vff.). He wrestled with the problem of the injustice of his son's premature death (Bevilacqua, V, fols. 97v–98). How hard to lose a child; how harsh that premature death; such promise unfulfilled! (Bevilacqua, V, fols. 10v–11, 99, 104r–v; Orsini, M, fol. 20v; Nogarola, ed. Abel, 171; George, ed. Mon., esp. 236–39; Mascarello, G, 176; Guarini, G, 182; Perleone, G, 214–17, 232, 235; Anon. A, 253). His grief was torrential grief; all Venice grieved with him, wrote Guarini, reflecting what seems to be the case, that Marcello's state became a public spectacle (G, 182). He considered but rejected suicide (Bevilacqua, V, fols. 162v–71). He insisted on the right of a father to grieve and appealed to his friend, Duke René, to understand his case which he had set in the Glasgow codex before us alongside the arguments of consolation extended him (Bevilacqua, V, esp. fols. 7–10, 99, 171v–73).

How are we to assess this episode of love, death, grief, consolation, and consolation rebuffed? If all is as it seems, it poses an example counter to what some historians suggest is the usual pattern of family relations in this premodern era. Children died with horrible frequency in medieval and Renaissance Europe. They may have shrunk from loving their children too much, it has been suggested, to save themselves the wearing sorrow when, implacably, death struck. Perhaps. This may have been a frequent, maybe even a typical response. But clearly it was not universal. Other evidence shows considerable warmth of family feeling despite the evidence of frequent neglect and indifference. Among the Italian humanists, scholars have pointed to four cases in the fifteenth century of fathers who vocally declare and defend their grief for the loss of children: sons in every case. Marcello is a fifth.

We can scarcely generalize from these few examples to speak about the experience of all families of all social classes in the Italian Renaissance. But the frequency among humanists of the theme of mourning a child is striking. Humanists as a group were more likely than most fathers to express such feelings as bereavement in writing—to write was their profession or their avocation; they may have put in words what others felt but left unexpressed. And what humanists wrote was more likely to be read, shared, and preserved than the words of less skilled or articulate persons. We are not entitled, therefore, to dismiss what they say as irrelevant to the experience of families outside of an intellectual elite. They may have in some immeasurable way given voice to feelings of paternal affection widespread in their culture.

To return to the Marcello episode: it may give us a clue to such family relations, but only if the record it offers is reliable. How much faith shall we place in the related humanist reports of filial excellence and paternal grief? The genre of consolation is a genre; it has its conventions, many of which are repeated here. The child's beauty, piety, obedience, the father's lamentations could be a web of words snatched from an established tradition by consolers more or less distant from the real events. In fact, some of the consolers may have had little or no contact with the family: Filelfo (one of the earliest and most eloquent!), Guarini, Mascarello, Anon. A and B. Others who knew Marcello personally may have, but there is no evidence of close relatedness: Sagundino, George, Nogarola, Fortebraccio, Bevilacqua. Two were clearly intimates and eyewitnesses of some of the events described: Perleone and Orsini. The father's voice we hear only as mimed by Bevilacqua; the child's, of course, never.

Thus many of the reporters of this incident are distanced from the events themselves. And the verisimilitude of their reports is further compromised by the presence of an invasive literary convention. Beyond these problems, there is something else definitely suspect about the construction of these texts. Elements in the description of Valerio and his death are present with suspicious consistency (and with equally puzzling variants) in many or most of the accounts: the early as well as the late ones, those by *famigliari* and those by strangers. The moment when Marcello first saw his son—Valerio's performance in the classroom—his behavior toward visitors—his recognition of the doctor Gerardo—his deathbed conversations with his father—how were these things made known to the authors of the Glasgow consolations? Did they each severally consult with the bereaved father? Did the first to write of each event compose a fiction in which he was followed by later imitators? Or did Marcello through a secretary publish a digest of anecdotes—a press release, in effect—for circulation to prospective authors? Close examination of the accounts of each incident in isolation could begin to point to an answer to this problem; but I believe it is ultimately unanswerable.

My own suspicion is that the last possibility presented above is correct. Marcello made known to Venice's *ordo litteratorum* that he would be interested in seeing works praising his lost Valerio. Perhaps he was inspired to do so after one or two works—those by Sagundino and George?—had arrived unprompted. He could have then supplied some anecdotes which different authors elaborated in distinctive ways. This hypothesis is consistent with two known facts. The first is that one and probably two of the Glasgow works were directly commissioned by Marcello (Bevilacqua's and Filelfo's). The second is that the works by those close to the family include, adjacent to anecdotes that are unique, and witnessed by those authors, some of the elements apparently circulated to nonintimates. The most knowledgeable writers, in other words, do not reject the incidents described by others, but are able to inject fresh matter of their own.

Marcello then may have to a greater or lesser degree—by direct commission or by suggestion and encouragement—stirred up this flurry of literary consolations. Must we therefore dismiss the whole episode as a concoction of a dilettante nobleman titillated by the prospect of fame? I think not: the framework of artifice does not need to invalidate the event which lies at its center. Some heart can be taken from the anecdotes of Valerio's brief life which appear uniquely in the works of authors belonging to Marcello's intimate circle: these seem deeply genuine, and suggest the plausibility of the whole series of events in which they take their place. The comment that Valerio made at the tomb of Vettor Pisani, as an example, was made in Orsini's own church and in that cleric's presence, for he stresses that he himself conversed with the boy. Orsini also was sole witness to Valerio's conversation with his father's academic friends

(M, fols. 19v–20, 20v). Also convincing is Perleone's account of Doctor Gerardo's visit—not a unique account, but a uniquely detailed one, suggesting the humanist's presence (G, 229ff., 245). Elsewhere, Perleone is a sole witness: of Valerio's confrontation with neighborhood children (G, 233–34), and, beyond our immediate concerns here, of some aspects of Marcello's military career (G, 197ff.). That these incidents should be invented I find quite implausible.

Their credibility lends stature to some others: the infant's eager greeting of his father at three months, conversations with senators and other prominent men, Marcello's vow offered in exchange for Valerio's recovery and Valerio's self-sacrificing intervention. These are repeated by several authors and are rich in detail; Orsini witnessed the conversations (M, fol. 20). Also convincing is the description of the child's intelligence and his father's role in providing for him a humanist education. Valerio's ability to share his father's interests in this direction may have aroused unique affection in the heart of this amateur *letterato*.

The contention made here—that this incident obliquely reflects real feelings and events—is best supported, however, by the evidence of Marcello's response. The very intensity of his paternal affection and extremity of despair are convincing: these emotions exceeded the norm. (Valerio's mother, whose nobility is duly praised [Perleone, G, 194–96], is not even mentioned as a mourner.) Struck, Perleone wonders: why such excess of feeling here? (G, 190–92). Marcello had always shouldered well the death of others—and his family had been ruthlessly dealt with by the angel of that name. He had lost his father Francesco whom he loved as much as any child; his mother Magdalucia, who had borne twenty-six children, nineteen boys and seven girls, the latter, he notes, all married to noblemen; Marcello had lost his brother, the Bishop Pietro Marcello, a second father, and had been present at the deathbed; he had lost other brothers and sisters, unspecified; a daughter; other sons. Why, asks Perleone, is Valerio alone so mourned? Did his represent the accumulation of all those other deaths? And other children, full of promise, survive. Perleone is justly puzzled. For this was a case of paternal love and filial love that surpassed his and most observers' experience. Here I believe is the key to this incident.

The Florentine humanist Giannozzo Manetti had a similar experience. He lost a son younger than Valerio—four years and two months old at death. Antonino was neither his first nor his last child, not his first nor his last son. (Marcello's grief is perhaps easier to understand, for Valerio was the last of his children, and it was especially painful for a father to lose that embodiment of the future at the verge of his own old age and death.) Yet Manetti, like Marcello, was inconsolable. In a self-consolatory dialogue which was his first substantial humanist work, Manetti presents through interlocutors consolatory arguments foreshadowing in some ways those encountered in the Marcello episode. In his own voice, he resists them, and defends his own despair. Here, too, was a case of exceptional attachment.

Further exploration of episodes such as these will strengthen, I suggest, a hypothesis that fathers and sons and even daughters, brothers, uncles and nephews, loved each other deeply. And it will also tell us more about the cultural expectations of young children in the Renaissance, at least in the social groups for which we have literary records. For Venice, these main avenues of study lie open: letters between humanists, especially fathers and sons, and teachers and sons, and school, university, and funeral orations. Attention to such sources will reveal, I think, the same intense interest in humanist studies linked to the same moral values of purity and obedience that has been found in the portrayal of Valerio Marcello.

The sincerity of Jacopo Antonio Marcello's fatherly affection, in closing, should not be discounted because of the artful literary form in which we find it described. Is it extraordinary that a bereft father should turn to literary modes to express and appease his grief? Such is often the balance between lives and words—even our own. Who of us, having lost a child, would not seek consolation even in conventional words, and not, unconsoled, reject it?

NOTE

I thank the audiences of the Renaissance Society of America National Conference and the Renaissance Seminar of Columbia University, whose comments on earlier versions of this essay have greatly strengthened it. Thanks are due to the National Endowment for the Humanities, which supported research for this study, and to Professor P. O. Kristeller for alerting me to the Glasgow codex and its importance. I am presently preparing a monograph on the Marcello episode which will examine its many dimensions. Since that work is underway, and since in smaller compass I have written previously on the matter, I forebear making references here to the secondary literature, and shall not supply the Latin text to passages quoted. The Bibliographical Note following this essay provides guidance to that secondary literature as well as to the body of texts upon which this study is based.

Bibliographical Note

I am preparing a monograph on the subject of Valerio Marcello's death and the consolation of Jacopo Antonio Marcello. In time, therefore, that volume should be consulted for guidance to the secondary literature pertinent to this problem. In the meantime, a general introduction to the Marcello episode is in my essay "An Inconsolable Father and His Humanist Consolers: Jacopo Antonio Marcello, Venetian Nobleman, Patron and Man of Letters," in *Iter Festivum* (a volume of essays in honor of Paul Oskar Kristeller), ed. J. Hankins, J. Monfasani, and F. Purnell, forthcoming in the Medieval and Renaissance Studies series (Binghamton: MRTS [SUNY Press], 1987). A brief discussion of the literary record of that episode can be found in my *Venetian Humanism in an Age of Patrician Dominance* (Princeton, N.J.: Princeton University Press, 1986), part II, Profile of Jacopo Antonio Marcello. In that volume can also be found profiles of the Venetian participants in the consolation of Marcello. The whole incident is discussed from the vantage point of Francesco Filelfo's consolation by R. Fabbri, "Le *Consolationes de obitu Valerii Marcelli* ed il Filelfo," in *Miscellanea di studi in onore di Vittore Branca*, Biblioteca dell'"Archivum Romanicum," ser. I, vols. 178–81 (4 vols. in 6; Florence: Olschki, 1983), III, i, 227–50. The bibliographical apparatus of these works provides adequate guidance to specialized studies on Marcello and his humanist colleagues.

The Marcello incident should be viewed in the light of the wider issues of the history of the family, and of death, grief, and consolation. Of a large literature on the history of the family, see esp. P. Ariès, *Centuries of Childhood: A Social History of Family Life*, trans. R. Baldick (1960; New York: Vintage, 1965); J.-L. Flandrin, *Families in Former Times: Kinship, Household and Sexuality*, trans. R. Southern (1976; Cambridge: Cambridge University Press, 1979); D. Hunt, *Parents and Children in History: The Psychology of Family Life in Early Modern France* (New York: Basic Books, 1970); L. de Mause, ed., *The History of Childhood* (New York: Psychohistory Press, 1976), esp. de Mause, "The Evolution of Childhood," pp. 1–73, and J. B. Ross, "The Middle-Class Child in Urban Italy, Fourteenth to Early Sixteenth Century," pp. 183–228; L. Stone, "The Massacre of the Innocents," *New York Review of Books*, 21 (11/14/74), 25–31, reviewing Ariès, Hunt, and de Mause; Stone, *Family, Marriage and Sex in England, 1500–1800* (New York: Oxford University Press, 1977).

On the whole, these works suggest the absence of familial affection in premodern times. Among the voices for the other side, S. E. Ozment's *When Fathers Ruled: Family Life in Reformation Europe* (Cambridge, Mass.: Harvard University Press, 1983) has argued the existence of warm familial feeling. The letters of Renaissance humanists often contain expressions of strong familial affection and should be systematically searched for this. G. W. McClure, Jr., "The Humanist Art of Mourning: Autobiographical Writings on the Loss of a Son in Italian Humanist Thought (1400–1461)," *Renaissance Quarterly* 39 (1986), 440–75, has focused on works of self-consolation by the humanist fathers Coluccio Salutati, Giovanni Conversini, Giannozzo Manetti, and Francesco Filelfo, all of whom felt deeply the loss of sons. See his work for additional studies of Manetti's famous consolatory dialogue. The Filelfo consolation is in fact that written to Marcello but contains references to Filelfo's own son Olimpio, recently dead. Filelfo's work circulated widely in manuscript and printed versions independent of the other Marcello consolations.

For entry to a complex literature on the genre of consolation, see the notes to McClure's "Humanist Art of Mourning," and the same author's dissertation, "The Renaissance Vision of Solace and Tranquility: Consolation and Therapeutic Wisdom in Italian Humanist Thought" (2 vols.; University of Michigan, 1981); and G. W. Pigman III, *Grief and Mourning in Elizabethan England* (Cambridge: Cambridge University Press, 1985).

Most of the consolatory texts (and the most important) are found in the University of Glasgow manuscript (Hunterian Museum Library, cod. 201 [U.1.5]), henceforth cited as G, upon which this essay is principally founded. What follows is a summary list of the literature associated with the consolation of Jacopo Antonio Marcello for the death of his son Valerio. It lists: (1) the main manuscript sources and printed works for the texts, including G itself; (2) all the works appearing in G and their alternate manuscript and printed versions; (3) the works not appearing in G. Where an alternate version has been preferred to G for citation in this essay, the preferred version is marked by an asterisk. Pages are given unless folios are specified.

All references to these works in the text appear in parentheses, and give the author's name, the abbreviation identifying the appropriate manuscript or printed source, and page or folio numbers.

CONSOLATORY WORKS TO JACOPO ANTONIO MARCELLO FOR THE DEATH OF VALERIO

1. Principal collections and other sources cited

G	Glasgow, University of Glasgow, Hunterian Museum Library, cod. 201 (U.1.5), paginated; entitled *De obitu Valerii Marcelli* [*consolationes*] *Nicolae Secundini et aliorum*
F	Ferrara, Biblioteca Comunale Ariostea, cod. II, 135
M	Milan, Biblioteca Ambrosiana, cod. H 122 inf., fols. 2–28 (autograph)
V	Verona, Bibl. Civica, cod. 1472 (Biadego #224)
Abel	E. Abel, ed., *Isotae Nogarolae Veronensis opera quae supersunt omnia* (2 vols.; Vienna: apud Gerold & socios, 1886)

Benadduci	G. Benadduci, *A Jacopo Antonio Marcello patrizio veneto parte di orazione consolatoria ed elegia di Francesco Filelfo e lettera di Giovanni Mario Filelfo* (Tolentino: Stabilimento Tipografico Francesco Filelfo, 1894)
Fabbri	R. Fabbri, "Le *Consolationes de obitu Valerii Marcelli*," etc., in *Miscellanea di studi in onore di Vittore Branca* (4 vols. in 6; Florence: Olschki, 1983), III, i, 227–50
Mon.	J. Monfasani, ed., *Collectanea trapezuntiana: Texts, Documents and Bibliographies of George of Trebizond* (Binghamton: MRTS [SUNY Press] 1984)
Iter	P. O. Kristeller, *Iter Italicum*, etc. (3 vols. and continuing; London: E. J. Brill, 1963, 1967, 1983)

2. Works appearing in G

1-25*

Sagundino, Niccolò, *De obitu Valerii filii consolatio* (Venice, 1461)
Also Vat. Ottob. lat. 1732, fols. 1–13; F, fols. 92–105v

25-38

George of Trebizond, consolatory letter (Venice, 7 April 1461 [Mon.])
Ed. Mon., 235–48*; many manuscript versions there cited, including F, fols. 85–91v

38-126*

Filelfo, Francesco, *De obitu Valerii filii consolatio* ([Milan] 25 December 1461)
Also autograph version (Vat. Lat. 1790, fols. 3–154v) and other manuscript versions, several printings in fifteenth–sixteenth centuries; partially printed by Benadduci, pp. 1–15. See also Benadduci, xxvi n.12; Fabbri, "Le *Consolationes*," pp. 233ff.

127-29

Filelfo, Francesco, Greek elegy
Ed. Fabbri, 243–45; also many manuscript versions, including Vat. Lat. 1790, fols. 155–58, and printed editions. Translated by Ludovico Carbone (see below) and Ludovico Grifo (see under #3).

130-33

Carbone, Ludovico, translation of F. Filelfo's Greek elegy
Also in Venice, cod. Marc. Lat. XIV, 246 (4683), fols. 139–41, and elsewhere; see Fabbri, "Le *Consolationes*," pp. 233ff.

133-41

Nogarola, Isotta, *Ad Jacopum Antonium Marcellum eius dulcissimi filii . . . in obitu consolatoria* (Verona, 9 August 1461 [Abel])
Ed. Abel, II, 161–78*; many manuscript versions, including F, fols. 115–19

141-60*

Fortebraccio, Carlo, da Montone, *De obitu Valerii filii consolatio* ([1463])

161-74*

Mascarello, Montorio, *Dialogus consolatorius*, with prefatory letter (Venice, Kal. Febr.)

175-79*

Mascarello, Montorio, consolatory letter

*179–88**
Guarini, Battista, consolatory letter (Ferrara [F])
Also F, fols. 109v–14v; Rome, Bibl. Naz. Centrale Vittorio Emanuele II,
cod. Varia 10 (619), fol. 360 (barely legible; cf. *Iter,* II, 360)
*189–248**
Perleone, Pietro, *Laudatio in Valerium eius filium eximium* (Udine, 1
November 1463)
Also West Berlin, Staatsbibl. Preuss. Kulturbesitz, cod. lat. qu. 557, fols.
3–108v (cf. *Iter,* III, 490). Actually written 1462, probably Sept. [text]
*249–68**
Anonymous A, consolatory letter (Venice, 15 July 1463)
269–94
Orsini, Michele, *Francisci Philelphi opinio de summa venetorum origine . . .
improbata* (Venice, S. Antonio Vienensis, 26 August 1462 [M])
M*; actually written May 1462 (fol. 28)
*295–308**
Anonymous B, consolatory letter (Padua, 1 October 1463)
309–426
Bevilacqua, Giorgio, da Lazise, *Excusatio adversus consolatores in obitu
Valerii filii* ([Udine] 13 November [1463]), in name of Jacopo Antonio
Marcello, to King René d'Anjou
V, fols. 7–173*, with letter of 3 November 1463, fols. 4–6

3. Works not appearing in G

Carbone, Ludovico, *Carmen . . . in consolationem de obitu . . . filioli sui Valerii*
(Latin elegy) [Ferrara, 1463?]
Venice, cod. Marc. Lat. XIV, 246 (4683), fols. 126–38; see also Fabbri,
"Le *Consolationes,*" p. 235, n. 28
Filelfo, Francesco, *Ad Iacobum Antonium Marcellum equitem aureum nomine
Francisci Sfortzie Mediolanensium ducis consolatio de obitu Valerii filii*
(Latin elegy)
Ed. Benadduci, 17–23
Filelfo, Giovanni Mario, *Consolatio marcellina* (as named by Benadduci)
Location unknown; see Benadduci, pp. xx–xxi, xxvii n. 18, 25–26
Grifo, Ludovico, translation of Francesco Filelfo's Greek elegy
Venice, cod. Marc. Lat. XIV, 246 (4683), fols. 142–44; see Fabbri, "Le
Consolationes," pp. 233ff.
Perleone, Pietro, consolatory letter
Venice, cod. Marc. Lat. XIV, 266 (4502), fols. 218–22; F, fols. 106–9;
Munich, Bayerische Staatsbibl., cod. Mon. Lat. 362, fols. 94–100; Vat.
Chis. J VII, 215, fols. 103–6v; also Padua, Bibl. del Seminario, cod.
126 (cf. *Iter,* II, 9)
Tifernate, Gregorio, *Oratio . . . de obitu Valerii filii*
Vicenza, Bibl. Comunale Bertoliana, cod. 7.1.31 (formerly 6.7.31), fols.
126v–131 (with epigram to Valerio on 131r–v); also Trent, Bibl. Capitolare,
cod. s.n. (temp #258), fols. nn. (cf. *Iter,* II, 189)

LANCE K. DONALDSON-EVANS

Demons, Portents, and Visions: Fantastic and Supernatural Elements in Ronsard's Poetry

For anyone who is familiar with much of the recent criticism devoted to *le fantastique*, the idea of viewing certain poetic texts of Ronsard as examples of this genre might well seem preposterous, anachronistic— indeed fantastic! First of all, Todorov, in his perceptive *Introduction à la littérature fantastique*, seems to preclude any such possibility when he states categorically: "We see now why the poetic reading constitutes a danger for the fantastic. If as we read a text we reject all representation, considering each sentence as a pure semantic combination, the fantastic could not appear ... the fantastic can subsist only within fiction: poetry cannot be fantastic."[1]

A second problem confronting anyone rash enough to consider Ronsard from the perspective of the fantastic is the chronological dilemma. Many critics follow the lead of Castex in equating the rise of the fantastic with Romanticism. Now, while there is little doubt that the nineteenth century represents the Golden Age of fantastic literature, it is my contention— and fortunately I am not alone—that the fantastic is far from being a Romantic invention but is instead a phenomenon which resists such precise dating, one which occurs at least as early as the Renaissance.

However, for the moment, I want to return to the first problem and address Todorov's claim that poetry and the fantastic are incompatible. Obviously the first step in attempting to reconcile Todorov's view and my own is to arrive at a satisfactory working definition as to what constitutes the fantastic.

The etymological source of the word *fantastique* is a useful, indeed a necessary, place to begin: *fantaisie, fantastique, fantasque, fantasme* in all their meanings derive from the Greek verb *phantazein* (to make visible) and *phantazesthai* (to have visions) which produced the noun *phantasia* meaning "appearance" and later "phantom," as well as "faculty of imagination." So when Ronsard describes himself as being "fantastique d'esprit" as he does in "L'Hymne de l'autonne," although the primary meaning of the adjective is something like "inventive" or perhaps even "visionary," it is neither illegitimate nor anachronistic to suggest important etymological and conceptual links between Ronsard's description of himself and the modern literary sense of *fantastique*. Of course, in sixteenth-century French, as Huguet's dictionary attests, the adjective *fantastique* also has a negative connotation, since it can mean "fou, insensé, extravagant" (mad or crazy). However, as madness was often considered to be related to the supernatural as well as to the process of literary creation, these meanings complement, without excluding, the etymological content of the word, a content which would be well known to a French Renaissance poet who had studied Greek at the Collège de Coqueret, as had Ronsard.

Perhaps one of the most practical definitions of the fantastic, however, is that given by Pierre-Georges Castex: "The fantastic is characterised by . . . the brutal intrusion of the mysterious into the context of everyday life."[2] Such a definition has the advantage of receiving the approval of Todorov himself and has been glossed by other critics such as Jacques Finné, who proposes the following version: "We can consider as fantastic any human being or in fact any entity encountered on the fringe of everyday human experience and whose sudden appearance violates the accepted rules of human existence."[3] It is this definition which I shall adopt as being the most fundamental account of the fantastic, a definition which aptly describes the many intrusions of the mysterious in Ronsard's verse as well as the many apparitions of beings which come from the periphery of everyday human experience.

Before proceeding, we need to return for a moment to Todorov for whom the *fantastique* is a peculiarly volatile, even fragile genre, being situated between *l'étrange* and *le merveilleux*. Indeed, for him, the *fantastique* lasts only as long as a certain hesitation either on the part of the reader or of one of the characters in a story as to whether apparently inexplicable events can be explained according to the laws of nature, or whether in fact they are the result of supernatural intervention. Once this hesitation passes, the *fantastique* will be incorporated either into the category of *l'étrange* (the supernatural explained) or *le merveilleux* (the supernatural accepted).[4] If we were to apply this criterion with total rigor, all the fantastic elements in Ronsard's verse would probably be assimilable to the *le merveilleux* and yet, as we shall see, there is often a feeling of the uncanny, which creates an atmosphere similar to that found in literature characterized "officially" as *fantastique*. In fact, Todorov's account of the fantastic is much less rigid than it first appears, and later in his text, when analyzing a story from the *Thousand and One Nights,* he recognizes the presence of supernatural beings as one of the pervasive features of the *fantastique:* "The other group of fantastic elements is based on the very existence of supernatural beings, such as the genie and the princess-sorceress, and on their power over human destiny. Both are capable of transforming themselves and others, and both can fly or transport beings and objects in space, etc. This is one of the constants of the literature of the fantastic: the existence of supernatural beings more powerful than men."[5] In his hymn "Les Daimons," Ronsard represents such supernatural beings and stresses their capacity for metamorphosis:

> Just as the Demons, whose body is so nimble,
> Pliable, supple, active, and transformable,
> Quickly change their shape, so that their agile body
> Is metamorphosed into whatever form it pleases: (ll. 91–94)
> . . . .
> One ofttimes sees them changed into strange beasts,
> Their bodies cut into pieces: one of them has but a head,
> Another only eyes, another has but arms,
> While only the shaggy feet of yet another remain visible. (ll. 99–102)[6]

If Todorov can include stories from the *Thousand and One Nights* in his discussion, it does not seem unreasonable to examine this particular Ronsard text, and in fact many others, from the perspective of the fantastic.

However, what of his objection that the *fantastique* and poetry are mutually exclusive? Once again we find ourselves confronted by a rigid definition which is less rigid than it appears. In the first place, Todorov himself admits that the differentiation he has already established between poetry and fiction (that fiction is representative while poetic images are nondescriptive) is a matter of degree rather than of binary opposition.[7] And if we move away from a structuralist/formalist approach, we can allow a certain referentiality, a certain fictionality to be inherent to some and perhaps all poetic genres. While "pure" lyric poetry might best be considered as a hermetic, self-referential verbal construct, other poetic genres, particularly in a period like the Renaissance, are replete with representational, fictional elements which cannot be reduced to a simple "verbal chain" or "semantic combination." Most of the Ronsard texts we are dealing with fall into such a referential category, which means that these examples of his poetry can in fact be considered to be perfectly legitimate vehicles for the *fantastique* (as, incidentally, Vax and Vircondelet among others, have already suggested).[8]

Most of the fantastic/supernatural elements in Ronsard's poetry are concentrated in the figure of the demon, that curiously ambiguous creature who makes his appearance in Ronsard's poetry quite early as a positive presence often associated directly with poetic inspiration. In the "Ode à Joachim du Bellay" from the first book of the *Odes*, Ronsard describes the ministrations of the demons to poets:

> A Demon accompanies them,
> The most learned Demon of all,
> And he instructs them every night, as they dream
> So that they learn from him without effort.
> Although demigod, he is willing
> Mere mortals to inform,
> So that man, while yet asleep,
> Can learn all knowledge. (ll. 25–33)[9]

In texts such as this one, Ronsard's portrayal of the demons is positive: they are seen as benevolent manifestations of the supernatural world order which forms part of the poet's cosmos. They do not in any way constitute an incursion into the fantastic.

However, this is far from always being the case and when demons come to personify not only the good, but also the malevolent forces in the universe, it is then that they trigger the *frisson* and the hesitation which are signs of the fantastic. One of the texts where this is most clearly seen is the enigmatic "Le Chat" from *Le Premier Livre des Poemes*. This fascinating poem, which begins with a strongly affirmative declaration of religious faith ("God is omnipresent, and is everywhere active, / Beginning, end and middle / Of every living thing, and His soul is contained / In everything and gives life to all creatures, / Just as our soul gives life to our bodies" [ll. 1–5]),[10] quickly reveals a fundamental tension between faith and superstition, between the Christian and the pagan supernatural, a tension which is only superficially resolved in the final lines by the assertion of man's God-given preeminence over the animal kingdom. However, this closing affirmation stands in sharp contrast to the general movement of the poem. The initial paean of praise to an omnipresent divinity leads to a discussion of divination by means of animals, birds, and plants, and includes a number of examples which the poet claims come from his own personal experience.

Firstly, there is the story of the "Thessalienne," the daphne, a variety of laurel, upon which the poet had been lavishing his most careful attention ("I watered it, kept it free from weeds, dug up the soil around it / Morning and evening; my intention was / To use its branches to make a fine wreath for my head..." [ll. 77–79]). Mysteriously, one brief hour after having given the plant its morning watering, the poet found the formerly thriving plant dying. The only possible explanation was a supernatural one ("One hour later I found it uprooted / By a Demon;

no mortal hand / Could have been responsible: it all happened too suddenly" [ll. 84–86]). This was not only an act of malevolence on the part
of the Demon in question (and all this in a universe in which God is
everywhere, infused in all beings), but a prophecy, since, subsequently,
Ronsard fell ill and languished like the daphne, although, unlike the
plant, he did not die. The "murder" (Ronsard calls it thus) of the daphne
was coupled with another bad omen, as, two months later, one of his
servants, mortally wounded by a horse's kick, called to him and fixed his
eyes on him at the moment of his death. Both of these omens proved to
be accurate and for eleven long months, Ronsard's broken body was
wracked by persistent fever. While the attribution of Ronsard's illness to
the intervention of a demon might seem to be simply a continuation of a
long-standing tradition which goes back to biblical times, the omens
themselves, particularly the mysterious death of the plant, represent
precisely that transgression of natural laws, that brutal intrusion of the
mysterious into everyday life, which constitute the very stuff of the
fantastic.

The poet's dread reaches a paroxysm when, after more than a hundred
lines, he finally turns his attention to the animal after which the poem is
named. The "triste Chat" is the creature which has the most "esprit
prophetique" (and which therefore should logically be one of the animals
which is closest to God). However, the cat fills the poet with utter dread:

> There was never a man living
> Who hates cats more than I do;
> I hate their staring eyes, their faces,
> And when I see them, I flee from their presence,
> Trembling all over from head to foot. . . . (ll. 114–18)

Throughout this section of the poem a subtle link between demon, cat,
and poet is established, a link which perhaps helps to explain the astonish-
ing apprehension Ronsard feels for this particular animal. It is significant
that the plant attacked and destroyed by the demon is a daphne, long
associated with poetic creation, a plant which Ronsard specifically identifies
with his own textual activity by stating that he intended to make a crown
of laurel for himself from its leaves. As for the cat, Ronsard establishes a
double correlation between it and poetic creation. Firstly, the adjective
he uses to describe the dreaded animal is *triste,* an epithet which suggests
melancholy, the temperament favorable to poetic production. Secondly
the cat, like the demon, is endowed with prophetic powers, a gift also
shared by the poet in Ronsard's literary universe. In this poem the
demon (and the cat) represent the reverse face of the demon of poetic
inspiration, and the dread Ronsard feels in the face of their intrusion
into his everyday world is in fact a metonymy for the ultimate dread of

any poet of any age: the fear of the Muses' flight, the phobia of poetic sterility. If all writing is about writing and all poetry about the poetic act, then the inscrutable and unpredictable intrusion of the fantastic into everyday life is the perfect figure for that most unpredictable of events: the outpouring of inspiration, variously seen by poets across the ages as the gift of the gods or as arising from some dark, demonic source.

Of course the poetic text where demons and demonology are most prevalent is the hymn "Les Daimons." This is a poem which has always particularly intrigued me and which has been the object of a great deal of commentary, thanks in part to Albert-Marie Schmidt's excellent critical edition. Nowhere is both the omnipresence and the ambiguity of the demon more abundantly clear. The demons are the inhabitants of the air and are thus intermediaries between the residents of the heavens (the angels and ultimately God) and those of the earth, mankind. Part air, part fire, their domain of predilection is the turbulent troposphere, "tousjours remply de vents, de foudres et d'orages." The demons are like their fellow inhabitants of this domain, the clouds, and, as we have already seen they have the same power of metamorphosis, the same ability to create monsters, except that the demons can bring these monsters to earth to frighten mortal men. Just as the air transmits to our eyes the images of objects in the material world, so the demons, creatures of air, transmit to the eyes of our mind, to our imagination, visions:

> Just as the Demons reveal their masquerades
> To our imagination which is capable of perceiving such things,
> Then our imagination transmits them to our minds,
> In the same fashion and way
> As it imagines them sleeping, or waking,
> Then our hearts are assailed by a sudden fear,
> Our hair stands up straight upon our heads,
> And from our brows, drop by drop,
> Sweat drips down to our feet.
> If we are abed, we dare not lift our arms,
> Nor even turn our body under the sheets;
> At such times we think we see our fathers
> Dead in their winding sheet, and we hear our poor, dead mothers,
> Speaking to us in the night, and we see in visions
> Our friends perishing in shipwrecks. (ll. 125–38)[11]

And the list of *terreurs nocturnes* goes on as these supernatural creatures are presented as the source of such phenomena. As we can see from these verses, demons are held responsible for nightmares and portents. They are also associated with what many consider to be the fantastic subject par excellence: the ghost.

There are, however, good demons and it is through these creatures of the air that man receives the gift of prophecy:

> The good Demons come down to earth from the heavens
> To reveal the will of the Gods to us,
> And then transmit to God our prayers and actions.
> They free our fettered souls from our bodies
> To take them up there, so that they can imagine
> What we need to know for our instruction.
> They show us in the night, through marvelous dreams,
> The true presages of the good and ill that is to befall us.
>
> (ll. 209–16)[12]

These good demons inspire no horror, just as the supernatural elements in fairy stories do not per se provoke fear, so perhaps we should modify Todorov's treatment of the relationship between the fantastic and the supernatural to state that benign supernatural beings and events do not produce the uncanny sensation associated with the fantastic, while malevolent, capricious spirits do. In any case, Ronsard appears to be far more fascinated by the malevolent variety than by the good, and in subsequent verses of the poem he details the activities of the bad demons, which range from the transmission of "pestes, fièvres, langueurs" to the production of apocalyptic signs in the heavens:

> They make noises in the air to frighten us,
> They make our human eyes see two suns in the sky,
> They turn the moon black
> And cause a bloody rain to fall from the sky. (ll. 225–28)

Ronsard then goes on to discuss "Incubes, Larves, Lares, Lemurs, Penates, et Succubes," all favorite subjects of later fantastic literature, and does not even neglect the somewhat playful, if frightening, activity of the poltergeists:

> They move seats, tables and tressles in the night,
> Keys, doors, sideboards, beds, chairs and stools,
> They count our treasure or hurl to the ground
> Now a sword, now a glass. . . . (ll. 245–48)

However, the most striking example of *le fantastique* in this poem is the recital of an encounter with supernatural and diabolical beings which is found in lines 347–70. The poem's persona recounts how, one night, at the witching hour ("Un soir, vers la minuict . . .") he was on his way to visit his mistress when he found himself pursued by supernatural hellhounds ("I heard, or so it seemed to me, a barking pack / Of dogs following in my footsteps . . ." [ll. 351–52]). Leading the hunt is a disquieting skeletonlike figure mounted on a black horse, who stretches out his bony hand to Ronsard:

> I saw close to me on a large black horse
> A man who was nothing but bones,
> Holding out his hand to invite me to mount upon the horse behind him. . . .
>
> (ll. 353–55)

The protagonist is seized with dread at the sight of these terrible apparitions and although he is wearing armor and is carrying a dagger, sword, and shield, he is nonetheless paralyzed with fear. It is only thanks to the remembrance that demons fear the naked blade of a sword, a remembrance which he sees as divinely inspired, that the poem's protagonist draws his weapon, with the result that the horrible specters flee. Ronsard's persona, when confronted by these demonic manifestations of the supernatural, gives voice to a feeling of dread which even his religious faith seems unable to overcome completely. The poem finishes with a prayer addressed to God which asks for protection from the evil variety of demonic forces and then, in an ironic twist which acts as a kind of poetic exorcism to dispel the fears which the poem has so eloquently expressed, Ronsard calls for the visitation of the demons upon the heads of those who are unappreciative of his poetry:

> O Lord God, in whom I put my trust,
> For the honor of your name, please grant,
> Oh please, that never again will I find
> Such apparitions in my path, but rather, Oh Lord,
> Send them far from Christendom, send the Turks
> These Goblins, Demons, Ghosts and Spirits,
> Or else call them down upon the heads of those
> Who dare say ill of the poems I sing on my new lyre. (ll. 421–28)

The perfect revenge of the poet!

However, although demons (good and bad) are treated in many other texts of Ronsard in similar fashion to their portrayal in "Le Chat" and "Les Daimons," they are not always associated with the uncanny and the fantastic. Even ghosts do not always give rise to a feeling of the numinous in Ronsard's verse. A case in point is the curious "Prosopopée de Louys de Ronsard," a short work from the *Second Livre des Poemes* which recounts the appearing in a dream or a vision (it is not quite clear which) of Louis de Ronsard, the poet's deceased father. The poem purports to be a rebuttal of those philosophies which deny any immortality to the soul and is highly stylized with Vergilian overtones of Anchises appearing to Aeneas. It is just before dawn (the most propitious time for reliable dreams or visions) that the poet has this particular encounter with the supernatural:

> I saw hovering over my bed an apparition,
> Thin, without bones, which possessed the eyes, the face,
> The body, the shape, and the voice
> Of my dear father when he was of this world. (ll. 9–12)[13]

The apparition becomes more frightening when it touches him three times, then leaves the bed three times, finally returning to take the poet's left hand and admonish him. What follows this evocation of the specter of his father is however quite unexceptional and we leave the threshold of the fantastic to fall into the sermon, since Louis's advice to his son is a standard paternal homily. At the end of his speech, Louis de Ronsard vanishes, leaving his son literally grasping at thin air:

> but the shadowy Form,
> Escaping from my clutch, flew away like the wind

and as night yields to day, the poet awakens, marveling ("tout esmerveillé"). Here the *merveilleux* is relatively benign, even if the image of the father is described as terrifying ("affreuse") in line 15, and the realm of the fantastic is approached from afar without being entered. What the supernatural frame of the poem does do, however, is to add interest to the rather banal advice the ghost gives to his son, advice he could have found in the Bible or in any number of pious treaties. Here the supernatural is an effective device to capture the reader's attention and to give weight to the father's words, although it does perhaps also bear witness to Ronsard's abiding fascination with the fantastic in its most primal sense.

Are we then justified in considering Ronsard to be a *poète fantastique?* Perhaps not in the same way or to the same degree as some of the poets of the nineteenth century. I believe, however, we can legitimately describe certain elements in his work as fantastic and we can discover an uncanny, fantastic atmosphere in a small but significant number of his poems. If his brand of the *fantastique* belongs above all to Todorov's category of the *fantastique-merveilleux,* we are nonetheless in the presence of an embryonic *auteur fantastique* whose superstition is never fully conquered by his religious faith and who is able to portray effectively the feeling of the uncanny which results from the brutal intrusion of supernatural forces into everyday reality. The visceral fear of malevolent demons which Ronsard portrays so graphically in his poetry may well be the verbalization of that archetypal poetic fear: poetic impotence and sterility. Harold Bloom would perhaps see in this fear of the demon a metaphor for the anxiety of influence, since, as he says: "our daemon . . . came to us not from the fire but from our precursors."[14] However, no matter what psychological or literary explanations we might propose, the fact remains that Ronsard is a poet who is quite capable of provoking in his reader what Louis Vax has called "le frisson du fantastique."[15]

NOTES

1. Tzvetan Todorov, *The Fantastic: A Structural Approach to a Literary Genre,* trans. Richard Howard (Cleveland: Case Western Reserve University Press, 1973), p. 60.

2. Pierre-Georges Castex, *Le conte fantastique en France de Nodier à Maupassant* (Paris: José Corti, 1951), p. 8 ("Le fantastique se caractérise ... par une intrusion brutale du mystère dans le cadre de la vie réelle"). Unless otherwise indicated, all translations from the French are my own.

3. Jacques Finné, *La littérature fantastique* (Bruxelles: Editions de l'Université de Bruxelles, 1980), p. 13 ("Peut être considéré comme fantastique tout être humain ou toute entité dont la rencontre se situe en marge de l'expérience humaine courante; dont l'apparition viole les règles préétablies ... ").

4. Todorov, *Fantastic,* pp. 41ff.

5. Todorov, *Fantastic,* p. 109.

6. Pierre de Ronsard, *Oeuvres complètes,* ed. Paul Laumonier (Paris: Société des Textes Français Modernes, 1935), VIII ("Tout ainsi les Daimons qui ont le corps habile, / Aisé, souple, dispost, à se muer facile, / Changent bien tost de forme, et leur corps agile est / Transformé tout soudain en tout ce que leur plaist:" [ll. 91–94]; "Bien souvent on les voit, se transformer en beste, / Tronqués par la moytié: l'une n'a que la teste, / L'autre n'a que les yeux, l'autre n'a que les bras, / Et l'autre que les piedz tous veluz par-à-bas" [ll. 99–102]).

7. Todorov, *Fantastic,* p. 59 ("Poetry too includes certain representative elements, and fiction properties which render the text, opaque, intransitive").

8. See Louis Vax, *La séduction de l'étrange* (Paris: Presses Universitaire de France, 1965) and Alain Vircondelet, *La poésie fantastique française* (Paris: Seghers, 1973).

9. Laumonier, I ("Un Démon les accompaigne / Par-sur tous le mieux instruit, / Qui en songes toute nuit / Sans nul travail les enseigne, / Et demy-dieu ne desdeigne / De les aller informant, / Afin que l'homme en dormant / Toutes sciences appreigne" [ll. 25–33]).

10. Laumonier, XV, "Le Chat," ll. 1–5: ("Dieu est par tout, par tout se mesle Dieu, / Commencement, la fin et le millieu / De ce qui vit, et dont l'Ame est enclose / Par tout, et tient en vigueur toute chose, / Comme nostre ame infuse dans noz corps"). The French texts for the other sections of this poem are as follows: ll. 77–79 "Je l'arrosois, la cerclois et bechois / Matin et soir; la voyant je pensois / M'en faire au chef une belle couronne ... "; ll. 84–86: "Une heure apres je la vis arrachée / Par un Démon; une mortelle main / Ne fist le coup: le fait fut trop soudain"; and ll. 114–18: "Homme ne vit qui tant haïsse au monde / Les Chats que moy d'une haine profonde; / Je hay leurs yeux, leur front et leur regard, / Et les voyant je m'enfuy d'autrepart, / Tremblant de nerfs, de veines et de membre' ... ".

11. "Les Daimons," ll. 125–38: "Tout ainsi les Daimons font leurs masqueures voir / A nostre fantaisie apte à les recevoir, / Puis nostre fantaisie à l'esprit les r'apporte / De la mesme façon et de la mesme sorte / Qu'elle les imagine ou dormant, ou veillant, / Et lors une grand'peur va noz coeurs assaillant, / Le poil nous dresse au chef, et du front, goutte-à-goutte, / Jusques à noz talons la sueur

nous degoutte. / Si nous sommes au lict, n'osons lever les bras, / Ny tant soit peu tourner le corps entre les draps; / Adoncq' nous est advis que nous voyons noz peres / Morts dedans un linçueil, et noz defunctes meres / Parler à nous la nuict, et que voyons dans l'eau / Quelcun de noz amis perir dans un bateau." See also Albert-Marie Schmidt, *Les Daimons* (Paris: Albin Michel, 1939), for an excellent commentary on this poem.

12. "Les Daimons," ll. 209–16 ("Les bons viennent de l'air jusques en ces bas lieux / Pour nous faire sçavoir la volonté des Dieux, / Puis r'emportent à Dieu nos faictz et noz prieres, / Et detachent du corps noz ames prisonnieres / Pour les mener là-haut, à fin d'imaginer / Ce qui se doit sçavoir pour nous endoctriner. / Ils nous montrent de nuict par songes admirables / De noz biens et noz maux les signes veritables . . . ").

The text of the other quotations from this hymn are as follows: ll. 225–28 ("Ilz font des sons en l'air pour nous espovanter, / Ilz font aux yeux humains deux Soleilz presenter, / Ilz font noircir la Lune horriblement hydeuse, / Et font pleurer le Ciel d'une pluye saigneuse"); ll. 245–48 ("Ilz remuent de nuict bancz, tables, et treteaux, / Clefz, huys, portes, buffetz, lictz, chaires, escabeaux, / Ou comptent noz tresors, ou gectent contre terre / Maintenant une espée, et maintenant un verre"); ll. 351–52 ("J'oüy, ce me sembloit, une aboyante chasse / De chiens qui me suyvoit pas-à-pas à la trace"); ll. 353–55 ("Je vy aupres de moy sur un grand cheval noir / Un homme qui n'avoit que les ôs, à le voir, / Me tendant une main pour me monter en crope"); and ll. 421–28 ("O Seigneur eternel, en qui seul gist ma foy, / Pour l'honneur de ton nom, de grace, donne moy, / Donne moy que jamais je ne trouve en ma voye / Ces paniques terreurs, mais, ô Seigneur, envoye / Loin de la Chrestienté, dans le païs des Turcz / Ces Larves, ces Daimons, ces Lares et Lemurs, / Ou sur le chef de ceux qui oseront mesdire / Des chansons que j'accorde à ma nouvelle lyre").

13. "Prosopopée," ll. 9–12: "j'apperceu sur mon lict une image / Gresle, sans oz, qui l'oeil et le visage, / Le corps, la taille, et la parole avoit / Du pere mien quand au monde il vivoit"; and ll. 61–62: "mais la nueuse Idole, / Fraudant mes doigts, ainsi que vent s'envole."

14. Harold Bloom, *The Anxiety of Influence* (London: Oxford University Press, 1973), p. 139.

15. Vax, *Séduction,* p. 60.

MARYANNE CLINE HOROWITZ

Michel de Montaigne's Stoic Insights into Peasant Death

Michel de Montaigne's openness to the wisdom of commoners distinguishes him as an uncommon sage. Socrates, who regularly conversed with farmers and artisans, served as a model, and Montaigne's *Essays* are sprinkled with anecdotes of his conversations with peasants of Périgord.[1] Since the peasantry is not as sensational a topic as, say, cannibals, and peasants have not been the major commentators on Michel de Montaigne, Montaigne's discussion of peasant life and death in southwest France has not received much attention;[2] yet as a contribution to scholarship on Montaigne's thoughts on death, a focus on peasant death rather than on the more individualistic topic of Montaigne's thoughts on his own death would further substantiate the broad base of Montaigne's comprehension of and empathy for the human condition.

This study applies in sequence the methodologies of narrative history, the history of ideas, and the history of mentalities in order to recreate the multilayered context of Montaigne's value-laden description of peasants dying from the plague on his estate in the mid-1580s. Multiple methodologies are needed to encompass the interplay between a claimed observation (*referentialité*) of an event of dying, use of Stoic vocabulary (*intertextualité*) for describing the dying within an internal dialogue (*autotextualité*) on the value of texts versus experience, and a perception of communal contexts of attitudes (*mentalités*) toward death.[3] An irony is that the vividness of Montaigne's description of experiential observations supports the contention that by the mid-1580s observation and experience were overriding texts as his source for knowledge, yet his intertextual use of observations as anecdotes in a dialogue with the ancients suggests that his library continued to influence his observations. My goal is to analyze a small segment of Montaigne's prose as a case study in contextual and intertextual readings.

This study will attempt to illuminate two poignant value-laden descriptions of what Montaigne claimed he saw from his library window and while walking on his estate during the plague in Périgord in 1586–87:

> To what end do we keep forcing our nature with these efforts of learning? Let us look on the earth at the poor people we see scattered there, heads bowed over their toil, who know neither Aristotle nor Cato, neither example nor precept. From them Nature every day draws deeds of constancy and endurance purer and harder than those that we study with such care in school. How many of them I see all the time who ignore poverty! How many who desire death, or who meet it without alarm and without affliction! This man who is digging up my garden, this morning he buried his father or his son. [III: 12, P 1017, S 795–796 (b)]
>
> See these people: because they are dying in the same month, children, young people, old people, they are no longer stunned, they no longer bewail one another. I saw some who feared to remain behind as in a horrible solitude; and found them generally to be concerned only about their burial. It pained them to see the bodies scattered amid the fields, at the mercy of the animals that promptly appeared in swarms. . . . Here a man, healthy, was already digging his grave; others lay down in them while still alive. And one of my laborers with his hands and feet, pulled the earth over him as he was dying. . . . In short, a whole nation was suddenly, by habit alone, placed on a level that concedes nothing in firmness to any studied and premeditated fortitude. [III: 12, P 1025, S 802–803 (b)][4]

The first passage above was likely written during the siege of Castillon which lasted from July 10 to the end of August 1586.[5] About five miles away from the Château de Montaigne, the royal Catholic forces under Mayenne were besieging Turenne's Protestant stronghold of Castillon. An epidemic of the plague, which had killed more than 14,000 people in Bordeaux from June to December 1585, broke out thirty miles east in Périgord in August 1586.[6] The plague ravaged soldiers and countrymen alike, and was background to the downfall of Castillon by September 1, 1586. As the "history" is recorded by Pierre L'Estoile and repeated by De Thou, the plague marked the affection of Mayenne and the king's army for the people of Castillon. Like his contemporaries Pierre L'Estoile, De Thou, and Philippe Duplessis-Mornay, Michel de Montaigne documented the violence of the pillagers to crops and peasants, as well as the deadliness of the plague.[7] They, like Montaigne, reveal a certain fondness for exaggeration that is endemic to contemporary chroniclers, and it may be that "all" in the next quotation from Montaigne documents the mentality of despair more accurately perhaps than it does the condition of the land. Montaigne commented that troops "pillaged them, and consequently me too, even of hope, snatching from them all they had to provide for their living for many years,"[8] that "the very salubrious air of my place, where in the memory of man no contagion, even though in the neighborhood, had been able to get a foothold, became poisoned. . . . "⁹ The literary flair of Renaissance chroniclers notwithstanding, the cumulative effect of the several accounts is to document swift devastation and sudden death.

In September 1586, Montaigne interrupted his writing to travel with his family in search of hospitality away from the threat of the plague. After he returned in March 1587, he continued his essaying, and the second passage above was composed before January 1588, when he left for Paris. En route to publish a new edition of the *Essays* and to try to negotiate peace between Henry of Navarre (who had received hospitality from Montaigne in October 1587) and King Henry III, Montaigne experienced the two dangerous incidents documented at the close of the chapter: he was accosted by a Huguenot band, whose leader was likely Condé, and later by a group from the Catholic League.[10] The chapter "De la Phisionomie" takes its title partly from the physiognomy of Montaigne's face and the Huguenot leader's statement "that I owed my deliverance to my face and the freedom and firmness of my speech."[11]

Understressed in the critical literature on Montaigne is his "survivor guilt" at his equally striking deliverance from the fate of the peasants whose deaths he vicariously experienced. He recognized that such deliverance was aided by his noble position — his ability to depart from a scene of famine and plague. His juxtaposition of his physiognomy with the physiognomy of dying peasant workers reveals his awareness of the unjust "privileges" of noble position. In a letter to King Henry III dated August 31, 1583, Montaigne, as mayor of Bordeaux, had already expressed commiseration for the poor: he requested their relief from burdensome additional taxes on the egalitarian principle that "all impositions must be made equally upon all persons, the strong supporting the weak and . . . it is more reasonable that those who have the greater means should feel the burden more than those who live only precariously and by sweat of their body."[12]

Though empathetic, Montaigne's ethic — unlike the ethic of a ship captain going down with his ship and his crew — did allow for preserving the life of the one in charge, whether mayor or landed gentleman, especially one who did not fear to remain behind in solitude. During the summer of 1585, at the end of his second term as mayor of Bordeaux, while the plague was taking its toll of his constituents Montaigne was in Sainte-Foy negotiating with Henry of Navarre. He wrote the jurats about "risking going into the city in view of the bad condition it is in, especially for people coming from as pure an air as I do," and of his decision not to return for the last days of his mayoral term: "I will come as close to you as I can, to Feuillas [across the river from Bordeaux] if the disease has not reached there."[13] Ever since the Black Death of 1348 in Florence, when

Boccaccio in his *Decameron* vividly described the people dying in the city while his aristocratic storytellers retreated to an unpolluted scenic haven, the one known effective measure against the plague, amid the many ludicrous and superstitious remedies suggested by the medical doctors, was to flee from contagion.[14] Montaigne's behavior of quarantining himself and his family accorded with reasonable upper-class behavior when faced with the plague.

Intertextual comparison of Montaigne's portrayal with other portrayals of commoners dying from the plague might yield further insights. Strowski cited comparable accounts read by Montaigne: Pierre Boaistuau, *Le Théâtre du monde*, 1559, and Ambroise Paré, *Traité de la Peste*, 1568. Boaistuau described someone looking into a window to offer a remedy to a woman who, reconciled to death, covered herself with a sheet. That singular scene of care and self-sufficient serenity contrasted with his overall description of people dying in unseemly poses bereft of human charity. Both he and the doctor Paré, like most writers on the plague, described events in the urban scene. Paré stressed the coldhearted abandonment of ill family members, evoked the putrefying smell of corpses decaying, and described suicides committed in rage. Both authors accepted that the plague was the scourge of God for human sin; Boaistuau's main point was to highlight the misery of humankind, and Paré's was to discourage quarantining and encourage compatriots to give Christian charity to plague victims.[15]

The two (c) passages Montaigne interspersed in the second passage after the 1588 edition are also historical accounts. Questioning whether burial is a universal notion, he cited a people subjugated by Alexander who thought the happiest of the dead were those devoured by animals. More significantly, Livy's account of Roman soldiers at the battle of Cannae committing suicide by burying their heads in the ground Montaigne cited expressly to stress the loftiness of the peasant self-burial. Montaigne's intertexts derived from authors who claimed to be recording events, and his description emerged distinct from each in content and language. In "Of Physiognomy" Montaigne purported to be writing about the context of his own life; thus he recorded threats to his own life—which have been corroborated—as well as noble deaths among commoners on his own estate. Montaigne's naturalistic description of the debilitating effects of famine in a rural context perhaps provides a key to the unusualness of the scene.

The mention of famine brought on by the brigandage of the troops contrasts strikingly with Montaigne's dwelling on his eating habits in the next and final essay, "On Experience." While Jules Brody had a delightful time giving renewed significance to those passages and to the "literacity" of Montaigne's palate,[16] it should be stressed as well that Montaigne was aware that eating adequately was a matter of class differentiation in a time of widespread starvation. During the siege of Castillon, Montaigne realized that devastation of fields would cause much hardship then and for the generation to come. In living elsewhere for six months, Montaigne provided for his own family by the aid of friends and by a generous payment from the queen mother Catherine de Médicis which accompanied his work as negotiator.[17] Returning to his estate, he experienced his own economic loss of revenue-producing manpower together with his sympathy with the loss of the lives of his workers: he linked peasant death—"not the hundredth part could save themselves"—to Virgil's description of fields deserted and to the naturalistic, economic image: "the land that a hundred men worked for me has lain idle for a long time."[18] The gross statistics in this statement are likely a literary exaggeration, as a 99 percent death toll far exceeds the estimate among historical demographers of a European death toll from the bubonic plague in the range of 23 to 45 per cent. Nevertheless, war and famine did add to the death toll in Périgord. To Montaigne, "grapes hanging on the vines" brought to mind an image of peasants dying without hope of a livelihood. Montaigne had the insight to recognize that hunger and hopelessness were the likely causes of calm and indifferent acceptance of death by masses of dying people.[19]

The French religious wars provided many opportunities to observe peasants' endurance of torture in the process of dying. Particularly noteworthy to Montaigne was their willingness to suffer a variety of grotesque tortures from mounted musketeers rather than to give up their religious beliefs; however, he admired his peasant neighbors more in their natural subjection to disease than in their willful endurance of torture "for opinions borrowed from others, unknown, and not understood."[20]

While Montaigne questioned the validity of peasants suffering on behalf of theological disputes that they barely understood, he saw the moral justification for peasants revolting on behalf of their economic livelihood. With regard to the revolts in Guyenne in 1548 against the economic burdens of the salt tax and taille, Montaigne placed responsibility for the murder of the king's lieutenant in Guyenne on his vacillation before a mob he should have controlled. In "Of Cannibals" Montaigne claimed as a comment of Indians from Brazil who visited Rouen in 1562 (a year after the peasant revolt in Agen and the murder of baron de Fumel) that "they had noticed that there were among us men full and gorged with all sorts of good things, and that their other halves were beggars at their doors, emaciated with hunger and poverty; and they thought it strange that these needy halves could endure such an injustice, and did not take the others by the throat, or set fire to their houses."[21] Given the upper-class stereotype of the individual peasant in revolt and the burst of peasant uprisings during the French religious wars, that was an inflammatory statement.[22] Contemporaries reading the above passage from "Of Cannibals" in its 1580 publication would think of the peasant disturbances which since 1575 had been erupting along the Rhone River — a peasant revolt that gained notoriety in the terrible backlash of a three-day massacre during the carnival season in Romans in 1580.[23]

Peasant leaders then, as traditionally in France, were faced with the extremist accusation of acts of "cannibalism" upon nobility;[24] the peasants' petition of February 1579 to the king gave more evidence of the kinds of "noble" torture of the peasantry documented by Montaigne: peasants buried alive to be eaten by animals and peasants' heads bound between ropes until their eyes spurted from their sockets.[25] Not surprisingly, peasant death from the plague, in contrast to peasant death by torture and violence, appealed to Montaigne: "it is generally quick, numbed, painless, consoled by the public situation without ceremony, without mourning, without a crowd around."[26] In placing before his reader the sympathy-producing model of the noble peasant succumbing to the plague, Montaigne was distracting his upper-class reader from the fearsome repercussion-producing stereotype of the peasant in arms against the nobility.

"Of Physiognomy" has been compared frequently to the 1580 version of Montaigne's "That to Philosophize Is to Learn to Die" (I: 20). While passages of I: 20, written 1572–74, emphasized the value of reading Stoic philosophers to prepare for death and ridiculed those who do not think ahead to death, passages of III: 12, written 1585–88, praised his peasant neighbors for their serenity before sudden death and ridiculed readers of Cicero's *Tusculan Disputations.* This contrast was one basis for Villey's theory that the *Essays* evolved from Stoicism through Skepticism to Epicureanism;[27] and subsequently, critics of the historicist method of Villey have pointed out the unity and subtle interplay of the two essays.[28] Montaigne's shifting emphasis may be traced not so much to different readings, but to the temporary suspension of reading as he looked out his library window and saw the effects of brigandage and plague, and his later identification with the deaths that continued to take place at the Château de Montaigne while he and his family were in flight, far from his library and his essaying. Overall, however, there are underlying consistencies in his contrast of the fearsome imagination of death with the acceptable reality of experiencing death; in his contrast of vicariously preparing for death through reading versus observing and facing death; and in his contrast of the artificial death rituals of the upper classes to the common folk's natural process of dying. The passages on peasant death from the plague represent the culmination of Montaigne's respect for Stoic virtue learned and attained not from books but from "following nature."

Michel de Montaigne meditated much about death and preparation for death. In I: 20, he talked about preparing for it with Stoic strength, and stressed that philosophy was an aid to prepare us not to fear death. He scorned those who did not prepare for it: "The remedy of the common herd is not to think about it. But from what brutish stupidity can come so gross a blindness!"[29] Because they do not think about death, the vulgar cross themselves at even the mention of death, as at the mention of the devil.

The term "common herd" or "the vulgar" for Montaigne is a broad category, marking off the masses from the man of understanding ("l'homme d'entendement"). To the extent that the terms are class categories, the "common herd" in the above passage from I: 20 likely does not refer to peasants at all, but to those wealthy enough to summon notaries and doctors, for he cites their not writing a will until a doctor has determined their imminent death.[30] At the close of that early essay, he noted that humble village folk manage the event of death more serenely than those in great houses, who have elaborate rituals to prepare.[31] The later essay revealed fuller experiential understanding of that tranquility which had made him ponder before: peasant neighbors do not cogitate over the last hour until it is there; the exercise of imagination expands anticipatory suffering.[32] The worker placidly planting the garden during the plague of 1586 was Montaigne's ideal back in the 1570s: "I want death to find me planting my cabbages, but careless of death, and still more of my unfinished garden."[33]

Literacy, as well as imagination, came under critique. In his essay "Of Physiognomy" Montaigne ridiculed Cicero's *Tusculan Disputations*, which he had utilized for the title and main theme of I: 20, on the grounds that dying would be as cheerful whether or not one had read Cicero's work.[34] Echoing his highly intellectual critique of intellectuality in I: 25 "On Pedantry" and II: 12 "Apology of Raymond Sebond," Montaigne proclaimed the chasm between words about death and the lived reality of dying. In the important first passage above, his introduction contrasted our "efforts of learning" with peasants acting "according to nature." And in the second passage above, he showed that the peasants accepted the universal sentence of death, learning from one another, from common experience, how to accept it. He contrasted their naturalness with "studied and premeditated fortitude."[35] Their only concern appeared to be to cover themselves with soil to prevent molestation by scavenger animals.

What was in question was the whole literature of preparation for death, the *Ars moriendi* ("Art of Dying") that became a vogue in the late Middle Ages and Renaissance and was pouring off the printing presses, volume after volume, in the early sixteenth century.[36] By Montaigne's time the popularity of the genre had waned; he objected to the artificial fears that had been produced by that literature. In juxtaposing "studied" dying with the illiterate natural dying of peasants, Montaigne was criticizing the *ars moriendi* genre, as well as contributing to it one more *exemplum* of a beautiful death. He juxtaposed peasant death with the famous death of Socrates, whose speech on his likely sentence of death Montaigne praised for its "pure and primary impression of Nature" and "unstudied and artless boldness."[37] Peasants, he suggested, were spared the partial reading and partial comprehension from which the semiliterate received their exaggerated fears of death.[38] In both I: 20 and III: 12 Montaigne stressed that familiarity with the thought of death would reduce frenzy at the reality of death: "I did not wrinkle my forehead any more over that thought than any other."[39] Especially in (c) passages of III: 12, he quoted Seneca against misinterpretations of Seneca: "The possibility of suffering makes us as unhappy as the suffering"; and "He suffers more than is necessary who suffers before it is necessary."[40] The citation of the Stoic Seneca gave additional support to his observation that peasants dying so gracefully were a schoolhouse better than proof texts: commoners suffer from death only when the reality is upon them.[41]

In that poignant vicarious experiencing of a dying unaided by books, Montaigne passed from the book-lined closed circle of his study to the wide open spaces of his fields; he interpreted his observations, however, in the language of his Stoic philosophical readings. Directly after describing the mass deaths of peasants in his time, he remarked that "We have abandoned Nature and we want to teach her her lesson, she who used to guide us so happily and so surely. And yet the traces of her teaching and the little that remains of her image — imprinted, by the benefit of ignorance, on the life of that rustic, unpolished mob — learning is constrained every day to go and borrow, to give its disciples models of constancy, innocence, and tranquility."[42] In the scholarly debate on Montaigne's Stoicism, attention needs to be directed to some "words in a corner" in this passage: therein he utilized Stoic phraseology for the common notions of goodness "imprinted" on a soil not overly corrupted from nature. Ancient Stoics, such as Seneca or Epictetus, as well as French neo-Stoics, such as Guillaume du Vair, held that right reason is imprinted with common notions, which provide the potential to attain knowledge of goodness and justice.[43] Montaigne conformed to the traditional Stoic identification of "imprinted notions" with "seeds of virtue" and "reason," innovating in his phraseology by emphasizing "virtue" as the source of true law without directly mentioning the term "natural law," and linking "seed" with "reason" by the phrase "seed of universal reason": "What I like is the virtue that laws and religions do not make but perfect and authorize, that feels in itself enough to sustain itself without help, born in us from its own roots, from the seed of universal reason that is implanted in every man who is not denatured."[44] The Stoic image of the "imprinted" notions reinforced the imagery of natural "seeds" of virtue "rooted" in the natural human being. Furthermore, "Of Physiognomy" began with the admonition that we need a clear sight to find the secret light hiding underneath our artifice of opinions; the "secret light," indicating, for example, the wisdom expressed in the sayings of Socrates, was a standard abbreviated Stoic phrase for the light of virtue shining in human nature.[45]

Throughout the *Essays,* he sometimes applied the term "raison" (reason), which appears four hundred and seventy-two times, and sometimes applied the term "conscience" (conscience), which appears one hundred and seventy-four times, to indicate the source within human nature for virtue.[46] Nevertheless, missing is a consistent epistemological theory explaining how the human mind attains knowledge of virtue. What is of such intertextual interest in "On Physiognomy" is the rarity within Montaigne's *Essays* of such a full-blown statement of Stoic confidence in human capacity to know and achieve virtue. The obstacle for Montaigne was his skepticism explicated in II: 12 "Apology of Raymond Sebond": applying the ancient test for "common notions," that they be ideas or customs universally upheld, Montaigne despaired of finding such notions. Not knowing how to distinguish natural law amid the morass of human law, he suggested that we might find such law among the animals.[47] That clue to where to look for natural law helps elucidate the passage on peasant death; the image of peasants dying in tranquility led him to discuss animal behavior, for in peasants and animals he saw traces of constant and universal nature uncorrupted by cultures.[48] In contrast to Jean Bodin, who defended the view that the seeds of virtue, acknowledged by the major schools of philosophy, are present for full development only in an elite of sages, Montaigne gave anecdotal evidence that nature's teaching is present in laborers and animals.[49] Skeptical of the intricacies of highly educated human reason, Montaigne's best passage incorporating the Stoic intertexts for the internal source for rational conduct was one describing an apparently silent communal self-burial. He wrote "traces ... imprinted" and "seed of universal reason" in "On Physiognomy" to highlight his discovery of humans living and dying "in accordance with nature."

In a complex interweaving of texts and experiences, Montaigne offered the image of peasants calmly digging their coffinless graves as a model for a peaceful and natural mode of dying to contrast with the violent and anguished dying everywhere in evidence during the French religious wars, and a model for a natural self-initiated burial to contrast with the artificial public ritual of burial prevalent among the upper classes of sixteenth-century France. A contextual study through *l'histoire des mentalités* of his discomfort with the elaborate Renaissance death rituals of the upper classes described in his early essay I: 20 will help illuminate his idealization of the virtuous natural deaths in III: 12.[50]

Montaigne reacted against the ceremonies and rituals developed around death in sixteenth-century Europe. From the thirteenth century on, in Europe except for Italy and Spain, it became customary while the deceased was lying in state to conceal the corpse beneath a shroud, and sometimes to enclose the body in a coffin.[51] Montaigne said, "There we are already shrouded and buried."[52] As Philippe Ariès has documented, it became customary to cover the face of a great lord with a mask made immediately after death. Refusal to look at the body was denial of physical death, with art showing by its fascination with the macabre what people did not want to see in real life.[53] Montaigne's description of peasant death, by contrast, is restrained and concise, with mystery absent. The importance of this contrast of naked appearance and masking for Montaigne is evidenced by "To the Reader": in the first paragraph his book appears as a literary substitute for a death monument, and in the second paragraph, he vouches for the naturalness with which he has portrayed himself.[54]

The emblematic peasant death scene in II: 12 relates intratextually to the upper-class death scene in I: 20. The image of digging one's grave without grieving witnesses contrasts with the image of awaiting one's death inundated by the sounds of grieving relatives, servants, and visitors. In the noble household, the sight of a darkened room with lighted candles overstimulated the imagination of the dying and the grieving. The dying individual was "besieged" by doctors and preachers. Montaigne far preferred what he perceived as the less-frightening death of a servant.[55]

It may well be that Montaigne was personally more distanced from the fear-provoking aspects of peasant mentality toward death, and personally more bothered by the fearsome aspects of the upper-class mentality. From the perspective of the history of mentalities, Montaigne's passages on peasant death from the plague in "Of Physiognomy" are so striking because they present unusual exemplars of peasant behavior, based, according to Montaigne, on nature instead of on culture. Montaigne implied that the special natural circumstances of hunger, plague, and mass death brought on a mentality of tranquility. Likewise, at least two seventeenth-century accounts of the plague likewise described self-burials; evidence abounds, nonetheless, both within Montaigne's *Essays* and in the literature on early modern popular culture, that peasants often faced death with fear, superstition, and magical rites.[56]

Despite Montaigne's disapproval of the upper-class "spectacular death," he personally was involved in a long-range preparation for death and did much to make public the memory of individual acts of dying. Montaigne's writing was in part a memorial to his father and his friend

Etienne de la Boétie as well as himself.[57] In recording with relish the details of individuals' behavior at death, he reflected the new trend toward death epitomized in Ariès's words, "In the mirror of his own death each man would discover the secret of his individuality."[58] The literary rituals of memorializing the individual life and death Montaigne helped to encourage; in "Of Physiognomy" he memorialized some of his laborers as well.

Montaigne's fascination with mass dying in war and plague mirrored his fascination with bones visible in charnel houses near churches.[59] After the fourteenth century, with a sensibility oriented toward the macabre, interest had grown in the custom of piling up bones near the church. Montaigne argued for the realistic benefits of the spectacle; cemeteries are near churches and in the busiest part of town, and thus people would not get panicky at the sight of the dead.[60] Like the sight of peasants dying in a common field, the mingling of bones of the dead in the church cemetery suited his sensibility for the individual submitting himself to "the common human pattern, with order, but without miracle and without eccentricity."[61]

To the exemplary image of peasants dying calmly from the plague in Périgord in 1587, Montaigne responded with respect and admiration. The natural virtue of their deaths impressed him: their deaths took place "without ceremony, without mourning, without a crowd around."[62] The artificial masking of death in the upper classes had driven Montaigne to look lower down in society for some evidence of earlier, more natural, less literate approaches to the end shared by human and animal alike. Whether reading or observing, Montaigne's attitude toward the last hour remained imbued with Stoicism; the peasants he portrayed as calmly digging their own coffinless graves provided an inspiring image of "the traces of nature's teaching" from which we might learn innocence and tranquility.

NOTES

This paper is dedicated to the memory of Isidor Horowitz. Appreciation extends to the following colleagues for their helpful suggestions: Marc Bensimon, UCLA; Philippe Desan, University of Chicago; Jon Snyder, UC San Diego; and especially Donald Stone, Harvard University.

1. I: 12, P 1013–14, S 792–94. Citations to the *Essais* give book: chapter, P page, S page. P refers to the Pléiade edition, Michel de Montaigne, *Oeuvres complètes*, ed. Albert Thibaudet and Maurice Rat (Paris: Editions Gallimard, 1962). S refers to the Stanford English translation: Michel de Montaigne, *The Complete Works*, trans. Donald M. Frame (Stanford: Stanford University Press,

1967). An (a) refers to text written before 1580, a (b) to text written between 1580 and 1588, and a (c) to text written between the edition of 1588 and Montaigne's death in 1592.

2. Géralde Nakam has called attention to "On Physiognomy" as a document of "l'histoire événementielle," reflecting the events in the early years of the eighth war of religion (1585-94). See Nakam, *Montaigne et son temps, Les événements et les Essais, L'histoire, la vie, le livre* (Paris: Nizet, 1982), pp. 13, 103, 169-84; and "Index historique des *Essais*," p. 246. Also Nakam interprets the plague as not only an event, but also a metaphor of Montaigne's perception of living in unhealthy times—"un temps malade"—in *Les Essais de Montaigne, Miroir et procès de leur temps, Témoignage historique et création littéraire* (Paris: Nizet, 1984), pp. 278-85, 304-10.

3. A brief selection of diverse publications on methodology follow. François Rigolot, "Référentialité, Intertextualité, Autotextualité dans les *Essais* de Montaigne," *Oeuvres & Critiques* 8 (1983), 87-101; Natalie Z. Davis, "A Renaissance Text for the Historian's Eye: The Gifts of Montaigne," *Journal of Medieval and Renaissance Studies* 15, 1 (1985), 47-56. For "l'histoire événementielle" and "l'histoire des mentalités," see Emmanuel Le Roy Ladurie, *Le Territoire de l'historien* (Paris: Gallimard, 1973), esp. chaps. 7, 15; Traian Stoianovich, *French Historical Method: The Annales Paradigm* (Ithaca, N.Y.: Cornell University Press, 1976); and Patrick H. Hutton, "The History of Mentalities: The New Map of Cultural History," *History and Theory* 20, 1 (1981), 237-59. For history of ideas, see Quentin Skinner, "Meaning and Understanding in the History of Ideas," *History and Theory* 8 (1968), 3-53; and for the related literary analysis of intertextuality, see Antoine Compagnon, *La seconde main ou le travail de la citation* (Paris: Seuil, 1979). The suggestion of the beneficial overlap of methodologies appears in Ernst Schulin, "German 'Geistesgeschichte,' American 'Intellectual History,' and French 'Histoire des Mentalités' since 1900. A Comparison," *History of European Ideas* 1 (1981), 195-214, as well as in Maryanne C. Horowitz, "Complementary Methodologies in the History of Ideas," *Journal of the History of Philosophy* 12 (1974), 501-9.

4. III: 12, P 1017, S 795-96 (b): "A quoi faire nous allons nous gendarmant par ces efforts de la science? Regardons à terre les pauvres gens que nous y voyons espandus, la teste penchante après leur besongne, qui ne sçavent ny Aristote ny Caton, ny exemple, ny precepte; de ceux là tire nature tous les jours des effects de constance et de patience, plus purs et plus roides que ne sont ceux que nous estudions si curieusement en l'escole. Combien en vois-je ordinairement, qui mescognoissent la pauvreté? combien qui desirent la mort, ou qui la passent sans alarme et sans affliction? Celuy là qui fouyt mon jardin, il a ce matin enterré son pere ou son fils. ... "

III: 12, P 1025, S 802-3 (b): "Voyez ceux cy: pour ce qu'ils meurent en mesme mois, enfans, jeunes, vieillards, ils ne s'estonnent plus, ils ne se pleurent plus. J'en vis qui craignoient de demeurer derriere, comme en une horrible solitude; et n'y conneu communéement autre soing que des sepultures; il leur faschoit de voir les corps espars emmy les champs, à la mercy des bestes, qui y peoplerent incontinent. ... Tel, sain, faisoit desjà sa fosse; d'autres à s'y couchoient encore vivans. Et un maneuvre des miens à tout ses mains et ses pieds attira sur soy la terre en mourant: . . . . Somme, toute une nation fut incontinent, par usage, logée en une marche qui ne cede en roideur à aucune resolution estudiée et consultée."

5. I disagree with Tournon's arguments that the first passage was written after 1587: A. Tournon, *Montaigne: La glose et l'essai* (Lyon: Presses Universitaires de Lyon, 1983), pp. 274–76. Montaigne's statement in the next paragraph, "J'escrivois cecy environ le temps qu'une forte charge de nos troubles se croupit plusieurs mois, de tout son pois, droict sur moy" [II: 12, P 1017, S 796 (b)], indicates that his writing in his tower library was interrupted by the crushing reality around him symbolized by the image of the worker digging in the garden below.

6. Donald M. Frame, *Montaigne: A Biography* (New York: Harcourt, Brace & World, 1965), pp. 240–41.

7. Pierre L'Estoille, *Memoires pour servir à l'histoire de France,* I (Cologne: Herman Demen, 1719), 212–13 (Houghton Library edition) in his 1586 entry cites the fall of Castillon as an example of the roles of famine, plague, and brigandage in the suffering of laborers: "En ce mois d'Aoust presque par toute la France les pauvres gens mourans de faim, alloient par troupes couper les epis à demy murs qu'ils mangeoient sur le champ, menançans les laboureurs de les manger eux-meme s'ils ne leurs permettoient de prendre ces epis.

"Au commencement de Septembre arriverent à Paris les nouvelles de Castilon rendu, où il n'y avoit plus que deux femmes pour secourir les pestiférez; la ville fut donné au pillage, mais on ny trouva que quelques haillos pestiferés, en quoy se remarqua la bonne affection du Duc de Mayenne à l'endroit de l'armée du Roy, à laquelle il donne liberallement la peste au pillage. . . . " Likewise, see selections from Jacques-Auguste de Thou, *Histoire universelle,* IX (London, 1734) and Philippe Duplessis-Mornay, *Fidelle Exposition sur la Declaration du Duc de Mayenne, contenant les Exploicts de guerre qu'il a fait en Guyenne* (1587) in Nakam, *Montaigne et son temps,* pp. 181–83.

8. III: 12, P 1020, S 798 (b).

9. III: 12, P 1024, S 801 (b).

10. III: 12, P 1039–41, S 813–14. Donald Frame, "Du nouveau sur le voyage de Montaigne à Paris en 1588," *Bulletin de la Société des Amis de Montaigne* (1962) and Nakam, *Montaigne et son temps,* pp. 184–85. Rumor reported that Montaigne was dead; Maryanne C. Horowitz, "Marie de Gournay, Editor of the *Essais* of Michel de Montaigne: A Case-Study in Mentor-Protégée Friendship," *Sixteenth Century Journal* 7, 3 (1986), 278.

11. III: 12, P 1040, S 814 (b).

12. Letter of Remonstrance from the Mayor and Jurats of Bordeaux to King Henry III, August 31, 1583, P 1374, S 1068–69.

13. Frame, *Montaigne: A Biography,* pp. 240–41, P 1394.

14. Boccaccio, *The Decameron* (Middlesex, Eng.: Penguin, 1973), pp. 49–68. Raymond Crawfurd, *Plague and Pestilence in Literature and Art* (Oxford: Clarendon Press, 1914), pp. 116–18 on Boccaccio and p. 158 on Paré; Montaigne is not mentioned. Anna M. Campbell, *The Black Death and Men of Learning* (New York: Columbia University Press, 1931); Philip Ziegler, *The Black Death* (New York: Harper & Row, 1969), pp. 63–84; Robert Mandrou, *Introduction to Modern France*

1500-1640: An Essay in Historical Psychology, trans. R. E. Hallmark (New York: Holmes & Meier, 1975), pp. 35–37.

15. Michel de Montaigne, *Essais,* ed. Fortunat Strowski, photocopy of "Bordeaux Copy" of 1588 edition (Paris: Hachette, 1912), notes to I: 12, pp. 338–42. Boaistuau, *Le théâtre du monde* (1559), 70r. Ambroise Paré, *Oeuvres complètes* (Paris: Baillière, 1841), III, 457–64.

16. Jules Brody, *Lectures de Montaigne* (Lexington, Ky.: French Forum, 1982), chap. 3, pp. 55–93.

17. Roger Trinquet, "Aperçus généraux sur l'attitude de Montaigne après la mairie de Bordeaux (1585–1592)," *Bulletin de la Société des Amis de Montaigne* series 4, 11 (1967), 7–10.

18. III: 12, P 1025, S 802 (b): "Mais quant au monde des environs, la centiesme partie des ames ne se peust sauver: 'videas desertàque regna Pastorum, et longè salutus latéque vacantes.' En ce lieu mon meilleur revenu est manuel: ce que cent hommes travailloient pour moy chaume pour longtemps."

19. III: 12, P 1025, S 802 (b): "Les raisins demeurerent suspendus aux vignes, le bien principal de pays, tout indifferemment se preparans et attendans la mort...." For a document of people eating boiled leather and a few eating human flesh, see Jean de Lery, selection in Julien Cody, ed., *The Huguenot Wars,* trans. Julie Kernan (Philadelphia: Chilton Book Co., 1969), pp. 228–33. On demographic correlation of undernourishment and plague, see Robert Favre, *La Mort dans la littérature et la pensée françaises au siècle des lumières* (Lyon: Presses Universitaires de Lyon, 1978), pp. 47–49. For historical demography, see Jean-Noël Biraben, *Les hommes et la peste en France et dans les pays européens et Méditerranéens* (Paris: Mouton, 1975–76), and for exaggeration among chroniclers, see Ziegler, *Black Death,* pp. 224–31.

20. II: 32, P 702, S 548 (a).

21. I: 31, P 213, S 159 (a). See R. A. Sayce, "The Conservative and the Revolutionary," *The Essays of Montaigne: A Critical Exploration* (Evanston, Ill.: Northwestern University Press, 1972), pp. 233–60, esp. p. 259.

22. I: 24, P 129–30, S 95–96. Natalie Z. Davis, "The Rites of Violence," *Society and Culture in Early Modern France* (Stanford: Stanford University Press, 1975), pp. 152–87; Peter Burke, *Popular Culture in Early Modern Europe* (New York: Harper & Row, 1978), pp. 189, 201–4; and Roland Mousnier, *Fureurs Paysannes* (Paris: Calmann-Lévy, 1967).

23. J. H. M. Salmon, *Society in Crisis: France in the Sixteenth Century* (New York: St. Martin's Press, 1975), pp. 276–309. Emmanuel Le Roy Ladurie, *Le Carnaval de Romans: De la Chandeleur au mercredi des Cendres 1579–1580* (Paris: Gallimard, 1979).

24. Emmanuel Le Roy Ladurie, *The Peasants of Languedoc,* trans. John Day (Urbana: University of Illinois Press, 1974), p. 197. On the origins of the cannibal accusation in the Jacquerie of 1358, see Barbara W. Tuchman, *A Distant Mirror: The Calamitous 14th Century* (New York: Ballantine Books, 1978), p. 177, note p. 630. Montaigne cited the Stoics Chrysippus and Zeno to justify cannibalism to relieve famine, I, 31, P 208, S 155 (a).

25. J. H. M. Salmon, "Peasant Revolt in Vivarais, 1575–1580," *French Historical*

Studies 11 (1979), 1–28, esp. p. 15. Compare to II: 32, P 702, S 548 and to I: 31, P 200, S 155.

26. I: 12, P 1095, S 809 (b) "C'est une mort qui ne semble des pires; elle est communéement courte, d'estourdissement, sans douleur, consolée par la condition publique, sans ceremonie, sans deuil, sans presse."

27. Pierre Villey, *Les Sources et l'evolution des Essais de Montaigne,* 2 vols. (Paris: Hachette, 1908), II, 390–98, esp. p. 392.

28. Floyd Gray, "The Unity of Montaigne in the *Essais,*" *Modern Language Quarterly* 22 (1961), 79–86; Donald Stone, "Death in the Third Book," *L'Esprit Créateur* 7 (1963), 185–93. Jules Brody, "Montaigne et la mort: deux études sur 'Que philosopher c'est apprendre à mourir (I, 20),' " *Lectures de Montaigne,* chap. 4, pp. 93–144, analyzing (b) and (c) additions as amplifications of ideas in I: 20 (a), is the most definitive recent statement rejecting Villey's theory that Montaigne's attitudes toward death evolved.

29. I: 20, P 82, S 57–58 (a). See Claude Blum, "La Mort des hommes et la mort des bêtes dans les *Essais* de Montaigne: Sur les functions paradigmatiques de deux exemples," *French Forum* 5 (1980), 3–13.

30. I: 20, P 82, S 58 (a).

31. I: 20, P 94–95, S 68 (a).

32. III: 12, P 1029, S 805 (b).

33. I: 20, P 87, S 62 (a). The first passage, quoted at note 4, echoes this earlier one.

34. III: 12, P 1016, S 794 (c).

35. See n. 4.

36. Pierre Chaunu, "Mourir à Paris (XVIe–XVIIe–XVIIIe siècles)," *Annales* 31 (1976), 29–51; Roger Chartier, "Les Arts de mourir, 1450–1600," *Annales* 31 (1976), 51–75; Daniel Roche, " 'La Memoire de la Mort': recherche sur la place des arts de mourir dans la Librairie et le lecture en France aux XVIIe et XVIIIe siècles," *Annales* 31 (1976), 76–120; Nancy Lee Beaty, *The Craft of Dying: A Study in the Literary Tradition of the Ars Moriendi in England* (New Haven, Conn.: Yale University Press, 1970).

37. I: 25, P 1032, S 807: "(b) . . . il représente (c) en une hardiesse inartificielle et niaise, en une securité puérile, (b) la pure et premiere impression (c) et ignorance (b) de nature." Frame, *Montaigne: A Biography,* p. 263, said: "the peasants are not his real heroes. They are a corrective; Socrates is a model."

38. The semiliterate "heard" oral readings: Davis, "Printing and the People," *Society and Culture in Early Modern France,* pp. 194–209. The culture gap between the literate and illiterate was suggested by Elizabeth Eisenstein, *The Printing Press as an Agent of Social Change* (Cambridge: Cambridge University Press, 1979).

39. I: 20, P 86, S 61 (a).

40. III: 12, P 1027, S 803 (c): "Parem passis tristitiam facit, pati posse." III: 12, P 1029, S 805 (c): "Plus dolet quàm necesse est, qui antè dolet quàm necesse est."

41. III: 12, P 1029, S 805 (b).

42. III: 12, P 1026, S 803 (b): "Nous avons abandonné nature et luy voulons apprendre sa leçon, elle qui nous menoit si heureusement et si seurement. Et cependant les traces de son instruction et ce peu qui, par le benefice de l'ignorance,

reste de son image empreint en la vie de cette tourbe rustique d'hommes impolis, la science est contrainte de l'aller tous les jours empruntant, pour en faire patron à ses disciples de constance, d'innocence et de tranquillité."

43. For a methodological model, see Mary B. McKinley, *Words in a Corner: Studies in Montaigne's Latin Quotations* (Lexington, Ky.: French Forum, 1981). Maryanne C. Horowitz, "The Stoic Synthesis of the Idea of Natural Law in Man: Four Themes," *Journal of the History of Ideas* 35 (1974), 3–16, analyzes the seed image in Seneca's *Epistles,* which had a direct impact on Montaigne. Camilla Hill Hay, *Montaigne: Lecteur et Imitateur de Sénèca* (Poitiers: Société française d'Imprimerie, 1938), pp. 77–86, 120–24. Another source was Guillaume du Vair, *De la sainte philosophie, Philosophie morale de Stoïques* (Paris: Librairie Philosophique J. Vrin, 1946), pp. 63–68.

44. III: 12, P 1037, S 811 (c): "Je l'aime telle que les loix et religions non facent, mais parfacent et authorisent, qui se sente de quoy se soustenir sans aide, née en nous de ses propres racines par la semence de la raison universelle empreinte en tout homme non desnaturé."

45. III: 12, P 1013, S 793: "il faut la veuë nette et bien purgée pour descouvrir cette secrette lumière."

46. Roy E. Leaky, *Concordance des Essais de Montaigne,* 2 vols. (Genève: Librairie Droz, 1981), I, 226 and II, 1060–63.

47. II: 12, P 563–64, S 437–38.

48. III: 12, P 1026, S 803.

49. Jean Bodin, *Le Théâtre de la nature universelle,* trans. F. de Gourgerolles (Lyon: Jean Pillehotte, 1597), pp. 687–90. Maryanne C. Horowitz, "Natural Law as the Foundation for an Autonomous Ethic: Pierre Charron's *De la Sagesse,*" *Studies· in the Renaissance* 21 (1974), 204–26.

50. Philippe Ariès, *Western Attitudes toward Death: From the Middle Ages to the Present,* trans. Patricia M. Ranum (Baltimore: The Johns Hopkins University Press, 1974). Ariés, *L'Homme devant la mort* (Paris: Seuil, 1977). Michel Vovelle, *Mourir autrefois: Attitudes collectives devant la mort aux XVIIe et XVIIIe siècles* (Paris: Gallimard, 1974). Michel Vovelle, "Les attitudes devant la mort: Problèmes de méthode, approches et lectures différentes," *Annales* 31 (1976), 120–33. Jacques Truchet, "Note sur la mort-spectacle dans la littérature française du XVIIe Siècle," *Topique: Revue Freudienne* 11–12 (Oct. 1973), 281–98. Compare the quotation in note 26 to the stereotypical household death scene ritual at the close of I: 20, P 94–95, S 67–68 (a).

51. Ariès, *L'Homme devant la mort,* pp. 168–72.

52. I: 20, P 94, S 68: "Nous voylà desjà ensevelis et enterrez."

53. Ariès, *L'Homme devant la mort,* pp. 125–33, 171–72.

54. "Au Lecteur," P 9, S 2.

55. I: 20, P 9495, S 6768. Brody, *Lectures de Montaigne,* chap. 4, illus. p. 100.

56. Jean Delumeau, *La peur en occident* (Paris: Fayard, 1978), p. 121 for examples of self-burial and pp. 1–2, 98–143. Robert Muchembled, *Culture populaire et culture des élites* (Paris: Flammarion, 1978), p. 40; Jean Delumeau, *Le Péché et la peur: La culpabilisation en Occident, 13e-18e siècle* (Paris: Fayard, 1983). Stuart Clark has pointed out that the description of the peasantry as "primitive" and "super-

stitious" in the above books reflects an older tradition of normative history, as much as it reflects the Annales school: "French Historians and Early Modern Popular Culture," *Past and Present* 100 (1983), 69–78. Thus, one cannot substantiate a claim that current historians are "neutral" observers in comparison with eyewitness, yet literary, observers, such as L'Estoille and Montaigne. See Nakam, *Essais de Montaigne,* chap. 11 "Phobies," for evidence that Montaigne also recorded numerous examples of popular fears.

57. Richard L. Regosin, *The Matter of My Book* (Berkeley: University of California Press, 1977).

58. Ariès, *Western Attitudes toward Death,* pp. 51–52.

59. Ariès, *L'Homme devant la mort,* pp. 59–60.

60. I: 20 P 8788, S 62 (a).

61. III: 13, P 1096, S 857: (b) "Les plus belles vies sont, à mon gré, celles qui se rangent au modelle commun (c) et humain, avec ordre, mais (b) sans miracle et sans extravagance."

62. See n. 26.

VI

CONTEXTUALITY:
Text in Community

JEANNE HARRIE

Renaissance Hermeticism as a Formula for Peace: Some Responses along Confessional Lines

Recent historiographical trends have suggested that Renaissance Hermeticism fostered religious irenicism and reconciliation. Frances Yates, D. P. Walker, and Jean Dagens have argued that the ancient theology, and in particular Hermetic philosophy, provided support for "eirenic, reunionist opinions" and practical efforts to reconcile warring Catholics and Protestants.[1] It appears that Renaissance thinkers liberal enough to explore Hermetic literature, with its magical overtones, as a way of enhancing the Christian religious experience were more likely than their contemporaries to entertain intellectual and practical rapprochement with rival Christians. The very process of reconciling a non-Christian text with Christian orthodoxy fostered an emphasis on the essentials, a positive approach to what is shared, and a de-emphasis of differences. The Hermetic literature, with its account of creation reminiscent of Genesis, its description of man's fall and redemption, and the terminology employed to describe the Godhead, "Father" and "Son of God,"[2] allowed those seeking an alternative to the orthodox Christianity of the schools to maintain an aura of orthodoxy. Hermes Trismegistus served them as a model of one antedating Christ who had appropriated the essentials of Christianity. Many of the same men whose disenchantment with scholastic Christianity led them to embrace warmly the Neoplatonism of Hermeticism openly expressed their dismay at the squabbling which rapidly came to characterize relations between Catholics and Protestants. It was often these men, Yates and others contend, who wrote in favor of reconciliation through a universal religion which preserved the essentials of the Christian faith.[3]

It is one thing to espouse an idea and another to work for its implementation. One wonders how many exponents of Hermetic philosophy continued to hope and work for religious unity amid the heat of religious controversy, when reputations, property, and even lives might be affected by one's support of a religious position. In an earlier article which focused on the enthusiastic Hermetist François Foix de Candale and the Protestant apologist Philippe Duplessis-Mornay, I examined the relationship of Hermetic philosophy to irenic, reunionist opinions within the context of the French religious wars and found little evidence of such a connection in the thoughts and actions of Foix de Candale and Mornay. Mornay's support of toleration was pragmatic in origin and not causally related to his interest in Hermeticism or other ancient theologies. Foix de Candale expressed irenic views which he supported with Hermetic philosophy, but he did not support the views of the *politiques* nor actively work for toleration as a practical solution to the religious wars.[4]

In this essay I intend to pursue a similar theme but in a slightly earlier historical context and with a different subject, Gabriel du Préau (Prateolus).[5] Du Préau (1511–88), a minor Catholic theologian and a contemporary of Foix de Candale (1512–94) and the somewhat younger Mornay (1549–1623), was the first to translate the *Corpus Hermeticum* into French. His interest in the Hermetic literature began sometime in the 1540s and appears to have ended by 1562. It thus antedated both the religious wars and that period Dagens called "the golden age of religious hermetism," from the 1570s to the middle of the seventeenth century, which saw the appearance of Guy and Nicholas Le Fèvre de la Boderie's translations of works by Ficino, Pico, and Francesco Giorgio and the publication of François Foix de Candale's various Hermetic and mathematical works.[6] Du Préau, with Jacques Lefèvre d'Étaples, Adrien Turnèbe, and Symphorien Champier, provided the textual foundation for the "golden age" which followed.

Du Préau, unlike Lefèvre, who for a time was interested in the apologetic possibilities of Hermetic philosophy, offers a challenge to those who would link Hermeticism and irenicism because his career included both enthusiasm for Hermetic literature and philosophy and a reputation as a zealous combatant of Protestantism. Recent historiography has led us to expect an exponent of the *Hermetica* to entertain more liberal views of other philosophies and religions, to stress similarities rather than differences. How is it that one responsible for two editions of the *Hermetica* could display such bellicose behavior toward his fellow Christians? Through du Préau, this paper will explore the relationship of Hermeticism to irenicism and religious toleration and the degree to which Hermeticism was a liberal, i.e., liberating, intellectual movement.

Details of Gabriel du Préau's life are sketchy.[7] He was born in 1511 into a noble family at Marcoussis, south of Paris. Skilled in languages, he taught *belles lettres* at the Collège de Navarre for some thirty years, and later directed the Collège de Peronne. Considered an excellent grammarian, a good translator, and a respected Latinist, he published several translations and numerous works of grammar, church history, religious apology, and anti-Protestant polemic. According to one source, he traveled to Italy, a common object of pilgrimage for French humanists, where he learned the language.[8] Judging from his writings, his early interests appear to have been those of a humanistically influenced schoolman; his earliest publications include translations of two works by the jurist Claude Coterau [Cottereau], a translation of Christophe de Cattan's [Cristoforo Cattaneo] *Geomancy,* and the French editions of the *Hermetica.* Although respected by his contemporaries as a theologian and prominent enough to appear in the standard reference works of the sixteenth and seventeenth centuries, had he not translated the *Hermetica* it is likely he would have remained in historical obscurity.

Jacques Lefèvre d'Étaples's 1494 edition of Ficino's *Pimander* introduced the Hermetic works to France and stimulated a long and active tradition of translation and commentary which included the work of Symphorien Champier, Gabriel du Préau, Foix de Candale, and others. In 1505, Lefèvre again published the *Pimander,* adding in the same volume the *Asclepius,* his own commentaries on the Hermetic treatises, and Lodovico Lazzarelli's *Crater Hermetis,* a dialogue resembling a Hermetic regeneration treatise. To this tradition Gabriel du Préau contributed the first two translations of the *Hermetica* into French. The first appeared in 1549, was translated from Lefèvre d'Étaples's edition of Ficino's Latin translation, and was dedicated to a churchman, Cardinal Charles de Lorraine.[9] A second edition appeared in 1557, shortly after Adrien Turnèbe published the first edition of the Greek text in 1554. Du Préau claimed to have worked directly from the Greek but, as Frederick Purnell has shown, his version is "simply a free rendering of Ficino's Latin."[10] Du Préau dedicated the second edition to Ja[c]ques de Basordan, "apostolic protonotary" and one of the king's councillors and confessors.[11] The 1557 edition included the *Pimander,* the *Asclepius,* Ficino's *Argumentum,* Lefèvre's commentaries, Lazzarelli's *Crater Hermetis,* and an additional work, Lazzarelli's translation of the *Definitions of Asclepius.* Champier had first published the *Definitions* in his *De Quadruplici Vita* in 1507 in a Latin translation by Lazzarelli. Turnèbe's Greek edition also included the *Definitions,* and du Préau probably used it when preparing his French translation.[12] Thus, du Préau was familiar with most of the Hermetic writings available in French humanistic circles at mid-century. His two editions remained the only French translations of the *Hermetica* until François Foix de Candale's translation appeared in 1574.[13]

Like others before and after him, du Préau embraced the Hermetic literature with warm enthusiasm. In the preface to the 1557 edition, he justified his translation on the grounds that the "natural" arguments it contained would help the "shield of faith" discredit the "false prophets, unbelievers, and unfaithful atheists" he believed responsible for the intellectual and religious turmoil of his age.[14] In a later work, he described atheists as "men without God who mock all the world's religions, customs, laws, and ceremonies, and who live like Epicureans without hope of another life than this."[15] The Hermetic writings were tools which could be used against such men for whom arguments from Scripture or tradition had no credibility. While the Christian argues from the revelation of divine truth contained in Scripture, Hermes argues from an understanding of the natural world. While the atheists might dismiss supernatural revelation, they could hardly reject arguments founded in natural reason. Mornay later used the Hermetic literature and other pagan sources in a similar way in his *De la Verité de la Religion Chrestienne*.[16]

Although careful to assert the priority of scriptural revelation, du Préau was himself impressed by the antiquity and wisdom of the Hermetic literature. In rhapsodic language, du Préau praised Hermes as a prophet who foretold such future events as the destruction of the old religion and the rise of a new faith, the coming of the Messiah, the resurrection of the dead, and the Last Judgment. He found that Hermes' revelation of profound mysteries resembled that of Moses and his understanding of God accorded with Christian truth: "It was he [Hermes] who first among all philosophers after having carefully versed himself in physics and the mathematical arts and having perfectly understood them, raised his spirit to contemplate the divine things. It was he who first before all humans very wisely debated the majesty of God, the angelic order, the mutation of souls . . . [and] for this reason was in ancient times called the creator of theology."[17]

Such enthusiasm notwithstanding, Gabriel du Préau and French Hermetists in general followed Lefèvre's lead and approached Hermetic ideas with a measure of restraint. Recognizing that the *Hermetica* could lead to dangerous magic and heresy, Lefèvre adopted a cautious approach to its use which became a hallmark of French Hermeticism, termed by Yates "religious Hermetism" because of its adherents' avoidance of magic and their concern to subject the Hermetic works to the canon of orthodox Catholic doctrine.[18] As enthusiastic as he was in the preface to his translation and in his brief commentaries, du Préau never raised Hermetic philosophy to the level of Christian doctrine. Lazzarelli, whose *Crater Hermetis* du Préau published with little commentary, had done so. The *Crater*, a dialogue between Lazzarelli who acts as master and King Ferdinand of Aragon, his disciple, includes an exchange in which Lazzarelli responds to the king's observation that Lazzarelli appears to be a "Hermetist" with the following: "I am a Christian, Sire, and so am not ashamed to be called a Hermetist. For if you diligently consider his precepts and teachings, you will yourself confirm them to be very much in accord with Christian doctrine."[19] Du Préau did not comment either upon this or Lazzarelli's identification of Jesus Christ and Pimander.[20] But, unlike Lazzarelli, who placed Moses after Hermes Trismegistus in the chronology of ancient theologians, du Préau followed Ficino and Lefèvre in accepting Hermes' spiritual descent from Moses, thereby preserving the priority of God's revelation to the Jews.[21] Thus Hermes offered a confirmation of God's existence and of divine revelation but was not himself a direct recipient of that revelation.

But du Préau was not uncritical of the *Hermetica.* He cautioned the reader that Hermes used words in a different manner than does a Christian philosopher and that his understanding of the role of the stars "draws man into the error of the pagans." In the eighth dialogue of the *Asclepius,* Hermes had termed the stars "gods," and in the ninth, he had suggested the existence of a multiplicity of gods. It was the *Asclepius*'s approval of idolatry in the ninth and thirteenth chapters that du Préau found abhorrent. He dismissed Lazzarelli's analogical and mystical interpretation of the idol-making passages as "invented with good and Christian affection, but perhaps violating the letter." Du Préau feared the magic the *Hermetica* contained enough to treat the entire work with caution, but there were respectable precedents for not dismissing it entirely. In his handling of the controversial ninth and thirteenth chapters of the *Asclepius,* du Préau followed Lefèvre d'Étaples (and St. Augustine) in condemning the idol-making passages.[22] Du Préau's dedication of the 1549 translation to Cardinal de Lorraine and that of 1557 to Basordan suggests that Hermeticism of this cautious or religious variety was acceptable in ecclesiastical, and perhaps even royal, circles.[23]

A measure of the influence of Hermetic philosophy upon an individual's intellectual makeup is the degree to which it shaped his intellectual interests and interpretations. François Foix de Candale's enthusiasm for Hermetic philosophy is apparent throughout his writings and influenced his interests in mathematics, natural philosophy, and alchemy, as well as his interpretation of Catholic doctrine on the Eucharist. By contrast, the Protestant Philippe Duplessis-Mornay made use of the *Hermetica* only when writing of natural theology. Similarly, du Préau manifested Hermetic influence in only one of his works. In the prologue to a work published in 1559, *De la cognoissance de soymesme pour parvenir à celle de Dieu,* du Préau called Hermes the author whom, after Catholic authors, he most admires and recommends.[24] Hermes' belief that piety and knowledge of God provide the only way to lasting happiness summarized for du Préau his own work. To see and know God, one must contemplate the cosmic order, as Hermes reminds us in several of his dialogues. Du Préau quoted Hermes as saying that "if you do not know the light which is in you, i.e., your soul and understanding, how are you able to know God?"[25] Thus knowledge of the world, of which knowledge of self is foremost, is necessary for true knowledge of God, an echo of Lazzarelli's *Crater Hermetis*, which treated the manner of knowing God and oneself and which du Préau had included in his *Deux Livres*. In three books, du Préau's *De la cognoissance* offered a path to divine knowledge which involved a series of meditations on the natural and moral states of man and on the spiritual remedies given man by divine providence. By the latter du Préau meant "the divine commandments and laws which man knows through proper consideration and diligent investigation of the Scriptures."[26] It is a kind of gnosis akin to that found in the Hermetic dialogues themselves and typical of the Christian Socratism which marked much of the writing of the sixteenth century.[27] Similarly, Foix de Candale, in his elaborate commentaries on the *Hermetica*, had proffered a doctrine of salvation which involved self-knowledge as a key to spiritual regeneration.[28]

Shortly after the second edition of his translation of the *Hermetica* appeared, du Préau published a translation of Christophe de Cattan's *Geomancy*, a work of divination employing dots or lines on paper.[29] Given his condemnation of the magical passages in the *Asclepius*, du Préau's translation of a work of magic might appear surprising. St. Augustine had condemned hydromancy, one kind of divination,[30] and the Church continued to view the magical arts with suspicion throughout the sixteenth century. Symphorien Champier, with whose works du Préau may have been familiar, had viewed geomancy as illicit divination, a fact in itself surprising since Champier had absolved the *Hermetica* of the charge of promoting demonic magic by ascribing the idol-making passages in the *Asclepius* to its translator, Apuleius of Madaura.[31] Du Préau was, in a sense, more consistent. He had repudiated the magical elements in the *Hermetica* and he took care in his preface to Cattan's work to avoid any hint of dangerous magic. He claimed the author's intent was only "to give pleasure and recreation." While acknowledging that the stars can influence "lesser beings" through the order and will of God, he warned his readers not to view the art as certain in its predictions for that would defy God's first commandment.[32] In his preface to the work, Cattan himself had denied any linkage of geomancy to divination or "diabolical invocation" and had described it as a "part of natural magic, called by several great persons, daughter of astrology." It was, as Cattan reminded the reader, permitted by no less a figure than Thomas Aquinas.[33]

Du Préau's attraction to Hermetic philosophy and natural magic was relatively short-lived. In the 1560s his work clearly began to change in character and in tone. Although his publications during this period included *Flores et sententiae scribendique formulae illustriores, ex M. T. Ciceronis epistolis familiaribus selectae* (1562) and a "revised and corrected" edition of the *Geomancy* (1567), more typically his works addressed the issues raised by the Reformation and the French religious wars. The growing strength of Protestantism in France appears to have been a significant factor in changing the direction and shape of his thought.

In 1559 French members of the Reformed Church held their first national synod. Under the leadership of Catherine de Médicis, Catholic and Protestant theologians met at Poissy in 1561 to consider religious reconciliation. The failure of the colloquy and the duke of Guise's massacre of the Protestant congregation of Vassy in 1562 opened an era of religious war that lasted nearly forty years. As Donald Kelley recently has shown, the constitutional crisis brought about by the death of Henry II and the politicization of religious conflicts provoked an outpouring of polemical literature generally characterized by its lack of understanding and tolerance. Protestant confidence in the "Word" meant that the war among Christians would be fought, at least in part, through the press, with Catholics matching Protestants in volume and vitriol.[34] In this context, it is perhaps understandable that the devotee of Hermes Trismegistus, whose initial targets had been the "Epicureans and Atheists," abandoned "the creator of theology" and began to write religious polemic and propaganda, composing several fiery pieces against a formidable enemy, the Protestants. The tone of his attacks on the Protestants was as vituperative as his praise of Hermes Trismegistus had been enthusiastic. One wonders if du Préau regretted his "youthful" dabbling in unorthodox literature and his relatively liberal attitude toward its ideas and sought to atone for his sins.

Du Préau's first published polemical piece was *Harangue sur les causes de la guerre entreprise contre les rebelles & seditieux...*, a twelve-page tract directed at the Protestants and arguing against freedom of religious practice.[35] In it he declared that there is nothing more beautiful nor more desirable than peace and union and condemned the religious divisions he believed responsible for the wars. Citing Germany as an example of the loss of souls, general depopulation, ruin of churches, and increased vulnerability to external threat to which religious division leads, he called for an end to religious freedom. Protestantism, he argued, is not only a heresy; it is political sedition which leads to political dissension and disunity. Not only are souls lost, but the temporal felicity which depends on religious truth is shattered when each soul is free to follow whichever religion pleases him. "There is no kingdom ... which can long remain in peace where each is free and permitted to embrace and follow whichever religion pleases him." The reformers, Luther, Zwingli, and Calvin, are false prophets who have divided the body of Christ; their followers are guilty of idolatry for revering them as gods.

Because of them, France is divided into Lutherans, Sacramentarians, Anabaptists, and atheists, "without God, without law, without faith, and without King."[36]

Du Préau developed this essentially antitoleration theme over the next twenty years. Toleration, in his opinion, does not lead to peaceful unity but dissension, war, and cruelty. Moreover, as he made clear in a later work of church history, Protestantism appeals to the common people who are moved by "folly, temerity, and ambition to anger and rage against kings and princes."[37] Such religious and political division leads to conquest, union to strength and invulnerability. Thus, he considered the war against the Huguenots just[38] for both political and religious reasons and the preservation of the "république" almost as important as preventing the loss of souls to heresy. Ignoring the zealous excesses perpetrated by Catholics, he castigated the Protestants for their cruelties toward Catholics. "What," he asked, "could the brute beasts or the cruel Tartars do that was more inhuman or abominable?" "This," he added, "is the fruit of the fifth Gospel sowed by Luther and cultivated by the venerable Calvin."[39]

Du Préau argued that Catholics must reject Protestant doctrine and should consider any contact with those who espouse it as offensive to God. Characteristic of du Préau's approach to the Protestants is a work he entitled *Declaration des abus, hipocrisie, et subtilitee des faux prophetes & seducteurs du peuple*. Published in 1579, the work first appeared in 1564 with a slightly different title and is a blend of religious apology, sectarian polemic, and pastoral guidance.[40] Du Préau declared in the dedication that he intended to refute the arguments of a "heretic" whose writings he had encountered, yet he identifies neither the author nor the work. He does make it clear that the targets of his criticisms are the Protestants, the "false prophets and seducers" of the title.[41] God, he warns, has given us signs by which to recognize false prophets, savage wolves who come to us in sheep's clothing. He takes pains to demonstrate that Protestants were indeed the false prophets Christ warned against in Matt. 7:15. Although they claim to be the true interpreters of Christianity, it is not enough that they take their words from Scripture; they must take them "in the sense of God's spirit, and of the true prophets, apostles, and holy doctors through whom God has manifested and declared his word." Moreover, the false teachers appeal to our will and our carnal attachments, unlike the true servants of God who constantly battle the flesh.[42]

One of du Préau's concerns in writing the book was to provide faithful Catholics with an answer to the practical question, "How much contact may Catholics have with Protestant 'heretics' and ceremonies without offending God and causing scandal?" His near-obsession with the first commandment led him to examine the Protestant baptismal, Eucharistic, marriage, and funeral services at some length to test the degree of idolatry found in each and thus determine the legitimacy of Catholic participation. Maintaining that the form of baptism had remained the same for fifteen hundred years, du Préau defended Catholic use of oil, salt, and chrism, added by the ancient fathers to increase the honor of the sacrament and the reverence in which it was held, against the "heretics' " charge that those forms are unscriptural.[43] Although du Préau considered the Protestants followers of the Antichrist and responsible for the "horrible desolation and dissipation" into which the Church had fallen, he regarded the Protestant baptism performed by an ordained, if wayward, priest to be efficacious. If conditions offered good Catholic parents only the options of baptism of their child in a heretic ceremony or leaving the child unbaptized, they must choose the former. "Sacramentaires" who refuse to baptize infants he considered abominable.[44] Du Préau had more trouble accepting Catholic participation in the Protestant ceremonies surrounding marriage and death. Because a religious ceremony was less necessary for marriage than for baptism, du Préau urged Catholic couples to hold a ceremony in a Catholic home rather than resort to a Protestant "conventicle." "For where there is a promise and legitimate contract between the husband and wife, there is no doubt that the marriage be solid and legitimate before God."[45] Under certain circumstances, a Catholic could attend a Protestant funeral ceremony but Protestant denial of the doctrine of purgatory made even such limited consorting with heretics dangerous.

Clearly, if participation in Protestant weddings and funerals could offend God, assisting at their celebration of the Lord's Supper ("La Cene") was an intolerable act for, in du Préau's opinion, the Protestants completely misunderstand the nature of the sacrament. Du Préau read the scriptural accounts of Jesus' last supper not as an injunction to commemorate the Paschal supper but as His institution of a holy sacrament. He scornfully wrote of the Protestant "Supper" as "nothing more than an act of drinking together which one can as easily do in a tavern."[46] He found no foundation either in natural reason or in Scripture for the Protestant arguments against transubstantiation.[47] Even Protestants, he contended, recognize that something is wrong with their interpretation. After their communion service, "they go from bad to worse, disfigured and displaying in their face bad color which indicates that their conscience is not in repose but always in fear."[48]

The issue of the true character of the Eucharistic sacrament proved to be among the most divisive factors separating sixteenth-century Protestants and Catholics. The long, tendentious tract in which an author defended a sectarian interpretation of the sacrament and attacked those of rival sects was a staple of the sixteenth century. However, there is some evidence that enthusiastic Hermetists viewed the sacrament as a mode of reconciliation rather than a bone of contention. Giordano Bruno saw the resolution of differences regarding the Eucharist as the key to ending the religious troubles and sought to end discussions of scholastic subtleties involving the Eucharist which fueled the debate.[49] Foix de Candale expressed similar views in both his commentary on the *Pimander* and in an unpublished treatise on the "holy sacrament" which he dedicated to the French king, Henry III. In the dedication to his work on the Eucharist, Foix de Candale expressed the view that warring Christians could be reunited under the leadership of Henry III and through the sacrament of the Eucharist. Foix de Candale consciously set himself apart from the usual polemics which characterized discussion of the issue, criticizing both Catholic and Protestant apologists and declaring that his intent was to draw out and reconcile all errant opinions in one fold under one shepherd.[50]

Du Préau also saw concord and union as the "true mark of truth." But unlike Foix de Candale, du Préau attacked Protestant doctrine, especially that of Calvin and Beza, not only in *Declaration* but also in *Du Souverain et unique sacrifice de l'eglise catholique et apostolique . . .*, a work on the Eucharist which he published in 1574.[51] In a far-from-conciliatory tone, he called the Calvinist interpretation "a wretched and damned invention of the devil."[52] He saw Calvinist doctrine as conforming to that of Marcion and the Manichees,[53] by which he apparently meant that it separated too distinctly the spiritual and material worlds, a measure of the distance he had traversed since his earlier advocacy of the essentially gnostic philosophy of Hermes. Citing Scripture, he argued against a "spiritual" interpretation of the Eucharist. The words, "This is my body, this is my blood," refer to "a true body, essential and of substance which has been given up and shed for us on the cross."[54]

In his *Declaration* du Préau established one firm rule: "never to consent to heresy and false religion nor approve it in any manner nor frequent the places and assemblies where one makes profession of it, if it is in any way possible."[55] He devoted most of the book to distinguishing Catholic and Protestant belief and practice, defending the one and demonstrating the falsity of the other. Protestants, he argued, deceive the "simple people" with their misuse of Scripture. The Protestant clergy, and here he specifically mentioned Pierre Viret, Guillaume Farel, Calvin, and Beza, he branded "ministers of Satan" and compared them to "Epicureans and Atheists." After demonstrating the errors of Protestant ceremony and the doctrines on which they were based, he drew from the Old and New Testaments to argue for separation of Catholic and Protestant communities and practices. Just as Judah remained faithful to God in the face of Israel's idolatrous worship and the early Christians lived apart from the Jews, so Catholics in war-torn Europe must preserve the integrity of the ancient faith.[56]

Du Préau largely abandoned the conciliatory tone he had used when introducing the Epicureans and atheists to Hermes Trismegistus; heresy is like gangrene in the manner in which it corrupts and only under certain limited conditions may Catholics participate in Protestant ceremonies. Du Préau was not willing to soften the doctrinal and liturgical lines separating Catholic and Protestant. To the contrary, he explicitly cautioned against "moderators" who wish to soften distinctions and ease rules "for the good of peace."[57] Terming them "Herodiens" after Herod who sought to please the Romans, he criticized their desire "to bring into accord the religion of Jesus Christ and that of the Antichrist so that by this means they are better able to live in peace with each other."[58] The true Christian must make known the differences between Catholics and Protestants even to taking a stance against errant princes who promote heresy just as Moses stood against Pharaoh in leading his people out of Egypt.[59] But separation of rival religions was not to be permanent. Du Préau scorned the religious liberty and diversity characteristic of Germany and Switzerland and ascribed it to the regions' historical political diversity.[60] Ultimately, du Préau sought the union of Christians in the "ancient" Catholic faith, by force if necessary. He did not stop short of violence, as his history of the Church makes clear. There he lauded the duke of Guise and Blaise de Monluc for their exploits against the Protestants, whose cruelty toward Catholics he considered inhuman. Monluc he praised for several "beautiful" massacres ("belle boucherie") of Protestants.[61] Such sincerely tendered praise of violence makes it difficult to credit du Préau with what Yates called that "distinctive badge of religious Hermetism. . . . the disapproval of the use of force in religious matters." To the contrary, any acceptance of heresy and false religion constituted for him "a form of idolatry and superstition."[62]

The case of Gabriel du Préau indicates the dangers of generalizing about the effects exploration of Hermetic literature had upon Renaissance writers. While some who used the *Hermetica* stressed "similarities rather than differences between various philosophies and religions" (Mornay and, to some extent, Foix de Candale), others remained wary of any unorthodoxy (du Préau). One factor appears to be the degree of commitment one made to Hermetic ideas. Gabriel du Préau embraced Hermetic philosophy in the early years of his career as a weapon against the "atheists" whose rejection of Christianity was based on rational arguments. He abandoned it when he perceived the enemy to be those Protestants willing to go to war for their cause. Du Préau never became a Hermetist in the manner of Foix de Candale or Giordano Bruno. He did not offer Hermetic philosophy as a substitute for Catholic doctrine or even a buttress to it, equivalent in stature. Like the Protestant Mornay, he saw it as a kind of natural theology, a confirmation in rational terms of the spiritual truths revealed in Scripture. Because he was convinced, at least after 1560, that Scripture was being misused to lead many away from God and salvation, he may have had trouble justifying the use of a body of literature already corrupted by idolatry. Certainly, after 1560, his writings display no sign, explicitly or implicitly, of Hermetic influence.[63] Mornay was at least willing to consider religious toleration as a temporary political solution. Du Préau not only argued against toleration of Protestant ideas and practices but considered unnecessary contact with such heretics idolatrous. Any similarities between Catholic and Protestant were forgotten in his passion to shear the wool of the false sheep and reveal them for the ravaging wolves they are. To be fair to du Préau, we must also remember that the ideological battle between Catholic and Protestant ceased in 1560 to be a dispute among clerks. The blood-and-guts struggle between rival religious and political factions involved families in death and suffering. Hermes did not speak to the survivors nor, apparently, to those like du Préau who witnessed the carnage. At least in the case of du Préau, contact with Renaissance Hermeticism did not foster religious irenicism and reconciliation.

NOTES

1. Frances A. Yates, *The French Academies of the Sixteenth Century* (London: Warburg Institute, 1947), esp. pp. 199ff.; D. P. Walker, *The Ancient Theology: Studies in Christian Platonism from the Fifteenth to the Eighteenth Century* (London: Duckworth, 1972), p. 131; Jean Dagens, "Hermétisme et cabale en France de Lèfevre d'Étaples à Bossuet," *Revue de littérature comparée* 35 (1961), 5–16.

2. Frances A. Yates, *Giordano Bruno and the Hermetic Tradition* (New York: Vintage, 1969 [1964]), pp. 6–12.

3. Yates, *Giordano Bruno,* pp. 169–89, 229–34.

4. Jeanne Harrie, "Duplessis-Mornay, Foix-Candale, and the Hermetic Religion of the World," *Renaissance Quarterly* 31 (Winter 1978), 499–514.

5. See below, n. 7.

6. Dagens, p. 6.

7. There is no complete biography of du Préau, but see: *Dictionnaire de biographie française,* 12 (Paris, 1970), 543–44; [Michaud], *Biographie Universelle, ancienne et moderne,* 12 (Paris, n.d.), 49–50; *Nouvelle biographie générale,* 15 (1856), 365–66; La Croix du Maine et du Verdier, *Les Bibliothéques françoises,* 6 vols. (Paris: Saillant & Nyon and Michel Lambert, 1772–73), I, 253–54; Jean de Launoy [De Launoi], *Regii Navarrae Gymnasii Parisiensis historia,* 2 parts (Paris, 1677), 757–58.

8. "Italiam profectus gentis linguam didicit, & conscriptos ea libros in Gallicum convertit." De Launoy, p. 758.

9. Yates, *Giordano Bruno,* pp. 170–73.

10. Frederick Purnell, Jr., "Hermes and the Sibyl: A Note on Ficino's *Pimander,*" *Renaissance Quarterly* 30 (1977), 305–10. I have not had occasion to compare du Préau and Ficino. See also Walker, pp. 68, 107, n. 4; Paul Oskar Kristeller, "Marsilio Ficino e Lodovico Lazzarelli: Contributo alla diffusione delle idee ermetiche nel Rinascimento," *Studies in Renaissance Thought and Letters* (Rome: Edizioni di Storia e Letteratura, 1956), pp. 221–42.

11. Gabriel du Préau, *Deux livres de Mercure Trismegiste Hermés tres ancien Theologien, et excellant Philozophe, l'un de la puissance et sapience de Dieu. L'autre de la volonté de Dieu. Avecq'un Dialogue de Loys Lazarel, poëte Chrestien intitulé le Bassin d'Hermés* (Paris: Estienne Groulleau, 1557). All references in this essay are to the 1557 edition.

12. Kristeller, p. 227.

13. Foix de Candale's French translation appeared in Bordeaux the same year as his Latin edition and was dedicated to the queen mother, Catherine de Medici. Jeanne Harrie, "François Foix de Candale and the Hermetic Tradition in Sixteenth Century France" (Diss., University of California, Riverside, 1975), p. 8.

14. Du Préau's motives for translating the work were "L'une à fin que soyons muniz non seulement du bouclier de la foy, mais aussi de toutes autres armeures (qui sont les choses naturelles, par lesquelles cestuy cy avec divine inspiration, a cogneu Dieu . . .) pour ruyner et desconsire plusieurs fauz prophetes, mescreans, et infideles Atheistes, qui pour le iourd'huy sont sortiz au monde des infernalles contrées et stigieux palluz avec leur chef et Capitaine Sathan" and "d'exerciter mon esprit, & d'atenter si je pourroys faire quelque chose plus que beaucoup de gens doctes." Du Préau, *Deux livres,* fol. a vi.

15. " . . . d'hommes sans Dieu . . . qui se moquent de toutes les religions, coustumes, ordonnances, & ceremonies du monde, & qui vivent comme Epicuriens, sans attente d'autre vie que de ceste cy. . . . " Du Préau, *Declaration des abus, hipocrisie, et subtilitee des faux prophetes & seducteurs du peuple. Ensemble les Marques & enseignes comme il les faut cognoistre & segarder d'eux* (Paris: Jean Poupy, 1579), fol. 97v.

16. Philippe du Plessis de Mornay, *De la Verité de la Religion Chrestienne contre les Athées, Epicuriens, Payens, Juifs, Mahumedistes et autres Infideles* (Antwerp: Plantin, 1581). See Harrie, "Duplessis-Mornay," pp. 505–7.

17. "Ce fut luy [Hermes], qui premier entre tous philosophes apres avoir soigneusement versé en Phisique, et artz Mathematiques, et les avoir parfaitement compris, esleva son esprit a contempler les choses divines. Ce fut luy qui premier avant tous humains, tres sagement disputa de la maiesté de Dieu, de l'ordre des Anges, du changement et mutation des ames. . . . pour ceste cause fut iadis appellé autheur de Theologie. . . . Il semble que Mercure traite mesmes mysteres que Moyse, occultement toutesfoys, et souz paroles couvertes." Du Préau, *Deux livres,* fols. a v, 1, 12.

18. Yates, *Giordano Bruno,* p. 170; Kristeller, p. 241.

19. "Ie suis Chrestien, Sire, et si n'ay honte de me dire Hermetiste. Car si diligemment tu consideres ses preceptz & enseignemens, le confermeras toy mesme n'estre de beaucoup reculé de la doctrine Chrestienne." Du Préau, *Deux livres,* fol. 131.

20. Lazzarelli wrote "ie louëray Iesus Christ, soubz le nom de Pimander, lequel est d'Hermés interpreté pensée divine." Du Préau, *Deux livres,* fol. 166.

21. Kristeller, p. 229. According to du Préau, Moses was born in 1598 B.C. At the same time there flourished in Egypt "un astrologue de fort grand renom et experience, nommé Athlas, frere de Prometheus... ayeul du costé maternel du grand Mercure, du quel fut neveu Mercure Trismegiste." *Deux livres,* fol. a iiii.

22. Du Préau, *Deux livres,* fol. 76v: "Mercure use bien autrement de ce mot animal, et de ce vocable ame, que n'avons coustume d'user"; fol. 93: "Mais il semble que tout cecy ne soient que fainctises, et inventions diaboliques, et autres vaines illusions, lesquelles attirent l'homme en l'erreur des Payens"; fols. 98–99: "de bonne & chrestienne affection inventée: mais peut estre violées quant à la lettre"; fol. 114: "Ce tresiesme est infectionné de pareille souilleure, que le neufiesme, auquel Mercure dit l'homme estre tres divin, et tres admirable, en ce qu'il a trouvé idolatrie, et inventé la maniere d'invoquer les diables."

23. Yates, *Giordano Bruno,* p. 172.

24. Du Préau, *De la cognoissance de soymesme pour parvenir a celle de Dieu. Livre utile & necessaire à tous Chrestiens: auquel sont traités plusieurs poincts difficiles de Theologie, Philosophie, & Medecine* (Paris: Estienne Groulleau, 1559), fol. e vii.

25. "Car (comme dit ledit Hermes) si tu ne cognois ceste lumiere qui est en toy cest à dire, ton ame & entendement, comme pourrois tu cognoistre Dieu?" Du Préau, *De la cognoissance,* fol. e i-vo.

26. "... les divins commandemens, ordonnances, & institutions de Dieu par bonne consideration & diligente inquisition des escritures." Du Préau, *De la cognoissance,* fol. 228v.

27. Dagens, p. 6.

28. Harrie, "Foix de Candale," pp. 102–61.

29. Du Préau, *La Geomance du seigneur Christofe de Cattan Gentilhomme Genevoys. Livre non moins plaisant & recreatif, que d'ingenieuse invention, pour scavoir toutes choses, presentes, passées, & à advenir. Avec la Roüe de Pythagoras* (Paris: Gilles Gilles, 1558).

30. St. Augustine, *The City of God,* VII, 35.

31. Walker, pp. 234–39; Brian P. Copenhaver, *Symphorien Champier and the Reception of the Occultist Tradition in Renaissance France* (The Hague: Mouton, 1978), pp. 210–22.

32. The planets and stars "influent & dispersent es choses inferieures par l'ordre & volonte de Dieu" [but to ascribe certainty to the astrological arts is] "contrevenir au premier commandement de Dieu." Du Préau, *La Geomance,* fols. eij, 4-vo.

33. "Car ceste science n'est point art d'enchanterie... ou de devination, qui se fait par invocation diabolique: ains est une partie de Magie naturelle, appellee de plusieurs grands personnages, fille d'Astrologie." Du Préau, *La Geomance,* fol. 8.

34. Donald R. Kelley, *The Beginning of Ideology: Consciousness and Society in the French Reformation* (Cambridge: Cambridge University Press, 1981), pp. 230–38, 249–51.

35. Du Préau, *Harangue sur les causes de la guerre entreprise contre les rebelles, & seditieux qui en forme d'hostilité ont pris les armes contre le Roy en son Royaume: &*

mesme des causes d'ou proviennent toutes autre calamitez, & miseres qui iournellement nous surviennent (Paris: N. Chesneau, 1562).

36. "...qu'il ny a Royaume... qui long temps puisse demeurer en paix ou il est à un chacun libre & permis d'embrasser & suyvre telle religion qu'il luy plaist." Du Préau, *Harangue*, fol. A iij-vo—A iiij-vo.

37. The Protestant "secte est du tout populaire, & beaucoup meilleure & plus propre à exciter le commun peuple, & à l'esmouvoir par folie, temerité, & ambition à ire & fureur contre les Roys & Princes." Du Préau, *Histoire de l'estat et success de l'Eglise dressee en forme de chronique generalle et universelle...*, 2 vols. (Paris: Jacques Kerver, 1583), II, fol. 617.

38. Du Préau, *Harangue*, fols. A ij, A vi.

39. "Que pourroient faire les bestes brutes, ou les cruels Tartares, qui fust plus inhumain & abominable? C'est le fruict du cinquiesme Evangile, semé par Luther, & cultivé par le venerable Calvin." Du Préau, *Histoire*, II, fol. 546v.

40. See above n. 15. The work first appeared as *Des Faux Prophetes, seducteurs et hypochrites, qui viennent à nous en habit de brebis, mais au dedans sont loups ravissans...* (Paris, 1564).

41. "Car combien sont ils venuz de Ministres, faux prophetes & loups ravissans de Geneve (receptacle & sentine de toutes les ordures Francoyses)...?" Du Préau, *Declaration*, fol. 14v.

42. "...mais aussi si elles sont prises au sens de l'esprit de Dieu, & des vrays Prophetes, Apostres, & saincts docteurs, par lesquels Dieu nous a manifesté & declaré sa parole." Du Préau, *Declaration*, fols. 7v–9v.

43. Du Préau, *Declaration*, fol. 29.

44. Du Préau, *Declaration*, fol. 50 [mispag. 52].

45. "Car la ou il y a promesse & contract legitime, entre le mary et la femme, il ny a point de doubt que le mariage ne soit ferme et legitime devant Dieu...." Du Préau, *Declaration*, fol. 51v.

46. "...leur Cene n'est... autre chose, qu'une buvette ou compotation, qui se peult aussi bien faire en une taverne." Du Préau, *Declaration*, fol. 62.

47. "...ilz ne sont fondez ny en raison naturelle, ny en escriture." Du Préau, *Declaration*, fol. 59v.

48. "...portans en leur visage mauvaise couleur, laquelle demonstre assez leur conscience n'estre en repos, mais tousiours en craincte." Du Préau, *Declaration*, fol. 62v.

49. Yates, *Giordano Bruno*, p. 230; Edward A. Gosselin, "'Doctor' Bruno's Solar Medicine," *Sixteenth Century Journal* 15 (1984), 212–20.

50. François Foix de Candale, "Traicte du Saint-Sacrement par lequel plusieurs intelligences divines, jusques a present couvertes, sont esclaircies pour rendre la [sic] disputes qui perturbent ce jourd'huy grand nombre de peuple de Dieu, le tout prins des sainctes lettres," Bibliothèque nationale, Fonds Français, 1886. See Harrie, "Duplessis-Mornay," p. 509.

51. Gabriel du Préau, *Du Souverain et unique sacrifice de l'eglise catholique et apostolique. Qui est la reale, substantielle, & corporelle presence de l'humanité de Iesus Christ en la Messe, sous les especes de pain et de vin* (Paris: Gervais Mallot, 1574).

52. "... une malheureuse & damnée invention du diable qui les conduit à sa volonté...." Du Préau, *Du Souverain,* p. 204-vo.

53. Du Préau, *Du Souvrain,* p. 32.

54. "... d'un vray corps essentiel, & de substance qui a esté livrée & espandue pour nous en la croix." Du Préau, *Du Souverain,* fol. 33v.

55. "... c'est qu'il fault tousiours tenir ceste reigle ... iamais consentir à heresie & fauce religion, ny l'approuver en quelque maniere que ce soit, ny frequenter les lieux & assemblees ou l'on en face profession, s'il est aucunement possible." Du Préau, *Declaration,* fols. 84v–85.

56. Du Préau, *Declaration,* fols. 65–82.

57. Du Préau, *Declaration,* fols. 42, 62–vo, 85, 118, 128–vo.

58. "... accorder la religion de Iesus Christ, & de l'Antichrist tout ensemble, à fin que par ce moyen ils puissent myeux vivre en paix avec un chacun." Du Préau, *Declaration,* fol. 124.

59. Du Préau, *Declaration,* fols. 147–58.

60. Du Préau, *Declaration,* fol. 78.

61. Du Préau, *Histoire,* II, 546–47.

62. Yates, *Giordano Bruno,* p. 186; "tout consentement donné à idolatrie, heresie, & fauce religion, contient approbation d'icelle" and is "une espece d'idolatrie, & de superstition." Du Préau, *Declaration,* p. 58.

63. The biographical notices cited in n. 7 above contain partial bibliographies of his published works which testify to du Préau's strong interest in heresy and antipathy to the Protestant "heresy."

HOWARD ADELMAN

Rabbi Leon Modena and the Christian Kabbalists

Much insight into Jewish-Christian relations during the sixteenth and seventeenth centuries can be derived from the writings of the Venetian rabbi Leon Modena (1571–1648) on Christianity and Jewish mysticism, commonly known as Kabbalah. Although a prolific writer on Jewish communal and religious issues, Modena is remembered for his polemics against Kabbalah and Christianity,[1] which most interestingly contain views favorable to both mysticism and Jesus. The development of his thinking can only be understood in light of his close association with many Christians and kabbalists,[2] even though he himself was not a kabbalist.

The fact which is central to all of Modena's relationships with Christians and kabbalists is the emergence of the published book as a factor in intellectual life during the sixteenth century. Until this time the study of esoteric subjects had been limited for many reasons, such as restrictions imposed by religious authorities and the high cost of rare manuscripts, but as progress was made in the publication of books, access to these materials became much easier, for Christians as well as Jews.[3] Modena, who worked regularly for the Christian publishers of Hebrew books, and who was sought out by Jews and Christians because of his interest in books, was able to gauge the power of published books to promulgate ideas which once had been peripheral, such as Christian uses of Kabbalah and new schools of Jewish Kabbalah, which will be discussed below. Gradually he came to realize that even the publication of the Zohar, the major source of kabbalistic teachings, posed a threat to traditional Judaism, and he began to undermine the integrity of the work. Modena never published any of his own writings on Christianity or Kabbalah; but, on the basis of remarks he noted in the margins of books and manuscripts he owned, incidental statements he made in letters and rabbinic decisions on other subjects, and treatises he composed late in life, it is possible to reconstruct the evolution of his attitude toward Kabbalah and Christianity.

I

In addition to buying, selling, sharing, and editing books, Modena's relationships with Christians involved studying Hebrew, discussing theology, and occasionally engaging in disputations and fracases. Soon after Modena returned to his birthplace of Venice at the age of twenty-one in 1592,[4] he began to attend meetings of Christian societies, and esteemed Christians came to hear him preach.[5] Thus to an old friend in Montagnana, where he had grown up, Modena wrote with great enthusiasm about the sermons and discussions in which he and other Jews participated at meetings of Christian scholars, adding that he would love to tell what had been discussed, but that certain matters must be presented only orally.[6] In 1593 Modena's first published poem appeared at the beginning of *Tevat Noah* by the Christian Hebrew scholar Marco Marini. Modena had many other Christian associates who knew Hebrew, including members of the monastery of San Antonio. Later in life, among his Italian Christian associates were Giovanni Vislingio (1598–1649), an important professor of anatomy and botany at Padua, whose accomplishments included pioneering work in the dissection of humans and a trip to the Land of Israel to study its flora; Vincent Noghera, theologian to Cardinal Sacchetti, archbishop of Bologna; Giovanni Argoli, a scholar and author in Bologna; Fulgenzio Micanzio, monk, censor, and later counselor to the Venetian Republic; Ozario Spinola, cardinal and papal nuncio in Ferrara; and perhaps Paolo Sarpi (1552–1623), Servite monk, historian, and counselor to the Venetian Republic during the period of controversy with the pope which culminated in the papal interdict of Venice. Renewed diplomatic relations between Venice and England, after a forty-five-year hiatus, heightened interest in Hebrew after the inauguration of a new translation of the Bible by King James I in 1604, and absence of an official Jewish community in England turned the attention of many English Christian Hebraists to the Jewish scholars in the ghetto of Venice. Modena's circle of English Christian acquaintances included Henry Wotton (1568–1639), the English ambassador to Venice; William Bedell (1577–1644), Wotton's secretary and later provost of Trinity College in Dublin, then Protestant bishop of Kilmore in Ireland and translator of the Bible into Gaelic; William Boswell (d. 1649), a scholar and politician who had served in Parliament and as secretary to several English ambassadors; John Selden (1584–1654), a member of Parliament, and a prominent scholar and Christian Hebraist; and perhaps Thomas Coryat (1577–1617), a traveler and writer who recorded a lengthy religious discussion with an unnamed Venetian rabbi who may have been Modena.[7] Because there also was no Jewish community in France at this time, French Christians interested in meeting Jews came to the ghetto of Venice. Modena's French associates included Henri duc de Rohan (1579–1638), the leader of the French Huguenots and then commander-in-chief of Venetian forces; Henri duc de Candale, an intimate acquaintance of the duke of Rohan; Gabriel Naudé (1600–1651), bibliographer, librarian, physician, and historian who worked for Cardinal Francesco Barberini (1597–1679) and Cardinal Giulio Mazarin (1602–61); Jean de Plantavit de la Pause (1576–1659), a French Protestant who converted to Catholicism and later became a bishop; Jacques Gaffarel (1601–81), a Catholic orientalist, Hebraist, mystic, and bibliophile; a brother of King Louis XIII, probably the rebellious Gaston duc d'Orleans (1608–60);[8] and several ambassadors.[9] One Frenchman, a Louis Iselin, who had studied Italian with Modena, commissioned the noted artist Tiberio Tinelli (1586–1638) to paint Modena's portrait, but Tinelli died, probably by his own hand, before the picture was completed.[10]

An example typical of Modena's support of a rapprochement between Christians and Jews was his defense of a Jewish moneylender, in which he condemned moneylending at interest but emphasized that if the Jews had alternative ways of earning a living they would not be moneylenders.[11] With the same goal in mind, he once wrote a Hebrew letter to an English Protestant in which he defended the Jews against the charge of having crucified Jesus.[12] Perhaps most important was his *Historia degli riti Hebraici*, the first systematic outline of Jewish practice in the vernacular. Modena wrote this between 1614 and 1615 at the request of an English lord, probably Wotton, for presentation to King James I. The goal of the *Riti* was to present Judaism sympathetically before Christian readers. The *Riti* circulated in manuscript and was finally published in 1637, followed by many subsequent editions and translations.[13]

II

By the time Modena had settled in Venice he had also known and studied Hebrew with many Jewish kabbalists. He had begun the formal study of Kabbalah by the age of eighteen[14] and regularly used kabbalistic expressions in his writings. He soon became involved in the publication of kabbalistic books for which he wrote dedicatory poems. Modena had many contacts with Shomrim Laboker societies, "Guardians of the Morning," who engaged in kabbalistic rites which had originated in the Land of Israel, such as rising early for penitential and flagellation ceremonies.[15] One of the leading kabbalists with whom Modena had close ties was Menahem Azariah Fano (1548–1620), the man who had circumcised him. Later in life Modena helped Fano publish at least one of his books, and corresponded with him about his own aspirations to be a writer and his frustrations as a teacher. Modena also owned many

kabbalistic books and manuscripts,[16] and in his writings he related anecdotes about prominent kabbalists, such as Moses Cordovero (1522–70),
Moses Basola (1480–1560), Isaac Luria (1534–72), Jacob Abulafia, Jedidiah
Galante, Naftali Ashkenazi (1540–1602), and Isaiah Horowitz (c. 1565–1630),
which are available in no other sources.[17]

Soon after settling in Venice, however, Modena began to turn against
Kabbalah, possibly as a result of his many conversations with Israel
Sarug, a popular itinerant kabbalist and preacher who was in Venice
from about 1592 to 1598. Indeed, most of the information available about
Sarug's activities in Venice is found in Modena's writings. Sarug claimed
to have been a student of Isaac Luria, the founder of Lurianic Kabbalah,
which differed from the accepted kabbalistic thinking of the time in Italy.
Sarug believed that there was no difference between philosophy and
Kabbalah. Modena's writings about Kabbalah from the 1590s, in which
he argued that philosophy and Kabbalah are separate realms, that there
is a difference between the seven sciences and the ten sephirot, and that
some truths are a matter of faith while others can be tested by investigation,
may reflect his controversies with Sarug.[18]

Modena's reaction against Sarug could have been motivated by concerns about Sarug's legitimacy as a disciple of Luria, whose doctrine was
not supposed to have been spread outside the Land of Israel, and Modena's
own attachments to earlier interpretations of Kabbalah, particularly those
of Moses Cordovero, whose views had been accepted by most of Modena's
teachers. There also was a personal aspect to Modena's reactions against
Sarug, who had attracted a wide following in Venice which included
thirty or forty devoted disciples, including Menahem Azariah Fano
and Aaron Berechiah of Modena, Leon Modena's cousin. According to
Modena, Sarug curried favor with the wealthy and important people by
telling them that in earlier incarnations their souls had resided in great
men. Modena viewed Sarug as arrogant. At a circumcision, a quarrel
between the two of them almost came to fisticuffs when Sarug threat-
ened Modena with a loaf of bread. Modena's descriptions of Sarug
employed expressions of contempt, and he questioned Sarug's miracles,
mental capacities, and character. Modena, the struggling preacher and
teacher, may have perceived Sarug, a foreign charismatic leader who was
winning the support of prominent Venetian Jews, as a threat to his own
chances for success in the community. The need for adorning his sermons with kabbalistic references was probably particularly strong during
his early years in Venice when he had to compete against Sarug's
popularity. In any case, whatever the main reason, Modena's initial
reactions against Kabbalah were not as an opponent of it per se, but
rather a rejection of particular teachings and a specific individual propa-
gating them.[19]

Around 1608 Modena seems to have broken off his close relations with Fano, perhaps because of Fano's devotion to Sarug. As Modena's closest students, such as Joseph Solomon Delmedigo (1591–1655) and Joseph Hamitz (d. c. 1676), became involved with Lurianic Kabbalah, his opposition to their new loyalties led him to a rejection of Kabbalah in general. These confrontations culminated later in his life in his two major literary polemics against Kabbalah, but already between 1608 and 1610 he had begun to include some subtle attacks on Kabbalah in his writings. To David Farar, a former Marrano who had returned to Judaism in Amsterdam and who engaged in polemics with Christians, Modena raised doubts about the relation between the names of angels and their actions in Kabbalah. From this discussion of the fact that the names of the angels had changed at the time of the destruction of the Temple, it would be possible to conclude, as Farar did, that ancient formulas transmitted by kabbalists which relied on angelic names were no longer valid and that practical Kabbalah was no longer effective.[20] Subsequently, an incident which occurred in about 1613 contributed to Modena's negative views of Kabbalah in general and Lurianic Kabbalah in particular. Modena was present when the famous former Marrano and defender of Judaism, Dr. Elijah Montalto (d. 1616), just before leaving to serve Marie de Médicis of France as her personal physician, accused Jedidiah Galante of fabricating stories about miracles attributed to Isaac Luria.[21] At this time Modena also publicly insisted, contrary to Jewish custom as well as Venetian law, that, according to rabbinic law, head covering was optional for Jews. These protests may have been a reaction against kabbalists who, basing themselves on the Zohar rather than Jewish law, claimed that head covering was mandatory for all Jews.[22]

Around 1618, in a rabbinic responsum in defense of David Farar of Amsterdam, who had been influenced by the letters Modena had sent him almost a decade earlier, Modena first expressed his objection to rabbis who considered Kabbalah so essential to Judaism that they excommunicated those who did not share their enthusiasm.[23] In the same responsum, he also began to challenge the legitimacy of Kabbalah, asking how oral traditions could have been transmitted from Moses to contemporary kabbalists without having been known to the early rabbis of the Talmud. He further contended that, despite the claims of kabbalists, the second-century rabbi Simon bar Yohai had not written the Zohar. Modena's view on this subject caused him to quarrel regularly with Jacob Halevi (d. 1629), a kabbalist as well as a music and dance teacher who became engaged to his daughter in 1613.[24] Though still reluctant to express his opinions in public, in his unpublished writings Modena began around this time to disavow kabbalistic references which had appeared in his earlier writings, to omit reference in his autobiography to the kabbalistic works for which he had written prefaces, and to compile a bibliography of antikabbalistic authors.[25]

Between 1618 and 1622 Modena expressed his strongest arguments against the antiquity of the Zohar.[26] By way of background, at the beginning of the sixteenth century, Elijah Levita (c. 1469–1549), a prominent Hebrew grammarian, had claimed that the Hebrew vowels had been created later than the consonantal text of the Bible on the grounds that they were not mentioned in the early rabbinic writings, the Talmud, or the Zohar.[27] To refute Levita's assertions, Azariah de Rossi (c. 1511–c. 1578), the leading critical Jewish thinker in Italy during the sixteenth century, had responded in 1573 in his *Meor 'eynayim* that the vowels had indeed been mentioned in early rabbinic writings, the Talmud, and the Zohar, arguing that the transmission of the vowels proved that the kabbalists possessed oral traditions from the time of Moses. De Rossi concluded: "If he [Levita] stood with us today he would surely say that 'I have been answered.' "[28] To this Modena retorted privately in the margins of his copy of *Meor 'eynayim:*

> If he stood with us today, I am sure that to one who would want to prove to him the antiquity of the vowels and accents from kabbalistic books which appeared in our times he too would reply to him and say: "It is easier for me to believe that all of these books are fabrications from scratch which arrived recently after the vowels and the accents, than for me to believe that the vowels and accents are earlier than these books, because he would not seek from him other proofs from those books which point a finger at belief in their newness.... " It is obvious for me because he would say it and so I will believe.[29]

Modena took de Rossi's use of kabbalistic texts as proof of the antiquity of the Hebrew vowels and accent marks and turned it around against the antiquity of the kabbalistic texts: the references to vowels and accents in these books were proof that they were not as old as the kabbalists claimed and did not contain ancient revealed truths, but only modern inventions.

III

At the same time that Modena was turning against Kabbalah, contacts with Christians showed him the dangers to Jewish loyalty posed by Christian uses of the most basic concepts of Kabbalah.[30] In 1609 in Florence—from 1609 to 1610 he left Venice to seek a living in Florence— Modena taught Hebrew, Bible, and rabbinics to Jean de Plantavit de la Pause.[31] The next year, Plantavit offered Modena the chair of oriental languages in Paris. It is almost certain that the offer depended upon Modena's conversion to Christianity because no professing Jews had lived in Paris since the expulsions of the Jews from France in the late fourteenth century.[32] At this time, too, Modena wrote a letter in Hebrew to a Christian student of his in which he tried to dissuade him from studying Kabbalah.[33] In 1611 Modena bought, with the intention of refuting, a fourteenth-century manuscript by Abner of Burgos (c. 1270–1340), the first Jewish apostate to Christianity who had used Kabbalah to justify his conversion.[34]

Modena was aware that in addition to Christians who used Kabbalah to entice Jews to Christianity, some Christians, such as Johannes Buxtorf the elder (1564–1629), author of *Synagoga judaica,* used it to denigrate Judaism.[35] Therefore in 1614, when writing his exposition of Judaism in the *Riti,* partially as a response to Buxtorf, Modena avoided using the word "Kabbalah" and excluded favorable explanations of kabbalistic teachings or practices. The only time he did mention Kabbalah in that book was to distinguish it from the Talmud or to ridicule it.[36] In the same vein, in his handwritten notes in the margins of *Meor 'eynayim,* Modena claimed that Christians used beliefs prominent in Kabbalah, such as the ten sephirot or divine emanations, to justify Christological beliefs.[37] During the 1620s Modena was reading a Latin book that used Kabbalah to support Christianity. This was *Bibliotheca sancta* of Sixtus of Siena (1520–69), a convert from Judaism in the sixteenth century who believed that the Zohar confirmed the doctrines of Christianity, that "Christians can stab the Jews with their own weapons," and that Kabbalah was a secret exposition of divine laws.[38] Around this time, Modena also annotated his copy of Pietro Galatino's *De arcanus catholicae veritatis,* one of the most popular Christian kabbalistic books of the Renaissance.[39]

In 1624, in a conversation with Andreas Colvius of Dort (1594–1671), a Christian preacher who was in the service of Johan Berck (1565–1627), Dutch ambassador to Venice, Modena discussed popular Christian interpretations of the Bible which involved the use of Kabbalah.[40] Colvius considered that the gematria, the numerical equivalent for the Hebrew letters, for the expression "Jesus and Mary" was the same as for the term "foreign gods of the land" in Deuteronomy 31:16 and that this showed that the Jews would accept Jesus and Mary.[41] In response, Modena gave Colvius a manuscript which mocked Christian uses of gematria, repeating the same arithmetic but emphasizing the idolatrous aspect of the formula. He then showed that the name "Jesus Nazarean" added up to 666, the number attributed to the Antichrist in the Apocalypse of John.[42]

In 1626, Modena allowed his increasingly critical position concerning Kabbalah to appear publicly in a rabbinic responsum.[43] He wrote that Kabbalah did not contain ancient traditions but rather consisted of recent creations. He supported his views by referring to Isaac ben Sheshet Perfet (1326–1408), a rabbi from Spain.[44] Comparing the ten sephirot to the Christian belief in the Trinity, Perfet had argued that by ascribing different attributes to the sephirot, kabbalists jeopardized the principle of the unity of God. Modena then wrote that proliferation of kabbalistic writings could bring great disaster and confusion for Jews and that Kabbalah would be a source of shame for them because Christians would either blame the Jews when Kabbalah contradicted Christianity or would use it to convert them when it confirmed aspects of their faith.

During the 1620s Modena developed a friendship with Jacques Gaffarel, who, after being appointed librarian to Cardinal Richelieu (1585–1642), had been sent to Italy in search of books and manuscripts. Drawing upon Johannes Reuchlin (1455–1522) and Pico della Mirandola (1463–94), leading Christian Hebraists of the Renaissance, Gaffarel had used the Zohar, *Sefer yetzirah*, and kabbalistic methods, especially gematria, to justify Christian doctrines in his *Abdita divinae cabbalae mysteria* in 1625. Gaffarel, who would later prepare a catalogue of Pico's manuscripts, may have been responsible for drawing Modena's attention to specific works by Pico.[45]

Between 1636 and 1639, Modena wrote *Ari nohem*,[46] his major polemic against Kabbalah, which was, in part, a reaction to Gaffarel. In *Ari nohem*, Chapter 12, Modena suggested that Pico had been the first Christian to study Kabbalah, and he began and ended his book with references to Pico. Modena wrote that of the 900 theses which Pico had posted in Rome in 1486, 116 were based on Kabbalah, 45 on Hebrew kabbalists, and 71 on his own inventions based on Kabbalah.[47] Modena's attention to Pico is evidence that Pico's writings, although not influential during his own time and, despite support from the pope, often opposed by many Christians, had become influential during the seventeenth century.[48]

In *Ari nohem*, Chapter 3, in addition to defending rabbinic Judaism against Kabbalah and attacking Lurianic Kabbalah, Modena drew attention to the relationship between his program against Kabbalah and his controversies with apostates. He accused the kabbalists of rejecting the literal meaning of the Bible and speaking like Christians when they described Scripture in terms of an outer garment with deep inner truths which were not shared by all Jews.[49] For similar reasons, Modena also attacked gematria because Jewish apostates used it to demonstrate biblical proof of their new faith, and he further warned his readers in Chapter 10 that some Christian uses of the Bible would "make their skin crawl." He also repeated the concern in Chapters 7 and 27 that the sephirot posed a threat to the unity of God and added that they resembled the doctrine of the multiplicity of God in Christianity. Although Modena adduced many arguments to prove that the Zohar was not an ancient text, he never presented proofs which relied on suspicions of the recent origins of the Hebrew vowels, realizing that this argument would have played into the hands of Christian critics of Jewish tradition who used arguments against the antiquity of the vowels to enhance their polemical claim that the rabbis had corrupted the Bible to suppress prophecies about Jesus.[50]

In the last chapter of *Ari nohem* Modena wrote that Pico "went to great lengths to show them [Christians] that its [Kabbalah's] ways and principles are all a foundation of the chief principles of their religion: of the trinity, of the incarnation, of the deity, of the virgin mother, of the birth, of the name Jesus, of the sin of Adam, which caused the death of the soul and the death of the messiah."[51] That these topics became, for the most part, the chapter headings of *Magen veherev*, Modena's final polemic against Christianity, which he had begun to write in 1645, shows the significant link in his thinking between his writings against Kabbalah and against Christianity.

Although in *Magen veherev* Modena offered many refutations of Christianity based on biblical verses, the New Testament, and Thomas Aquinas, his chief purpose was to oppose the use of Kabbalah by Christian missionaries, especially those who relied upon Galatino. For example, Modena undermined the proofs for Mary's virginity which had been based on gematria,[52] and showed that the messiahship and divinity of Jesus could not be demonstrated on the basis of his Hebrew name.[53]

In *Magen veherev* Modena also continued his struggle to defend traditional Judaism against Christian uses of Kabbalah, without however compromising the essentials of Kabbalah. Thus he affirmed the idea of creation through divine emanations and argued that the attributes which the kabbalists gave to the sephirot were descriptive, unlike the distinctive quality of each member of the Trinity (II:1, III:7). He explained that the sephirot played an intermediary role between God, the angels, and the lower world (II:7) and did not eschew using the mystical Torah commentary of Menahem Recanati upon which Galatino and other Christian kabbalists had also relied.[54] Modena also presented the kabbalistic teaching that all human souls had originated at the time of creation, a belief necessary to counter the Christian idea that souls were created at conception and hence were tainted by original sin (I:5).

Moreover, in *Magen veherev* Modena made concessions to the validity of aspects of Christianity, or at least to civility and good manners. First (in I:10), unlike most Jews, he called the Gospels *Evangelae* in Hebrew rather than *Aven gilayon*, meaning "sin sheet." Modena referred to non-Jews as *gentili* rather than *goyim*, a term based on the Hebrew word for "nations" which took on derogatory connotations (IV:12). Also, he defended Jesus against many Jewish accusations, writing that these were a disgrace to the Jews who believed them. Modena stated that he tried to write about Christianity as if he had lived in Jesus' generation and had sat with him, perhaps one of the earliest Jewish attempts at presenting a historical Jesus (III:9).

Additionally, he wrote that Jews would concede that certain verses in the Bible could be interpreted according to Christian interpretations and that the Trinity would be acceptable to Jews were it not for the doctrine of the incarnation.[55] Moreover, he admitted the logical possibility of the antepartum virginity of Mary because, he argued, if God could create the world He could create a fetus in a woman if He wanted (IV:7).

Modena's sympathetic attitude toward Jesus was consistent with the specific goals of *Magen veherev* and with what he may have said about Jesus on other occasions. A student of his, who later became an apostate under the name Giulio Morosini, reported in his *Via della fede* that Modena had said that Christians were virtuous and that Jesus was a good man, *huomo da bene,* probably the promised messiah, and that Modena's only remaining difficulty with Christianity was the belief that Jesus was God incarnate.[56] Nevertheless, Modena had no great love for Christianity, and privately, in the margins of his manuscript copy of Abner of Burgos's writings, Modena was somewhat harsher towards Jesus and Christianity:

This sage . . . was neither a Jew nor a Christian.
This is complete stupidity.
. . . Jesus was the son of Joseph and the son of David. This is impossible.[57]

Therefore, we can consider *Magen veherev* to have been the work of a seasoned polemicist who was writing for a specific audience of Christian Hebraists and the Jews who would have to respond to them.

IV

In conclusion, Modena's attitude toward Kabbalah went through four stages. His early attitude was one of using kabbalistic citations and ideas common to educated Jews in Italy to make his point as a teacher and preacher. During the second stage Modena confused his antipathy for Sarug with hostility to Kabbalah in general. During the third stage Modena's hostility to Kabbalah in general increased for different reasons. Now he saw the dangers to Judaism posed by Christian use of kabbalistic methods. Finally, as Modena's thinking matured, although aware of its misuses and dangers, he nevertheless developed a positive attitude to Kabbalah and, as a pioneer among Jewish scholars, acknowledged what he saw as good in Christianity.

Underlying Modena's polemics was the reality that Kabbalah had much in common with both Judaism and Christianity. Thus he challenged aspects of Kabbalah which could be used to confirm doctrines of Christianity, such as trinitarian aspects of the deity and the manipulation of scriptural passages to find secret truths. Simultaneously he defended aspects of Kabbalah which were also fundamental to rabbinic Judaism, such as the authority of the Hebrew Bible and the legitimacy of the oral tradition of the rabbis. In formulating his critique of Kabbalah, Modena strove not only to protect rabbinic Judaism from Christian missionaries but also from his own critique of Kabbalah.

NOTES

1. For a thorough bibliographic essay on Kabbalah, see Jochanan H. A. Wijnhoven, "Medieval Jewish Mysticism," *Bibliographic Essays in Medieval Jewish Studies: The Study of Judaism,* II (New York: Ktav Publishing House, 1976), 269–332.

2. The interpretation presented in this paper is a revision of the standard view, first offered by Abraham Geiger, *Leon da Modena: Rabbiner zu Venedig (1571-1648), und seine Stellung zur Kabbala, zum Thalmud und zum Christenthume* (Breslau: Joh. Urban Kern, 1856), p. 15, that Modena had attacked Kabbalah in order to undermine rabbinic Judaism with which Geiger felt it was closely aligned. Elsewhere I have argued that Modena was a staunch supporter of rabbinic Judaism and that nineteenth-century writers who attributed antirabbinic writings to him did so for their own tendentious reasons without any convincing textual evidence. See my "New Light on the Life and Writings of Leon Modena," *Approaches to the Study of Medieval Judaism,* II, ed. David Blumenthal (Chico: Scholars Press, 1985), 109–22. For a full discussion, see my "Success and Failure in the Seventeenth Century Ghetto of Venice: The Life and Thought of Leon Modena" (Diss., Brandeis University, 1985).

3. On the role played by printing in making Hebrew literature available to a large Christian audience in Europe during the sixteenth century, see Lucien Febvre and Henri-Jean Martin, *The Coming of the Book,* trans. David Gerard (London: Verso Editions, 1976), pp. 268–72.

4. For the details of Modena's life, see Mark R. Cohen's forthcoming English translation of his Hebrew autobiography, *Hayye Yehudah,* which, in addition to introductions by Natalie Z. Davis, Theodore K. Rabb, and myself, will contain historical notes I have prepared in conjunction with Benjamin C. I. Ravid.

5. Modena, *Hayye Yehudah,* ed. Abraham Kahana (Kiev: Mekorot Lehistoria Israelit, 1911), p. 25.

6. *Kitve haRav Yehudah Aryeh miModena,* ed. Judah Blau (Budapest: Adolf Alkalay & Sohn, 1905, 1906; Strassburg: Karl J. Trübner, 1907), #47; cf. Yosef Hayyim Yerushalmi, *From Spanish Court to Italian Ghetto* (New York: Columbia University Press, 1971), pp. 353–54.

7. Coryat recorded his observations about the Jews of Venice in *Coryat's Crudities* (London, 1611), pp. 231–37; (Glasgow: James MacLehose and Sons, 1905), pp. 370–76; reprinted in part in Cecil Roth, "Leone da Modena and England," *Transactions of the Jewish Historical Society of England* 11 (1924/27), 216–25.

8. Gaston duc d'Orleans was the only brother of the king alive when Modena wrote in his autobiography (*Hayye,* p. 47) that he had met the king's brother. Letters from Gaston duc d'Orleans in Venice to his brother King Louis XIII as well as several manifestos by the duke, mostly dating from 1632, are preserved in the Biblioteca Nazionale Marciani in Venice.

9. Modena received a generous gift from the ambassador for a poem he had written in honor of the birth of a son (who would become King Louis XIII) to King Henry IV and Marie de Médicis. See *The Divan of Leo de Modena,* ed. Simon Bernstein (Philadelphia: Jewish Publication Society, 1932), #56; Isaac min Haleviim, "Introduction," *Magen veherev,* ed. Abraham Geiger (Breslau: H. Salzbach, 1856), fol. 11a.

10. *Hayye,* pp. 53–54.

11. While in Ferrara between 1604 and 1607, Modena had been summoned by Cardinal Ozario Spinola to help with this case between a Jewish moneylender and a Christian nobleman. See Clemente Ancona, "Attachi contro il Talmud di Fra Sisto da Siena e la riposta finora inedita di Leon Modena, rabbino in Venezia," *Bollettino dell'istituto di storia della società e della stato veneziano* 5–6 (1963–64), 297–323. For Jewish views on moneylending at this time, see Benjamin Ravid, "Moneylending in Seventeenth Century Jewish Vernacular Apologetica," in *Jewish Thought in the Seventeenth Century,* ed. Isadore Twersky and Bernard Septimus (Cambridge, Mass.: Harvard University Press, 1987), pp. 257–84.

12. This letter was written between 1612 and 1618. See *Zikne Yehudah,* ed. Shlomo Simonsohn (Jerusalem: Mosad Harav Kook, 1956), #32, and Roth, "Leone da Modena and England," p. 209.

13. For a complete analysis of the *Riti,* see Mark R. Cohen, "Leone da Modena's Riti: A Seventeenth Century Plea for Toleration of Jews," *Jewish Social Studies* 37 (1972), 287–321.

14. *Hayye,* pp. 15, 16; *Ari nohem,* ed. Nehemiah Libowitz (Jerusalem: Eretz Yisrael, 1929), p. 84.

15. Modena owned a list of regulations of a Shomrim Laboker society. See Library of the Jewish Community of Ancona MS. 7, fol. 6a; cf. Solomon Schechter, "Safed," *Studies in Judaism,* II (Philadelphia: Jewish Publication Society, 1908), 289–301, 238–40, and Yaakov Toledano, *Otzar genazim* (Jerusalem: Mosad Harav Kook, 1960), pp. 48–51. Sometime before 1623 Modena wrote a poem called *Yom zeh yehi mishkal* for the eve of the new moon for a Shomrim Laboker society. See *Hayye,* p. 44; *Divan,* #197. He also wrote an introduction to *Seder hamalkot,* a flagellation rite, for a Shomrim Laboker society. See Blau, *Kitve,* #11; British Library Or. 5396, fols. 9b–10a.

16. A bibliography of books which may have been in Modena's own library listed seventeen kabbalistic books. See Ancona 7, fol. 6b. At the time of his death, after pawning and giving away many books, Modena still owned kabbalistic books, including a complete Zohar. See Clemente Ancona, "L'inventario dei beni di Leon da Modena," *Bolletino dell'istituto di storia della società e dello stato veneziano* 10 (1967), 257–68.

17. *Ari nohem,* chaps. 25, 26, 14, 23, 2, and 13.

18. On Sarug, see Gershom Scholem, "Israel Sarug—talmid haAri?" *Tzion* 5 (1940), 214–43; Blau, *Kitve,* #46 and 48; Yaacov Boksenboim, *Iggrot Rabbi Yehudah Aryeh miModena* (Tel Aviv: Chaim Rosenberg School of Jewish Studies, 1984), #19; *Ari nohem,* pp. 42, 53, 81, and 85.

19. Evidence that Modena's polemic was primarily directed against Lurianic Kabbalah is found in his ambivalent endorsement during the summer of 1625 of

Knaf renanim, a hymnal with Cordoverian kabbalistic overtones which Joseph Jedidiah Carmi wrote for a Shomrim Laboker society. Further proof that Modena was not completely opposed to the contents of this book was that he used some prayers from it in his own anthology, *Tefilot yesharim* (Venice, 1642), last two pages; cf. *Knaf renanim,* fol. 12a. In his response to this paper when it was first offered at the annual meeting of the Renaissance Society of America, Bernard Cooperman suggested that Modena's reactions against Lurianic Kabbalah may have been a result of his position as one of the last defenders of the native Italian Jews against the encroachments of a movement of ideas and personalities arriving from the east. Cooperman's suggestion that this was as much an ethnic struggle as a religious controversy corresponds with our findings about this case and about other communal controversies in Venice.

20. Moshe Idel, "Differing Conceptions of Kabbalah in the Early Seventeenth Century," in *Jewish Thought in the Seventeenth Century,* pp. 137–200; Isaiah Sonne, "Leon Modena and the da Costa Circle," *Hebrew Union College Annual* 21 (1948), 16–28.

21. *Ari nohem,* p. 80.

22. *Zikne,* #21, 22. Isaac Rivkind, "Teshuvat haRav Yehudah Aryeh Modena 'al gillui rosh," *Sefer hayovel likhvod Levi Ginzberg* (New York: American Academy for Jewish Research, 1946), p. 414. For a full treatment of the relationship between Jewish law and Jewish mysticism, see Jacob Katz, "Post-Zoharic Relations between Halakhah and Kabbalah," *Jewish Thought in the Sixteenth Century,* ed. Bernard Dov Cooperman (Cambridge, Mass.: Harvard University Press, 1983), pp. 283–307.

23. Joel Sirkes, *Sheelot utshuvot bayit hadash,* #4b, and *Pahad Yitzhak,* ed. Isaac Lampronti, "Rofe rasha'."

24. *Hayye,* pp. 33, 48; *Ari nohem,* pp. 2, 57, 21, 52, 60, 61. See Moshe Idel, "Major Currents in Italian Kabbalah between 1560–1660," *Italia judaica* II (Rome, 1986), 260–61.

25. *Zikne,* #33, 35, and 55; *Ari nohem,* p. 7; Ancona 7, fol. 13b.

26. *Meor 'eynayim,* Parma 983, chap. 59; cf. fols. 85b–86b and *Meor 'eynayim,* ed. David Cassel (Vilna: S. I. Fin A. G. Rozenkants, 1866), p. 230.

27. *Massoreth ha massoreth,* ed. Christian D. Ginsburg (Liverpool, 1867), pp. 44–53, 121–34.

28. *Meor 'eynayim,* ed. Cassel, pp. 471–73.

29. *Meor 'eynayim,* Parma 983, fol. 129b. For a detailed description of de Rossi's polemical method which suggests some interesting parallels with that of Modena, see Robert Bonfil, "Some Reflections on the Place of Azariah de Rossi's *Meor 'eynayim* in the Cultural Milieu of Italian Renaissance Jewry," *Jewish Thought in the Sixteenth Century,* pp. 23–48.

30. From his earliest days, Modena recalled his father's admonitions about the dangers of Christian Kabbalah. See *Ari nohem,* the last chapter. Modena's above-mentioned antikabbalistic remarks to David Farar between 1608 and 1610 may have been prompted by Farar's disputations with Hugh Broughton (1564–1617), a missionary to the Jews who had quoted kabbalistic books such as the Zohar. At this time one of Modena's students in Venice was Samuel Slade (1568–c. 1612) and the disputations between Broughton and Farar were held in the Latin

school of his brother, Matthew Slade (1569–1628). See A. Schwartz, "Aus der Briefsammalung Sebastian Tegnagels," *Zeitschrift fuer Hebraeische Bibliographie* 20 (1917), 73.

31. Judah Blau, "Plantavits Lehrer in Rabbinischen," *Zeitschrift fuer Hebraeische Bibliographie* 10 (1907), 113–21, and *Divan,* #44. In a letter Modena also mentioned that three times a week he taught a monk who served in the court of the duke of Florence (Boksenboim, *Iggrot,* #104).

32. Cecil Roth, "Leone da Modena and the Christian Hebraists of His Age," *Jewish Studies in Memory of Israel Abrahams* (New York: Press of the Jewish Institute of Religion, 1927), pp. 388, 394. The first known Jews to return to Paris were Dr. Elijah Montalto and Rabbi Saul Levi Morteira in 1613.

33. Boksenboim, *Iggrot,* #104. In a similar vein, Plantavit would cite Modena, "R. Juda Leo Mutinas our teacher in rabbinics . . . warned us that this book is a kabbalistic one" (Blau, "Plantavits Lehrer," p. 115).

34. The description of the conversion of Abner of Burgos, or Alfonso de Valladelid (1270–1340), that Modena found in ibn Yahyah's *Shalshelet hakabbalah* (Jerusalem: Hadorot Harishonim Vekorotam, 1962), p. 128, showed clearly the influence of mysticism on his apostasy. In his introduction to Abner's manuscript Modena quoted ibn Yahyah's description extensively. Modena saw that the pivotal event in Abner's conversion was Nahmanides's (1194–c. 1270) allegedly teaching him that all the commandments were somehow contained in the Torah Portion *Ha-azinu* (Deuteronomy 32:1–32:52). Abner's Christian teachings also relied on other aspects of kabbalistic thought, such as the sephirot, to support Christian ideas such as the Incarnation and the Trinity. See Yitzhak Baer, *A History of the Jews in Christian Spain,* trans. I. Schoffman, II (Philadelphia: Jewish Publication Society, 1961), pp. 330, 334, 377, 343; Scholem, "Zur Geschichte der Anfange der christlichen Kabbala," *Essays Presented to Leo Baeck on the Occasion of His Eightieth Birthday* (London: Council for the Protection of the Rights and Interests of Jews from Germany, 1954), pp. 170–76; Francois Secret, *Les Kabbalistes Chrétiens de la Renaissance* (Paris: Dunod, 1964), p. 13; Yitzhak Baer, "Torat hakabbalah bemishnato hakristologit shel Avner miBurgos," *Sefer hayovel likhvod Gershom Scholem* (Jerusalem: Y. L. Magnes Press of the Hebrew University, 1958), pp. 152–63; and Parma (533) 2440, fols. 2a–6a, 10b–12a, 15a–21b. Modena realized that Kabbalah could teach apostates methods which could prove that absolutely any teaching was found in the Bible and that these had potential to do great harm to Judaism (Parma 2440, fols. 1a–1b).

35. Cohen, "Riti," p. 304.

36. *Riti,* II, II, 2; Cohen, "Riti," p. 304.

37. *Meor 'eynayim,* Parma 983, fol. 35a.

38. Modena wrote in May of 1627 that he had finally sat down to write a refutation of *Bibliotheca sancta* (Ancona, "Attachi contro il Talmud," p. 313). In June 1627, however, Fra Fulgenzio Micanzio refused to allow Modena's response to be published.

39. Galatino's book was published in 1518 and 1603. The location of Modena's annotated copy of it is not known. His annotations are mentioned in *Magen veherev,* V:1 and Haleviim's introduction. Modena, unaware of Galatino's sources,

viewed Galatino as "the king of the liars" and as the chief source of teaching which Modena considered dangerous.

40. This discussion is reported in Francois Secret, "Notes sur les Hebraisants Chrétiens," *Revue des etudes juives* 124 (1965), 157–58 based on Gisbertus Voetius, *Selectarum disputationum theologicarum,* II (1648–69), 97, 123, 79; cf. Jacques Basnage, *L'Histoire des Juifs depuis Jésus Christ jusqu'à present,* IX, part 2 (The Hague: H. Scheurlee, 1719), pp. 891–93, and Johan Wolf, *Bibliotheca hebraea,* I (Hamburg, 1715), 416.

41. *Yeshu u miryam, elohe nekher-ha aretz.*

42. Apocalypse of John 13:11–18. The Hebrew was *Yeshu notzri.* This polemical interpretation was used in other contexts in Venice during the period. For example, the Protestants noted that the name and title of Pope Paul V (1605–21), *Paulo V vice-Deo,* added up to 666. See Burnett, *The Life of William Bedell* (Dublin: M. Rhames, 1736), p. 9.

43. *Zikne,* #55, written in 1626.

44. Isaac ben Sheshet Perfet (Ribash), *Sheelot utshuvot Ribash,* #157; Abraham M. Hershman, *Rabbi Isaac ben Sheshet Perfet and His Times* (New York: Jewish Theological Seminary, 1943), pp. 91–92, 173, 192, 197–99; *Ari nohem,* chap. 9.

45. Modena wrote that the year he had begun to work on *Ari nohem,* a French Christian had shown him twelve of the choicest kabbalistic manuscripts from Pico's collection. Modena realized that these, contrary to claims of their antiquity, were recent works. See *Ari nohem,* chap. 13.

46. *Hayye,* p. 60; the date of 1638 on the manuscripts is probably wrong.

47. In the last chapter the numbers given were 47 and 72; perhaps in rereading Pico while writing *Ari nohem* Modena notice the discrepancy in Pico's numbers. One of the most important of these these was: "No science yields greater proof of the divinity of Christ than magic and Kabbalah," Ginsburg, *Massoreth,* p. 11. See Joseph Blau, *The Christian Interpretation of the Cabbalah in the Renaissance* (New York: Columbia University Press, 1944), p. 34.

48. On Pico, see Secret, *Les Kabbalistes Chrétiens,* pp. 260–61 and David Ruderman, *The World of a Renaissance Jew: The Life and Thought of Abraham Farissol* (Cincinnati: Hebrew Union College Press, 1981), pp. 51–52.

49. *Ari nohem,* chap. 5; on the spiritual understanding of the Torah held by converted Jews, see Ruderman, *World of a Renaissance Jew,* pp. 43, 50.

50. These included Raymond Martini (1220–87), Nicholas de Lyra (1270–1340), Jacob Perez da Valencia (1420–41), Luther (1483–1546), Zwingli (1484–1537), and Calvin (1509–64). Subsequent Protestants, however, such as Broughton and Johannes Buxtorf (1564–1629), found much succor for their views by accepting the antiquity of the vowels. During Modena's day, Christians such as J. J. Scaliger (1540–1609), Jean Morin (1591–1659), and Louis Cappellus (1585–1658) continued to attack the trustworthiness of the Hebrew Scriptures. See Francois Secret, *Le Zohar chez Kabbalistes Chrétiens* (Paris: Librairie Durlacher, 1958), pp. 99–103. Thus when Modena sent Selden a biblical codex from 1304, he wrote that this manuscript was "ancient, real, true, and good" (Roth, "Leone da Modena and His English Correspondents," p. 42). Indeed, elsewhere Modena defended the vowels as an essential component of rabbinic Judaism.

See Peninah Naveh, *Leket ketavim* (Jerusalem: Mosad Bialik, 1968), pp. 287–88; *Divan,* #38.

51. *Ari nohem,* p. 96. Modena referred to Galatino in many chapters and devoted an entire section to a direct attack on him. See *Magen veherev,* ed. Shlomo Simonsohn (Jerusalem: Mekitze Nirdamim, 1960), IV:4.

52. *Magen veherev,* IV:8.

53. Modena tried to show, using the same list of calculations he had given one of his Christian Hebrew students in 1624, that the numerical equivalent of the Hebrew expression "Jesus Nazarean" (*Yeshu Notzri*) also equals the number for the Antichrist, 666. He then repeated several other calculations to show the results against Jesus' divinity, messianism, and saving powers, that could be produced by using this spelling of Jesus' name as the Christians insisted. See *Magen veherev,* V:7.

54. *Magen veherev,* III:4. He included this in his kabbalistic bibliography; see above.

55. *Magen veherev,* II:4; Daniel Lasker, *Jewish Philosophical Polemics against Christianity in the Middle Ages* (New York: Ktav Publishing House, 1977), pp. 81–82, 102, 105, 215, 225.

56. Lou H. Silberman, "The Magen V'Herev of R. Judah Aryeh of Modena" (D. H. L. Thesis, Hebrew Union College, May, 1943), p. 33; David Simonsen, "Giulio Morosini's Mitteilungen ueber seinen Lehrer Leon da Modena und seine juedischen Zeitgenossen," *Festschrift zum siebzigsten Geburtstage A. Berliner's* (Frankfurt: J. Kauffmann, 1903), p. 340; Benjamin Ravid, "*Contra Judaeos* in Seventeenth Century Italy: Two Responses to the Discorso of Simone Luzzatto by Melchiore Palontrotti and Giulio Morosini," *Association for Jewish Studies Review* 7–8 (1983), 301–52. The expression of Jesus being a good man and a great prophet had also been offered by the Jew in the above-mentioned disputation with Coryat in 1608, strengthening the possibility that he indeed was Modena.

57. Parma 2440, fols. 14a, 53a, 96b.

Notes on Contributors

HOWARD ADELMAN is Assistant Professor and Director of Jewish Studies at Smith College. He collaborated in the introduction and historical notes of *The Autobiography of a Seventeenth-Century Venetian Rabbi: Leon Modena's "Life of Judah."* He is currently researching the literary salon of Sarra Copia Sulam, a seventeenth-century Venetian Jewish writer and poet.

ANNE J. CRUZ, coeditor, is Associate Professor of Spanish and Portuguese at the University of California, Irvine. Her publications include *Imitación y transformación: El petrarquismo en la poesía de Boscán y Garcilaso de la Vega,* and articles in *Ideologies & Literature, Romance Notes,* and *Romanic Review.* She is currently working on a book entitled *Discourses of Poverty: A Study of the Spanish Golden Age Picaresque Novels.*

PHILIPPE DESAN is Assistant Professor of Romance Languages and Literatures at the University of Chicago. He has published a book on *Naissance de la méthode: Machiavel, La Ramée, Bodin, Montaigne, Descartes* and is currently working on a book on Montaigne. His articles have appeared in, among other journals, *Pacific Coast Philology, Dialogue, Rinascimento, French Literature Series,* and *Essays in French Studies.*

LANCE K. DONALDSON-EVANS is Professor of Romance Languages at the University of Pennsylvania. He has written *Poésie et méditation chez Jean de La Ceppède* and *Love's Fatal Glance: A Study of Eye Imagery in the Poetry of the Ecole Lyonnaise.* He has also published articles in *French Forum* and *Neophilologus,* among other journals, and has edited Lazare de Selve's *Les Oeuvres spirituelles.*

WENDY A. FURMAN, coeditor, is Associate Professor of English at Whittier College. She is currently at work on a book-length study tentatively entitled *Augustinian Homiletics and English Nativity Poetry.* She is also co-authoring with Virginia J. Tufte, University of Southern California, *Visualizing Paradise Lost: The Illustrations of 1688, Blake, Doré, and Groom as Aids in Reading Milton.* She has published in *Philological Quarterly.*

JEANNE E. HARRIE is Professor of History at California State College, Bakersfield. Her fields of interest include Renaissance occult philosophy and Irenicism. She has published in *Renaissance Quarterly* and in the *Proceedings of the Western Society for French History.*

WYMAN H. HERENDEEN is Associate Professor of English at the University of Windsor. His publications include *From Landscape to Literature: The River and the Myth of Geography,* and articles in *Journal of Medieval and Renaissance Studies, Studies in Philology,* and *Medievalia et Humanistica.* Professor Herendeen is currently working on a critical biography of William Camden.

MARYANNE CLINE HOROWITZ, coordinating editor, is Associate Professor of History at Occidental College. She is completing a book to be entitled *Seeds of Virtue and Knowledge,* which explores diverse uses of this Stoic commonplace in the Italian and French Renaissance. The journals in which her articles have appeared include *Journal of the History of Ideas, Harvard Theological Review, History of European Ideas,* and *Sixteenth Century Journal.*

ELISE BICKFORD JORGENS is Associate Professor of English at Western Michigan University. Her publications include *The Well-Tun'd Word: Musical Interpretations of English Poetry, 1597-1651,* and articles in *Comparative Drama, English Literary Renaissance,* and *Parnassus: Poetry in Review.* She is the editor of *English Song, 1600-1675,* a facsimile edition of twenty-six song manuscripts with companion volumes containing the song texts in modern edition.

MARGARET L. KING is Professor of History at Brooklyn College and at the Graduate Center, CUNY. She has published *Venetian Humanism in an Age of Patrician Dominance,* and has coedited, with Albert Rabil, Jr., *"Her Immaculate Hand": Selected Works by and about the Women Humanists of Quattrocento Italy.* Her articles have appeared in *Renaissance Quarterly, Journal of Medieval and Renaissance Studies,* and *Medievalia et Humanistica,* among other journals. Professor King is an editor of *Renaissance Quarterly.*

ARTHUR M. LESLEY is Associate Professor of Modern Hebrew Language and Literature at Baltimore Hebrew College. His articles have appeared in *Aspects of Medieval Judaism, Ficino and Renaissance Neoplatonism,* and *Prooftexts.* He is currently preparing a book on Yohanan Alemanno in collaboration with Moshe Idel of the Hebrew University.

HARRY LEVIN, Irving Babbit Professor Emeritus of Comparative Literature, Harvard University, has written widely on Renaissance literatures. His many publications include *The Gates of Horn: A Study of Five French Realists, The Myth of the Golden Age in the Renaissance,* and *Shakespeare and the Revolution of the Times.* Professor Levin's latest book is entitled *Playboys and Killjoys: An Essay on the Theory and Practice of Comedy.*

MARÍA CRISTINA QUINTERO is Assistant Professor of Spanish and Portuguese at the University of Southern California. Her research interests include the political theater of Hapsburg Spain, and she is currently working on a book tentatively entitled *Poetry as Play: Gongorismo and the Comedia.* Her articles have appeared in *Bulletin of the Comediantes, Revista de Estudios Hispánicos, Romance Notes,* and *Symposium.*

RICHARD L. REGOSIN is Professor of French at the University of California, Irvine. He is the author of *Agrippa d'Aubigné's* Les Tragiques: *The Poetry of Inspira-*

tion and *The Matter of My Book: Montaigne's* Essais *as the Book of the Self.* The journals where his articles appear include *PMLA, Romanic Review,* and *Renaissance Quarterly.*

FRANÇOIS RIGOLOT is Meredith Howland Pyne Professor of French Literature at Princeton University. His publications include *Les Langages de Rabelais, Poétique et Onomastique: L'Exemple de la Renaissance,* and *Le Texte de la Renaissance: Des Rhétoriqueurs à Montaigne.* His many articles have appeared in *Yale French Studies, Poétique, Renaissance Quarterly,* and *Romanic Review,* among other journals.

JULIE A. SMITH is Lecturer of English at the University of Wisconsin at Whitewater. Her fields of interest include the author portraits in early English printed books. She has published in *Gutenberg-Jahrbuch.*

PAUL F. WATSON is Associate Professor of Art History at the University of Pennsylvania. His publications include *The Garden of Love in Tuscan Art of the Early Renaissance,* and articles in, among other journals, *Artibus et Historiae, Renaissance Quarterly, Trivium,* and *Modern Language Notes.*

Index

Note: Page numbers of illustrations
are given in italics.

Abdita divinae cabbalae mysteria (Gaffarel),
278
Abner of Burgos (c. 1270–1340), 277, 280,
284 n. 34
Abravanel, Isaac (1437–1508), 52
Abulafia, Jacob, 274
Accolti, Bernardo (1458–1535), 166
Acerba (Stabili), 166, *178*
Addison, Joseph, 8, 9, 12, 15
Advancement of Learning, The (Bacon), 5–6,
9, 10–11, 151
Aeneid (Virgil): as model for *La Franciade*,
67–77 passim; as precursor of Renaissance
works, 123; translated by Leonardo de
Argensola, 107
Aesop, 164–65, *177*
Aesop (trans. Tuppo), 164–65
Agaynste a Comely Coystrowne (Skelton), 159,
169, *175*
"Agenst Garnesche" (Skelton), 168
Agrippa, Menenius, 10, 12
Albertus Magnus, 6
Alejandra (Leonardo de Argensola), 107
Alemanno, Yohanan (1433/34–c. 1504),
62–63
Alexander and Campaspe (Lyly), 41, 42
al-Ghazzali, Abu Hamid, 62
Amphitruo (Plautus), 100, 103
Amyot, Jacques, 199 n. 9
Andromache (Euripides), 99, 109 n. 10
Apollonius of Rhodes, 70, 76
"Apology of Raymond Sebond" (Montaigne),
242, 244
Apophthegms (Bacon), 3
Apuleius of Madaura, 260

Arcadia (Bacon), 14
Arcadia (Sannazaro), 86
Argensola, Lupercio Leonardo de, 105,
106–7, 108
Argoli, Giovanni, 272
Argumentum (Ficino), 257
Ariadne (classical sculpture), 119
Ariès, Philippe, 245, 246
Ari nohem (Modena), 278–79
Aristophanes, 36
Aristotle, 97; Averroes' commentary on, 57;
in Hebrew learning, 51, 53; in Raphael's
School of Athens, 114; views on poetry, 7,
12, 20
Armies of the Night (Mailer), 153
Arraignment of Paris, The (Peele), 38, 42, 43,
44
Ars morendi ("Art of Dying"), 242
Ars poetica (Horace), 68, 98, 114, 118
Art poëtique (Peletier), 68, 74
Art poetique (Ronsard), 194
Art Poëtique François (Sebillet), 188
Asclepius, 257, 259, 260
Ashkenazi, Naftali, 274
As You Like It (Shakespeare), 13,
39–40
Ausonius, Decimus Maximus, 120
Authors, portraits of, 159–69 passim
Autobiography (Freud), 8
Avantentrée du Roi treschrestien à Paris
(Ronsard), 188
Averroes (Ibn Rushd), 57

Bacon, Francis: collected works of, 5; as
follower of Camden, 151; and Freud, 8; as

Bacon, Francis (*continued*)
  historian, 6–7, 10; image of "light" used
  by, 4, 15; and imagination, 8–9, 10–11, 14;
  modernity of, 5; as poet vs. scientist, 3–4,
  6, 7, 11, 15; and rhetoric, 14; views on
  poetry, 7, 9, 10–11. *See also names of*
  individual works
Baconianism, 4
Baïf, Jean-Antoine de, 187, 190
Bakhtin, M. M., 18
Baldacci, Luigi, 86
Barberini, Cardinal Francesco (1597–1679),
  273
bar Yohai, Simon, 275
Barzizza, Gasparino (1370–1431), 165
Basola, Moses (1480–1560), 274
Basordan, Jacques de, 257, 259
Baumgarten, A. G., 15
Bedell, William (1577–1644), 272
Bellay, Joachim du. *See* Du Bellay, Joachim
Belleau, Rémy, 190
Bellori, Giovanni Pietro, 113, 117
Bembo, Pietro, 81–82, 84, 85, 86
Bentham, Jeremy, 14
ben Yehiel, Yehuda. *See* Messer Leon
Berck, Johan (1565–1627), 277
Berechiah, Aaron, 274
Berger, Bertran, 190
Bergson, Henri-Louis, 6
Bermúdez, Pedro, 106
Bevilacqua da Lazise, Giorgio, 206–18 passim
Beza, Theodore de, 264
Bible: as basis for Efodi's grammar, 54, 55;
  precedents for Hebrew literature in, 57–59,
  63
Biblicist hebraism: combined with humanist
  rhetoric, 56–58; formulated, 54–55
Biblioteca sancta (Sixtus of Siena), 277
Bibliothèque françoise (La Croix du Maine),
  187
Binet, Claude, 187
Biography, in Hebrew literature, 62–63
Blake, William, 3
Bloom, Harold, 92, 233
Boaistuau, Pierre, 239
Boccaccio, Giovanni: as Italian classic, 105,
  114; plague described by, 239; in Raphael's
  Parnassus, 117, 118, 120; as vernacular poet,
  81; wearing laurels, 163
Bodin, Jean, 147, 244
Boileau, Nicolas, 72

Book of the Honeycomb's Flow, The (Messer
  Leon), 57, 58
Boscán, Juan: imitation of Petrarchan models
  by, 80–93 passim; translations by, 99
Boswell, William (d. 1649), 272
Bouju, Jacques, 192
Bright, Timothie, 36, 37, 38
Britannia (Camden): debt to Sidney in,
  146–47, 152; method of, 148–49;
  patriotism in, 144–45; poetry and history
  in, 145, 149–51, 153; subject of, 150
Brocense, El (Francisco Sánchez de las
  Brozas), 99
Brody, Jules, 239
Broughton, Hugh (1564–1617), 283–84 n. 30,
  285–86 n. 50
Browne, Sir Thomas, 5, 151
Bruno, Giordano, 264, 265
Burghley, Lord (William Cecil), 5, 154–55
  n. 5
Burney, Charles, 34
Butcher, S. H., 7
Buxtorf, Johannes, the elder (1564–1629), 277,
  285–86 n. 50

Calvin, John (1509–64), 261, 264, 285–86
  n. 50
Camden, William, as poet and historian,
  143–54 passim
Campion, Thomas, 146
Cantar de los cantares (León), 96
Canzoniere (Petrarch), Spanish imitation of,
  80–93 passim
Capella, Martianus, 122, 159, 160
Cappellus, Louis (1585–1658), 285–86 n. 50
Caracciolo, Giulio Cesare, 86
Caracciolo, Fra Robert (1425–95), 166
Carbone, Lodovico, 115, 120, *131*, 208, 209
Cariteo, Il (Benedetto Gareth), 82
Carmi, Joseph Jedidiah, 282–83 n. 19
Cascales, Francisco de, 96
Case, John, defense of music by, 33, 34, 35,
  39, 44
Castiglione, Baldassare, 37
Castle of Health, The (Elyot, 1541), 37
Castex, Pierre-Georges, 225, 226
Castillon, siege of, 237, 240
Castor, Grahame, 72, 75
Cathedra, symbolism of, 161–63
Catherine de Médicis, 240, 261
Cato, Dionysius, 166–67

Cattan, Christophe de. *See* Cattaneo, Cristoforo

Cattaneo, Cristoforo, 257, 260

Caxton, William, 166, 168

Cervantes, Miguel de, 107

Champier, Symphorien, 256, 257, 260

Charles IX (king of France), 187, 188, 199 n. 9

Charles de Lorraine (cardinal) (1524–74), 257, 259

Charles de Lorraine (1554–1611). *See* Mayenne, duc de

Chartres Cathedral, 160

"Chat, Le" (Ronsard), 228, 230

Cicero, Marcus Tullius, 55, 80; as model of Latin writing, 63, 81; read by Montaigne, 24; rejected by Camden, 151; and *Rhetorica ad Herennium,* 57; ridiculed, 241, 242; views on poetry, 114; views on translation, 97–98, 107

Civile Wares (Daniel), 151, 152, 156 n. 24

Classical mythology: Bacon's use of, 10, 11; Vico's use of, 10

Cogan, Thomas, 37

Coignet, Matthieu, 142

Coleridge, Samuel Taylor, 3, 14

Coligny, Odet de, 196

Colvius, Andreas, of Dort (1594–1671), 277

Comedy of Betrothal (Sommo), 59–60

Comedy of Errors (Shakespeare), 11

Compotus manualis ad vsū Oxoniēsiū (Kryfoth, 1519), 167–68, *179*

Concordat of Bologna (1516), 186

Condé, Henri I, prince de, 238

Conversini, Giovanni, 222

Cooperman, Bernard, 282–83 n. 19

Cordovero, Moses (1522–70), 274

Coriolanus (Shakespeare), 10

"Coronation Oration" (Petrarch), 114

Corpus Hermeticum, 256, 257, 259, 260

Cortesi, Paolo, 81

Coryat, Thomas (1577–1617), 272, 286 n. 56

Coseriu, Eugenio, 109 n. 7

Cottereau, Claude, 257

Cotton, Robert, 154–55 n. 5

Cowley, Abraham, 4

Crater Hermetis (Lazzarelli), 257, 258, 260

Criterion of Action (al-Ghazzali), 62

Dagens, Jean, 255, 256

"Daimons, Les" (Ronsard), 227, 230–32

Damon and Pithias (Edward), 39

Daniel, Samuel, 146, 151, 152–53

Daniello, Bernardino, 84

Dante: as Italian classic, 105; poetry of, 114, 120; in Raphael's *Parnassus,* 113, 114, 115, 117, 118, 119, 123, 124; wearing laurels, 163

Dassonville, Michel, 191

De arcanus catholicae veritatis (Galatino), 277

De arte poetica (Vida), 115, 118

Death: of peasants, 236–46 passim; of Renaissance children, 205–20 passim

De Augmentis Scientiarum (Bacon), 5, 6, 9–10, 11

Decameron (Boccaccio), 239

Declaration des abus, hipocrisie, et subtilitee des faux prophetes & seducteurs du peuple (du Préau), 262, 264

De concinnitates grāmatices (Whittinton), 167, *179*

de Connubio Tamae et Isis (Camden), 150, 151

Defence of Poesie (Sidney): influence on Bacon, 12; influence on Spenser and Camden, 145, 146, 147–48, 151, 152

Deffence et Illustration de la Langue Françoise, La (Du Bellay), 72, 74

Definitions of Asclepius (trans. Lazarelli), 257

de Imitatione (Bembo), 81

de Inventione (Cicero), 98

De la cognoissance de soymesme pour parvenir à celle de Dieu (du Préau), 259, 260

"De la force de l'imagination" (Montaigne), 8

De la Verité de la Religion Chrestienne (Mornay), 258

Delbene, Alphonse, 194

Delmedigo, Joseph Solomon (1591–1655), 275

Delorme, Philibert, 188

De obitu Valerii filii consolatio (Filelfo), 208, 209

De partibus aedium (Grapaldi), 165, *178*

De Quadruplici Vita (Champier), 257

de Rossi, Azariah (c. 1511/20–c. 1578), 59, 276

Descartes, René, 6

Description of the Intellectual Globe, A (Descriptio Globi Intellectualis) (Bacon), 10

De syllabarum quantitate (Quintianus), 165

de Thou, Jacques-Auguste, 237

Deux Livres (du Préau), 260

de Worde, Wynkyn, 167, 168
Dialogic Imagination, The (Bakhtin), 18
Diálogo de la lengua (Valdés), 105
Dido en Carthagine (Pozzi de' Medici), 106
Didone (Dolce), 106
Disputà (Raphael), 114, 116, 123, *132*
Divine Comedy (Dante), 114, 118
Doctrinal du Temps Présent, Le (Michault), 163, *176*
Dolce, Ludovico, 106, 107
Donatello (Donato de Betto di Bardi), 118, *135*
Donatus, Aelius, 160, 165, *177*
Dorat, Jean, 190, 191
Drama: Bacon's suspicions of, 11; Hebrew, 59–60
Drayton, Michael, 146, 151, 152, 153
Dryden, John, 97, 107
Du Bellay, Jean (cardinal), 199 n. 9
Du Bellay, Joachim, 74; on balance between work and inspiration in poetry, 72, 73; education of, 190; as Pléiade poet, 67; royal epitaphs by, 188; support for, 187
Dundas, Judith, 140–41 n. 24
Duplessis-Mornay, Philippe. *See* Mornay, Philippe Duplessis-
du Préau, Gabriel (Prateolus) (1511–88): and hermeticism, 256, 257–66; life of, 256–57
Duran, Profiat. *See* Efodi
d'Urvoy, René, 190
Du Souverain et unique sacrifice de l'eglise catholique et apostolique (du Préau), 264
Dyuers Balettys and Dyties Solacyous (Skelton), 159, 169

Edward, Richard, 39
Efodi (Duran, Profiat), cultural reform introduced by, 53–55. *See also* Biblicist hebraism
Electra (Sophocles), 99
Eliot, T. S., 14
Elisa Dido (Virués), 106
Elizabeth (queen of England), 44, 154–55 n. 5
Elyot, Thomas, 37
Emile, Paul, 190
English Renaissance, 3–17, 33–47, 142–56, 159–83
Ennius, Quintus, 138 n. 8
Epictetus, 243
Epistles (Ovid), 165, *177*

Epithalame d'Antoine de Bourbon et Jeanne de Navarre (Ronsard), 188
Erasmus, Desiderius, 81
Essays (Bacon), 3
Essays (Montaigne): conversations with peasants recorded in, 236; evolution of, 241; as historical document, 18, 20–21, 22, 25; interpretation as subject of, 19, 23; learning discussed in, 26–27; as literary-rhetorical document, 19, 21–22; new editions of, 238; physiognomy as emblem in, 23; relationship between text and context in, 20, 21, 22–23, 29–30; role of Socrates in, 19, 23, 24–25, 26, 27, 28, 29, 236, 243
Euripides, 99, 100
Excusatio adversus consolatores in obitu Valerii filii (Bevilacqua da Lazise), 208, 210

Faerie Queene, The (Spenser), 146, 150, 151, 152, 153
Fano, Menahem Azariah (1548–1620), 273, 274–75
Fantastique poetry, 225–33
Farar, David, 275, 283–84 n. 30
Farel, Guillaume, 264
Ferdinand (king of Aragon), 258
Ficino, Marsilio, 62, 63, 256, 257, 259
Fideism, 6, 7
Filelfo, Francesco, 208–22 passim
Filelfo, Giovanni Mario, 208, 209
Finné, Jacques, 226
Flores et sententiae scribendique formulae illustriores, ex M. T. Ciceronis epistolis familiaribus selectae (du Préau), 261
Floriani, Pietro, 81
Foix de Candale, François (1512–94), 256, 257, 259, 260, 264, 265
Folena, Gianfranco, 103
Fortebraccio da Montone, Carlo, 208, 210, 212, 217
Fourth Book (Boscán), 86
France: civil war in, 25–26, 237–38, 261–66; Renaissance social organization of, 185–86
Franciade, La (Ronsard): imitation of *Iliad* and *Aeneid* in, 67–77 passim; patronage for, 187; political premise of, 69–70; prefaces to, 70–71, 72, 75, 76
François I (king of France), 186
Freccero, John, 83
Frederick II (Holy Roman emperor), 164

French Renaissance, 18–32, 67–79, 184–202, 225–70

Freud, Sigmund, 8

Freudian psychoanalysis, 6

Fry, Roger, 8

Fuller, Thomas, 151

Fumel, baron de, 240

Fussner, Smith, 144

Gaffarel, Jacques (1601–81), 273, 278

Galante, Jedidiah, 274, 275

Galatino, Pietro, 277, 279

García Yebra, Valentín, 109 n. 7

Garcilaso de la Vega, imitation of Petrarchan models by, 80–93 passim

Garland of Laurel (Skelton), 168

Garnesche, Christopher, 168

Gaston, duc d'Orleans (1608–60), 273

Gelli, Giovanbattista, 100

Genealogy of the Gods (Boccaccio), 114, 117

Geomancy (Cattaneo), 257, 260, 261

George of Trebizond, 207, 209, 212, 217, 218

Georgics (Virgil), 189

Gerardo Bolderio, Doctor, 205–6, 212, 218, 219

Gesta Grayorum, 11

Giorgio, Francesco, 256

Giovanni Santi, 115, 124

Giraldi Cinthio, Giovambattista, 106, 107

Glanvill, Joseph, 15

Gosson, Stephen, criticism of music by, 33, 34, 35–36, 38, 41, 44, 45, 154 n. 2

Grammar, depicted as a schoolmistress, 159–60

Grammaticales regulae (Veronensis), 165

Grapaldi, Francesco Maria (1465?–1515), 165, *178*

Greek Grammar (Camden), 154–55 n. 5

Greek tragedies, translated into Spanish, 99–103

Greene, Thomas M., 81, 108

Guarini, Battista, 208, 209, 210, 214, 216, 217

Guicciardini, Francesco, 147

Guise, duke of, 261, 265

Habert, François, 188

Halevi, Jacob (d. 1629), 275

Halevi, Yehuda (1075–1141), 53

Hall, Joseph, 146, 147, 153

Hamitz, Joseph, (d. c. 1676), 275

Harangue sur les causes de la guerre entreprise

contre les rebelles & seditieux ... (du Préau), 261

Haven of Health Chiefly made for the comfort of Students, The (Cogan, 1612), 37

Hebrew literature (in Italy): adoption of humanism into, 51–53, 56–58, 63–64; and biography, 62–63; and drama, 59–60; and historiography, 60–61; Kabbalah, 271–81 passim; and moral philosophy, 62–63; and poetry, 58–59

Hecuba (Euripides), 99, 100

Hecuba triste (Pérez de Oliva), 100, 101–2, 103, 104

Henri, duc de Candale, 273

Henri, duc de Rohan (1579–1638), 273

Henri I, prince de Condé, 238

Henri II (king of France): death of, 261; offices sold by, 185; and Ronsard, 187, 188, 190, 192, 195, 196

Henri III (king of France), 199 n. 9, 238, 264

Henri IV (king of France). *See* Henri de Navarre

Henri de Navarre, 238, 282 n. 9

Heraclitus, 4

Hermenegildo, Alfredo, 99, 100

Hermes Trismegistus, 255, 258, 259, 260, 261

Hermeticism: of du Préau, 256, 257–66; influence of, 259; introduced into France, 257–58; and reconciliation, 255–56, 261

Herodiens, 265

Herodotus, 165

Heywood, Thomas, 47 n. 25

Historia (Herodotus), 165

Historia degli riti Hebraici (Modena), 273, 277

Historia Philippicae (Justin), 106

History: and Bacon, 6–7, 10; and fiction, 30 n. 7; Hebrew, 60–61; and Montaigne, 18, 20–21, 236; and poetry, 142–54 passim

History of Britain (Daniel), 153

Hobbes, Thomas, 14

Hoby, Edward, 142

Homer: poetry of, 120; in Raphael's *Parnassus,* 113, 114, 115, 117, 118, 119, 123; Ronsard's imitation of, 67–77 passim

Hooker, Richard, 35

Horace, 68; depictions of, 164, 165; as model poet, 188; on poetry, 114, 115, 118; translations of, 97–98

Horowitz, Isaiah (c. 1565–1630), 274

Huguet's dictionary, 226
Humanism, adopted into Hebrew literature, 51–53, 56–58, 63–64
Hunter, Dr. William, 207
Hylas, L' (Ronsard), 75
Hymne de France (Ronsard), 189
"Hymne de l'autonne, L' " (Ronsard), 226

Ibn Yaḥya, Tam, 61
Idola Theatri (Bacon), 5, 11
Iliad (Homer), as model for *La Franciade,* 67–77 passim
Imagination: Bacon's view of, 8–9, 10–11, 14; differing views of poetic, 8–9; Montaigne's views on, 20
In Cold Blood (Capote), 153
Instauratio Magna (Bacon), 5
Institutio Oratoria (Quintilian), 71, 98
Introduction à la littérature fantastique (Todorov), 225
Introductory Lectures (Freud), 8
In vita humana (Bacon), 3
Iselin, Louis, 273
Italian Renaissance, 51–66, 80–95, 113–41, 205–24, 271–85

Jakobson, Roman, 99
James, D. G., 3
James I (king of Great Britain), 272, 273
Jamyn, Amadis, 76
Jeanne de Navarre, 188
Jerome, Saint, 98
Jews, in France, 277
Jews, Italian: cultural reform among, 53–55; grammatical studies in, 55–56; humanism adapted by, 51–53, 56–58, 63–64; and Kabbalah, 271–81 passim; and precedence of Hebrew over classical learning, 52–53, 56; settlements of, 53, 272. *See also* Hebrew literature
Jews, Spanish, 54
Jodelle, Étienne, 190
Johnson, Dr. Samuel, 8
Jones, Roger, 119
Jonson, Ben: and Bacon, 11; and Camden, 143, 145–46, 149, 151, 152, 153, 154–55 n. 5
Josephus, Flavius, 60
Julius II (pope), 113, 114, 115
Justin (Marcus Justianus Justinus), 106
Justus van Ghent, 115

Kabbalah, 271–81 passim
Kant, Immanuel, 10
Kelley, Donald, 261
Kendrick, Thomas, 144
King Edward the Fourth (Heywood), 47 n. 25
King James I, and Bible translation, 272
Knaf renanim (Carmi), 282–83 n. 19
Kryfoth, Charles, 167, 169
Kuzari (Halevi), 53

Labé, Louise, 185
La Boétie, Etienne de, 246
La Croix du Maine, Francois, 187
Landino, Cristoforo, 114, 117, 124
Lando, Vitale, 210
Lange, Paul, 67
Laocoön (classical sculpture), 117
La Péruse, comte de (Jean-François de Galaup), 190
Lapesa, Rafael, 93 n. 1
Laudatio in Valerium eius filium puerum eximium (Perleone), 208, 209
Laumonier, Paul, 67
Laurels: for poet laureates, 159, 163–66; in Raphael's *Parnassus,* 121–22
Laurence of Durham, 162, *175*
Lazzarelli, Lodovico, 257, 258, 259
Lebègue, Raymond, 187
Le Fèvre de la Boderie, Guy, 256
Le Fèvre de la Boderie, Nicholas, 256
Lefèvre d'Étaples, Jacques, 256, 257, 258, 259
Leland, John, 152
Leo X (pope), 115, 166, 186
León, Fray Luis de, 96, 99, 109 n. 10
Leonardo da Vinci, 11–12
Leslie, Bruce R., 67
L'Estoile, Pierre, 237
Lévi-Strauss, Claude, 184
Levita, Elijah (c. 1469–1549), 56, 276
Levy, F. J., 144
L'Hospital, Michel de, 192
Livy (Titus Livius), 60, 63, 239
Lodge, Thomas, 36
López Pinciano, Alonso, 97
Loyseau, Charles, 186–87
Luria, Isaac (1534–72), 274, 275
Luther, Martin (1483–1546), 261, 285–86 n. 50
Lyly, John, 41, 42
Lyra, Nicholas de (1270–1340), 285–86 n. 50

Lysias, 24

Macaulay, Lord, 4
Machiavelli, Niccolò, 13
Macrobius, Ambrosius Theodosius, 139
 n. 15
Magen veherev (Modena), 279–80
Maimonides, Moses (1135–1204), 60
Malipiero, Pasquale, 210
Manetti, Antonino, 219
Manetti, Giannozzo, 219, 222
Mantegna, Andrea, 115, 141 n. 29, 207
Marcello, Francesco, 219
Marcello, Girolamo, 212
Marcello, Jacopo Antonio, 205–7, 210, 211,
 213, 214, 215, 216–19, 220; works composed
 to console, 207–10, 216, 217
Marcello, Madgalucia, 219
Marcello, Bp. Pietro, 219
Marcello, Valerio, 205–6, 210–16
Marguerite de Navarre, 185, 192
Marguerite of Savoy, 188
Marianna (Dolce), 107
Marie de Médicis, 275, 282 n. 9
Marini, Marco, 272
Martin, Jean, 188, 192
Martini, Raymond (1220–87), 285–86
 n. 50
Martini, Simone, 138 n. 10
Marullo, Michael Tarchiniota, 120
Mascarello, Montorio, 208, 209, 210, 217
Mayenne, duc de (Charles de Lorraine)
 (1554–1611), 237
Mazarin, Cardinal Giulio (1602–61), 273
Mazzoni, Jacopo, 142
Measure for Measure (Shakespeare), 39
Melancholy, and music, 38–40
Melanges (Ronsard), 196
Ménager, Daniel, 67, 70, 188
Meor 'eynayim (de Rossi), 276, 277
Messer Leon (Yehuda ben Yehiel), 57–58
Metamorphoses (Ovid), 90
Micanzio, Fra Fulgenzio, 272, 284 n. 38
Michault, Pierre, 163, *176*
Midsummer Night's Dream, A (Shakespeare),
 8–9
Milton, John, 153
Missy, Caesar de, 207
Modena, Rabbi Leon: and Kabbalists, 271–81
 passim
Modernity, of Bacon, 5

Monluc, seigneur de (Blaise de Lasseran
 Massencôme), 265
Montaigne, Michel Eyquem de: description
 of peasant deaths by, 236–46 passim; and
 imagination, 8; sympathy for peasants,
 236–37, 238; views on learning, 26–27, 28,
 32 n. 30. *See also names of individual works*
Montalto, Dr. Elijah (d. 1616), 275, 284 n. 32
More, Sir Thomas, 15, 120, 168
Morelli, Jacopo, 207
Morin, Jean (1591–1651), 285–86 n. 50
Mornay, Philippe Duplessis- (1549–1623),
 237, 256, 258, 259, 265
Morosini, Giulio, 280
Morteira, Rabbi Saul Levi, 284 n. 32
Mulcaster, Richard, 36, 37
Muret, Marc-Antoine, 190
Music: abuse of, 35, 37, 38, 43–44; defended,
 34–35, 36–37, 44; difficulty of categorizing,
 35; as incitement to wickedness, 33–34, 35,
 36, 38
Mussato, Albertino, 181 n. 14
Myrrour of the worlde (Caxton, 1481), 166, *178*
Mythomystes (Reynolds), 11

Nahmanides (1194–c. 1270), 284 n. 34
Narcissus, myth of, 87
Nashe, Thomas, 143
Natural Philosophy, of Bacon, 6
Nature: contaminated, 25, 27; and true
 knowledge, 27, 28, 29, 243–44
Naudé, Gabriel (1600–1651), 273
Navagiero, Andrea, 80
New Atlantis, The (Bacon), 4, 14, 15
New Philosophy, 5, 15
Newton, Isaac, 9
Nogarola, Isotta, 208, 210, 217
Noghera, Vincent, 272
Notes toward a Supreme Fiction (Stevens), 14
Novum Organon (Bacon), 5

"Ode a Joachim du Bellay" (Ronsard), 228
Odes (Ronsard), 188, 192, 194, 195–96, 197, 228
Odyssey (Homer), 68
"Of Cannibals" (Montaigne), 240–41
"Of Experience" (Montaigne), 239
"Of Masques and Triumphs" (Bacon), 11
"Of Pedantry" (Montaigne), 242
"Of Physiognomy" (Montaigne), 23, 24, 25,
 29–30; death in, 238, 239, 241, 242, 244,
 245, 246

"Of the Power of the Imagination"
  (Montaigne), 8, 20–21, 22, 29
"Of Youth and Age" (Bacon), 8
Old Wives' Tale, The (Peele), 41, 44
Olympics (Pindar), 191, 195
"On Truth" (Bacon), 9
Opere (Horace), 165
Opere (Thibaldeo da Ferrara, 1519), 165
Orbecche (Cinthio), 107
Origen, 52
Orsini, Michele, 208, 209–10, 212, 217, 219
Othello (Shakespeare), 39
Ovid, 164, 165, *177*
Ovidian myths, 90–93

Painting: as science, 12
Paragone (Leonardo), 12
Paré, Ambroise, 239
Parnassus (Raphael), *127–28, 133–34;* artist in,
  113, 119, 123, 124; description of, 113–15,
  116–19, 121–24; precedents for, 115–16
Paruus Chato (Caxton, 1481[?]), 166–67, *178*
Paschal, Pierre, 190–91
Pasquier, Etienne, 191
Passerat, Jean, 75, 76
Peale, George, 101
Peasants, Montaigne's interest in, 236–37,
  238
Peccate, Julien, 190
Peckham, John, 182 n. 25
Peele, George, 38, 41, 42, 43, 44
Peletier du Mans, Jacques, 67, 68, 69, 72, 73,
  74, 190
Penny, Nicholas, 119
Perez da Valencia, Jacob (1420–41), 285–86
  n. 50
Pérez de Oliva, Fernán, 99–102, 103, 104, 107,
  108
Perfet, Isaac ben Sheshet (1326–1408),
  277–78
Perleone, Pietro, 206–19 passim
Peter, Saint, 161–62, *175*
Petrarch, 114; on imitation, 120; as Italian
  classic, 105; laureation of, 159, 163–64,
  166; medal of, 122, *136;* as model for
  Spanish poets, 80–93 passim; Raphael's
  familiarity with poetry of, 116, 141
  n. 28
Petri Paschali Elogium (Ronsard), 190
Philo, 62
Pico, Gianfrancesco, 81, 82, 86, 89, 256

Pico della Mirandola, Giovanni (1463–94),
  62, 63, 278, 279
Pimander (Ficino), 257
Pindar, 188, 191, 193, 195
Pisani, Vettor, 212, 218
Pisseleu (bishop of Condom), 199 n. 9
Plague: in Florence (1348), 238; in Périgord
  (1586–87), 237–38, 239, 242, 246; in Venice,
  209
Plantavit de la Pause, Jean de (1576–1659),
  273, 276
Plato, 13, 97; Bacon compared to, 4; in
  Hebrew learning, 51; and poetry, 12, 15,
  114, 120; in Raphael's *Parnassus,* 114
Plautus, 100, 103
Pléiade poets: called *Brigade,* 189; competi-
  tion among, 187; dependence on benefices,
  187; education of, 190; lack of money
  among, 186; Ronsard as example of, 69,
  185
Plutarch, 20, 24, 30
Poesy. *See* Poetry
Poetic license, 10
Poetics (Aristotle), 7, 12
Poetry: Aristotle's views on, 7; Bacon's
  views on, 3, 7, 10–11, 15; criticism of, 9,
  33, 147, 154 n. 2; depicted in Raphael's
  Parnassus, 113–24 passim, *130;* epic,
  68–69; Hebrew, 58–59; historical, 142–54
  passim; and imagination, 9; Leonardo's
  deprecation of, 11–12; Richards's views
  on, 13; Sidney's defense of, 12–13, 15;
  Spanish, 80–93 passim; translation of, 99;
  work vs. labor in, 194. *See also* Poetic
  license; Poets
Poets: dependence on patrons, 186–87;
  laureated, 166; as liars, 9, 12; male vs.
  female, 184–85; myth of, 184; professional
  status of, 184–85, 186; tasks of, 187. *See also
  names of individual poets*
Poliziano (Angelo Ambrogini), 81, 120
Poly Olbion (Drayton), 151, 152, 156 n. 23
Polyphemus, 7
Pope, Alexander, 3, 13
Pozzi de' Medici, Alessandro, 106
"Praise of Musicke, The" (Case, 1586), 33
"Preface to the Translation of Ovid's Epistles"
  (Dryden), 97
Premier Livre des Poemes, Le (Ronsard), 228
Price, David, 34
Priscian (Priscianus Caesariensis), 160

"Prosopopée de Louys de Ronsard" (Ronsard), 232–33
Provenzal, David, 56, 59
Psalms, King James's Authorized Version, 3
Pseudodoxia Epidemica (Browne), 151
Puritans, and music, 33, 34
Purnell, Frederick, 257
Puttenham, George, 9, 142

Quint, David, 73
Quintianus, Joannes (1484–1537), 165
Quintilian (Marcus Fabius Quintilianus), 71, 97, 100

Raimondi, Marcantonio, 137 n. 2, 137 n. 18
Raphael Santi: in *Parnassus*, 113, 119, 123, 124; poetry by, 116
Rasselas (Johnson), 8
Rastell, John, 159
Recanati, Menahem, 279
Recreation, and music, 38, 40–41
"Relation of the Poet to Day-Dreaming, The" (Freud), 8
Remains (Camden), 148, 149
René I (duke of Anjou), 207, 208, 209, 216
Republic, The (Plato), 15
Reuchlin, Johannes (1455–1522), 278
Reynolds, Henry, 11
Rhetoric (Aristotle), 57
Rhetorica ad Herennium, 57
Richards, I. A., 13
Richelieu, Cardinal (1585–1642), 278
Rime (Bembo), 82, 84
Robert the Wise (king of Naples), 163–64, 183 n. 33
Robortello, Francesco, 105
Romanticism, 225
Ronsard, Louis de, 232–33
Ronsard, Pierre de: admiration for Homer and Virgil, 74–75; ambition of, 67, 69; criticism of, 191; education of, 190; epitaphs by, 188; *le fantastique* in poetry of, 225–33; as French Pindar, 193; poetry of, 71–72, 188–89, 190–91; as professional poet, 185, 187–88, 194; struggle for employment, 87–98. *See also names of individual works*
Roth, Cecil, 63, 281 n. 7, 284 n. 32
Ruines of Time, The (Spenser), 145

Sacchetti (archbishop of Bologna), 272
Sackville, Thomas, 152

Sagundino, Niccolò, 208, 209, 217, 218
Saint-Gelais, Mellin de, 188, 189, 190, 192
Salutati, Coliccio, 222
Sannazaro, Jacopo, 86
Santillana, marqués de, 93 n. 1
Sappho of Lesbos, in Raphael's *Parnassus*, 114, 116, 117, 118, 119, 120
Sarpi, Paolo (1552–1623), 272
Sartre, Jean-Paul, 193
Sarug, Israel, 274, 275, 280
Sasso, Pamphilo (c. 1455–1527), 165, 166
Saturnalia (Macrobius), 139 n. 15
Savile, Sir Henry, 3
Scaliger, J. J. (1540–1609), 285–86 n. 80
Scaliger, Julius Caesar, 13, 105, 142
Schiller, Johann Christoph Friedrich von, 10
Schmidt, Albert-Marie, 230
"Schoole of Abuse" (Gosson, 1579), 33
School of Athens (Raphael), 114, 123, 139 n. 18
Scienza Nuova (Vico), 10
Sebillet, Thomas, 188
Second Book (Boscán), 84, 85
Second Livre des Poemes, Le (Ronsard), 232
Sefer Ma'aseh Efod (Efodi), 53–54
Sefer yetzirah, 278
Sefer Yosippon, 60, 61
Selden, John (1584–1654), 152, 272, 285–86 n. 50
Seneca: depictions of, 164; read by Montaigne, 24; Stoicism of, 243; and tragedy, 104, 105, 106, 107, 139 n. 15
Serafino di'Ciminelli dall'Aquila, 82
Severitanus, Joannes Policarpus (1470–1525?), 165
Seznec, Jean, 3
Sforza, Francesco, 208
Shakespeare, William, 8–9, 10, 11, 13, 39
Shelley, Percy Bysshe, 3
Shomrin Laboker societies, 273
Sidney, Sir Philip: and Bacon, 12, 13, 15; and Camden, 142, 144, 145, 146–48, 149, 151, 153
Silver, Isidore, 67, 193
Sixtus of Siena (1520–69), 277
Skelton, John, portrait of, 159, 168–69, *175*
Skinner, B. F., 7
Slack, Paul, 47 n. 31
Slade, Matthew (1569–1628), 283–84 n. 30
Slade, Samuel (1568–c. 1612), 283–84 n. 30
Snow, C. P., 14

Socrates, and Montaigne, 19, 236, 244
Sofonisba (Trissino), 106
Sommo Portaleone, Yehuda (1527–92),
  59–60
Sonetti (Accolti), 166
Sonetti, Capitoli, Egloge (Sasso, 1519), 165
Song of Solomon's Ascents, The (Alemanno),
  62–63
Sophocles, 99
Spanish Renaissance: and poetry, 80–93
  passim; and tragedies, 99–108; and
  translation, 96–108 passim
Spenser, Edmund: and Camden, 143, 144,
  145, 146–47, 150–51, 153; popularity of, 144,
  145–46
Sperandio of Mantua, 115–16, 119, 120
Spingarn, J. E., 12
Spinola, Ozario, 272, 282 n. 11
Spurgeon, Caroline, 4
Stabili, Francesco degli (1269–1327), 166, *178*
Statius, Publius Papinius, 123, 124, 137 n. 1,
  141 n. 26
Stevens, Wallace, 14
Storer, Walter H., 67
Strabo, 207, 210
Strachey, Lytton, 4
Strowski, Fortunat, 239
Suetonius, 62
Synagoga judaica (Buxtorf), 277

*Table of Colours or Appearances of Good and
  Evil* (Bacon), 14
Tacitus, Cornelius, 151
Tansillo, Luigi, 86
Tasso, Bernardo, 86
Terence, 55, 165
Terry, Arthur, 81
Tevat Noah (Marini), 272
"That to Philosophize Is to Learn to Die"
  (Montaigne), 241
Theater: abuse of music in, 38–45; as
  incitement to wickedness, 33, 34, 45
Théâtre du monde, Le (Boaistuau, 1559), 239
Thebaid (Statius), 123
"Thessalienne" (Ronsard), 228–29
Thibaldeo da Ferrara (1463–1534), 165, *177*
Thomas Aquinas, 260, 279
Thyard, Pontus de, 187
Tifernate, Gregorio, 208, 209
Timaeus (Plato), 13
Timon (Anon.), 40–41, 43, 46–47 n. 19

Tinelli, Tiberio, 273
Tintoretto (Jacopo Robusti), 193
Todorov, Tzvetan, 225, 226–27, 233
Traité de le Peste (Paré, 1568), 239
Translation: classical, 97–98; as imitation, 97;
  role of during Spanish Renaissance,
  96–108 passim; vertical vs. horizontal, 103;
  Vives's views on, 98–99, 107
Treatise of Melancholie, A (Bright, 1586), 36
Trevor-Roper, Hugh, 144
Trionfi (Petrarch), 141 n. 28
Trissino, Giangiorgio, 106
Tuppo, Francesco del, 164
Turenne, vicomte de (Henri de La Tour
  d'Auvergne), 237
Turnèbe, Adrien, 256, 257
Tusculan Disputations (Cicero), 241, 242
Twelfth Night (Shakespeare), 33

Udall, Nicholas, 42–43
Utopia (More), 15

Vaihinger, Hans, 14
Vair, Guillaume du, 243
Valdés, Juan de, 100, 105
Vascosan, Michel, 189
Vatican, Stanza della Segnatura in, 113, 116,
  123, *127–29, 133–34*
Vax, Louis, 233
Venganza de Agamenón, La (Pérez de Oliva),
  100, 102, 103, 104
Venice, 205–20 passim, 272–86 passim
Vergil. *See* Virgil
Veronese, Guarino (Veronensis, Guarinus)
  (1374–1460), 165, 207, 210
Via della fede (Morosini), 280
Vico, Giambattista, 10
Vida, Marco Girolamo, 115, 117, 118, 120,
  124
Vies et eloges des hommes illustres (Emile),
  190
Villey, Pierre, 241
Viret, Pierre, 264
Virgil, 240; imitated by Ronsard, 189; as
  model of Latin writing, 81; poetry of, 120;
  portrait of, 164; in Raphael's *Parnassus*, 113,
  115, 117, 118, 119, 123, 124; Ronsard's
  imitation of, 67–77 passim
Virués, Cristóbal de, 105–6, 107, 108
Vislingio, Giovanni (1598–1649), 272
Vives, Juan, 96, 98–99, 104, 107

Vocabularium (Barzizza), 165
Voltaire, 5

Walker, D. P., 255
Weber, Henri, 186
Whittinton, Robert, 167, 168
Wilkins, Ernest Hatch, 83
Wisdom of the Ancients, The (*De Sapientia Veterum*) (Bacon), 9, 10
Wooing, and music, 38, 41–44
Worde, Wynkyn de. *See* de Worde, Wynkyn

Wotton, Henry (1569–1639), 272, 273

Xenophon, 15, 62

Yates, Frances, 255, 265
Yom zeh yehi mishkal (Modena), 282 n. 15

Zeno, Apostolo, 207
Zohar, 271, 275, 276, 278
Zwingli, Huldrych (1484–1537), 261, 285–86 n. 50